THE OPERA HANDBOOK

John Lazarus

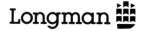

Longman Group UK Limited,
Longman House, Burnt Mill, Harlow, Essex CM20 2JE, England
and Associated Companies throughout the world.

First published 1987

British Library Cataloguing in Publication Data

Lazarus, John
    The opera handbook.
    1. Opera – Dictionaries
    I. Title
    782.1'03'21   ML102.06
    ISBN 0-582-00107-2

Typeset in 8 pt Rockwell and printed in Great Britain by The Bath Press, Avon.

CONTENTS

Kiri Te Kanawa, Herman Prey, Placido Domingo and Benjamin Luxon at the end of *Die Fledermaus*

Acknowledgements

MANY PEOPLE helped me in preparing this book, in ways that those who have undertaken a similar project would recognise as crucial. Chief among these is my wife, Shelley; she put up with me throughout while coping with heavy demands in her own work, and her critical insights were indispensable. Our young son, Micha, took a lively interest, and trained me to keep the plots simple.

For their unstinting help and valuable perspective I am permanently indebted to Delayne and Max Loppert. Michael Blake, Ruth Thackeray and Lindsay Wentworth made specific and useful contributions. Evelyn Dalberg has probably forgotten how much she stimulated my interest in opera, years ago. The patience shown by my editors – Philip Dodd, Rosemary Dooley and Jenny Hicks – was greatly appreciated.

Practical help was provided by the excellent National Sound Archive, the Central Music Library at Victoria, the Marylebone Music Library, and above all the staff of the Central (Music) Library at Kensington, who have assembled an impressive collection of recordings and scores. I am also grateful to Sally Groves of Schott & Co. and the Librarian of Opera North, each of whom solved a particular problem.

The Publishers would like to thank Lesley Davy for picture research; Julian Grant for editorial support; Malcolm Walker for discographical advice; and *Opera* magazine (particularly Deidre Tilley) for supplying essential information.

by Jeremy Isaacs

Chief Executive of Channel 4; future General Director of the Royal Opera House, Covent Garden.

OPERA REFRESHES the parts that other arts cannot reach. It is able to do this because the combination of dramatic and musical pleasures – drama *through* music – provides, at its best, a rare exhilaration and excitement.

Opera, it used to be thought, was for the few. No longer. The audience for opera, urged on by radio, by recordings and by television, grows each year as millions discover the pleasure that music drama can bring.

Many people who say they do not care for opera can still sing you their favourite tunes from Puccini, Verdi, Mozart and Rossini; they enjoy opera without knowing it. Many more roll up, in city after city, for performances by the remarkable opera companies active in Britain and around the world.

It is often simply a question of getting started. I was lucky: for the price of a day return from Glasgow, I heard Glyndebourne in Edinburgh in the fifties (eight shillings and sixpence in the circle). When Sena Jurinac, in the Prologue to Strauss's *Ariadne auf Naxos*, sang that music was a holy art, I got prickles down the back of my neck which have never really gone away.

But opera, although more widely available than ever, is not always as accessible as it needs to be. The more we understand it, the more satisfaction we can derive. Sub-titles on television, clear diction in the theatre and now sur-titles too, help us to grasp precisely what is sung, and make us laugh, cry and appreciate it all the more.

A book like this one accelerates the process. The information *The Opera Handbook* contains will be useful to all those just entering or still exploring opera's magic world, as each of us discovers new favourites to add to our personal list of pleasures.

Britten and Janáček, Birtwistle and Glass. The list, thank goodness, grows longer each year.

Jeremy Isaacs

HOW TO USE
THE OPERA HANDBOOK

The Opera Handbook is a compact
guide offering a structured approach to
the extensive – and sometimes daunting
– repertoire of opera. By starting from
a framework of major operas, it should
encourage you, through a system of
cross-references, to encounter as wide
a range of opera as possible.

The Handbook's role is to prepare
the groundwork for building up an
overall view of operas in the context of
their history, and to encourage you to
develop your own personal tastes. The
different routes you can take are clearly
marked; it is up to you whether or not
you choose to pursue them.

Above all, the Handbook is intended
to be an active reference book: it has
been designed for ease of use, and ease
of access. Ideally, you should act on its
recommendations and suggestions, and
experience individual operas in
performance whenever you have the
chance.

To support you, the Handbook
provides back-up facts and information;
although compact, it is crammed with
data. In conjunction with the critical
advice provided, it will give you a set
of landmarks to refer to when you see
opera on TV, on film or live, or when
you hear it on record, compact disc or
radio.

The entries

At the heart of the Handbook are the
two hundred main entries. The operas
have been deliberately chosen
according to how often they have been
performed by major companies in the
1980s. The selection aims to provide
various starting-points, ranging from the
early works of Peri and Monteverdi
through the more familiar ground of
Verdi, Puccini and Wagner to
contemporary works such as Philip
Glass's Akhnaten or Aulis Sallinen's The
King Goes Forth to France. We have not
intended to include all operas; the
Handbook is not a comprehensive
encyclopedia, but rather a stimulus and
a springboard for further exploration.

All the main entries can cross-refer
to each other, but they also refer to an
outer band of operas, all indexed at the
back of the book. You could start with
an opera you already know, look it up
in the Index (where the page number

of its main entry will be given in bold)
and then follow the links; equally, you
could start reading through one of the
chapters, each of which covers the
development of a national school of
opera.

The operas have been grouped into
these national schools to create an
instant framework, which helps when
you are dealing with what may appear
to be the amorphous world of opera.
You should bear in mind that:

☐ The use of the term 'national' school
of opera does not necessarily imply
that all the composers within it are
of that nationality. The crucial factor
is the style of opera. Consequently,
in the French chapter, you will find
operas by Rossini and Verdi, who
were both Italian.

☐ The national schools are those
generally used by the opera writers
and historians you may refer to.

☐ The order of the chapters broadly
reflects the chronological
development of opera in those
national schools. So Italian opera was
the first to have an identifiable
tradition, American the most recent.

☐ A two-page spread opens each
chapter with a summary of the
salient features which bind the
school together, and the significant
points of its history.

Within the national schools, the works
of each composer are listed in order of
composer's date of birth and the date
of each opera's first performance.
For example:

BIZET (born 1838)
       The Pearl Fishers (1863)
       Carmen (1875)
MASSENET (born 1842)
       Manon (1884)
       Werther (1892) etc.

For each composer, the following
information is given:

1 A short block of biographical
information (date and place of birth
and death).
2 A brief note setting their opera works
within the development of opera and
in the context of their own musical
output.
3 Suggestions for further reading.

This information is given at the first entry, where a composer appears within two national schools.

Main opera entries contain the following elements:

1 **Title:** The main title given is that which an English-speaking audience is most likely to see: there are many foreign-language operas which are most popularly known by their English title (for example The Magic Flute, The Flying Dutchman). In those cases, the original title is given immediately beneath the main entry title. Conversely, if an opera is primarily known in its original language (eg La traviata), an English translation is also provided. Apart (obviously) from British and American operas, the exception to the rule is if the title is formed by a proper name or names, in which case, the word for 'and' has not been translated (eg Tristan und Isolde).

2 **Factual data:**
   – Number of acts
   – The librettist(s), often a vital element, plus major original sources
   – The place and year of first performance (and major revisions)

3 A **plot outline** gives the core of those convoluted plots so beloved of opera. If you wish to read the plots in much greater details and at full length, we recommend Kobbé (see the Opera Books section on page 229) or any of the many books which consist purely of storylines.

4 A critique of each work (called **The opera**), concentrating on the main musical, dramatic and thematic elements of the opera – what is important and individual about it, and what to listen and look for. References to other main entries are indicated in bold, and words featured in the Glossary (see Databank below) are marked by an arrow symbol (>). The titles of individual arias, songs, etc. are in italics; individual phrases or lines are in quote marks.

5 The **Overview** is the section which suggests links and new directions to follow. These links can range from the musical to more adventurous thematic and dramatic links, encouraging you to cut across different opera styles rather than getting stuck in any particular one.

We can't guarantee you will like these suggestions, but they will certainly give you a sense of the breadth of the genre. Again cross-references to main entries are in bold.

6 **Further reading:** suggested books and guides which focus in detail on the particular opera.

7 **Listening:** a suggested recording or recordings of the opera, with discographical information. The recordings are recommended on the basis of quality, not necessarily because they are the most recent. Note that some historically important recordings may be deleted at present, but available through record libraries or through re-issue. Compact disc options are supplied where possible, reflecting the importance that this medium is gaining in the opera market.

The Databank

Following the main chapters is a Databank of additional information, including:

☐ A guide to major **opera singers**: a representative selection of singers you may come across on recordings or performance with brief biographical information, and a rundown on their individual qualities and most successful roles. Again cross-references to main entries are in bold.

☐ A **glossary** listing opera-related terms in the Handbook which may require some clarification. These are marked throughout the text by the arrow symbol (>).

☐ **Opera books**: includes titles which will give further background or detail, and also provide an additional entrée to the world of opera.

☐ A country-by-country listing of **information sources**: magazines, festivals, opera companies and other bodies which can supply useful information and act as contact points.

☐ **Index**: an A-Z of all the operas and composers mentioned in the Handbook.

The Opera Handbook is the second title in a series of Longman Handbooks on the arts; see the back cover for further details.

ITALIAN OPERA

Italy is the home of opera. In the 1590s and early 1600s a group of artistic Florentine amateurs, fascinated by theories about the relationship between music and drama, tried to recreate classical Greek theatre. Their first efforts, sung and acted versions of Greek legends such as Orpheus and Eurydice, were presented as court entertainment for connoisseurs and like-minded lovers of art as well as for aristocrats intrigued by such experiments.

These early works are not enormously interesting – it was difficult for their composers to breathe life into the narrow forms they had imposed on themselves, with the solo voice predominant at the expense of ensemble or chorus, earnestly imitating the rhythms and inflections of the verse it set. But with Monteverdi, whose *Orfeo* was produced in 1607, opera found its first great composer, who could depict intense human passions as well as delightful comedy with a range and variety which remains fresh today.

In 1637 the first public opera house opened in Venice. After this, a great work of Italian opera had to be primarily a popular entertainment – it had to be accessible to, and approved by, the public. Cavalli and Cicognini became the 17th century's most popular composers, with audiences relishing the comedy and intrigue they incorporated. Now >recitative, with its snappy, pointed rhythms familiar from comic speech patter, took over from the more melodic >arioso – and in an established form emerging in strong contrast to recitative, the >aria illuminated the moments of deepest feeling. This scheme allowed for plenty of emotion, and, with the marvels of stage machinery given full scope, for dramatic excitement as well.

The early 18th century was the heyday of >opera seria. Scenic extravagance gave way to formal, static settings; classical tragedy flourished within the strict parameters were developed by the poet Metastasio. His libretti were the basis of numerous operas. Their high points were the arias; more a response to a dramatic situation than a development of it, they concentrated on opera's particular marvel, the human voice.

In other countries, opera might demonstrate high principles of art, invent spectacular scenery, aim to express the spirit of the nation, or cultivate orchestral complexity. But Italian opera's most striking feature remained the most natural form of self-expression, sung melody. The Italian language, with its open vowels, lends itself to song, and natural joy in singing enriched the stage medium. So singers were paramount in Italian opera and audiences could identify with them: they became such popular heroes that anyone might take up the cudgels on their behalf. Their singing and their song spoke directly to their listeners – and indeed so dominated European opera for nearly three centuries that those great non-Italians, Handel, Gluck and Mozart, produced some of their most glorious masterpieces in the medium of Italian opera, albeit with their own refinements.

Of course there was competitiveness among singers; often vocal agility became valued as much as >bel canto. So when Rossini harnessed the traditional virtuosity of the singers and the orchestra, he was developing a new operatic style. Vocal acrobatics began to make more sense as a part of the dramatic action – listen to a Donizetti or Bellini mad scene. And listen too to a Verdi heroine's intensely real emotions – the kind which everyone in the audience could identify with – or to the partnership between passionate feeling and melody in Puccini.

The special relationship between singers and audiences gave opera the power to change events. In the 1840s the Italians, oppressed by the French and the Austrians, hungered to unite the country under their own rulers. Verdi was the right composer at the right time: his vivid depictions of the suffering of oppressed peoples became a rallying cry to revolution, and people poured out of the opera house to riot.

Nowadays Italian opera no longer travels much to other parts of the world, but the passions may still be roused. The great domination by scene and song, blood and guts, art and instinct, is over for the time being.

The great Italian tenor Enrico Caruso

Jacopo Peri

Born: 20th August 1561/Rome
Died: 12th August 1633/Florence

At a time of experimentation with sung drama, Peri wrote the works we think of as the first operas, including *Dafne*, which has not survived, and *Euridice*.

EURIDICE

Prologue and five scenes
Libretto: Ottavio Rinuccini
First performance: Florence 1600

Plot: Shortly after Orpheus and Eurydice's wedding, Eurydice is fatally bitten by a snake. Orpheus wants to die too but the Goddess Venus invites him instead to petition Pluto for the return of his beloved. Orpheus gains entry to the Underworld, where he persuades the unwilling King of the Dead to release Eurydice, and takes her back to their joyous friends.

The opera: *Euridice* is the earliest extant opera. Written as a rather appropriate wedding present for Maria de Medici, it was first performed for a small, invited audience as part of the nuptial celebrations. The twist at the end, where Orpheus's music successfully rescues Eurydice from death, is symbolic: Peri was one of a group of Florentine artists who set out to restore the ideal Greek drama by combining it with music.

Peri, apparently a wonderfully expressive singer himself, probably took the part of Orpheus in the performance, accompanying himself on the lute. Expressive singing with improvised ornamentation is crucial to the effectiveness of this work, as the main substance of the opera is in a mildly declamatory style close to the rhythms and inflections of natural speech, neither varying the rhythm nor exploiting the wider range of the voice. So the set pieces are the most moving, notably Orpheus's reaction to the news of Eurydice's death, and his song at the gates of Hell.

Overview: Hell as depicted by **Don Giovanni** (Mozart) or **The Damnation of Faust** (Berlioz) certainly carries terrors more substantial than that faced by Peri's Orpheus. Yet *Euridice*, de facto our first opera, has some unexpected links with its successors, for three centuries later in **Pelléas et Mélisande**, Debussy, too, carefully coordinated the voice and the text, and in **Erwartung** Schoenberg developed the same principle with >sprechgesang. Peri and his contemporaries, notably Caccini, who wrote a rival *Euridice*, took these giant steps forward partly to flesh out an aesthetic argument, as did Gluck in the 18th century and Wagner in the 19th.

In making claims for the power of the new music, Peri gave himself 'operatic licence', and fundamentally altered a great myth to suit his purpose. Opera composers have freely reshaped stories ever since, aiming at what is effective in the opera house.

Listening

Harmonia Mundi HM2.478(2)
Solisti di Milano/Ephrikian

Claudio Monteverdi

Born: 15th May 1567/Cremona
Died: 29th November 1643/Venice

Monteverdi was the first truly great opera composer. Apart from *Il ritorno d'Ulisse in patria* and the two dealt with here, none of his operas has survived. Other stage works are *Il ballo delle ingrate* (opera–ballet) and *Il combattimento di Tancredi e Clorinda* (a dramatic cantata, sometimes staged). Monteverdi was famous as a composer of madrigals and other works and an innovator in harmony and orchestration.

Further reading: Denis Arnold – 'Monteverdi' *The New Grove Italian Baroque Masters* (London 1984).

L'ORFEO

Prologue and five acts
Libretto: Alessandro Striggio
First performance: Mantua 1607

Plot: Rejoicing over his wedding, Orpheus receives the news of Eurydice's sudden death. Determined to rescue her or die, he is escorted by Hope to the river at the edge of the Underworld. He overpowers the hostile Charon with the beauty of his singing, and rows himself over.

Pluto grants Orpheus his request, on condition he restrains himself from looking at Eurydice as she follows him. Orpheus sets out jauntily, but, pricked on by anxiety, and over-confident of the supreme power of Love, he turns – and sees her fading from him.

Lamenting his loss, he is taken to Heaven by his father, Apollo, where he will see Eurydice in the stars. (Some productions use Striggio's earlier intention of having him torn to pieces by the Bacchantes for rejecting the love of women, or combine the two by having Apollo save him from the Bacchantes.)

The opera: To the new medium of opera, Monteverdi brought rich general experience as a composer. Unlike Peri's earlier **Euridice**, *Orfeo* displays diversity in style and form, and variety in rhythm. Each scene is punctuated with instrumental pieces, vocal choruses and short songs, throwing into relief the crucial moments depicted in >recitative. And what recitative! It is the core of the opera, always compelling, immediate and emotional. Through it Monteverdi illuminates the human qualities of his characters – the Messenger, appalled at having to bring such tidings; Orpheus, setting out to melt Charon's resolve with his dazzling song, then in despair reducing it to a simple plea for compassion, and Charon, doggedly proclaiming the strength of his resolve, simply falling asleep; again Orpheus, permitted to take Eurydice back with him, cockily praising his own music-making well before his feelings of love assert themselves. Orpheus is a three-dimensional character, full of instinctive

bravery, who 'conquered Hell and was then conquered by his own emotions'.

Overview: In the Orpheus myth, there is greater legitimacy for Striggio's original ending than for the apotheosis with which the opera ends. The convention of >deus ex machina, used by Monteverdi to resolve the question of what to do with Orpheus once he has lost his Eurydice, dominated operas with mythological plots throughout the 17th century. This was court entertainment, and so the intervention of a god (symbol for the princely patron) had to be seen to produce the requisite happy ending. It also afforded opportunities for lavish and spectacular production effects.

Monteverdi's recitative remained an important element, but it was rarely used by later composers with the same expressive flexibility or psychological immediacy, and the >aria took over as the fullest expression of feeling at crucial moments.

Further reading: John Whenham – *Claudio Monteverdi: Orfeo* (Cambridge 1986).

Listening

EMI EX270 131-3 4 EX270 131-5
CD: CD57 47142-8
Angel DSX-3964 4 4DSX-3964
CD: CDCB-47141
London Baroque/Medlam
London Cornett & Sackbut Ens./Caudle
(Chiaroscuro/Rogers)
1985

THE CORONATION OF POPPAEA
L'incoronazione di Poppea

Prologue and two/three acts
Libretto: Giovanni Busenello
First performance: Venice 1642

Plot: In thrall to Poppaea, the Roman Emperor Nero decides to crown her as his Empress despite the bitter objections of his wife Octavia and the

11

Maria Ewing and Dennis Bailey in *The Coronation of Poppaea*

philosopher–statesman Seneca. Seneca readily accepts the Imperial order to commit suicide; Octavia, her plot to murder Poppaea thwarted by the God of Love, is exiled. Poppaea's husband, Otho, had been forced by Octavia to attempt the murder; he is an anguished soul, but has at least found a loyal lover, Drusilla. Poppaea is crowned, her ambitions fulfilled, and she and Nero contemplate uninterrupted sexual fulfilment together.

The opera: Scholars dispute the reliability of the scores from which reconstructions of *Poppaea* are made (hence the possible division into two or three acts, according to whose version is used). Yet the opera is acknowledged as a masterpiece. It was written, not as a court entertainment, but for a public theatre, which is the key to much that makes it special: it is the first opera peopled with figures from history rather than from myth or legend. As in Shakespeare, who also wrote for a cross-section of the public, the audience is presented with characters from all classes, their behaviour realistic rather than idealised. There is no moral tone or final judgement, no out-and-out villain or flawless hero;

good is not rewarded, destructive ambition may be. The tragic and the comic alternate as in everyday life.

Monteverdi uses free >recitative to express the specific psychology of each person: outraged patricians driven to suicide or to murder, a monarch whose neurotic obsession verges on insanity, lovers obsessed with one another, an ambitious courtesan, a rejected husband. We can hear in his music the garrulous nurse ambitious for her mistress and blind to her faults, flirting servants, grumbling soldiers with a shrewd insight into their leaders. Crucial to this flexibility of style is the small continuo orchestra, whose role is mainly to support the singer's free line.

Overview: Last works, especially those of an old person, often carry a special fascination. At the age of seventy-five Monteverdi wrote love music of a startling sexuality. Its rapture approaches Verdi's for **Otello** and Desdemona, composed at the age of seventy-three; its sensuousness equals Wagner's for **Tristan und Isolde**, written when the composer was half Monteverdi's age. For breadth of canvas and sharpness of social observation *Poppaea* approaches Mozart's **Figaro**. We are fortunate: we live in a period when Monteverdi has been revalued and revived.

Listening

Telefunken 6.35247; 4.35376
CD: 8.35247
Vienna Concentus Musicus/Harnoncourt
(Söderström, Esswood, Donath)
1974

Francesco Cavalli

Born: 14th February 1602/Crema
Died: 14th January 1676/Venice

Cavalli wrote about forty operas, including *La callisto*, *L'Egisto*, *Erismena*, and much church music. His operas are quite commonly revived.

ORMINDO

Three acts
Libretto: Giovanni Faustini
First performance: Venice 1644

Plot: Erisbe feels trapped in her marriage to an aged king, and plays with the emotions of Ormindo and Amida until Amida's previous beloved, Sicle, reveals that he has abandoned her. Confronted with the darker side of love, Erisbe cleaves to Ormindo. They elope, but are captured; furious, the king sentences them to death by poison.

Amida rediscovers his passion for Sicle through her nurse's clever piece of stage management (a theatrical convention); Ormindo and Erisbe find they have been given a sleeping draught instead of a poison (another convention); the king forgives them and offers Ormindo his throne.

The opera: Typically for its time, the plot of *Ormindo* contained little that was new. The challenge for Faustini and Cavalli was to give it life. One device was to have mundane servants do a comic monologue in front of the curtain – to disguise scene changes – while offering comment on the current

situation. This was the theatrical function of the lower classes, and here it appears fresh and effective. But opera stands or falls by its power to stir the emotions at crucial moments, and Cavalli, judged by a 20th-century ear, may sometimes be found wanting, despite some beautiful writing, notably in the duets between Erisbe and her maid (Scene 5), and between Amida and Sicle as they reveal their renewed feelings to one another. The darkening of the music of Act II suggests that the main characters, each in their own way, are going through a deep inner experience, and this takes the story beyond the superficial.

Overview: Cavalli's operas helped popularise the medium throughout Italy. The successful relationship between composer and audience is a two-way process, and the substance of a Cavalli opera contained the kind of structural organisation designed to respond to popular taste. >Strophic arias might easily become familiar; ritornelli prepared the ear for the vocal melodies which followed. At the same time >recitative became less dominant, and once the organic closeness of words and music was lost, dramatic immediacy was dissipated. You must decide whether this is the conventions crystallising, or the rot setting in.

Further reading: Jane Glover – *Cavalli* (London 1978).

Listening

Decca Argo ZNF8/10
London Phil. Orch./Leppard
1968

George Frideric Handel

Born: 23rd February 1685/Halle
Died: 14th April 1759/London

A great all-round composer, Handel's body of some forty-six operas (written mainly in the highly competitive theatre world of London) brought >opera seria to perfection. Within its conventions, convolutions of plot were necessary so that the leading characters could experience changes in their emotional state, to be expressed in >arias. In this way the composer could offer his singers (the dominant party) a satisfactory number of opportunities to display their abilities to a knowledgeable audience. And the audience delighted in seeing how it was all handled – a character manoeuvred offstage, an aria following a >recitative, a variation in the form of the aria itself. Some of Handel's operas are heroic, some 'magic', some a mixture of humour and more serious elements. Neglected for many years, they have now become a standard part of the repertory. There are also oratorios so dramatic that they are regularly staged.

Further reading: Winton Dean – *Handel and the Opera Seria* (Berkeley and Los Angeles, 1969); Winton Dean and John Merrill Knapp – *Handel's Operas 1704–1726* (Oxford 1987); Stanley Sadie – 'The Operas of Handel' in *Opera on Record 2* (London 1983).

RINALDO

Three acts
Libretto: Aaron Hill/Giacomo Rossi
First performance: London 1711

Plot: In the final stage of their conquest of the Holy Land, the Crusaders are besieging the Saracens in Jerusalem. If Jerusalem falls, the great hero Rinaldo will win Almirena, daughter of his leader.

The Saracens' leader, Argante, has the assistance of his lover, Armide, a sorceress. The only hope of defending Jerusalem lies in luring Rinaldo away from the Crusader cause, and Armide sets herself to seduce him. But Rinaldo remains unswerving in his love for Almirena, and Armide is deflected from destroying him because she falls in love with him.

The Crusaders cannot be vanquished by the powers of darkness. Through Rinaldo's valour they defeat the Saracens in battle, and take Argante and Armide prisoner. These two, recognising Christ Triumphant, embrace the faith, and are set free.

The opera: Handel's first opera for London, *Rinaldo* initiated a quarter-century of composition, production and management which, despite its uneven success, is one of the glories of opera history. As a 'magic' opera, it was not bound rigidly by the conventions of >opera seria, and its emotional denouement arrives early in the third act, leaving the actual battle, with its brilliant display music for orchestra and singers, as the main interest in the final scenes. The other high points of the music spring from moments of pure grief: *Cara sposa, Lascia ch'io pianga*, and *Ah, crudel, il pianto mio*, all three ravishing in intensity. Note also the glorious vocal and instrumental imitations of bird music (*Augelletti che cantate*) and of battle music (*Or la tromba*).

The two main types of magic spectacle are both associated with Armide: horrors and personal transformation. These, plus the extended scenes of armies and battles, give *Rinaldo* a Cecil B. de Mille quality. Doubtless he would have approved of Handel's writing one 'hit song' for each act.

Overview: Except in **Orlando**, the magicians in Handel's 'magic' operas are participants, whose own humanity may defeat them. At least in *Rinaldo* Armide emerges edified and morally sound (by the standards of 1711), whereas Gluck, in his **Armide**, emphasises the human/sexual weakness, and she ends up a tragic loser. *Rinaldo* is, by virtue of its final act, the first >grand opera of the sort made famous by Meyerbeer and Verdi's **Aida**. Whether the 20th century can stomach the epic show of armies and battles is for the producer and the audience to decide. The 17th- and 18th-century theatre's ability to produce mechanical spectacle, however, suggests that it could teach us the real meaning of theatrical magic.

Listening

CBS (Europe) 79308 4 40-79308
CBS (US) M3-34592

La Grande Ecurie et la Chambre du Roi/Malgoire
(Esswood, Cotrubas, Watkinson)
1977

JULIUS CAESAR
Giulio Cesare

Three acts
Libretto: Nicola Haym
First performance: London 1724

Plot: Having dispossessed his sister, Cleopatra, Ptolemy has secured the crown of Egypt by killing Pompey, and he now has plans to assassinate Caesar and establish absolute power. Pompey's widow, Cornelia, and their young son, Sextus, come to offer their loyalty to Caesar on his arrival in Egypt. They are all shocked that Ptolemy welcomes Caesar with the gift of Pompey's head, and Sextus swears revenge.

The position of these Romans is perilous. Cornelia is desired by both Ptolemy and his general, Achilla; she and her son are imprisoned, and Ptolemy forces her to join his harem.

Cleopatra has two objectives: she wishes to be Queen, and she wishes to ensnare Caesar. While there is time, she sets up an elaborate seduction. However, once she and Caesar have become lovers their passion is mutual, and when she believes him dead, she is stricken. Just when all appears lost, Caesar and Sextus contrive to destroy Ptolemy's power, and achieve a happy ending.

The opera: *Julius Caesar*, written when the composer was at the peak of his success in London, has always been one of Handel's most popular operas. It has a range of particularly convincing characters. Caesar is proud but not inflated, and we see him as lover, as brooding philosopher, as man of action. The two women are mature personalities of substantial presence; Cornelia the noble suffering Roman matron, Cleopatra vulnerable but resourceful, generating an entirely new atmosphere every time she appears. Her music is ravishing, showing great depth of soul – *Se pieta di me non senti,*

and *Piangero la sorte mia* are among the most wonderful Handel >arias. The villains, on the other hand, are rather two-dimensional characters, and they die unredeemed.

Overview: Because the characters are credible, their relationships become genuinely interesting. The suffering and anxiety shared by Cornelia and Sextus anticipates the Azucena–Manrico relationship (Verdi's **Il trovatore**) although this one is more tender; the open sexuality of Caesar and Cleopatra calls to mind Nero and Poppaea (Monteverdi's **The Coronation of Poppaea**), who also have to indulge in some intense power-play, but are never genuinely threatened as Caesar and Cleopatra are. And Caesar, ruminating, standing back from his experience – he and Hans Sachs (Wagner's **Die Meistersinger**) are brothers under the skin.

Listening

EMI EX270232-3 4 EX270232-5
Angel DS-3794
English National Opera/Mackerras
(Baker, Masterson)
1983

TAMERLANO

Three acts
Libretto: Nicola Haym adapted from Agostino Piovene
First performance: London 1724

Plot: Bajazet and his daughter Asteria have been taken prisoner by the tyrant Tamburlaine (Tamerlano) and are consumed with hatred for him. Tamburlaine has conceived a passion for Asteria, unaware that she and his ally Andronicus love one another. He offers Bajazet freedom in exchange for Asteria's love – and in order to clear the decks, he offers his own fiancée, Irene, to Andronicus.

Complications and misunderstandings ensue. Until Andronicus brings himself to declare his own feelings in front of both Asteria and Tamburlaine, she assumes that he no longer cares for her, and it is partly because of this, and partly to save her father's life, that she agrees to marry Tamburlaine, intending to assassinate him.

To show that he refuses to accept either death or clemency at the hands of the despised Tamburlaine, Bajazet commits suicide; this will free Asteria from any obligation to safeguard his life and, therefore, from Tamburlaine's offer. The tyrant, vanquished on this level, accepts that Asteria will wed Andronicus, and takes Irene as originally planned.

The opera: In *Tamerlano* the mould of >opera seria is broken – not by a change in the formula, but by a use of it so magnificent that the drama grips with elemental power. When Bajazet – who is certainly the most interesting character – defiantly commits suicide, this denouement, by providing honour for all, should neatly balance the plot. Yet it brings forth inspiration from Handel which, paradoxically, unbalances the whole opera, generating a new level of musical experience at the end which calls for deeply committed singing/acting, and an audience response to match. The suicide scene, and those generated by Bajazet's relationship with Asteria, are the core of the opera.

Overview: Asteria is the first of a series of young women torn between romantic and filial love, and shares the anguish of Pamina (Mozart's **The Magic Flute**) and **Aida** (Verdi). Bajazet, deeply anxious about his daughter, has less in common with Aida's father, Amonasro. Father–daughter relationships are good operatic fare (mother–son relationships tend to keep a lower profile).

Listening

Oryx 4XLC2
Copenhagen Chamber Orch./Moriarty
1970

RODELINDA

Three acts
Libretto: Nicola Haym
First performance: London 1725

Plot: Grimoaldo has usurped the throne of Bertaride, and wants Bertaride's queen, Rodelinda, as well. Although Bertaride is believed dead, Rodelinda vows eternal constancy. Grimoaldo and his unscrupulous ally Garibaldo compel Rodelinda to accept Grimoaldo: the alternative would be the death of her son. Rodelinda challenges Grimoaldo: if he marries her and becomes King, he must be the one to kill her son, the rightful heir. Faced with this, the logical conclusion of his actions, Grimoaldo starts to crack.

These events are witnessed from his hiding place by Bertaride, who reveals himself to Rodelinda. Their reunion is shattered when Grimoaldo has him thrown into a dungeon. He is helped to escape – just in time to save Grimoaldo, by now half-mad, from being murdered by the ambitious Garibaldo. Bertaride kills Garibaldo; Grimoaldo finds both his mental and his moral balance again, and returns the kingship to Bertaride. Rodelinda is reunited with her husband.

The opera: *Rodelinda* is one of Handel's masterpieces. The plot, with all the ingredients of the typical >opera seria, is better integrated than most. Handel's music for Grimoaldo shows us a complex and believable human being, whose inner consciousness restrains him from downright villainy, and ultimately redeems him. His moments on the edge of insanity reveal a soul at war with itself, in anguish. There is this quality of compassion in much of the music of *Rodelinda*, and the characteristic falling intervals of its lyrical melodies are like caressing gestures. The expressive melancholy which shows the King and Queen to be partners even while they are separated reaches its fulfilment in their one great scene together, with its incandescent duet of farewell.

Overview: There are important elements in *Rodelinda* that recur in the operas of later composers. The murky oppressiveness of the dungeon scene – surely a real horror in Georgian London society – foreshadows **Fidelio**, where Beethoven, in his own slow introduction, uses virtually the same phrase as Handel. Grimoaldo's threatened madness leads directly along a line of tormented usurpers to Musorgsky's **Boris Godunov**. And Rodelinda herself, fighting for survival against the very man who has caused her vulnerability,

Title page engraving for an early edition of *Rodelinda*

is not only a typical opera seria heroine: she has a sister in Puccini's **Tosca.**

Listening

Decca 414 667-1DH2 4 414 667 4DH2
CD: 414 667-2DH2
Welsh National Opera/Bonynge
(Sutherland, Nafé, Ramey)

ORLANDO

Three acts
Libretto: adapted from Capece, after Ludovico Ariosto
First performance: London 1733

Plot: Orlando, a mighty hero, cannot give up his passion for Angelica although it might lose him the glory of mighty deeds. His discovery that Angelica – despite professing love for him – is in love with Medoro unhinges his mind, and he runs amok. Only the compassionate guardianship of the magician Zoroastro protects those around him from harm at his hands.

When Zoroastro eventually restores Orlando's mental balance, it is the loving concern of his intended victims which saves him from a self-expiating suicide. And he comes to recognise that the hero's greatest glory is to triumph over love – over himself.

The opera: The formula so beloved of >opera seria – two lovers struggling to survive the passionate claim of a powerful prince – is retained as part of the framework of this 'magic' opera. A further part is the magic itself. This gives opportunities for the elaborate machinery of 18th-century theatre, with its capacity for spectacular transformations of scenery and lighting, to effect the most awe-inspiring magic of all – a change in the order of Nature. Zoroastro conjures up storms, clouds, fountains, gardens, an eagle, the temples of Love and of Mars; Handel creates music to match, which widens the imaginative scope and moral force of the opera. He delights in the scene-painting, even using bird-song.

Against this idealised sylvan background, Orlando's mad scenes appear strikingly disjointed. Handel treats his mental disorder by embodying disorder in the music itself. Irregular rhythms, strange harmonies, and abrupt phrases combine to express both the cataclysmic horror and the heartache of a broken hero. It is an extraordinary piece of music theatre.

Overview: Opera is singularly well equipped to convey madness, and Orlando joins an illustrious group of whom perhaps the best known are **Lucia di Lammermoor** (Donizetti), Lady **Macbeth** (Verdi), **Boris Godunov** (Musorgsky) and **Wozzeck** (Berg). (Strange that, while it predates the earliest of these by a hundred years or so, *Orlando* is probably the most recent to have become familiar to us.) The kinship of madness and grief brings Orlando closest to Purcell's tragic Carthaginian Queen **Dido**. Both Handel and Purcell use a dragging,

chromatically descending ground bass to underpin quintessential anguish.

Listening

RCA (UK) SRS 3006, (US) LSC 6197
Vienna Volksoper Orch./Simon
(Sciutti, Bogard, Stefan, Greevy)
1970

SERSE

Three acts
Libretto: adapted from earlier versions by Nicolò Minato and Silvio Stampiglia
First performance: London 1738

Plot: Serse (Xerxes), an autocrat, falls in love with Romilda. His brother Arsamene and Romilda are in love, but Serse has the power to prevent their marriage. Romilda's sister Atalanta has her eye on Arsamene and hopes Serse's passion will get Romilda out of her way. Serse himself forgets his promised marriage to Amastre, who spends the entire opera disguised as a soldier attempting to protect her interests.

As a result of some supremely unlikely misunderstandings, Arsamene and Romilda manage to get married under the mistaken impression they have been commanded to by Serse. Amastre confronts Serse; his brutal arrogance melts and he takes her back.

The opera: Towards the end of his 'golden' period of the 1720s, Handel made a five-month journey to the Continent where he must have tapped his sources anew after nearly twenty years. London's tastes, however, had altered, and with the reduced commercial success of his operas, Handel experienced some financial problems. In 1737 he suffered a stroke that partially crippled him for several months, and must also have affected his state of mind.

This all has bearing on *Serse*, where the self-imposed limitations of >opera seria give way to a richer anti-heroic mix incorporating comedy, with a strain of wry human insights reminiscent of Monteverdi.

The music of this mellower, more

human, Handel, is wonderfully beautiful. In the absence of his best singers, the >arias (excepting those for Serse) tend to be less virtuoso, more direct, often briefer. The style ranges from some exquisite lyrical >recitative accompagnato to the broken accents of a street-cry – and, to start with, the famous and mis-named 'Largo' itself, which, far from the religiose sentiments it has been assumed to express, might just be a send-up: in it, Serse speaks his love for his favourite plane-tree.

Overview: In both its musical atmosphere and its social comedy *Serse* constantly reminds us of Mozart's **Figaro**, and Arsamene's servant Elviro would relish a half-hour puncturing romantic pretensions with Leporello (**Don Giovanni**) or Despina (**Così**). All the main characters suffer some kind of jealousy; Mozart again springs to mind (*Così*, **Figaro**) and so too does Verdi – think of Ford (**Falstaff**), think of Eboli (**Don Carlos**). Yet the melodramatic contortions of this particular plot are hilarious: Handel is beating Gay's **The Beggar's Opera** at its own game in sending up opera seria. And Serse's final invocation to the Furies could represent two centuries of operatic rage. In this work Handel looks backward to Monteverdi and forward to Mozart, and takes in everything else that has happened so far on the way.

Listening

Westminster WST 8202
Vienna Radio Orch./Priestman
(Forrester, Popp, Braningan, Hemsley) 1965

Giovanni Battista Pergolesi

Born: 4th January 1710/Iesi
Died: 16th March 1736/Pozzuoli

Pergolesi was so famous after his death that many works were falsely attributed to him. He raised comic opera to a new level that remained fresh well into the 19th century. He also composed many fine >opere serie, and much beautiful sacred music (including a famous Stabat Mater).

LA SERVA PADRONA
The Maid Mistress

Intermezzo in two parts
Libretto: Gennaro Antonio Federico
First performance: Naples 1733

Plot: Uberto feels ill done by: he has looked after his maid, Serpina ('little snake'), so well that she now takes advantage of him; she wants to be treated like a mistress. Weary of being bossed, Uberto plans to marry: anyone would be better than Serpina. She announces he should marry her, and proceeds to trick him into doing so – and Uberto, while protesting otherwise, finds he is delighted to oblige.

The opera: >Intermezzi were generally performed between the acts of >opere serie. What mattered was contrast: this was real life, low-life, comical stuff, jibing at pretensions, parodying the holy cows of its operatic parent. >Recitative was a genuine conversational exchange spiced with lots of abuse, witty or otherwise, and in-jokes using dialect or foreign languages. Slapstick was part of the fun, coming naturally to the broadly drawn >buffa characters. Each of the two parts has one or two >arias, plus the final duet, all da capo. There is at least one non-singing part – a chance for a specialist comedian.
   La serva padrona is the freshest of the intermezzi (at its funniest done in the original Italian by Italian singers who know how to handle recitative). Serpina's arias are the most 'whistleable' before Mozart; *Stizzoso, mio stizzoso* is irresistible.

Overview: The maid catching her master is one type of the woman-catching-her-man theme so common in comedies, particularly intermezzi. The grotesque version had an old maid (often a >travesty part) forcing her attentions on a young man. Anything inappropriate in sex was fair game:

more often it was an old man lusting after a young woman. Serpina's determination to raise her socia' station, and Uberto's readiness to be the means, gives this light-hearted scene-shifter a touch of revolutionary prophecy that its protagonists would be hard put to understand. Comedy and satire are the safest mirror of social change: Pergolesi's little masterpiece looks straight ahead to Mozart's **The Marriage of Figaro**.

Further reading: Michael Robinson – *Naples and Neapolitan Opera* (Oxford 1972).

Listening

HM 20343/30.343.
(Bonifaccio, Nimsgern)

Christoph Willibald von Gluck

Born: 2nd July 1714/Erasbach, Upper Palatinate
Died: 15th November 1787/Vienna

A prolific composer of operas, including comedy and >singspiel, Gluck worked mainly in Vienna and Paris. One of the most important theorists about opera, his >reform operas were enormously influential even after his own time (Beethoven, Berlioz, Wagner). Other notable works include *Paride ed Elena*, *Iphigénie en Aulide*, *Armide*, *Alceste* and *Iphigénie en Tauride*.

ORFEO ED EURIDICE

Three acts
Libretto: Raniero de Calzabigi
First performance: Vienna 1762

Plot: Orpheus laments the death of Eurydice, and vows to find her in Hades.

Amor (Love) brings him permission to proceed, but he must not look at Eurydice until they have left the Underworld. His music breaks down the antipathy of the Furies; they send him on to the Elysian fields. Eurydice, at first ecstatic on being restored to him, becomes confused when he refuses to look at her, and an anguished argument develops. Eventually he turns to her, and she dies. Guilt-ridden, Orpheus cannot face life without his wife. Amor saves him from suicide and restores Eurydice to him.

The opera: *Orfeo ed Euridice* was Gluck's first >reform opera, reflecting contemporary thinking about 'noble simplicity and calm greatness'. (Ignore the overture and the happy ending; Gluck had to tack these on to the opera proper.) From the first notes of the lamenting chorus we find ourselves in a new world of classical restraint. There is little room for vocal display *per se*, and the melodic writing has a simple >diatonic outline, gaining its effect by its placing in the dramatic context. Gluck's objective is unity of language: >recitatives are integrated with the >arias, often fully accompanied by the orchestra, and melodic shapes recur. Note how the vocal line of the first chorus is the framework for the great climax, *Che farò?*, or how the orchestra echoes Orpheus in *Chiamo il mio ben*, strengthening the relationship between the elements of singer, chorus and orchestra. In this kind of opera the drama is not contrived to dazzle with its diversity and complexity; it carries its power within itself. Gluck expanded the opera for Paris in 1774, using a tenor for Orphée, and several productions now present combinations of the Vienna and Paris versions.

Overview: The myth of Orpheus was used by Gluck to give substance to an ideal of Greek drama; it had been used for the same purpose by Peri and Monteverdi over a century and a half earlier and it would be the basis for works by Haydn, Offenbach, Milhaud and Birtwistle. Both Peri and Gluck were attempting theatrical reform. But whereas Peri had imitated faithfully what he assumed to be the Greek manner, Gluck recreated the Greek spirit from what he found useful in the established traditions of opera –

recitative, aria, chorus, diversity of instrumentation, unity of form. The later Wagnerian reform was arguably a more thorough-going one, but Wagner could draw on a tradition that had incorporated Gluck's own achievements: greater significance for the orchestra, greater unity for the musical language, and organic truth for the drama.

Further reading: Patricia Howard – *Gluck and the Birth of Modern Opera* (London 1963); Patricia Howard – *C. W. von Gluck: Orfeo* (Cambridge 1981); Max Loppert – 'Orfeo ed Euridice' in *Opera on Record* ed Blyth (London 1979).

Listening

Combination of 1762 and 1774 versions:
Decca SET 4431
Royal Opera House/Solti
(Horne)

Janet Baker in Peter Hall's production of *Orfeo ed Euridice* at Glyndebourne (1982) – her last opera performance

Joseph Haydn

Born: 31st March 1732/Rohrau
Died: 31st May 1809/Vienna

Haydn was one of the great masters, especially of symphonies, chamber and piano music, and sacred music. His operas (around thirty) have only recently emerged from neglect.

ORLANDO PALADINO

Three acts
Libretto: Nunziato Porta, after C. F. Badini
First performance: Esterhaza 1782

Plot: Orlando, a valorous knight-errant (paladin), has been so maddened by his

love for Angelica that – to avoid his unbridled desire to destroy his rival – she and her lover Medoro must flee continually. The sorceress Alcina protects them, but when her powerful magic does not modify Orlando's crazed fury she uses the waters of Lethe to induce forgetfulness in him. He is thus restored to mental balance, forgetting Angelica, and the two lovers achieve peace at last. Two other characters – Eurilla, a shepherdess, and her suitor, Pasquale, who is Orlando's squire – also attain loving contentment at the end.

The opera: As Kapellmeister of the Court at Eszterháza, Haydn composed many of the operas he presented. Although there has been a revival of interest in these works, which have considerable appeal, few commentators praise them whole-heartedly, questioning their sense of theatre, and the quality of plot and characterisation.

The famous Song of Roland was a favourite source of material for the theatre. Haydn's *dramma eroicomico* presents Orlando (Roland) purely as a ridiculous figure, and our sympathy is reserved for the lovers, although they are somewhat lacking in resourcefulness. Some of his writing looks foward to 19th-century opera – Angelica's *Dell'estreme* is a >cavatina followed by a >cabaletta. In the midst of the constant comings and goings, findings and losings, the most effective characters are Eurilla and Pasquale: Pasquale is a glorious rogue (his *Ecce spiano* is a brilliant demonstration of musical wit) and Eurilla, shepherdess or no, is wise in the ways of the world.

Overview: Haydn was a great symphonist, a master of instrumental music, so it is only natural that his use of the orchestra should be more interesting than it is in many other contemporary >opere buffe. He echoed in the later operas of Mozart – Medoro, with his inability in travail to do much except sing beautifully, so like Don Ottavio (**Don Giovanni**); Pasquale, a real 'character of the people', an all-too-human cousin to Papageno (**The Magic Flute**) and Leporello (*Don Giovanni*), especially in his encounters with the supernatural. The weakness is in Haydn's treatment of Orlando himself – after experiencing Handel's **Orlando**

one cannot help wishing Haydn's hero had a little more psychological complexity.

Further reading: H. C. Robbins Landon – *Haydn: Chronicle and Works* (London 1976).

Listening

Philips 6707 029
Lausanne Chamber Orchestra/Dorati
(Shirley, Augér, Ameling)
1976

Giovanni Paisiello

Born: 9th May 1740/Roccaforzata, near Taranto
Died: 5th June 1816/Naples

Enormously popular in his time, Paisiello composed over eighty comic and serious operas, as well as chamber and sacred music. His sentimental comedy *Nina* achieved great success and started a vogue for that genre (*comédie larmoyante*). There was some exchange of influence between him and Mozart.

THE BARBER OF SEVILLE
Il barbiere di Siviglia

Two acts (four parts)
Libretto: Giuseppe Petrosellini after Pierre-Augustin Caron de Beaumarchais
First performance: St Petersburg 1782

Plot: The elderly Don Bartolo plans to marry his pretty young ward, Rosina. He keeps her a virtual prisoner away from any young suitors, but does not entirely succeed: Rosina is being wooed by Lindoro, unaware that he is the Count Almaviva in disguise. The Count enlists the help of his old servant, Figaro, newly returned to Seville, and they talk their way into the Bartolo household under various pretences. When Bartolo, alert to the danger, procures a Notary to draw up a marriage document, the Count gets his name inserted in the contract: he and Rosina have proved all Bartolo's precautions useless.

The opera: As his first comic opera for the Court at St Petersburg, Paisiello chose the familiar Beaumarchais play so that the Russians' lack of Italian would not be a handicap, and there is a simplicity and directness about the setting which makes it easy to follow. There is also considerable sophistication in the handling of ensembles, which broke new ground: the deft accumulation of voices ending the early trio between Bartolo and his sleepy servants, or the proportion of time given, without its being forced, to the concerted finale. And the part of Dr Bartolo is a gift for a good >buffa bass: he is the butt of the comedy, and the focal character of the entire opera.

Overview: When Paisiello composed *The Barber*, Mozart had not yet composed **Figaro**, and Rossini had not been born. Yet it is difficult to approach Paisiello's opera without hindsight: the style constantly reminds one of what was to come. His melodic ideas, undeveloped though they might be by comparison, must have made an impression on Mozart, for there are clear echoes of Paisiello's *Barber* in *Figaro*; and Rossini would not have been the same composer without Pergolesi, Paisiello and Cimarosa. Rossini's own **Barber** was at first viewed with suspicion as something of an upstart venture, Paisiello's opera having been universally admired for thirty-five years, but it eventually edged the earlier version out of the repertoire. Inevitably, now, Paisiello's *Barber* feels like Rossini manqué, but it has a healthy charm of its own, and had there been no Rossini it might still hold the stage.

Further reading: Michael Robinson – *Naples and Neapolitan Opera* (Oxford 1972).

Listening

Hungaroton SLPD12525/7

CD: HCD12525/6
Hungarian State Orch./A. Fischer
(Laki, Gulyás, Gáti, Sólyom-Nagy, Gregor)
1984

Domenico Cimarosa

Born: 17th December 1749/Aversa
Died: 11th January 1801/Venice

The most celebrated >opera buffa composer of his generation, Cimarosa wrote well over sixty operas of all types, as well as instrumental music, oratorios and sacred music.

THE SECRET MARRIAGE
Il matrimonio segreto

Two acts
Libretto: Giovanni Bertati, after George Colman and David Garrick
First performance: Vienna 1792

Plot: Carolina, younger daughter of a rich, deaf merchant, has secretly married his secretary, Paolino. The couple become involved with the proposed marriage of Carolina's spiteful older sister to an impecunious English Count; the Count prefers Carolina, and she is accused by the family of seducing him. To complicate matters the girls' elderly aunt has selected Paolino for herself. In the end Carolina can only be saved from being sent to a convent by revealing the truth of her marriage and receiving her family's pardon.

The opera: *The Secret Marriage*, once encored in its entirety, is Cimarosa's masterpiece, with all the ingredients of success: tunefulness and wit, rhythmic vitality and delightful instrumental colouring. Always sparkling, it whisks us onward, keeping itself fresh by mingling duets and trios with solos (unusual for this time), as well as the final ensemble in each act. The comic absurdities are easy to follow, aptly served by music which only rarely engages the listener. But note the wistful inner feeling of the lovers' duet which starts the final scene: surrounded by ridiculous posturings, these two transgressors are the only sane ones in the household.

Overview: Although at first the music might appear related to Mozart, its lyrical impulses tend to disintegrate. Closer familiarity shows Cimarosa taking comic opera forward from Pergolesi and Paisiello to Rossini. The clear, light patter lacks the realistic bite of Pergolesi's **La serva padrona**; it has become more amiable, more complacent. Cimarosa hints at the famous Rossini crescendo as he builds up excitement in the ensembles; Rossini would take over this sophisticated mix of romantic comedy and lightly sketched characters, and add his own brand of caricature. Audiences are still avid for this recipe.

Listening

DG 2740 141
ECO/Barenboim
(Varady, Augér, Davies, Fischer-Dieskau)
1977

Wolfgang Amadeus Mozart

Born: 27th January 1756/Salzburg
Died: 5th December 1791/Vienna

A supreme master in all genres of music, four of Mozart's operas are among the greatest works in the repertory. He wrote twenty-two sung stage works, mostly operas in the Italian style. His few German comedies and >singspiels were the first great works of the German opera tradition (see page 132). But he was by no means fully appreciated in his lifetime, though Prague was more responsive than his own Vienna.

Frank Hauser's production of *The Secret Marriage* (Glyndebourne 1965)

Further reading: William Mann – *The Operas of Mozart* (London 1977); Stanley Sadie – *The New Grove Mozart* (London 1982); Brigid Brophy – *Mozart The Dramatist* (London 1964); Joseph Kerman – *The Opera as Drama* (New York 1956)

IDOMENEO

Three acts
Libretto: Giambattista Varesco after Antoine Danchet
First performance: Munich 1781

Plot: The Trojan War has ended. To save himself during a sea-storm, King Idomeneo has sworn to Neptune that he will sacrifice the first person he meets after returning to Crete. He is horrified to be welcomed by his son Idamante. Idamante has his own problems: he is loved by the proud princess Electra, but is in love with a Trojan princess, Ilia, who rejects him.

Impatient for the promised sacrifice, Neptune sends a ravaging sea monster, and Idamante determines to fight it. Fearing for him, Ilia reveals that she loves him. But Idamante leaves, wretched at his father's unexplained hostility – and kills the monster. Now Idomeneo must carry out the sacrifice,

but Idamante is ready, for he has learnt why his father could not show his love before. As Idomeneo is about to strike, Ilia flings herself forward as victim in Idamante's place. Then the oracle pronounces: Idamante must become king, Ilia his bride. Electra departs in furious despair, leaving a united Crete, symbol of peace.

The opera: Mozart relished the early opportunity of working on a weighty work for an important opera house, and it shows: *Idomeneo* is his first operatic masterpiece. Already in the overture the intensity makes the writing of his contemporaries appear inconsequential. His use of wind instruments opens up a whole range of orchestral colouring (listen to the cries of the gulls and the wind in the storm), which enriches the emotional content with wonderful eloquence. You cannot avoid identifying with characters showing such force of feeling: Idomeneo's guilt towards the son he has unwittingly condemned to death before getting to know him; Ilia's anguish, a defeated Trojan in love with an enemy prince; Idamante, so loving, rejected by both his father and Ilia. Only Electra, brilliantly drawn, repels us with her arrogance. The action flows, arising naturally from the situations, as in the great Act III quartet which develops from the young lovers' avowal of their feelings.

Overview: Though basically an >opera seria, *Idomeneo* could claim to be >grand opera in embryo. The people of Crete neither initiate action, as in Musorgsky's **Boris Godunov**, nor contribute to it, as in Wagner's **The Twilight of the Gods**, but their responses *live* as in no earlier opera. The turbulent anxiety of Mozart's Cretans awaiting Idomeneo loses nothing compared with Verdi's Cypriots awaiting **Otello.** But the central characters are recalled when others of Mozart take the stage – Ilia's first >aria foreshadows Elvira's *Mi tradi* (**Don Giovanni**), Electra's angry >coloratura the Queen of the Night (**The Magic Flute**). And the embarkation chorus *Placido è il mar* shares a yearning for calm winds with the glorious *Soave sia il vento* in **Così**.

Listening

Teledec 6.355 47 4 4.35547
CD: 8. 35547
Zurich Mozart Opera Orch./Harnoncourt
(Yakar, Schmidt, Palmer, Hollweg)
1980

THE MARRIAGE OF FIGARO
Le nozze di Figaro

Four acts
Libretto: Lorenzo da Ponte, after Pierre-Augustin Caron de Beaumarchais
First performance: Vienna 1786

Plot: As servants, Figaro and Susanna need the Count's permission to marry. But the Count aims to seduce Susanna first, exercising an aristocratic right, the ancient droit de seigneur he is supposed to have renounced. To foil the Count's plans, the two servants conspire with the Countess, who is neglected by her husband. Young Cherubino introduces complications, his passion for the Countess – and indeed all women – wreaking havoc; subplots, disguises and secret letters do the rest. All is resolved when the Count finds himself secretly flirting not with Susanna but with his own wife; exposed, he begs her pardon, and blesses the marriage of Figaro and Susanna.

The opera: In conservative Vienna, *Figaro* was subversive. On the surface an amusing portrayal of domestic intrigues, it questioned the entire social order. An aristocrat is made to look ridiculous, outwitted by his servants: it is character, not class, that counts. The friendship between Countess and maidservant is given musical substance – in the final duet the two women are interchangeable – yet only at the wonderful moment of their reconciliation can the Count, emerging from his festering resentments and lusts, match the nobility of the Countess. Normally in >opera buffa the feverish activity at the end of each act generates complex ensembles, and nowhere so much as in *Figaro*. But while the finale becomes more and more crowded musically, individuals continue to develop their own qualities; no character sings mere patter or just fills in. Mozart has a genius for winning audience affection for his characters; his music can transform the most prosaic exchange, and paint the darkest or most exalted emotions behind the comic merry-go-round. In *Porgi amor* and *Dove sono?* it illuminates the grief of the

Countess, once wooed so passionately, now simply ignored; in *Non so più* the feverish teenage amorousness of Cherubino; in *Se vuol ballare* the rebellious irony of Figaro. Then there are Susanna's *Deh vieni*, Cherubino's *Voi che sapete*, Figaro's *Non più andrai* – all lovers of *Figaro* have their own favourites.

Overview: Mozart must have experienced life intensely: he composed *Figaro*, his first great comic opera, when he was only thirty. Verdi was seventy-nine when he wrote his great comic opera, **Falstaff**. Both works, with supreme lightness of touch, depict a whole society in a small world; both are life-enhancing. But in *Figaro*, with the Countess at its emotional centre, disappointment weighs heavily – something that strikes home in the worldweary 20th century. So it is not surprising that Strauss's **Der Rosenkavalier** pretends to echo *Figaro's* atmosphere (and Oktavian might be Cherubino a few years on). **The Barber of Seville** (Rossini) presents *Figaro's* characters at an earlier point in their lives.

William Shimell in Jonathan Miller's production of *Don Giovanni* for the English National Opera (1985)

in 17th-century Seville that he becomes the object of a chase. Highly amused, he takes refuge in a graveyard, where he is challenged by a statue placed over a fresh grave. It is the statue of a nobleman who had been killed by the Don when defending his daughter's honour. Don Giovanni invites the statue to his home to dine with him – but when it arrives it drags him, defiant, down to Hell.

The opera: The Marriage of Figaro had had such enormous success in Prague that Mozart was commissioned to write another work. His chosen theme was the defiant hero who is always triumphant and who can only be dragged down by supernatural powers. His Don, an amoral free-thinker, rejects the religious and sexual code of his society. The high emotions of those who suffer at his hands – Donna Elvira, Donna Anna and Don Ottavio – and the knockabout slapstick humour of his dealings with the peasants is punctuated by the ironic commentary of his servant, Leporello. This alternating of tragic and comic music delineates the social class of the characters: Donna Anna and Don Ottavio are noble and high flown, whereas the peasant Zerlina has simpler, more direct, more sensual music. Donna Elvira is always earnest, sometimes comically so, whether ardent or anguished. Don Giovanni's style adapts itself according to whom he is currently trying to seduce. Mozart's use of the orchestra at the beginning and end of the opera, and in several >recitatives (especially Anna's and Elvira's) foreshadowed the Romantic composers in its extreme expressive intensity and in evoking the mood of the characters, the atmosphere of the scene. Note the on-stage orchestra included as part of the action and in-joke quotations of popular music by other composers and by Mozart himself. Among the numerous magnificent numbers, *Là ci darem la mano* (the seduction duet between the Don and Zerlina) is probably the most famous, Zerlina's *Batti, batti* the most disarming, and Leporello's catalogue >aria the most staggering.

Further reading: Tim Carter – *W. A. Mozart The Marriage of Figaro* (Cambridge 1987).

Listening

1 Philips 6707 014 4 7699 005
BBC SO/C. Davis
(Wixell, Norman, Freni, Ganzarolli, Minton)
1970
2 Decca D267 D4/K267 K42
CD: 410 150-2
London LDR/5 74001
LPO/Solti
(Te Kanawa, Popp, Von Stade, Allen)

DON GIOVANNI

Two acts
Libretto: Lorenzo da Ponte
First performance: Prague 1787

Plot: The brazen sexual adventures of Don Giovanni, a notorious and obsessive seducer, cause such outrage

Overview: The first important combination of >opera seria and >opera buffa, *Don Giovanni* ranks high. Writing of such dramatic power was not to be found until **Fidelio** (Beethoven) in 1805. The Don Juan story, long popular in folklore, was probably first put on stage in the 1620s. In opera it was taken up by Gazzaniga at about the same time as by Mozart, the most important later version being *The Stone Guest* by Dargomizhsky. The Romantics loved to identify themselves with Mozart's revolutionary hero; the later 19th century patted itself on the back when he got his just deserts. The 20th century remains interested, Joseph Losey's stylish film emphasising the sexual corruption behind the elegance. In Mozart's opera seduction itself is the main source of entertainment; this theme of cruel sport with female emotions, already hinted at in **The Marriage of Figaro**, is given a refined twist in **Così fan tutte**; later, Verdi used it to underscore the drama of **Rigoletto**.

Further reading: John Higgins – *The Making of an Opera: Don Giovanni at Glyndebourne* (London 1978); Julian Rushton – *W. A. Mozart: Don Giovanni* (Cambridge 1981).

Listening

1 EMI SLS143 665-3 4 SLS 143 665-5
  CD: CD57 47037-8
  Angel DSX-3953
  CD: CDCC-47036
  Glyndebourne Festival/Haitink
  (Allen, Van Allen, Vaness)
  1984

COSÌ FAN TUTTE
All Women Behave Like That

Two acts
Libretto: Lorenzo da Ponte
First performance: Vienna 1790

Plot: Ferrando and Guglielmo, supremely confident of the faithfulness of their fiancées, the sisters Fiordiligi and Dorabella, make a bet with Don Alfonso. They pretend to depart for the wars; reappearing in disguise, each launches himself to woo the other's beloved.

The sisters are innocent of what is being perpetrated on them, with no apparent reason to mistrust either their maid Despina, who has been enlisted in the plot, or their friend Don Alfonso, its strategist. Moving from disdain and polite interest, they are eventually fascinated, gripped by passion. The men's light-hearted response to Don Alfonso's cynical challenge has become a destructive contest in seduction, which sours their friendship and rocks their own constancy. Once both women have agreed to marry their new lovers, Don Alfonso has won his bet. The original fiancés 'return', the plot is revealed and all is apparently forgiven.

The opera: Mozart plays with the permutations of six voices – high and low, male and female – in duets, trios and quartets. More than in his other operas the characters sing together in musical/social harmony (never more beautifully than in the trio *Soave sia il vento*). With so few characters, *Così* feels like a >chamber opera, especially in its focus on a single situation. The sub-title is the key to the real meaning: 'The School for Lovers'. In Mozart's time claims were mounting for the importance of passion, but it was still deeply mistrusted. While Don Alfonso manipulates his quartet of young people he is really teaching them a hard lesson: if you're choosing to marry, don't delude yourself that your sexual-romantic feelings can guide you, as these can change. Only when you learn that your feelings are unreliable can you make a conscious choice based on self-knowledge.

The opera presents itself as comic. The disguises and deceptions give opportunities for some amusing stage business, and Despina, a practical realist, comments ironically on the posturing of those she serves. Of the sisters, Dorabella is purely a creature of her feelings, Fiordiligi is more earnest and therefore more troubled. Each man, too, suffers as his comrade wins over his prey. But in the end, no matter that the women's emotions have been cruelly abused, there is apparently no tragedy and no bitterness.

Overview: Where **The Marriage of Figaro** idealises a female friendship which overcomes the age-old sexual threat, *Così* explores both the pressures women are put under by persuasive men, and the strains on male friendship made by unequal sexual prowess. Jealousy momentarily darkens the atmosphere of easy amusement just as in another seemingly light-hearted opera of love-games, **Falstaff** (Verdi). Mozart, who married the younger sister of the woman he had been in love with, and had occasion later to doubt her faithfulness, knew something of what his young men experience in *Così*. The 19th century rejected *Così* as immoral; in the 20th century, which has had to confront the murderous aspect of sexual jealousy in **The Twilight of the Gods** (Wagner) and **Pelléas et Mélisande** (Debussy), *Così* cannot be simply a charming comedy – it strikes home.

Further reading: *Così fan tutte* (English National Opera Guide, London 1983).

Listening

Philips 6707 025 47699 055
Royal Opera/C. Davis
(Caballié, Baker, Cotrubas, Gedda, Ganzarolli, Van Allen)

LA CLEMENZA DI TITO
The Clemency of Titus

Two acts
Libretto: Caterino Mazzola after Pietro Metastasio
First performance: Prague 1791

Plot: The Emperor Titus has to choose an Empress. Vitellia, daughter of a previous Emperor, is furious not to be chosen, and commands her lover, Sextus, to assassinate Titus. Sextus is a close friend of the Emperor and at the moment appointed for firing the Capitol he tries to stop his conspirators, but is too late. Although Titus survives, Sextus, full of self-loathing, confesses his guilt, and the Senate condemns him to death. To protect Vitellia, he refuses to explain his motives to Titus, at which point Vitellia, who had after all been chosen as Empress when the previous candidate was allowed to withdraw, rushes in and confesses. Faced with so many traitors, Titus shows extraordinary clemency by pardoning them all.

The opera: Mozart infused life into the >opera seria form with this, his last opera, written for the coronation of Leopold II. Most of the numbers are brief, there is relatively little display singing, even the march in Scene 2 is bright, not pompous. Vitellia's >coloratura dominates because *she* dominates; she shrieks melodramatically because her situation is genuinely melodramatic – what would *you* do on hearing you had finally been chosen as Empress, if you knew that you had one minute earlier dispatched someone to assassinate the Emperor? The Act I finale fuses drama and music: first Sextus, in a marvellous >recitative accompagnato, is torn between obeying his lover and honouring his friend; then characters are gradually added to the scene while the Capitol blazes; the crowds cry out and against their lamenting, as the music draws inward, the lovers face the appalling reality they have created.

Overview: Inevitably, Mozart invites comparison with himself; his is a rich world. The lyrically beautiful >arias of Titus are reminiscent of Don Ottavio (**Don Giovanni**) and were written for the same singer; the dramatic exchanges between singer and clarinet obbligato in Sextus's famous *Parto, parto* evoke the very different intimacy between Papageno and his pan-pipes (**The Magic Flute**). *La clemenza di Tito* was enormously popular during the Romantic era, and then lost favour. Until recently it was considered something of an aberration. But as opera seria has become better understood, its use in Mozart's hands has been better appreciated. Look at this opera as a period piece, if you prefer: it is a gem.

Listening

Philips 6703 079 4 7699 038
Royal Opera/C. Davis
(Burrows, Baker, Minton, von Stade, Popp, Lloyd)
1976

Gioacchino Rossini

Born: 29th February 1792/Pesaro
Died: 13th November 1868/Passy

Like Mozart, Rossini was a precocious genius, but his major achievements are almost entirely in his nearly forty operas, particularly the early comedies, and those associated with his periods in Naples and Paris. Most famous as an >opera buffa composer, he also developed >opera seria towards >grand opera. He composed very little after the age of thirty-seven and suffered from depression for twenty years or more. He dominated opera absolutely while he was active and was the measure by which all composers were judged for many years.

Further reading: Philip Gossett – 'Rossini' *The New Grove Masters of Italian Opera* (London 1986).

TANCREDI

Two acts
Libretto: Gaetano Rossi, after François-Marie Arouet Voltaire
First performance: Venice 1813

Plot: To save Syracuse from the Saracens, Argirio and the tyrant Orbazzano make a pact which includes Orbazzano marrying Amenaide, Argirio's daughter. Amenaide has secretly sent a letter asking her lover, Tancredi, to return from political exile, to reign over both Syracuse and her own heart. In fact Tancredi has arrived incognito, to fight for his ungrateful fatherland and his beloved Amenaide. But when he meets Amenaide secretly to declare his love, she shows only terror for his safety.

Events move swiftly. Orbazzano has intercepted the letter, in which Amenaide had taken care not to mention Tancredi's name; he accuses her of being secretly in love with the Saracen leader and inviting him to invade Syracuse. Everyone believes in her treachery, and she is imprisoned and condemned to death. Although convinced of her guilt, Tancredi, still incognito, fights as her champion and kills Orbazzano, after which he leads the battle against the Saracens. Only then does he learn from the vanquished leader that Amenaide is innocent; he returns amid general rejoicing, and asks her forgiveness.

The opera: One is tempted to ask Amenaide: 'But why didn't you *tell* him?' – but then half the opera would fall away if Tancredi accepted that she loved him alone. In the fresh spirit of Rossini's first >opera seria, the drama and the music move forward hand in hand, and the orchestration is crystal clear (note how the oboe combined with the subtlest string texture strikes the mood on Tancredi's arrival, or in Amenaide's prison scene). Tancredi's *Di tanti palpiti* became so popular that, according to legend, it was even hummed in court to show sympathy for defendants, opera being very much a part of daily life for the Italians at the time.

Overview: Rossini's more modern combination of solos, ensembles and choruses, where the dramatic and the lyrical were no longer strictly divided, became the pattern for the first half of the 19th century. Abandoning the >castrato voice, and using both the tenor and the mezzo-soprano or contralto in important roles, he paved the way for the vocal 'mix' we take as normal today. *Tancredi* contains some favourite devices, in particular the prison scene (a feature of Handel's **Rodelinda,** Beethoven's **Fidelio** and Smetana's **Dalibor**), and a brief >parlando letter-reading scene, whose special tension was further exploited by Rossini in **Semiramide**, and by Verdi in **Macbeth** and **La traviata**.

Listening

Fonit-Cetra ITL70070
Capella Coloniensis/Ferro
(Cossotto, Cuberli, Hollweg, Ghiuselev)
1980

THE ITALIAN GIRL IN ALGIERS
L'italiana in Algeri

Two acts
Libretto: Angelo Anelli
First performance: Venice 1813

Plot: Just at the moment that Mustafa, Bey of Algiers, decides to abandon his wife out of boredom, in the hope of finding a spirited Italian woman to marry, Isabella comes ashore from a shipwreck, and is captured for his harem. She has been seeking her lost lover, Lindoro, and now by chance she discovers him – as Mustafa's slave. A resourceful woman, she proceeds to do a little enslaving of her own, and soon has Mustafa virtually eating out of her hand. She then sets up a plan to escape with Lindoro and the other Italian prisoners. By initiating Mustafa into the select ranks of the Pappataci – those who are able to eat, drink and sleep no matter what their wives or lovers get up to – she tricks him into ignoring their departure under his very nose. Ruefully, Mustafa decides to go back to his wife.

The opera: This is the first of the Rossini comedies to gain a lasting place in the repertoire – the work of a young man just twenty-one. No matter how well you know it the opera can still be amusing, with its delightfully idiotic plot, and the verve and fun of the music. In many of his early operas, Rossini took >buffa patter to extremes (there are some delicious exchanges here between the humorous male characters), and relished exploiting the comic possibilities of nonsense words. There is a brilliant example of this in the crazy finale to Act I.

Overview: Rossini engaged in a fair amount of trading between his >opere serie and his opere buffe. Not only did he borrow overtures and whole numbers when it suited him (claiming later it would preserve the best music of his failures), he also mingled styles, adding his particular brand of rhythmic vitality to opera seria, and rather boldly bringing some of the high-mindedness of the older form into his comedies, as

in Isabella's stirring song to the Italian prisoners, *Pensa alla patria*. This song represents two 19th-century trends: it is a step towards the breakdown of clearly defined types of opera, and it hints at the future political role operas like *La muette de Portici* (Auber) and **Nabucco** (Verdi) were shortly to play in rallying audiences to the nationalist cause.

Listening

Erato STU 71394 4 MCE71394
RCA (US) ARL3-3855 4 ARK3-3855
I Solisti Veneti/Scimone
(Horne, Balfe, Ramey)
1980

THE BARBER OF SEVILLE
Il barbiere di Siviglia

Two acts
Libretto: Cesare Sterbini, after Pierre-Augustin Caron de Beaumarchais
First performance: Rome 1816

Plot: Count Almaviva, posing as Lindoro, is finding it difficult to woo Rosina: her guardian Dr Bartolo keeps her under lock and key, aided by the old rogue, Don Basilio. The ubiquitous Figaro comes to his help, and between them they insinuate the Count into Bartolo's household, first as a drunken soldier, then as an obsequious music teacher. Rosina contributes both wit and resourcefulness to the schemes, and eventually she and the Count are married in the nick of time by the very notary Dr Bartolo has sent for to solemnise his own marriage to Rosina.

The opera: Despite a disastrous first night, *The Barber* permanently established Rossini's reputation. It remains for many the most perfect comic opera ever written. Although it lacks the humanity of great comedy – an innocent heartlessness is at the very basis of the brilliance – it offers sheer delight instead: the effortless melodic and rhythmic verve, the youthful

Donald Adams (Bartolo) and William
Mackie (Basilio) in the 1986 Welsh
National Opera production of *The Barber
of Seville*

confidence, sweep all before them.
Rossini not only sets the superb
Beaumarchais original, he matches it,
creating a new genre of purely musical
humour. The big solo numbers are
stunning: Figaro's superb >cavatina, an
explosion of verbal patter, orchestral
effect and rhythmic vitality; Rosina's
arch cavatina, whose galloping
virtuosity is periodically reined back to
tease; Don Basilio's *La calunnia*, an
awesome piece of scurrility which
makes symbolic and practical use of the
Rossini crescendo. The overture and
the first act finale encapsulate the
special Rossini quality that was to
dominate Italian opera for twenty years.

Overview: Rossini started writing
operas in a relative vacuum: Italian
opera had at that time no major figure.
Written within a few weeks, *The Barber*
challenged the best works of Cimarosa
and Paisiello, reducing them to period
pieces and setting a standard for future
composers. This being still an age of
vocal virtuosity, star singers abounded;
Rossini both restrained and exploited
this situation, creating in Rosina one of
the first of the great female comic roles
written for a mezzo-soprano. With
Rosina and the Count, >buffa lovers
enter the 19th century as romantic hero
and heroine: Donizetti's **L'elisir
d'amore** and Berlioz's **Béatrice et
Bénédict** start here.

Further reading: *Il barbiere di Siviglia*
(English National Opera Guide,
London 1985).

Listening

CfP CFPD4704 4 TC-CFPD4704
RPO/Gui
(de los Angeles, Alva, Bruscantini)
1962

LA CENERENTOLA
Cinderella

Two acts
Libretto: Jacopo Ferretti after
Charles Perrault
First performance: Rome 1817

Plot: The Prince, advised by his tutor
to find a wife among the daughters of
Don Magnifico, exchanges roles with
his groom, Dandini. The Don and his
daughters fawn all over Dandini with
the vulgarity of snobbism, intermittently
abusing the Don's step-daughter,
Cinderella. Safe in his lowly disguise,
the Prince encounters her, and they are
both deeply affected. The family is
invited to the Prince's country home;
Cinderella, brought there by the tutor,
shows her love for 'the groom' in
rejecting the advances of 'the Prince'
(Dandini). She leaves, to give her lover
time to think about his feelings. When
Dandini reveals his identity to Don
Magnifico, the family troops home,
thoroughly disgusted. Shedding his
disguise, the Prince pursues them, and
claims Cinderella for his wife. Don
Magnifico and his daughters are furious
but Cinderella forgives them.

The opera: The fairy-tale is stripped of
its magic to reveal a human story whose
central element is Cinderella's search
for loving acceptance, both in her family
and in a romantic relationship; this gives
the opera an underlying seriousness.
Cinderella needs her relationship with
the Prince to find her identity, as her
family distorts true values. (This is not
yet fully clear at the end of Act I, and
so Rossini can use his typical crescendo
Finale to depict the insecurity shared
by everyone.) At first downtrodden and
restricted, Cinderella gradually gets
the chance to express her warmth and
moral clarity, and from her nostalgic
folk-tale ballad at the beginning she

moves through more personal
utterances to one full >aria at the end.
Rossini's >coloratura interferes with
some of her earlier expressions of
feeling, but at the end it is appropriate,
showing her at her most complete.

Overview: *La Cenerentola* has
become almost as popular as **The
Barber of Seville**, but it represents a
different concept of opera, which does
not fit easily into any category. It is
much more a work of the 19th century.
Cinderella looks ahead to the
sentimental heroines of Donizetti, while
the juxtaposition of her >buffa father
and sisters with a character and theme
of some depth is taken up by Verdi in
The Force of Destiny, to mention one
example. The use of a medieval-type
ballad, whose occasional partial
repetitions bind the role both musically
and psychologically, occurs also to
great effect in **The Damnation of Faust**
(Berlioz). And later, in *Cendrillon*,
Massenet gave the same story an 18th-
century atmosphere.

Further reading: *La Cenerentola*
(English National Opera Guide, London
1980).

Listening

DG 2709 039
CD: 415 698-2GH3
London Symphony Orch./Abbado
(Berganza)
1971

THE LADY OF THE
LAKE
La donna del lago

Two acts
Libretto: Leone (Andrea) Tottola,
after Sir Walter Scott
First performance: Naples 1819

Plot: The Highlanders, led by Roderick
and the Douglas of Angus, are rebelling
against James V. Partly to cement the
chieftains' alliance, Douglas has
promised his daughter Ellen to
Roderick, unaware that Ellen and the
young warrior Malcolm are in love. To

add to Ellen's distress, a hunter, Hubert, has fallen in love with her. There is a major battle against the King's forces, during which Roderick finds Hubert with Ellen; the men fight, and Roderick is killed. The Highlanders are defeated, Malcolm is captured, and Douglas gives himself up as hostage to peace. Ellen rushes to petition the King for the safety of her father and her friends, and discovers that Hubert has been James V in disguise. The King generously gives the men their freedom, offering his friendship, and Ellen is overjoyed.

The opera: The Highland setting inspired Rossini to some beautiful 'local colour'; during Scene 1 the hunters' echoing horn calls (sounded from the stage) alternate with shepherds' choruses, followed by Ellen's meditative *O mattutini albori* sung from a boat on the lake: they evoke a wistful, softened quality, idealising the misty lochs, waterfalls, woods and crags. There are also some stunning virtuoso numbers, Ellen's *Tanti affetti in tal momento* being the best known. Rossini was able to try out his more adventurous writing on the excellent Naples singers and they, in turn, influenced the development of his florid vocal style. This >opera seria is of its time – the chorus really plays a role, often sharing or even dominating the music. Listen too for the special instrumentation in the lovers' beautiful Act I duet.

Overview: Scott's poem came out in 1810, an unusually recent source for an opera seria (Rossini's was the first setting of Scott for the stage and Donizetti's **Lucia di Lammermoor** would be the most famous). The Romantics found Scotland fascinating – think of Mendelssohn's Scottish Symphony or Hebrides Overture – and the world of *The Lady of the Lake* is a Romantic one. The very brilliance of those first notes in the strings, and the use of the clarinet, suggest Weber's overture to **Oberon**, and with the horn calls we have come far from anything the 18th century would recognise. Add to this the presence of two tenors, both in love with the heroine, and Rossini has moved another step towards the soprano/tenor axis which came to dominate 19th-century opera.

SEMIRAMIDE

Two acts
Libretto: Gaetano Rossi, after
François-Marie Arouet Voltaire
First performance: Venice 1823

Plot: The people of Babylon want their Queen Semiramide to announce the successor to her dead husband, Ninus. Assur is confident of being chosen, but Semiramide is strangely hesitant, and terrifying signs show the displeasure of the gods. The young captain Arsace is received well by the High Priest, and Semiramide announces him as her consort and the new King. Arsace is unreceptive as he is in love with the Princess Azema, but the ghost of Ninus emerges, undertaking to confirm him as king-elect as long as he first avenges a crime, in Ninus's tomb. Then Arsace learns that he is the long-lost son of Semiramide and that she conspired with Assur to murder his father. He confronts his mother, who is deeply remorseful, and proceeds to the tomb where, despite great fear, he strikes down Assur and is proclaimed King of Babylon.

The opera: *Semiramide* was Rossini's last Italian opera. It combines all the diverse strands of true >opera seria, yet has a tense forward movement. The traditional turn-and-turn-about of >recitative and >aria is so embedded in the complex arrangement of ensembles, choral and orchestral sections that the effect is of an organic whole which fuses the personal concerns of powerful figures with their larger political roles. The two scenes with Semiramide and Arsace, in remarkable contrast to one another, cover between them the deepest emotions of their characters, yet the urgency of the overall drama is not lost. For the first time in an opera, a military band appears onstage. The overture, hinting at the musical material to come, is particularly fine.

Overview: Semiramide herself is far removed from the traditional opera seria tyrant whose misguided and misplaced love is the excuse for the plot: she is a complex person, both fallible and heroic, close in some ways to Gertrude in Thomas's **Hamlet**, Equally, Assur's 'mad scene' nearby Ninus's tomb is less blatant in madness, closer to Macbeth than to **Orlando.** It is Shakespeare who is evoked, and, through him, Verdi, who would have known Rossini's opera before writing **Macbeth**.

Listening

Decca SET 317; London OSA 1383
LSO
(Sutherland, Horne, Serge)

Gaetano Donizetti

Born: 29th November 1797/Bergamo
Died: 8th April 1848/Bergamo

Donizetti composed sixty-six operas of mixed achievement, his main works being enormously successful. He worked with amazing rapidity. He was a master craftsman in comic opera, and his tragic operas dominated the scene until his death around the time that Verdi was reaching his peak.

Further reading: William Ashbrook *Donizetti and His Operas* (Cambridge 1982).

ANNA BOLENA

Two acts
Libretto: Felice Romani
First performance: Milan 1830

Plot: Henry VIII (Enrico) needs to get rid of Anne Boleyn (Anna Bolena) before his new love, Jane Seymour (Giovanna), can become Queen. He recalls Lord Percy from exile, hoping that he can use Percy's former relationship with Anne to provide evidence of Anne's infidelity, and indeed Percy, by insisting on a private scene with Anne in which he threatens

suicide, is fulfilling Henry's designs. Anne's musician, Smeaton, in love with her, also unwittingly assists Henry. Jane Seymour is Anne's lady-in-waiting; she attempts continually to intercede on her behalf with Henry. The King will brook no interference; Anne is condemned and executed.

The opera: After some thirty operas, Donizetti found his own style in *Anna Bolena* and created his first notable opera, a powerful 'historical' drama of genuine conviction. Four substantial characters are locked in a personal and political struggle depicting Anne's attempt, and the attempt of those supporting her, to block Henry's drive to dishonour and destroy her. Henry, an unvarying force, is musically constant; he has no >arias, and it is against his role in ensembles that the others react. Anne's music expresses the full range of emotions. She has some fine moments, such as her prayer *Dio, che mi vedi in core*, and *Al dolce guidami* in the splendid final scene – and listen for *Giudici!... ad Anna!* (Act I Finale). Her part needs a >bel canto singer able to stand out against Jane (a heavy dramatic voice) and the male roles, especially in the duets, which are the dynamic element in the drama. The mounting tension in the scenes between Anne and Percy, and Anne and Jane, shows Donizetti at his best.

Overview: Politically, Anne's situation is a development of Octavia's in **The Coronation of Poppaea** (Monteverdi); emotionally it is closer to Bellini's **Norma**, although Anne cannot have Norma's authority (and it is interesting that Jane Seymour and Norma's younger rival, Adalgisa, take up similar positions). The use of the oboe in the visionary moments of Anne's final scene evokes the hopes of another ill-fated prisoner, Florestan (Beethoven's **Fidelio**). This scene is sometimes mistakenly referred to as a mad scene; it does incorporate nostalgic mental wandering as manifested by somnambulistic Romantic heroines, but psychologically and musically it is a much more complex achievement. Anne's young page, the musician Smeaton, is a >trouser role for a mezzo, very like Cherubino (Mozart's **Figaro**), although here the lad's adolescent passion for his mistress has tragic consequences. Cherubino/Smeaton will turn up again without romantic attachments as Oscar (Verdi's **Masked Ball**) and will become a full-blown lover, centre stage, as Oktavian (Strauss's **Der Rosenkavalier**).

Listening

1 Cetra CD: CD518
   La Scala/Gavazzeni
   (Callas)
   1957
2 Angel AVC-34031 4 4AXS-34031
   London Symphony Orchestra/Rudel
   (Sills)
   1972

L'ELISIR D'AMORE
The Elixir of Love

Two acts
Libretto: Felice Romani
First performance: Milan 1832

Plot: Nemorino is hopelessly in love with Adina, who finds the swaggering Sergeant Belcore more to her taste. Hearing how Tristan got Isolde to love him by drinking a love potion, he turns for help to the itinerant quack pedlar, Dulcamara. This worthy capitalises on the situation by selling him a bottle of Bordeaux wine. Its effect on Nemorino is startling – even Adina takes notice. She resents both his new-found popularity with other women and his feigned indifference to her, and agrees to marry Belcore just to spite her former suitor. Nemorino signs up with Belcore's platoon to get the ready cash for more elixir, but Adina buys back his freedom and declares her love. The opera ends with Dulcamara's triumphal exit as all the villagers possess themselves of the wonderful elixir.

The opera: Composed in fourteen days, L'elisir d'amore was an instant success. It is a story about the village itself rather than the two lovers and the whole opera moves forward in duets or larger ensembles. The few solo numbers are show-stoppers: Dulcamara's classic hard-sell, and Nemorino's deeply felt Una furtiva lagrima (a case of the composer's instinct being absolutely

right, for Romani was against a 'pathetic lamentation' at this point). Nemorino is actually so single-mindedly earnest as to be almost unfunny until he gets tipsy, and even Adina's more expansive moments tend to move away from comedy. Her reaction when she recognises the depth of Nemorino's love leads to a fascinating juxtaposition of styles, Adina singing a heartfelt 'serious' melody while Dulcamara patters on in clipped >buffa rhythms. The libretto is very funny – Donizetti must have congratulated himself for insisting on working with Romani – and the names Dulcamara, Nemorino and Belcore (Bitter-sweet, Little No-love and Beautiful Heart) are a give-away: the story comes from the >commedia dell'arte, and the rogue Dulcamara, a superb creation, is the lynch-pin of the fun.

Overview: Dulcamara would be recognised all over the world, for the quack pedlar is a favourite rogue in many cultures. (Full marks if you know the title of W. S. Gilbert's pre-Sullivan burlesque, Dulcamara; or The Little Duck and The Big Quack; or The Tipsy Gypsy and the Pipsy Wipsy.) With hindsight, L'elisir d'amore suggests how **La sonnambula** in different hands might have become a glorious send-up. Donizetti's village characters are gullible, Bellini's are suggestible, and love reduces both tenors to equal foolishness (the refined feeling of the exquisite tenor >aria, like O my beloved father in Puccini's **Gianni Schicchi**, strikes a new note, sitting like a jewel in its buffa setting). Donizetti's sentimental comedy also chuckles about **Tristan und Isolde** a quarter-century before Wagner built his great opera around the drinking of a love-potion. It shares its sense of fun with Smetana's **The Bartered Bride**; it is one of those rare operas which leaves you feeling sure that the composer has enjoyed writing it.

Listening

1 CBS (UK) 79210; (US) M3-34585
   Covent Garden/Pritchard
   (Cotrubas, Domingo, Wixell, Evans)
   1977
2 Philips 412 714-IPH2 4
   412 714-4PHZ
   CD: 412 714-2PH2

Turin Radio Orch./Scimone
(Ricciarelli, Carreras, Nucci, Trimarchi)
1982

LUCIA DI LAMMERMOOR

Three acts
Libretto: Salvatore Cammarano, after Sir Walter Scott
First performance: Naples 1835

Plot: Lucy Ashton (Lucia) is in love with an enemy of her family, Edgar Ravenswood (Edgardo). When Edgar leaves for France, Lucy's brother, Henry (Enrico), makes other plans for her: insecure at Court, he needs an alliance with someone of influence. He intercepts all Edgar's letters to Lucy, and pressures her into marrying Arthur Bucklaw (Arturo). On the appointed wedding day with Arthur, Henry produces a forged letter showing that Edgar loves another woman. Lucy, already morbidly depressed, and believing Edgar faithless, can no longer resist Henry's bullying. The marriage contract is signed – and Edgar arrives. His denunciation of Lucy breaks her: her hold on reality goes. In the nuptial chamber, she stabs Arthur; she wanders deranged among the guests, and dies shortly afterwards. Hearing of this, Edgar stabs himself.

The opera: Donizetti writes beautifully for the tenor voice, and it was *Lucia* which finally established the tenor as the romantic male supreme in opera, one singer being named 'the tenor of the curse' and another 'the tenor of the beautiful death' according to his rendering of Edgar. But as time went on the soprano became the dominant singer in this opera, and at one period the final scene was actually dropped in performance, giving the soprano the last word. Even now, *Lucia di Lammermoor* is considered a soprano vehicle, and both Lucia's lovely first >aria and her mad scene are famous tours de force. Lucy is more victim than initiator, and her singing is more ornamental than dramatic. Yet overall Donizetti achieves clear dramatic movement, despite the clutter of the

extra male roles (Norman, Raymond and Arthur, the latter two making up the party for the celebrated sextet) and he shows a splendid flair for nastiness with Henry Ashton.

Overview: Comparisons with Bellini's **I puritani** are inevitable; the operas were 'born' in the same year, they are drawn from Scottish themes, and their heroines, representative Romantic women, have extended mad scenes. In terms of dramatic motivation, Lucia's mad scene comes second to Elvira's – her >coloratura is gorgeous but gratuitous. But at least her madness leads to death, a very satisfying conclusion for a Romantic opera. And the regulation outburst from the betrayed tenor seems rather more legitimate than is usual. *Lucia*'s popularity received a fillip when it was included among the >bel canto operas revived for Maria Callas in the 1950s.

Listening

Decca SET 5281
London OSA 13103 4
OSA 513103
CD: 417 193-2DH3

Monica Pick-Hieronimi as *Lucia di Lammermoor* (Buxton Festival 1979)

Royal Opera/Bonynge
(Sutherland, Pavarotti, Milnes, Ghiaurov)
1971

MARIA STUARDA

Three acts
Libretto: Giuseppe Bardari, after
Friedrich Schiller
First performance: Milan 1835

Plot: Mary Stuart, previously Queen of
Scotland, imprisoned on the instructions
of Queen Elizabeth, is suspected of
plotting to take over the English throne.
Elizabeth is advised by Cecil in the
interests of security to execute Mary;
both Talbot and Leicester intercede
with her on Mary's behalf. Elizabeth is
jealous of Leicester's obvious romantic
involvement with the prisoner, but
agrees to meet her while out hunting.
Face to face, the two Queens find no
common ground; Elizabeth insults Mary,
who abandons her submissive attitude
and hurls abuse in return. After this
Elizabeth condemns her to death,
despite Leicester's exhortations. Mary
receives absolution for her rather spotty
past from Talbot, and goes to the block
with dignity.

The opera: The core of the opera is the
fictitious confrontation between the two
Queens, one of the great might-have-
beens of history. Even allowing for the
bad press given to Elizabeth I in the
19th century, and the natural sympathy
of Donizetti's public for a Catholic
Queen put to death by a Protestant
regime, its appeal to the composer is
understandable: the meeting is the very
stuff of drama, and Mary's outburst gives
us by proxy the glorious – and rare –
satisfaction of expressing exactly what
is felt just when the greatest restraint
ought to be exercised. The whole opera
builds up to this moment, with
Elizabeth's jealousy and Leicester's
resolve increasing the tension. Mary's
final scene is not simply a tableau, nor
pure sentiment, but a highly organised
mini-opera with overture, chorus, and
an intense musical–dramatic life of its
own. Leicester's and Mary's solo >arias
throughout the opera are consistently
fine, the melodies in several cases

being built from an ascending scale.

Overview: *Maria Stuarda* takes us back
to the beginnings of opera: it rewrites
history with the same concern for
theatrical appropriateness shown by
Peri and Monteverdi in rewriting the
myth of Orpheus. Its focus – the
confrontation of two women of
conviction – became a myth in its own
right, recurring in varying forms in
operas by Verdi (**Don Carlos**, **Aida**),
Ponchielli (**La Gioconda**), Cilea
(**Adriana Lecouvreur**) and Strauss
(**Elektra**). Let us hope that the singers
playing these roles do not repeat an
incident during rehearsals for the first
production of Donizetti's opera, when
the Elizabeth and the Mary, already
hostile to one another, took the
confrontation scene so seriously that
they turned it into a fist-fight.

Listening

1 Decca D2D3 4 K2A33
  London OSA 13117 4 OSA5-13117
  Teatro Comunale, Bologna/Bonynge
  (Sutherland)
  1974–5
2 HMV SLS 5277
  English National Opera/Mackerras
  (Baker)
  1983

DON PASQUALE

Three acts
Libretto: Giovanni Ruffini and the
composer, after Angelo Anelli
First performance: Paris 1843

Plot: Don Pasquale, an elderly
bachelor, is angry with his nephew
Ernesto: the lad is in love with Norina,
a penniless young widow. To marry her,
he would have to inherit his uncle's
wealth, and Pasquale has no intention of
subsidising such a marriage. To spite
Ernesto, he decides to disinherit him,
and choose a wife for himself. Doctor
Malatesta brings in his own sister,
Sofronia, fresh from a convent; Pasquale
is enchanted by Sofronia's meekness
and beauty, and they get married
immediately. Ernesto is witness, and is
barely restrained by Doctor Malatesta

from blurting out his horror – 'Sofronia' is his own Norina! The plan has been set up to help the young lovers, and to keep Pasquale from a real marriage. Once the contract is signed, 'Sofronia' becomes an absolute shrew, a spendthrift and a flirt, and Pasquale longs for the days of his freedom. When she undertakes to leave if Ernesto will bring a wife in to run the household, Pasquale readily settles a fat income on his nephew so that he can marry Norina – and finds, to his amazement and relief, that his own marriage has melted away.

The opera: This is Donizetti's masterpiece, a delight from start to finish. Its music has a marvellous freshness, compactness, great variety of rhythm, real tunes you can whistle, and delightful instrumentation (there are constant little surprises with trumpets, bassoons, cellos, flute). The characters come from the >*commedia dell'arte*, but – Ernesto apart – they are also real people from the day-to-day business of life. Norina's relish at playing Sofronia; Pasquale's pathetic attempts to assert himself as his picture of marital bliss takes a beating; the compassionate irony motivating Malatesta's puppet-mastering – all this shows the humanity behind the >buffa scheme. Yet shortly after *Don Pasquale* was written Donizetti manifested the effects of the syphilis that would paralyse and eventually kill him, and it was his last comic opera.

Overview: Although *Don Pasquale* is in the great buffa tradition of both Pergolesi and Mozart, it is a work of individual authority, which ranks with Rossini's **The Barber of Seville** – some would say higher. Rich as it is, there is nothing superfluous or included for display. Italian opera had to wait half a century for Verdi's **Falstaff** before any comic opera had more to say, or could say it as well. All three masterpieces ridicule old men who want young wives. All show young lovers battling for their love to survive – they have to snatch time together, but when they meet, the music is glorious.

Listening

EMI SLS143436-3 4 TC-SLS143436-5
Angel DSX-3938 4 4DSX-3938
Philharmonia/Muti

(Freni, Winberg, Nucci, Bruscantini) 1981

Vincenzo Bellini

Born: 3rd November 1801/Catania
Died: 23rd September 1835/Puteaux

Bellini was the arch-romantic opera composer, whose dramatic flair has been obscured by his achievement in the elegaic beauty of his >bel canto melodic line, and the intense emotion it conveys. His output was almost entirely in vocal writing, and his influence was widespread. Of his ten operas, four are popular – marvellous vehicles for singers specialising in the particular manner they require.

I CAPULETI E I MONTECCHI
The Capulets and the Montagues

Two acts
Libretto: Felice Romani, after William Shakespeare and other sources
First performance: Venice 1830

Plot: As leader of the Montagues, Romeo offers peace to his enemies the Capulets on condition that he marries Juliet (Giulietta), daughter of Capulet (Capellio) their leader. But he is rejected. Romeo and Juliet are secretly in love, but she is destined to marry Tybalt (Tebaldo). Romeo tries to persuade her to elope with him but Juliet will not cast family duty overboard. In desperation Romeo infiltrates the wedding with his followers and tries unsuccessfully to abduct Juliet. Lawrence (Lorenzo), a Capulet and the lovers' friend, gives Juliet a powerful potion; it makes her appear dead and she is laid in the family vault. But Lawrence comes under suspicion, and cannot get the information to Romeo. He, believing Juliet dead, gets into the vault to mourn her, taking poison just before she regains consciousness. After an affecting farewell, Romeo expires, and Juliet dies of grief.

The opera: Romani used several sources, including some Shakespeare had used, and the old tale gains swiftness and clarity. The constant warring between the two clans is in the foreground in Act I, giving both orchestra and chorus an important role. Romeo (written for a mezzo-soprano) initiates much of the action, and the music reflects his forceful energy; even his love-music is urgent, persuasive. The famous Bellini lyricism is given to Juliet; her plea to her father (*Ah, non poss'io partire*) is a marvellous instance of >bel canto, the voice expressing the deepest feeling with the simplest melodic means. She also shows maturity and strength of character, her rejection of Romeo's reckless plans creating a fascinating tension between the lovers. A feature in the score is Bellini's use of solo instruments at the start of the main >arias, the harp, the horn, the clarinet or the cello often voicing the lovers' feelings with a special poignancy. The tomb scene conveys exquisite feeling with remarkable psychological perception.

Overview: *I Capuleti e i Montecchi* has a quality of its own. Romeo's >ariosos, and Juliet's arias, are among Bellini's most beautiful. The >recitative in the tomb scene recalls Monteverdi (with recitative like that, who needs melody?). So does the even-handedness: Juliet is an unexpectedly complex heroine, Tybalt a most sympathetic 'enemy' figure; even Capulet, the stock villain, has a moment of soul-searching, and Romeo's impetuous heroics get only negative feedback. Had Bellini followed this line of development instead of aiming to move his audience to tears, 19th-century opera might have grown up sooner.

Listening

EMI EX270 192-3
Angel DS-3969
Royal Opera, Covent Garden/Muti
(Gruberova, Baltsa)
1983

LA SONNAMBULA
The Sleepwalker

Two acts
Libretto: Felice Romani
First performance: Milan 1831

Plot: In an Alpine village, Elvino and Amina are to be married. Elvino is a jealous type who reacts badly when the young Count, on his way to take up residence in the local castle, responds to Amina's charm and beauty. And when she is discovered sleeping in the Count's room at the inn, Elvino renounces her for betraying him. He cannot accept the Count's explanation that Amina was sleepwalking until he sees it for himself: she appears on the roof of the mill, walks along the edge, and gets across a rotten bridge, unconscious of the extreme danger. Still asleep, she murmurs sadly of Elvino's refusal to believe in her innocence, and the loss of their love. No more proof is needed, and Amina has an unusually joyful awakening.

The opera: With its lightweight treatment of the affections of the young villagers flowing easily from sentimental tragedy to sentimental happiness, *La sonnambula* is an >opera semiseria. Bellini's wonderful gift for long melancholy melodies is evident in the two tenor >arias, *Prendi l'anel ti dono* and *Tutti o sciolto* and attains quite remarkable beauty in the famous *Ah, non credea mirarti*, the centre-piece of the main sleepwalking scene. Bellini uses the sleepwalking to create, and then resolve, dramatic situations. For the early Romantics, *feeling* was paramount; since Amina's words while asleep simply confirm the evidence already presented, their effect is to intensify for the onlookers (and the audience) the pathos of this rejected lover. Although a genuine contemporary interest in somnambulism must have added a frisson, the story now seems rather dated, but it has a period charm, and is an adequate vehicle for some lovely music.

Overview: *La sonnambula* brought Bellini wide fame in Europe, which was

ENGLISH WORDS
PRICE 3/-

JENNY LIND'S
CELEBRATED

SONNAMBULA SONG,

WITH ITALIAN WORDS
PRICE 3/-

"AH NON GIUNGE", "DO NOT MINGLE",

An 1850 songsheet of 'Ah non giunge' from *La sonnambula*

consolidated with his subsequent operas, whose theme and treatment were more substantial (although *Beatrice di Tenda* was a failure). Different periods approached drama in different ways. Fifteen years after *La sonnambula* Verdi's treatment of Lady **Macbeth's** sleepwalking shows how opera had advanced: psychological insight forms the very basis of the drama. One is tempted to imagine a >verismo setting of *La sonnambula*

sixty years after Bellini's. It could have had a very different ending, for the Count would certainly have taken advantage of Amina's innocent visitation.

Further reading: Friedrich Lippman – 'Bellini' *The New Grove Masters of Italian Opera* (London 1986).

Listening

EMI EX290043-3 4 EX290043-5
CD: CD57 47378-8
Angel CD: CDCB 47377

41

La Scala/Votto
(Callas, Monti, Zaccaria)
1957

NORMA

Two acts
Libretto: Felice Romani
First performance: Milan 1831

Plot: The Druid prophetess, Norma, has secretly broken her vows of chastity and borne two children; her lover was Pollione, proconsul of the hated Romans occupying Gaul. Yet she has continued to officiate, and to restrain the Druids from revolt. Then she finds Pollione has been unfaithful to her with Adalgisa, a young priestess, and has demanded that Adalgisa return with him to Rome. Enraged, Norma decides that before killing herself she will murder her children, but she cannot bring herself to harm them. Pollione, arrested for trying to abduct Adalgisa from the sacred altar, is brought to Norma to be judged. She terrifies him with threats to kill Adalgisa. But when she summons the Druids, she names herself as guilty of breaking her vows and betraying her country, and – first extracting a promise from her father that he will care for the children – she mounts the sacrificial pyre with Pollione.

The opera: *Norma* is Bellini's most powerful opera, and his most beautiful. The glories are worth enumerating: Norma's exquisite invocation, *Casta diva*; the moving duet with Adalgisa, *Mira o Norma*; the wonderful scene when Norma's anguished love for her children conquers her destructive anger; the ecstatic Finale; even the single moment when she reveals her guilt – *Son io* – which fuses the drama with the expressive power of >bel canto. Norma is shown as Priestess, as guide, as mother, as friend, and as woman humiliated; she sings no love duet, and her end is no >*liebestod*: while Pollione is rediscovering his love for her at the end, she is achieving lasting understanding with her father. Adalgisa, who becomes a woman of substance and strength, is ultimately, like Pollione, a catalyst for the feelings of Norma herself. The Druids are a living presence – praying, grumbling, unleashing their fury, they add a forceful energy to the opera.

Overview: The theme of love across patriotic boundaries crops up frequently in opera, and the religious-cum-nationalist element in the Druids is vital to *Norma*. Also familiar is the priestess who breaks her vows for love (like Spontini's **La vestale,** Bizet's **The Pearl Fishers** and Delibes' **Lakmé**). But *Norma* is really concerned with an older, more potent story – the woman spurned, who in her vengeful fury destroys her children and/or her husband's new lover. Cherubini had not flinched from the ultimate horror in **Médée,** but for Bellini it was an inspiration to show the tortured Norma as a mother who protects, and, given his belief that the audience's emotions must be wrung, probably more effective (compare the tear-jerking aspects of Andromache's scene in Berlioz's **The Trojans**, or Puccini's **Madam Butterfly**). Still, there is one new, Romantic truth: Norma is among the very first operatic heroines to die.

Listening

EMI 3C 163 00535-7
Angel SCL 3615
La Scala/Serafin
(Callas, Ludwig, Corelli, Zaccaria)
1960

I PURITANI
The Puritans

Three acts
Libretto: Carlo Pepoli, after Jacques Ancelot and Xavier Boniface Saintine, after Sir Walter Scott
First performance: Paris 1835

Plot: With some stretching of boundaries, this Scottish tale is set in Plymouth, England. Civil War is raging. Elvira, daughter of a Puritan, is in love with Arthur, a Cavalier, and her father has reluctantly given them permission to marry. But, just before the wedding, Arthur helps the widowed Queen of Charles I to escape, and this is misinterpreted as an elopement. Elvira loses her sanity; Arthur is hunted as a traitor. He risks returning to see Elvira, who regains her clarity of mind. But when he wants to run from the approaching soldiers, she suffers a relapse, and, holding him back, attracts general attention. The soldiers want to execute Arthur; when Elvira hears this, she is shocked back into sanity, and everyone else – out of concern for her – tries to dissuade the soldiers. Just in time, news comes that the war is over and Cromwell has pardoned all prisoners. The lovers can now contemplate a joyful future together.

The opera: For Paris, Bellini enlarged the scale of his work, the active chorus and colourful instrumentation showing a move towards >grand opera. But *I puritani* is about Elvira; all sentiments centre on her. The Romantic male weeps for her and swears vengeance on those who wound her. She represents Romantic womanhood: she is passionately attached, but vulnerable, and her sensitive spirit cannot take the cruel shocks of Fate. Her >coloratura is thus dramatically true, an expression of her nervosity, either ecstatic or deranged; her >bel canto melodies convey the ardour or the suffering of a beautiful soul. Her healthiest outburst, in *Son vergin vezzosa*, shows her dangerously excitable. When you weep for Elvira, which is what Bellini wanted, you are responding to a major manifestation of Romantic art.

Overview: A century before Bellini, >opera seria presented a string of contrasting emotional states, each embodied in an >aria; now, in the Romantic period, composers aimed to present subtle shifts of emotion. A Baroque mad scene showed a breakdown of the victim's nature, a Romantic mad scene intensified the victim's nature, and this is why Bellini's Elvira or Donizetti's **Lucia** are sympathetic figures to all around them, whereas Handel's **Orlando** is regarded with fear and horror. Elvira has other reactions typical of the Romantic heroine: in her heart's loneliness, she sings a nostalgic ballad, as did **La Cenerentola** (Rossini), as will Marguerite (Berlioz's **The Damnation of Faust**) and Desdemona (Verdi's **Otello**). By contrast, Giorgio and

Riccardo swear common cause to martial rhythms; brotherhood, whether noble or evil, is a Romantic show-stopper, and will reappear in **The Force of Destiny** and **Don Carlos** (Verdi), **The Twilight of the Gods** (Wagner), and **The Pearl Fishers** (Bizet).

Listening

Decca SET587 4 R25K32
London OSA 13111 4 OSA5-13111
Royal Opera/Bonynge
(Sutherland, Pavarotti)
1975

Giuseppe Verdi

Born: 10th October 1813/Le Roncole
Died: 27th January 1901/Milan

Verdi is one of the few undisputed great opera composers whose most popular works have been the core of the repertory of every opera house in the world. He dominated Italian opera for fifty years, first with operas that were identified with the revolutionary movement, then with his early masterpieces at the halfway point of the century. He never stopped developing as a composer, and the two works of his old age are a towering achievement in the field of tragic and comic opera, which showed Italian opera the way forward in the face of the mounting influence of Wagner's work.

Further reading: Julian Budden *The Operas of Verdi* (London 1973–8).

NABUCCO

Four parts
Libretto: Temistocle Solera
First performance: Milan 1842

Plot: The Assyrians are led by King Nabucco, his daughter Fenena, and

43

Abigaille (she, thought to be Nabucco's daughter, is an ambitious slave). The Hebrews, led by Zaccaria, their High Priest, are conquered, and taken to Babylon. There, with Nabucco away, the Assyrian leadership comes into dispute: Fenena, acting as Regent, is in love with the Hebrew Prince Ismaele, and because she converts to the Hebrew faith and frees the Hebrews, she is unseated by Abigaille and the Priests of Baal. Nabucco returns, claims to be God, and is immediately struck mad. Abigaille, now absolute ruler, keeps Nabucco prisoner, planning to execute Fenena and all the Hebrews. Fearful for his daughter's safety, Nabucco prays to Jehovah; his mind clears, he regains power and saves the Hebrews. Abigaille takes poison; she dies acknowledging the Hebrew faith and asking for forgiveness.

The opera: Despite his depression after the death of his wife and two children, Verdi could not help responding to Solera's libretto. He brought to the stage opera that was stirring, exciting, full of ferocious energy (as when Nabucco storms out to save Fenena). Alongside this energy was a rich store of melody: the formidable Abigaille, after her fiery >recitative, reveals inner feelings of unexpected beauty (*Anch'io dischiuso un giorno*), and Zaccaria speaks to the Hebrew Lord with profound spiritual yearning (*Tu sul labbro de' veggenti*). (Verdi makes sublime use there of the strings, and, in several other >arias, of the flute, to represent God's comfort.) Above all, *Nabucco* spoke to the Italians' passionate desire to throw off foreign domination, to regain their country. Almost all the choral writing is given to the Hebrews; in a sense they are the central character in the opera, a people enslaved and in exile. How could the Italians fail to identify with them, how could they not thrill to the lament *Va pensiero* as it swelled at *O mia patria si bella e perduta?* This was the first of several Verdi operas to provoke demonstrations, even riots, against the Austrian oppressors. Verdi became a symbol of Italian resistance, his name in acronym the slogan proclaiming the King: VIVA VERDI (Vittorio Emanuele Re d'Italia).

Overview: Nabucco's moments of madness, contained within formal limits,

do not approach those of **Macbeth**, but Abigaille shares qualities of the she-devil with Lady Macbeth, which connect them both with Handel's sorceress Armide (**Rinaldo**). The opera's highly coloured, melodramatic changes of situation bring it close to Meyerbeer, yet its best qualities – passionate human feelings, lyrically expressed – are essentially Italian, fitting it for its role in the struggle for national independence.

Listening

Decca SET 298 4 K126K32
CD: 417 407-2DH2
London OSA 1382 4 OSA5-1382
CD: 417 407-2LH
Vienna State Opera/Gardelli
(Gobbi, Souliotis)
1965

MACBETH

Four acts
Libretto: Franceso Mario Piave and A. Maffei, after William Shakespeare; revised version Piave
First performance: Florence 1847; revised version Paris 1865

Plot: Macbeth and Banquo are hailed by witches prophesying kingship for Macbeth and kingly descendants for Banquo. Macbeth informs his wife; when he reaches home the intention to murder is already formed, and they kill King Duncan, who is their guest, in his sleep. Macbeth takes the throne, becomes fearful of the prophecy concerning Banquo, and has him killed – but his son escapes. At a banquet Macbeth, haunted by Banquo's ghost, cannot contain his horror. A visit to the witches gives him no peace of mind, and Lady Macbeth starts obsessive sleepwalking. The people of Scotland flee from Macbeth's bloody tyranny to Malcolm, Duncan's son, and Macduff, whose family has been wiped out. Ready for battle, Macbeth recognises that his existence is joyless, meaningless; even the death of his wife does not touch him. He is killed by Macduff, and the people are liberated.

Renato Bruson as Macbeth and Renata
Scotto as Lady Macbeth (Royal Opera
House 1981)

The opera: Verdi's revisions ensure
that *Macbeth* ends with the people and
their triumph rather than with
Macbeth's death. Despite this, the
fascination of the opera remains the
relationship of Macbeth and Lady
Macbeth, and the ravages made on
their inner spirit by their drive for
power. The banquet scene brilliantly
conveys the strain they are under, Lady
Macbeth's contrived joviality in the
drinking song being forced aside by
her husband's dramatic >recitative.

Her presence, as powerful as
Macbeth's until the last scenes, is
extended in the superb *La luce langue*;
her sleepwalking scene with its
tortured revelations over insistent note
patterns is the most riveting scene in
the opera. No wonder that Verdi
refused to cast a famous soprano whose
voice quality was too pure, too angelic.

Overview: The 1847 version was
dominated by Macbeth himself; the
revision placed the opera in a more
political context. This was a by-product
of the Parisian taste for >grand opera
compared with the Italians'
concentration on the individual; for very

different reasons, there was a similar shift of perspective with Musorgsky's **Boris Godunov**. In *Patria oppressa*, *Macbeth* shares with *I lombardi* and **Nabucco** a deeply moving cry for liberty, expressed as a refugees' lament. Few Italians in mid-century could fail to respond, and today it is these choruses, rather than the rallying cries to battle, which strike home. The problem of *Macbeth* for modern audiences, and therefore for modern directors, is the witches, on whom Verdi laboured so hard. Nowadays 19th-century macabre appears dated and ineffectual; Berlioz's devils in **The Damnation of Faust** aren't horrifying either. What grips us is individual angst: Macbeth's paranoid hallucinations or Lady Macbeth's neurotic hand-washings are the true witches of the criminally ambitious soul.

Further reading: David Rosen and Andrew Porter, eds. – *Verdi's Macbeth: A Sourcebook* (New York 1984).

Listening

DG 2709 062 4 3371 022
CD: 415 688-2GH3
La Scala/Abbado
(Verrett, Cappuccilli, Domingo, Ghiaurov)
1976

LUISA MILLER

Three acts
Libretto: Salvatore Cammarano after Friedrich Schiller
First performance: Naples 1849

Plot: Although the love of Carlo and Luisa is innocent, Luisa's father believes his suspicions justified when Count Walter's aide, Wurm, tells him that 'Carlo' is Rodolfo, the Count's son. Miller is not the only anxious father – the Count wants Rodolfo to make an advantageous marriage, and is prepared to break up the relationship with Luisa at all costs. He abuses Miller and his daughter in their own home, but is prevented by his son from arresting them. Then he has Miller thrown into chains, and sends Wurm to Luisa: to save her father's life she must write a letter proving she

loves Wurm. Distraught, Luisa complies. The letter is then leaked to Rodolfo, who is shattered to learn of Luisa's perfidy. When Miller is released, he has to dissuade his daughter from suicide, and they plan to start a new life elsewhere. But Rodolfo reappears, and engineers matters so that Luisa and he share a poisoned drink. As they are dying, she reveals the deception she has been forced into, and Rodolfo, in his last moments, manages to kill Wurm, flaunting his own death before his father as a punishment.

The opera: The three acts are labelled 'Love', 'Intrigue' and 'Poison', pastoral innocence darkening by degrees to the tragedy of the impressive third act. This gives a sense of overall unity, strengthened by occasional repetitions of the very first notes of the overture (or a variant of those notes). The musical language within each scene is also unified, for as the >recitatives do not obviously shape up for the >arias, the divisions do not obtrude, and the action can flow forward. Much of the music is contained in magnificent two-person exchanges, or in larger ensembles, one of which is sung >a capella, strangely effective in this richly orchestrated score.

Overview: *Luisa Miller* was part of Verdi's development towards the operas by which he became best known (**Rigoletto, Trovatore, Traviata**), but it does not boast any comparable high points. Its unity and inexorable forward movement give it the feeling of Greek tragedy, appropriate for an opera concerned with father-daughter and father-son relationships. As with Shakespeare, the father-daughter theme occupied Verdi continually up to **Falstaff**, and in this opera he exploits it fully with the kind of moral argument and reconciliation that Wagner transmuted in **The Valkyrie**. The similarity to Wagner, of course, ends there – although it would not be inappropriate to describe Verdi's last scene as a >*liebestod*.

Listening

Decca SET606 4 K2L25
London OSA 13114 4 0SA5-13114
National Philharmonic/Maag
(Caballé, Pavarotti, Milnes)
1975

RIGOLETTO

Three acts
Libretto: Francesco Mario Piave,
after Victor Hugo
First performance: Venice 1851

Plot: The hunchback Rigoletto, jester to the Duke of Mantua, strikes out with biting sarcasm, regardless of his victims' feelings, just as the libertine Duke seduces the wives and daughters of his courtiers at will. Unable to get at the Duke, some courtiers vent their hatred on Rigoletto; they abduct his 'mistress' to the palace, unaware that she and the Duke have already been attracted to one another. By the time Rigoletto blurts out that it is his daughter they have abducted, Gilda is beyond his reach, a not unwilling victim of the Duke. Rigoletto proclaims vengeance. He hires an assassin, whose sister will lure the Duke to a tavern where he will be killed. Rigoletto shows Gilda the

Duke flirting in the tavern; her love for him remains unshaken, and leads her later to offer herself as substitute victim. Gloating over the sack containing the corpse, Rigoletto discovers that he has brought about the murder of his own daughter.

The opera: With this grim melodrama Verdi took a further step forward in integrating drama and music. Originally called *La maledizione*, it plots the consequences of a courtier's curse on the Duke and Rigoletto for the seduction of his daughter; Rigoletto, adopting the curse to avenge the seduction of Gilda, is eventually its victim. The theme of the curse, sounded in the Prelude, broods over the opera; Rigoletto's own twisted anger merely hastens its effects, but, chillingly, the Duke's blithe *La donna è mobile* prevails, and becomes part of the drama (out of context it rapidly became universally popular). The other set pieces, used conventionally, are no less effective – Gilda's exquisite *Caro nome*, Rigoletto's revenge >cabaletta – and the famous quartet, although somewhat formal just before the denouement, is very beautiful.

Lucian Pintile's production of *Rigoletto* for the Welsh National Opera in 1985

Overview: The Duke, the assassin, Gilda and Rigoletto, all melodramatic types, are also genuine fleshed-out individuals. No other composer of that time achieved a comparable level of characterisation. The figure of Rigoletto, monster within and monster without, only partially redeemed by his love for his daughter, can be explained by any sociopolitical historian or indeed any psychologist (under an all-powerful, corrupt ruler, the servant classes are stunted, the creative perverted). Wagner's Alberich and Mime (**The Ring**), Verdi's own Azucena (**Il trovatore**) share some of these tendencies and their causes with the hunchback; so, in a narrow sense, do both Canio and Tonio in **Pagliacci** (Leoncavallo). The Duke, also a monster within, is of course everywhere; most notably, in opera, in **Don Giovanni**. *Rigoletto* has recently been set in both a Mafia-type underworld and Fascist Italy; it would lend itself to any setting where fear and corruption deform the soul.

Further reading: *Rigoletto* (English National Opera Guide, London 1982).

Listening

Decca SET 542-4 4 K 2A3
London OSA 13105 4 OSA5-13105
CD: 414 269-2DH2
LSO/Bonynge
(Sutherland, Pavarotti, Milnes)
1972

IL TROVATORE
The Troubadour

Four acts
Libretto: Salvatore Cammarano after Antonio Garcia Gutiérrez
First performance: Rome 1853

Plot: Knowing the background of this drastically condensed epic saves confusion. An old gypsy woman was burnt at the stake by the di Luna family for 'bewitching' their younger child. To avenge the gypsy, her daughter Azucena stole the 'bewitched' child, intending to throw him on the fire, but

in her confusion threw her own child on it instead. She has brought up the di Luna boy as her own Manrico, but broods on revenge. The elder boy, now Count di Luna, is a loyalist in the civil war; Manrico is a rebel calling himself The Troubadour of the title. Both men love Leonora. At the start, Leonora's passionate declaration of love for Manrico inflames the rivals to fight. Later, after a battle with di Luna's forces, Manrico is left for dead; hearing this, Leonora enters a convent; di Luna tries to abduct her, but Manrico, restored to health by Azucena, overpowers him and saves her. When Azucena falls into di Luna's hands, Manrico is captured trying to save her. Leonora offers herself to di Luna to buy Manrico's freedom, taking poison to prevent his possessing her, but dies unable to persuade Manrico to escape. Cheated, di Luna kills Manrico, forcing Azucena to watch – and she reveals that he has killed his own brother. Her mother is avenged at last.

The opera: With such a plot, Verdi was clearly not aiming for radical developments in unity or dramatic truth. But he decked out these blood-and-thunder events with music of great beauty and energy. The Chorus gets two splendid songs, including the 'Anvil' chorus; Leonora's >arias with their glorious wide-ranging phrases are a miracle of beauty; Manrico, rushing to save his mother, takes time off to hurl the quintessential tenor challenge, *Di quella pira*; there is a superb trio in the prison, and barely a single dry line of >recitative – in fact, the opera throbs with life. Azucena is a magnificent creation, whose important numbers at the beginning and the end are famous show-stoppers.

Overview: *Il trovatore* is often called the last great Italian Romantic opera, full of breathless action and vivid characters. Azucena, probably the most impressive old woman in opera, is in the mould of Fides (*Le prophète* by Meyerbeer); Azucena and Manrico have perhaps the most important mother–son relationship in opera. The two brothers, unwitting rivals, anticipate Verdi's own **The Force of Destiny** and also underpin the relationships of Hagen/Günther and Günther/Siegfried in **The Twilight of the Gods** (Wagner):

all good material for Freudian analysis. The heroine, as in Verdi's other operas of this period (**Luisa Miller, Rigoletto** and **La traviata**), is heart-rendingly put-upon but makes the supreme sacrifice for a tenor who little deserves it (though he may be capable of generous impulse). The melodramatic plot has contributed to much levity, not least in the Marx Brothers' crazy antics at the climax of *A Night at the Opera*. Yet Puccini built **Tosca** around a situation parallel to *Trovatore* Act IV. And in our cynical times, Verdi's great block-buster shows no signs of losing its audience.

Further reading: *Il trovatore* (English National Opera Guide, London 1983).

Listening

EMI SLS 879 4 TC-SLS 869
Angel M3554CL
La Scala/Karajan
(Callas, Barbieri, di Steffano)

LA TRAVIATA
The Woman Gone Astray

Three acts
Libretto: Francesco Mario Piave,
after Alexandre Dumas
First performance: Venice 1853

Plot: In Paris, the courtesan Violetta is the centre of a frenetic whirl of social activity. Ill with consumption, she cannot conceive of escaping to a love that would be stable and caring. The approach of Alfredo Germont, timid but ardent, touches her even while she deflects it. They set up house together in the country, fulfilling each other's deepest needs, and Violetta's health improves. But Alfredo's father, feeling the shame of his son's connection with a courtesan, appeals to Violetta to break off the relationship. To help Alfredo and his family, she returns abruptly to the old Parisian life, and Alfredo, outraged, denounces her bitterly in front of her friends. Violetta's condition worsens; she is dying, virtually alone. But old Germont, now an ally, tells Alfredo of Violetta's sacrifice, and the remorseful young man returns to her in time for a

few ecstatic minutes before her death.

The opera: With only three substantial characters, *La traviata* was unusual for its time: it is the most intimate, the most affecting, of Verdi's operas. In the unity of its musical language, it was particularly modern: most of the expressive melodies or melodic lines follow one of two shapes – the curve of an arch, or a clear descent from a high point – and this makes it especially accessible. There is no overture, but the beautiful, poignant Preludes before the first and third acts express intimate inner feelings in phrases which are only wrung out of the singers themselves at climactic moments. In the same way, the 'recall' of other key phrases integrates the drama, gathering singers (and audience) into a recognisable musical world. There are some superb self-contained numbers: Violetta's *Sempre libera* with its feverish >coloratura, her deeply touching *Addio del passato*, and the drinking song. But the centre of the drama is in Violetta's individual line within the ensembles (especially at the end of Act III), or in the composite duet scenes, each shift in relationship spontaneously shaping further musical growth. This is most striking in the scene between Violetta and old Germont, where the music shows the characters moving by degrees from opposite, hostile points to the sad harmony of mutual understanding.

Overview: The growth of understanding between Germont and Violetta contrasts strongly with the comparable situation in **Luisa Miller**, but *Traviata* is really about the demands placed by a (surrogate) father on his daughter's love for another. It is closer in that sense to Wotan and Brünnhilde (Wagner's **Ring**) or Bajazet and Asteria (Handel's **Tamerlano**). It is also about the development of a woman's capacity to love and to gain wisdom beyond loving; in this, it is almost unique. Dumas's story has been found potent in many versions, including the Garbo film *Camille*, Ashton's ballet *Marguerite and Armand* for Fonteyn and Nureyev, and Zeffirelli's wonderfully evocative film of the opera itself.

Further reading: *La traviata* (English National Opera Guide, London 1981).

Listening

SIMON BOCCANEGRA

Prologue and three acts
Libretto: Francesco Mario Piave,
then Arrigo Boito
First performance: Venice 1857;
revised version Milan 1881

Plot: In Genoa, patricians and plebeians jostle for power, full of mutual hate. When Simon Boccanegra, the plebeian sea-captain, seduced the daughter of the patrician, Fiesco, she was kept from him in her father's palace, and died; their child, looked after abroad, disappeared. Simon is elected Doge of Genoa; Fiesco goes underground, plotting to regain power for the patricians. To save the Grimaldi estates from confiscation, he grooms a young orphan as Amelia Grimaldi, unaware that she is his lost granddaughter, Maria, and encourages her love for his fellow-plotter, Gabriele Adorno. Simon's plebeian supporter, Paolo, turns against him when Simon, having discovered Amelia's identity, refuses to let him marry her. Paolo attempts to abduct her, has a finger pointed at him in Council, and poisons Simon's drink in revenge. By identifying his relationship with Amelia/Maria, Simon gains the loyalty of Gabriele, then Fiesco; by his wisdom, generosity and vision he gains the love of the people, and when he dies, a united Genoa mourns him.

The opera: A quarter-century after composing *Simon Boccanegra*, Verdi set about clarifying the plot with Boito's help. Inevitably, much of the music was changed, or added (the Council scene is new), and the orchestral scene-painting developed in richness, especially in evoking the movement and light of the sea, a definite presence in the score. Showing Genoese private and public life as intertwined, Verdi dispenses with a conventional hero-figure, nor does he dwell for long on individual characters' inner concerns. The duets remain in the mind; the lovers, ecstatic; Fiesco and Adorno, in deep empathy; Simon and Maria's recognition, gloriously ripe; the painful exchanges of the two fathers. Yet even these are superseded by the vast canvas of the Council scene and the final ensemble.

Overview: Apart from Debussy in **Pelléas et Mélisande**, no composer could show the ravages of jealousy like Verdi. The spotlight beamed on Gabriele's agonies will lay bare the hearts of Ford (**Falstaff**) and **Otello**; Paolo's last appearances are a study for the evil void that is Iago's soul. But this opera was composed by a man who had lost his children; hence the tenderness between the father and daughter, echoing **La traviata** Act II, or Handel's **Tamerlano**. It was also composed by a patriot who had learnt how sectarian self-interest could sabotage the dream of national unity; its great cry for love of country is more knowing than the nostalgic choruses of **Nabucco** and **Macbeth**. At least Simon dies believing in the possibility of peace in Genoa; when **Boris Godunov** dies, tormented, his Russia is still torn apart.

Further reading: *Simon Boccanegra* (English National Opera Guide, London 1985).

Listening

A MASKED BALL
Un ballo in maschera

Three acts
Libretto: Antonio Somma, after
Augustin Eugène Scribe
First performance: Rome 1859

Plot: (The opera takes place in colonial Boston, as the censors disallowed the historically accurate Swedish setting, but some modern productions return to Verdi's original intentions.) A group of conspirators aims to assassinate Riccardo, Governor of Boston. He ignores both the advice of his friend and counsellor, Renato, and the fortune-teller Ulrica's prediction of his imminent death; he is generally beloved by his people, and believes his own good faith will protect him. But his undeclared passion for Amelia, Renato's wife, proves his undoing and hers. Discovering that Amelia returns his love, he confronts her outside Boston at midnight. Renato, hurrying to protect Riccardo from the conspirators, interprets Amelia's presence with him as adultery; his trust destroyed, he immediately joins the conspiracy. Despite Amelia's desperate efforts to warn Riccardo, Renato stabs him at an official masked ball; as he dies, Riccardo clears Amelia's name and pardons Renato.

The opera: *A Masked Ball* is generally regarded as a masterpiece. Juxtaposing avid enjoyment with death plots, and love with the ties of society and friendship that frustrate it – all vividly depicted in the music, often in brilliantly devised ensembles – Verdi produced a drama of swiftness and economy. The two lovers are unusually complex, essentially decent people caught in an all-too-familiar situation. Amelia is prepared to destroy herself for the sake of her beloved, but also for the sake of her husband, whom she continues to protect even while trying to save Riccardo. Riccardo's eminent position masks a young man's unfulfilled need for love, reiterated in the yearning melody Verdi associates with it; when that love is revealed, all the wisdom of political maturity is flung aside. Once (like Ulrica) one sees the reality behind the appearance – behind Amelia's veil, the conspirators' anonymity, or the masks at the ball – one knows life as more savage, more naked, than any well-ruled society will admit to.

Overview: Amelia's deeply felt plea to Renato to see her son before being killed puts her with opera's great mothers – **Madam Butterfly**, **Suor Angelica**, **Norma**, Fides (*Le prophète*), Azucena (**Il trovatore**). Riccardo and Renato, singing of the emptiness of life

without love, share the sense of loss with King Philip (**Don Carlos**) and so many other men depicted by this composer who lost his wife before he was thirty. Central to the opera is the theme of male friendship, betrayed by love for the same woman, which ends in murder – and here *A Masked Ball* prefigures Wagner's **The Twilight of the Gods** with an uncanny resonance.

Listening

DG 415 685-1GX3 4 415 685 4GX2
CD: 415 685-2GH2
La Scala/Abbado
(Ricciarelli, Domingo, Bruson)
1980

THE FORCE OF DESTINY
La forza del destino

Four acts
Libretto: Francesco Mario Piave, after Angel Pérez de Saavedra; revised by Antonio Ghislanzoni
First performance: St Petersburg, 1862; revised version Milan 1869

Plot: Unacceptable to Leonora's family because of his Peruvian Inca lineage, Alvaro persuades Leonora to elope with him. Her father confronts them, and is accidentally shot. The lovers lose contact – Leonora seeks peace as a hermit, protected by a monastery; Alvaro volunteers for the army. But Leonora's brother, Carlo, wants to avenge his father's death. Under assumed names, he and Alvaro become friends, and in turn save one another's life. Discovering Alvaro's identity, Carlo insists on a duel. When they are separated by guards, Alvaro resolves to find peace in a monastery. After five years, Carlo catches up with him and this time Alvaro mortally wounds him. Alvaro seeks help from the 'hermit', and he and Leonora recognise each other. As she embraces her dying brother, he stabs her, but she, before she dies, persuades the anguished Alvaro to accept God's will.

The opera: In the original version Alvaro leaps to his death off the crags,

51

shrieking curses against humanity; the pious ending, and the fine overture (incorporating crucial themes recurrent in the opera), were the main alterations for Milan. The tragic plot advances in short, swift bursts, part of a sprawling epic spanning at least six years and two countries, a world peopled by beggars, soldiers, new recruits, camp followers, monks, pilgrims, peasants and travellers. The vivacious gypsy, Preziosilla, and the irritable >buffa monk, Melitone, generate delightful music (including the famous 'Rataplan'), contrasting with the stark buffetings of Fate experienced by the lovers, hunted by the obsessive Carlo. There are remarkable ensembles, especially when the main characters mingle with the crowds, and great >arias. Alvaro's Act III soliloquy concentrates the complex feelings of an outcast. Leonora's wonderful *Pace, pace, mio dio* confirms (revised ending notwithstanding) that cruel destiny claims its victims while God ignores her earlier plea, *Deh! non m'abbandonar*, one of Verdi's great arching phrases, the most eloquent in the opera.

Overview: Verdi felt that his grand operas *The Force of Destiny*, **Don Carlos** and **Aida** were modern in being made up of ideas, not numbers. *The Force of Destiny* is rich in ideas: it introduces a theme rare in opera – the racism experienced by Alvaro – which is also touched on in **Otello** and in Tippett's **The Knot Garden** and *The Ice Break*. It suggests that, in a religious withdrawal from the world, there is no escape from the consequences of our actions (an idea hinted at in **La traviata** and Puccini's **Suor Angelica**) but, in contrast with sexual involvement, it can bring fulfilment and peace (the theme of Donizetti's **La favorite** and Wagner's **Parsifal**).

Further reading: *La forza del destino* (English National Opera Guide, London 1983).

Listening

EMI EX 270522-3 4 EX 270 522-5
La Scala/Muti
(Freni, Zajic, Domingo, Zancanaro, Bruscantini)
1986

AIDA

Four acts
Libretto: Antonio Ghislanzoni, after Auguste-Edouard Mariette
First performance: Cairo 1871

Plot: The Ethiopians, under their king Amonasro, have attacked Egypt again. The young warrior Radames is chosen to lead the Egyptian forces; he is overjoyed, as is the princess Amneris, who loves him passionately. But her Ethiopian slave, Aida, is anguished: as Amonasro's daughter, she fears for her country and her family, yet she and Radames are secretly in love, and she cannot wish him defeated. Amneris makes her confess her love, and threatens her cruelly. Aida's father, defeated and brought back as a prisoner, forces her to trick military secrets out of Radames. Seeing them together, Amneris denounces Radames as a traitor; Aida escapes with her father. The priests, disregarding Amneris's desperate pleas, condemn Radames to be buried alive in a vault. Aida is already there, having chosen to die with him; as they await death, Amneris mourns above.

The opera: Written for the opening of the new Cairo Opera House, *Aida* combines ceremonial scenes on a vast scale with the individual passions of Italian melodrama. Although the many ensembles, dances, processions and ritual chantings are superb, the personal drama remains intense: already in the first scene Radames hymns his love gloriously in *Celeste Aida*, and Aida shows herself on the rack in the wonderful >scena *Ritorna vincitor*. Aida's emotions are the fulcrum of the drama: she is tossed this way and that by the pressures from Amneris, from her father, and from her love for Radames; her three duets are all magnificent wrangles. But Act IV belongs to Amneris, her wilful jealousy transformed to cold despair at the inexorable forces she has unleashed, and when the exalted final duet has faded, it is her voice we hear, praying for the peace she will never find.

Overview: Aida is the classic heroine torn between patriotic and personal love whom we meet in **Tamerlano** (Handel) and in **Idomeneo** (Mozart); her male equivalents are Arnold (**William Tell**) and Samson (**Samson et Dalila**). The awkwardness of being rival to a more powerful superior is echoed in other Verdi operas such as **Don Carlos** and **A Masked Ball**. The exotic aspect of much of the music outside the personal drama is more marked in Puccini (**Madam Butterfly**, **Turandot**), but not necessarily more convincing. In *Aida*, Verdi arrived at the fulfilment of his >grand opera style, beating the French at their own game.

Further reading: *Aida* (English National Opera Guide, London 1980).

Listening

Decca SET 427-9 4 K64K32
London OSA 1393 4 5-1393
Rome Opera/Solti
(L. Price, Gorr, Vickers, Merrill)
1961

OTELLO

Four acts
Libretto: Arrigo Boito, after William Shakespeare
First performance: Milan 1887

Plot: The brave Moor, Otello, who leads the Venetian fleet in defeating the Turks, is Governor of Cyprus; Cassio is his lieutenant. Otello's evil ensign, Iago, schemes to destroy him. He manoeuvres Cassio into a brawl, and Otello bans Cassio from his position. Into Otello's rapturous happiness with his wife, Desdemona, he inserts a question about Desdemona's faithfulness that becomes an obsession in Otello's mind. When Desdemona pleads for Cassio's reinstatement, and when, later, Iago has her handkerchief planted on Cassio, Otello becomes convinced she is unfaithful. Reaching a pitch of convulsive jealousy, he strangles her. When the truth comes to light, Otello, painfully aware of what he has destroyed, stabs himself to die next to his wife.

The opera: Surely the greatest Italian tragic opera – and perhaps the greatest of all – *Otello* matches Shakespeare's play in encompassing the vast complexity of human emotion. In this, the work of a septuagenarian (and Verdi's first new opera for nearly sixteen years), love, hate, jealousy, pain, and remorse are almost unbearable in their nakedness. From the astounding energy of the storm to the lonely anguish of Otello's last kisses with their swelling theme from the love scene, the score is masterly, the >recitative free and eloquent, the >arias of extreme psychological subtlety. Iago's joyless vitality is encapsulated in the drinking song; he is monstrous in the >Credo (the only material not taken from the play). Desdemona is shown only responding to an outside initiative, until in Act IV, when her inner feelings are fully exposed in the *Willow Song* and the succeeding prayer. Otello sings a series of climaxes – the love scene, the scene with Iago leading to his farewell to peace of mind (*Ora per sempre addio*) and the chilling 'oath' duet, the huge outburst before the great Act III ensemble – and then the last, low-key climax of pathos and pain gathered into the words he addresses to the body of his wife ('*E tu, come sei pallida!*') and the ineffable final moments.

Overview: It is terrible to watch Otello's jealousy burning through him and overwhelming Desdemona; only the jealousy of Golaud is more horrifying (**Pelléas et Mélisande**), although Debussy's method is wholly different from Verdi's. *Otello* demonstrates how an Italian opera about human experiences may use the orchestra to the fullest extent, may unify the musical 'action' with recurrent >motifs, may dissolve the barriers between numbers into a continuous flow so that the drama dictates the shape of what is sung, and yet maintain the supremacy of the voice as the ultimate expressive instrument. It is the culmination of nearly three centuries of development, and the ultimate retort to the Wagnerians' claim that Italian opera had lost its way.

Further reading: James Hepokoski – *Giuseppe Verdi: Otello* (Cambridge 1987).

Listening

1 RCA (UK) GL82951 4 GK82951
(US) CRL 3-2951 4 CRK 3-2951
CD: RD82951
National Phil./Levine
(Scotto, Domingo, Milnes)
1978

2 RCA (UK) m AT303 (US) m LM 6107
NBC SO/Toscanini
(Nelli, Vinay, Valdengo)
1947

FALSTAFF

Three acts
Libretto: Arrigo Boito after William Shakespeare
First performance: Milan 1893

Plot: Virtually broke, Falstaff plans to woo a rich matron. Since he does nothing by halves, he sends identical letters to Mistress Alice Ford and Mistress Meg Page. These two, with Mistress Quickly and Alice's daughter, Nanetta, decide to punish him lightly. They invite him to visit Alice, but Master Ford complicates matters: a dictatorial father (he disapproves of Nanetta's love for young Fenton) and a jealous husband, he has already, in disguise, bribed Falstaff to try Alice's constancy. While Falstaff is attempting to seduce Alice, Ford and his men scour the house for his wife's lover. Hidden in a laundry basket, Falstaff is turfed out into the River Thames. His spirits dampened, he warms himself with wine, and is invited to meet Alice in Windsor Forest at midnight. There he is tormented by 'fairy spirits' (Alice's friends), and later witnesses Ford blessing the union of Nanetta and an elderly suitor – who turns out to be Fenton in disguise. Ford is now discomfited, to Falstaff's delight. Young love has triumphed; old age can laugh, too.

The opera: Verdi came to *Falstaff*, effectively his only comedy, in his late

seventies. His is a generous old age. True, there is a coolness in the snatches of exquisite love music (which leave one yearning for more), but this is a score of unstinting vigour, humour, beauty and wisdom. From the rollicking exchanges at the Garter Inn and the chatter of the women, to the enchanting fairy music and the exhilarating final >fugue (the ultimate in-joke: 'All the world's a joke' set in this severe academic form), from Mistress Quickly's ironic reverence and Alice's gloriously beautiful send-up of Falstaff's letter, to Ford's tortured >aria and Falstaff's policy statements about honour and wine, there is an irresistible glow over the music – sunshine, not autumnal. *Falstaff* would win any melody-per-minute competition with ease. But the music is such a seamless weaving together of a myriad of musical ideas that it would be virtually impossible to lift any single number out of the score.

Overview: Verdi took no part in the banner-waving battle between adherents of Wagner's operas and those of his own, but he had the last word. *Falstaff* showed how to abandon the >number opera yet retain its sequence of special musical experiences, and how to use the orchestra in the forefront of the musical argument yet let the singers lead. It is the last great >opera buffa; it is both a romantic opera and a parody of the genre; it is an acknowledgment of 'German' principles but the most Italian of operas. It turns an anti-hero into a hero; it makes a celebration out of human weakness. And it understands the young, the middle-aged and the old as only the oldest among us can.

Further reading: James Hepokoski – *Giuseppe Verdi: Falstaff* (Cambridge 1983).

Listening

RCA (UK) m AT 301
(US) m LM 6 111
NBC SO/Toscanini
(Valdengo, Nelli, Stich-Randall, Elmo) 1950

Renato Bruson in the title role of *Falstaff* (Ronald Eyre's production for the Royal Opera House 1982)

Amilcare Ponchielli

Born: 31st August 1834/Paderno Fasolaro, near Cremona
Died: 17th January 1886/Milan

The last notable composer of the great romantic tradition, Ponchielli may also be called a father of >verismo, partly because of the veristic elements in *La Gioconda* and partly because he taught both Mascagni and Puccini at the Milan Conservatory. His other nine operas had mixed success, and contained worthwhile music, but they have not remained in the repertory. He composed ballets, piano duets, band music (he was in turn conductor of the Municipal Bands of Piacenza and Cremona) and sacred music (he was >maestro di capella in Bergamo).

LA GIOCONDA
The Joyful Woman

Four acts
Libretto: Arrigo Boito after Victor Hugo
First performance: Milan 1876

Plot: Badoero, married to Laura, is Chief of the Venetian Inquisition; Barnaba is his leading spy. Barnaba desires La Gioconda, a local singer, who finds him abhorrent; embittered, he whips up the crowd against her blind mother, claiming she is a witch. Only Laura's intervention saves the old woman, who gives her her rosary in gratitude. But Barnaba, determined to break Gioconda's heart, arranges for her lover, Enzo, to be reunited with his previous passion, Laura, informing Badoero so that they can be trapped together. Gioconda overhears his plans; distraught at losing Enzo, she confronts Laura, and is on the point of stabbing her when she recognises her mother's rosary around her neck. She is transformed – as Badoero approaches she helps Laura to escape, and later, when the outraged Badoero orders Laura to take poison, Gioconda gives her a sleeping draught to make her appear dead, and has her brought to meet Enzo. To buy Enzo's freedom she has made the supreme sacrifice of offering Barnaba her body. When he comes to claim it, she stabs herself, and dies.

The opera: By far Ponchielli's best-known work, *La Gioconda* combines French and Italian >grand opera. There are impressive *tableaux vivants* – the festive crowds, the mob, the church, the sailors, the masked ball (including the famous 'Dance of the Hours'). There are also passionate exchanges among the five main characters, an extended ensemble ending Act III, and several excellent solos, including Enzo's popular *Cielo e mar* and a remarkable suicide monologue for Gioconda. The blind woman's music – her duet with her daughter and her song of thanks to Laura – is a bonus, demonstrating the warmth of Ponchielli's writing, already evident in the overture.

Overview: Coming after Verdi's **Aida**, *La Gioconda* could be called the last of the great blockbusters. It also offers a first taste of >verismo in the artificial gaiety with which Gioconda prepares to stab herself before the slavering Barnaba. Barnaba is a fore-runner of both Iago (Verdi's **Otello**), in his relish for destruction, and Scarpia (Puccini's **Tosca**), in his sexual ruthlessness. *Tosca* is foreshadowed also in the terror surrounding the secret police, and the ploy by which the tenor gains his freedom. (Puccini was Ponchielli's pupil; he later turned Barnaba's image of ensnaring a butterfly to good use.) The confrontation between the two women is famous, and its shadow hovers over **Adriana Lecouvreur** (Cilea). The moving mother–daughter relationship here is rare in opera, although Janáček would take it up in **Jenůfa**; even rarer is Gioconda's capacity to grow by specific stages to an extraordinary unselfishness of which she herself is aware. (The 'Dance of the Hours' has had a life of its own, serving several ungainly animals in Walt Disney's *Fantasia*, and providing the perfect melody for Alan Sherman's 'Hello Muddah, Hello Fuddah, here I am at Camp Granada!'.)

Listening

Ruggero Leoncavallo

Born: 8th March 1858/Naples
Died: 9th August 1919/Montecatini

Leoncavallo was famous as a >verisimo composer. Of his twelve operas and ten operettas, only *La bohème*, which gradually had to give way before Puccini's version, and *Zazà*, achieved a success anywhere near that of his celebrated *Pagliacci*. Like Mascagni, his career went fairly steadily downhill after his first great sensation.

PAGLIACCI
Clowns

Prologue and two acts
Libretto: The composer
First performance: Milan 1892

Plot: (The deformed Tonio speaks a Prologue: the theatre is not just play-acting, but the arena of real life, and actors are living, feeling human beings.) A troupe of strolling players is in the village, including its director, Canio, his wife, Nedda, and Tonio. Tonio, his advances repulsed by Nedda, observes her with her lover Silvio, a local villager; he fetches Canio, who overhears the lovers planning to run away. Unable to catch Silvio, Canio threatens to kill Nedda – but the audience starts arriving for the performance, and he can only cry out at having to perform comedy when his heart is breaking. The stock characters enact a stock cuckolding, but the roles of Canio (Pagliaccio), Nedda (Colombina) and Tonio (Taddeo) are identical to their real situation, so much so that Canio cannot keep his feelings from breaking through. The performance becomes a horrific drama, and the audience's confusion prevents Silvio reaching the stage in time to stop Canio stabbing Nedda; Canio then turns on Silvio and kills him.

The opera: *Pagliacci* rivalled the success of Mascagni's **Cavalleria rusticana**, with a more cohesive and substantial plot written by Leoncavallo himself (the two – both short operas – are often performed as a double bill). Combining >comedia dell'arte and naturalistic >verismo to demonstrate that art and life are inseparable is nicely ironic. The central idea is echoed at many points, as in Canio's magnificent *Vesti la giubba*. (The opera's final line – '*La commedia e finita*' ['The comedy is over'] – given to Tonio, has now been appropriated by the tenor playing Canio.) The characters are not really developed; Tonio, leering and cynical, being potentially the most complex. The score is uneven, but its musical high points override this. With the >Intermezzo/Prelude continuing Canio's brooding, and phrases from *Vesti la giubba* recurring, the tight integration of music and drama adds to the sense of direction. It is the larger audience's awareness of impending doom, as compared with the stage audience's ignorance, that gives the opera its stark verismo horror.

Overview: The device of a play within a play appears also in Strauss's **Ariadne auf Naxos**; it is the overlapping between life and art that makes it so effective here. But Tonio is a melodramatic echo of Verdi's **Rigoletto**; Puccini's treatment of a similar love triangle, **Il tabarro**, gives us more substantial characters in a less diversified score.

Listening

HMV m ALP 1126-8
Seraphim IB6058
RCA Victor Orch./Cellini

(de los Angelos, Björling, Warren) 1954

Giacomo Puccini

Born: 22nd December 1858/Lucca
Died: 29th November 1924/Brussels

Puccini composed seven hugely successful operas (and three others), whose melodic flair and theatrical effectiveness have made them the backbone of the popular repertory. He composed a little other music, mainly sacred music and songs, most of it unpublished.

Further reading: Mosco Carner – *Puccini: a Critical Biography* (rev. edn., London 1974); William Ashbrook – *The Operas of Puccini* (rev. edn., Oxford 1985).

MANON LESCAUT

Four acts
Libretto: Ruggero Leoncavallo, Domenico Oliva, Giulio Ricordi, Luigi Illica, Giuseppe Giacosa and Mario Praga, after l'Abbé Prévost
First performance: Turin 1893

Plot: At first sight, des Grieux falls passionately in love with Manon Lescaut, and elopes with her before she can be abducted by old, wealthy Géronte. Her brother, Lescaut, persuades her to leave the impecunious des Grieux, and Géronte installs her as his mistress. Tiring of her life with him, she again responds to des Grieux, and Géronte has her arrested: she will be deported as a courtesan. When, despite Lescaut's help, des Grieux fails to abduct her from prison, he gets himself taken on as cabin boy for the voyage to America. In New Orleans Manon's beauty creates further problems, and the two lovers flee. Exhausted, feverish, Manon dies, proclaiming her love for des Grieux.

The opera: Puccini's earliest international success, *Manon Lescaut* exhibits many of the composer's hallmarks: masterly orchestral manipulation, passionate vocal writing, the capacity to present many strands of musical activity involving crowds, groups and soloists, or to focus on an extended statement of the most intense emotions. From the bustling, cheerful beginning with its almost impersonal liaison between the lovers the level of experience deepens by degrees, to the nakedly tragic feeling occupying the entire fourth act. A graph drawn from *Tra voi, belles*, a truly sunny popular melody, through the darkness of *In quelle trine morbide*, the desperate self-abasement of *Guardate, pazzo son, guardate*, to the wracked anguish of *Sola, perduta, abbandonata* will confirm the lovers' gradual loss of confidence in the world. How much you are moved by the hammering out of the great phrases in the final act is a measure of your response to Puccini's musical language.

Overview: With the >Intermezzo between Acts II and III Puccini followed Mascagni's **Cavalleria rusticana**; he also demonstrated how far >programme music had come south from Germany. We easily grasp what its musical ideas signify and recognise the inner emotions of its hero, as in the operas of Wagner – the shepherd's piping in **Tristan**, or the Good Friday music in **Parsifal**. But Puccini had an earlier Italian model for his Intermezzo – the Prelude to Act III of Verdi's **La traviata**. (Britten makes use of the method, although the intention is less personal, in **Peter Grimes**.) With Des Grieux, however, there is no earlier model: he is that rare being, a tenor lover whose ego is totally subsumed in concern for his woman.

Listening

1 DG 413 893-2GH2 4 413 893-4GH2
   CD: 413 893-2GH2
   Philharmonia/Sinopoli
   (Domingo, Freni)
   1984
2 EMI m EX290041-3 4 EX290041-5
   CD: CDS7 47398-8
   Seraphim m IC6089 4 4X3G-6089
   La Scala/Serafin
   (Callas, Di Stefano)
   1957

LA BOHEME
Bohemian Life

Four acts
Libretto: Giuseppe Giacosa and Luigi Illica after Henri Murger
First performance: Turin 1896

Plot: Four young men, artists all live in poverty in a Parisian garret, surviving precariously on good humour, their belief in their work, and occasional good luck. The painter Marcello is entangled in an on-off relationship with Musetta; the poet Rodolfo meets a young woman nicknamed Mimi who lives in the same building, and their new-found love seems to answer all their yearnings. But Mimi is ill with tuberculosis, and the stricken Rodolfo knows that the unheated garret is worsening her condition. They part, each believing it is for the good of the other – but Mimi comes back to die, and Rodolfo is at her side.

The opera: Puccini's gift is to present characters and situations of no great depth but with enough feeling to wring the emotions of his audience.
La bohème is made memorable by the intense melodic writing for Mimi and Rodolfo, charged with tenderness, passion, or pathos. Their ardent vocal phrases may expand suddenly and thrillingly, though with only a sketchy relation to what is actually said – this opera can be enjoyed even without a detailed translation of the text. Puccini's method is to give his leading singers repetitions of one note while the orchestra outlines the tune, then – at climactic moments – to underpin their melodies with big orchestral sound. He often sets their most poignant exchanges against a bustling background, or against the arguing of the other two lovers, creating a surface effect of realism. In the breaks between the big solos or duets, the conversational writing is kept fresh by its humour and gaiety, and by much entertaining stage action. There are several famous set pieces that have almost become part of our general heritage, including *Che gelida manina* (known as 'Your tiny hand is frozen'), *Mi*

chiamano Mimi, and the familiar
Musetta's Waltz.

Overview: Mimi is the prototype of the
frail, loving Puccini heroines, Liù
(**Turandot**) and **Madam Butterfly**.
They all suffer horribly, but in *La
bohème*, the gentlest of his works, the
ending is tearful rather than tragic. In
this sense it differs both from his other
operas and from the >verismo writing
popular at the turn of the century; it
romanticises the 'bohemian' life of its
characters, and sentimentalises their
sufferings, where verismo such as
Leoncavallo's **Pagliacci** deliberately
sets out to shock with the dramatic
harshness of reality.

Further reading: Arthur Groos and
Roger Parker – *Giacomo Puccini: La
bohème* (Cambridge 1986).

Listening

1 EMI e SLS 896 4 TC-SLS 896
   CD: CDS7 47235-8
   Seraphim e SIB 6099
   RCA Orch./Beecham
   (de los Angeles, Björling)
   1956

2 Decca SET 565 4 K2B5
   London OSA 1299 4 5-1299
   Berlin Phil./Karajan
   (Freni, Pavarotti)
   1973

TOSCA

Three acts
**Libretto: Giuseppe Giacosa and Luigi
Illica, after Victorien Sardou**
First performance: Rome 1900

Plot: Rome, 1800; the ruthless Scarpia
is Chief of Police. Tracing an escaped
political prisoner to a nearby church,
Scarpia finds he has disappeared with
the painter Cavaradossi. He tricks
Cavaradossi's lover, the famous singer
Tosca, into leading his men to
Cavaradossi, but finds nothing. With
Tosca present Scarpia tortures
Cavaradossi, who gives nothing away,
but Tosca, having tried every other
means of protecting her lover, reveals
the prisoner's whereabouts. Scarpia

then sends Cavaradossi to be executed;
but if Tosca accepts his sexual
demands, it will be a mock execution.
Finding Scarpia immovable, Tosca
agrees; but as he advances on her in
extreme sexual excitement, she stabs
him to death. She tells Cavaradossi to
expect a sham execution – but then
finds he has really been killed, and as
Scarpia's police come for her, she leaps
from the parapet to her death.

The opera: When Tosca cries
admiringly 'Ecco un artista!' as
Cavaradossi falls dead, the composer
achieves the true >verismo climax. Yet
in the church with the lovers we are still
in the musical world of **La bohème**. It
is Scarpia, from his three horrific chords
onwards, who destroys that illusion. He
has the soul of the sadistic rapist: his
>Credo (sung during the *Te deum*)
rates highest the power which
combines execution and sexual
intercourse. Although there are
Scarpias with us always, *Tosca* was
once condemned as a 'prolonged orgy
of lust and crime', as a 'shabby little
shocker'. But, beyond its theatrical
brilliance, audiences value the human
truth in Tosca's confrontation with
Scarpia. And the secret of Puccini's
success – his lyricism – is at its richest
here. *Recondita armonia*, *Vissi d'arte*
and *E lucevan le stelle*, with their
beautiful melodies and warm
instrumentation, are appropriate
dramatically, and equally memorable
out of context.

Overview: Interesting links: the
Sacristan, a grotesque relative of
Verdi's Melitone (**The Force of
Destiny**), hints at the Puccini to come
in **Gianni Schicchi**; the song of the
Shepherd opening Act III was a
convention already used by Wagner in
Tristan and Berlioz in **The Trojans**;
Cavaradossi's finest moments,
proclaiming his political stance, align
him with political rather than purely
amatory tenors, such as Florestan
(Beethoven's **Fidelio**), Macduff (Verdi's
Macbeth) and Smetana's **Dalibor**.
Although the choice facing Tosca was
prefigured in Handel's **Rodelinda**, and
the 19th century produced many a
brutal baritone before Scarpia, these
two protagonists are unique; they
require singer–actors of the highest
order. (They occasionally require
humour, too: a Tosca disliked by her

Tito Gobbi, Franco Zeffirelli, Maria Callas, Carlo Felice Cillario and Renato Cioni: a classic *Tosca* (Royal Opera House 1964)

colleagues once found herself leaping to her death onto a trampoline, thus making several post-suicidal reappearances above the parapet – much to the delight of the audience.) Callas and Gobbi, whose famous Act II is preserved live for television, cast a long shadow still.

Further reading: Mosco Carner – *Giacomo Puccini: Tosca* (Cambridge 1986).

Listening

EMI EX290039-3 4 EX290039-5
CD: CDS7 47175-8
Angel m 3508 BL
CD: CDCB 47174
La Scala/de Sabata
(Callas, di Stefano, Gobbi)
1953

MADAM BUTTERFLY

Three acts
Libretto: Luigi Illica and Giuseppe Giacosa, after David Belasco
First performance: Milan 1904

Plot: US Navy Lieutenant Pinkerton, visiting Nagasaki, makes a financial arrangement to 'marry' a young geisha, Madam Butterfly; he will stay with her briefly before returning to the United States to find an American wife. Butterfly takes it all seriously, even adopting Christianity, for which she is cut off by family and friends. Pinkerton, infatuated and charmed, does not disillusion her, and the marriage begins in a state of rapture. When Pinkerton leaves, promising to return, Butterfly waits faithfully, rejecting all indications that things are not as they should be. Three years later Pinkerton arrives – with his American wife, to fetch the son he has just heard about. He finds Butterfly dying – she has cut her throat – and their child waving an American flag.

The opera: The source of Belasco's play was a magazine story based on a real incident, and the opera rings horribly true; Pinkerton is the acme of self-indulgent, thoughtless cruelty, the appropriately-named Butterfly his willing, fluttering victim. Yet the charm of the Japonaiserie (Puccini carefully incorporated a Japanese element in the music), the rich melodic writing, and Butterfly's very vulnerability, tend to soften the experience until, as Butterfly says an agonised farewell to her child, killing herself so that he can enter the world denied to her, >verismo takes over with a vengeance. Although the opera seems >through-composed, there are several self-contained numbers whose theatrical effectiveness makes them individually memorable – *Un bel dì* (a household name as 'One fine day'), the Humming Chorus, the death scene, and the love duet, the last a perfect example of Puccini's capacity for working up the erotic ecstacy. And the composer's lyric facility is nowhere better demonstrated than in the Flower Duet, a true efflorescence of beautiful melodies.

THE GIRL OF THE GOLDEN WEST
La fanciulla del West

Three acts
Libretto: Guelfo Civinini and Carlo Zangarini, after David Belasco
First performance: New York 1910

Plot: Minnie runs the bar in a miners' camp in California during the gold rush. She is mother and sister to the men, bringing out their finest feelings. Into the camp comes Dick Johnson; he and Minnie are drawn to one another. But Johnson is a bandit hunted by the local sheriff, Rance – and Rance wants Minnie. He discovers the wounded Johnson sheltering in Minnie's cabin. Minnie offers Rance a game of poker: if he wins, he gets Johnson and herself; if he loses, she keeps Johnson. By cheating, Minnie wins. Later, when Johnson rides away to a new life, he is captured, and taken to be lynched. Again Minnie saves him, claiming him as her due from the miners, and she and Johnson leave together.

The opera: *The Girl of the Golden West* was Puccini's second 'exotic' opera, into which he incorporated American melodies such as 'Old Dog Tray' for local colour. He was moving towards 'harder' subject matter, and so there is less of the celebrated Puccini lyricism, more of the dramatic >recitative with heavy orchestration to underpin it (*Ch'ella mi creda*, Johnson's beautiful plea, is strangely out of place in this score). Careful characterisation of the lesser roles creates a chorus made up of individuals, so that Puccini can shift realistically between duet exchanges, larger ensembles and choral tutti. This makes possible the magnificent final ensemble, during which Minnie reminds the miners of what they have gone through together, while their murmur of sympathy grows; the action is all in the music. The theatrical high point, the poker game with life and love at stake, is a naturalistic treatment of the symbolic game with the Devil for the soul of a loved one.

Overview: Written in a period when Europe was looking to the East to enlarge its visual and musical horizons, *Madam Butterfly* offers a somewhat sentimentalised view of Japanese customs which has become entrenched through the opera's popularity. Once stripped of its exotic aspect it is one of the classic tales of lovin' and leavin', along with the two great Dido operas (Purcell's **Dido and Aeneas** and Berlioz's **The Trojans**), and Butterfly joins a gallery of heroines who make the ultimate sacrifice for their man, their child, or both – Liù (Puccini's **Turandot**), Verdi's Gilda (**Rigoletto**) and his Leonora (**Il trovatore**).

Further reading: *Madam Butterfly* (English National Opera Guide, London 1984).

Listening

EMI SLS 927 4 TC-SLS 927
Angel SCLX 3702
Rome Opera/Barbirolli
(Scotto, Bergonzi)
1966

Overview: There are themes running through Puccini's oeuvre: the story of

Minnie hints at **Turandot**, for the girl of the golden West has held herself from all comers until finding the man she wants; *The Girl of the Golden West* and **Tosca** are permutations of the same plot, Act II in both operas presenting a woman forced to offer herself to a villain to save her lover's life. The final rescue, in the grand tradition of heroines such as Leonore (**Fidelio**), goes back even further as a theatrical device, to the 17th century with its >deus ex machina; this is the convention mocked in Weill's **The Threepenny Opera**.

Listening

DG 413 285-1GX3
Royal Opera/Mehta
(Neblett, Domingo, Milnes)
1977

IL TRITTICO: IL TABARRO
The Triptych: The Cloak

One act
Libretto: Giuseppe Adami, after Didier Gold
First performance: New York 1918

Plot: It is evening on Michel's barge on the Seine. The stevedores are weary, the atmosphere good. But between Michel and his young wife Georgette there are dark areas. Their little boy died a year ago – Michel remembers how he used to shelter wife and child under his cloak – and since then Georgette has not responded to her husband. She and the young stevedore Louis share a feverish passion; the tormented Michel suspects it. Mistaking Michel's glowing pipe for Georgette's signal, Louis runs up the gangplank – and is throttled by Michel. In death, he clings to his killer, who covers him with his cloak. When Georgette comes out on deck, asking to be close to her husband under his cloak, he rolls out Louis's body and presses her against its face.

The opera: *Il tabarro* is not simply a piece of >verismo. While the numerous realistic details building a turn-of-the-century Parisian soundscape give it a strong sense of locale and period,

symbolic play with the gathering darkness and the cloak of the title create a sombre poetry as the protagonists' inner life unfolds. The out-of-tune barrel-organ, cleverly integrated, the interpolations of passers-by, and the comments of the lesser characters all heighten the turgid intensity of a score virtually unrelieved by lyricism. The sense of suffocation in the brooding prelude is felt between the lovers, their vocal lines unable to soar, and in Michel's soliloquy even as he shouts out his murderous frustration. Puccini's >recitative has become an element of the orchestration rather than a medium for conversational exchange.

Overview: *Il tabarro* belongs to the type of opera of which **Pagliacci** is the most famous – stark melodrama in which the displaced husband kills his wife and/or her lover. (Zemlinsky's **A Florentine Tragedy** offers a twist to this plot.) The characters do not develop – they are as they are. Motivation is clear; atmosphere is important; everything leads to the inevitable climax. The first, and heaviest, opera in *Il trittico*, it has recently gained greater critical respect. Yet in it Puccini began to break the limits of his own vocal tradition; he was moving guardedly towards the atmosphere of Schoenberg's **Erwartung**.

Listening

EMI e SW5066 TC-SLS 5066
Angel SCLX 3849E
Rome Opera/Belleza
(Gobbi)
1955

IL TRITTICO:
SUOR ANGELICA
The Triptych:
Sister Angelica

One act
Libretto: Giovacchino Forzano
First performance: New York 1918

Plot: Each nun in the convent has her own story. Sister Angelica, an unmarried mother, joined it seven years ago after giving birth. At last her Aunt, the Princess, comes to see her: Angelica must sign away her inheritance in favour of her sister who is getting married. When Angelica asks about her child, the Princess tells her flatly that he is dead. Consumed with grief, and appalled that he died without his mother, Angelica drinks poison – only to realise that she has committed a mortal sin. In despair, she begs the Blessed Virgin to save her, and as she dies the church fills with light and she sees the Virgin bringing her young child to meet her.

The opera: This, the second opera of *Il trittico*, is set in the 17th century but could equally be in the early 20th, and indeed the heavy, highly-coloured orchestration and the slightly exotic harmonies give it a contemporary feel. The Princess, hard, self-righteous and destructive, is one-dimensional but effective; Angelica is more substantial, her anguish in *Senza Mamma* fully believable. Their confrontation is the dramatic core of the opera. The other nuns, initially adding sentimental charm, perform at the end the appropriate function of an exalted choral background to the miracle.

Overview: Poulenc's **Dialogues des Carmélites**, set in a convent, also exploits the interplay of women's voices, contrasting the experience and attitudes of individual nuns. But Puccini's theatre inhabits another planet. Angelica's grief milks the same vein of emotion which makes **Madam Butterfly** so heart-rending; many of Puccini's operas are simply sob-stories expressed in music. Bellini might have applauded the later composer's application of his own theory that opera should get its audiences crying. But Bellini's heroines tend to suffer in stylised ways: they go mad, or dream, or become exalted; Puccini's heroines confront their plight without losing the clarity of their vision, and when they die it is because they know life is too cruel to continue.

Listening

EMI e SLS 4 TC-SLS 5066
Angel e SCLX 3849E
Rome Opera/Serafin
(de los Angeles, Barbieri)
1957

IL TRITTICO: GIANNI SCHICCHI
The Triptych: Gianni Schicchi

One act
Libretto: Giovacchino Forzano, developed from Dante Alighieri
First performance: New York 1918

Plot: The late Buoso's relatives, mourning round his deathbed, are mainly concerned with his will. Rinuccio hopes for money so that he can marry Lauretta, daughter of Gianni Schicchi; he sends for them both. When the will is discovered it confirms that everything has been left to a monastery. The relatives are devastated, the marriage is off. But Schicchi's plan is accepted with delight: disguised as the moribund Buoso, he will dictate to the notary a new will in favour of the relatives. Everything is set up – and when 'Buoso' bequeaths the most valuable property to 'my friend, Gianni Schicchi', the relatives can do nothing. Eventually Schicchi drives them out of his new house, leaving the young lovers blissfully happy.

The opera: The last of *Il trittico*, *Gianni Schicchi* is in the great >buffa tradition, Puccini's characteristic narrow-range >recitative suiting the rapid exchanges perfectly. The eponymous role has marvellous comic possibilities, but it is the relatives abandoning their praying to hear the rumour concerning the monastery, their frenzied hunt for the will, their bitter vision of the well-fed monks laughing at Buoso's poor relatives, and their fawning on Schicchi when they see him as a means of increasing their inheritance, that make this opera one of the funniest pieces of black humour in the repertory. Lauretta's short >aria, *O mio babbino caro*, is a sly dig at opera's thwarted heroines, although Puccini's setting confuses the issue by giving it the full treatment, even introducing the melody earlier to give it weight; Rinuccio's paean to Florence is much more in keeping with buffa style.

Overview: In his only comedy, Puccini's irony, unmodified by sentiment, makes him heir to Rossini, and to Pergolesi before him. Schicchi would have shared a laugh with Donizetti's Malatesta (**Don Pasquale**), but warily – there can only be one winner in the situations they engineer. As a brazen imposter, he has as much flair as Despina (Mozart's **Così**), the Count (Rossini's **Barber**) and Norina (Donizetti's *Don Pasquale*), but his wry perspective on society puts him among the great commentators, comic or serious – Mozart's **Figaro**, Wagner's Hans Sachs (**Die Meistersinger**), and Verdi's **Falstaff**.

Listening

EMI SLS 5066 4 TC-SLS 5066
Angel SCLX 3849E
Rome Opera/Santini
(Gobbi, de los Angeles)
1958

TURANDOT

Three acts
Libretto: Giuseppe Adami and Renato Simoni, after Carlo Gozzi
First performance: Milan 1926

Plot: In Peking, Prince Calaf finds his aged father, the exiled King Timur, cared for by a young slave woman, Liù. These three hear a proclamation: remembering her great ancestor, who was virgin ruler of China until being abducted and murdered by a barbarian invader, Princess Turandot has vowed to protect herself from men. Anyone choosing to woo her must answer three riddles, or be beheaded. Many have tried and lost. Seeing Turandot, Calaf's passion for her cannot be restrained. He challenges her – and answers the riddles correctly. Faced with her horror, he offers to die if she can discover his name before dawn. Captured and tortured, Liù, for love of Calaf, will not disclose his name, and commits suicide to ensure its secrecy. At dawn Calaf kisses Turandot, and she accepts his love.

The opera: With *Turandot* Puccini wanted to strike out on a new path. The idiom is grotesque-exotic (much dissonance, several true Chinese melodies), with a dollop of Puccinian lyricism at key moments (most notably in *Nessun dorma*, the music for Liù, and several of the choruses). With a much larger percussion section, the orchestral pallete shows many new colours; but although it threatens to overwhelm the signers, the Italian balance is preserved. The >commedia dell'arte masks – Ping, Pang and Pong – are partly humanised as State officials. Puccini's feeling for dramatic effect shows superbly in the climax to Act I, as Calaf breaks clear of the huge ensemble's dissuasion and strikes the gong three times (the number three recurs symbolically in this 'fairy-tale' opera). Completed by Franco Alfano after Puccini's death, from his notes, the ultimate climax – the symbolic kiss, accompanied by shocking, thrusting drumbeats – is less satisfactory, raising the whole question of sadism in Puccini. Must we really accept that the Turandot of *In questa reggia* 'only needs a good kiss' to stop rejecting men? Calaf recognises his cruelty in imposing himself on her, but the music for the kiss, a naked assertion of power, belies his insight. And what of Liù, with her gratuitous torture and suicide?

Overview: Liù's sacrifice compares with Verdi's Gilda (**Rigoletto**) and Leonora (**Trovatore**). But the opera's stronger link is with Wagner's **Ring**. Forced to accept a man, Brünnhilde protects herself with impenetrable fire, Turandot with unanswerable riddles: the victor will have to be heroic. When he materialises, their response is similar, which tells us more about Wagner and Puccini than about the battle of the sexes. Gozzi's play inspired several composers: Weber wrote incidental music for it; Busoni set it as a short opera; and it gave Puccini the basis for his magnum opus.

Further reading: *Turandot* (English National Opera Guide, London 1984).

Listening

Decca SET 561 4 K2A2
CD: 414 274-2DH2
LPO/Mehta
Sutherland, Pavarotti, Caballe)
1973

Pietro Mascagni

Born: 7th December 1863/Livorno
Died: 2nd August 1945/Rome

Mascagni struck the first blow for >verismo with *Cavalleria rusticana*, but the public's expectations remained unfulfilled by almost all his other operas (he wrote fifteen), in which he usually tried to break away from the style that had made him famous. He was associated with the Fascist regime from the twenties until his death near the end of World War II.

CAVALLERIA RUSTICANA
Rustic Chivalry

One act
Libretto: Giovanni Targioni-Tozzetti and Guido Menasci
First performance: Rome 1890

Plot: Turiddu, returning to his Sicilian village from the army, has found his sweetheart Lola married to Alfio, and has taken up with Santuzza. But on Easter day tragedy hovers: Santuzza informs Turiddu's mother that he and

Lola have renewed their relationship, leaving her dishonoured and abandoned. She then appeals to Turiddu, who rejects her violently, and in furious despair she tells Alfio of his wife's infidelity. There is a confrontation between the two men, and a challenge. Before the fight Turiddu accepts blame, asking his mother to care for Santuzza if he should die – and indeed it is he who is killed.

The opera: After an unimpressive period as a student (he was dismissed from the Milan conservatory) and some hack work as a professional musician, Mascagni won a prize for *Cavalleria rusticana* in a competition for one-act operas, and it soon gained enormous success. Its broad, accessible melodies sung with intense emotion by 'ordinary people' who are emphatically *not* larger than life but whose situations are violently melodramatic make it a classic >verismo opera. The overture, unusual in incorporating a serenade sung from behind the curtain, generates the mood of suppressed passion which continues in Santuzza's *Voi lo sapete, o mamma* and explodes in her later duet with Turiddu and his appeal to his mother before the fight. Although much of the chorus writing would not be out of place in a conventional opera, the Easter hymn and the drinking song stand out, and the >Intermezzo has become very popular.

Overview: *Cav*, as it is affectionately known, initiated the brief vogue for verismo at the end of the century. Of course the situation it presented was common to many operas; what made it special was the 'rustic' setting usually reserved for >opera buffa, here the basis of the starkest tragedy. Before Mascagni, village life had been idealised, tragedy deriving from intrusions by nobles (as in Verdi's **Luisa Miller**, or the ballet *Giselle*). Now village life itself was the subject, but not till Janáček's **Jenůfa** or Martinů's **The Greek Passion** would it be presented with equal power.

Listening

DG 413 275-1GX3 4 413 275-4GX2
La Scala/Karajan
(Cossotto, Bergonzi)
1965

Francesco Cilea

Born: 26th July 1866/Palmi di Calabria
Died: 20th November 1950/Varazze

A minor composer, Cilea composed six other operas and a fair amount of piano music, but only *Adriana Lecouvreur* achieved success, and its rewarding title role has remained popular with sopranos. Cilea was for much of his life a teacher and director at various conservatories of music.

ADRIANA LECOUVREUR

Four acts
Libretto: Arturo Colautti, after Augustin Eugène Scribe
First performance: Milan 1902

Plot: Maurice, Count of Saxony, is in love with the great actress Adrienne Lecouvreur, but he dallies with the Princess de Bouillon, and she considers him her property. To protect the Princess from discovery after a nocturnal meeting, Maurice charges Adrienne with helping her escape, and although neither woman knows the identity of the other, when they discover they are rivals a bitter confrontation develops. At a reception given by the Princess the women recognise one another; the Princess's hostility drives Adrienne to denounce her by means of a Racine speech she had been invited to recite. Adrienne now languishes without Maurice; when she receives a bunch of violets she had recently given him she assumes this is his way of saying goodbye, and she weeps over the flowers, sniffing their remaining scent. Just as Maurice arrives to reaffirm his love for her, it becomes clear that Adrienne is dying, poisoned by the violets – they were sent by the Princess.

The opera: Adrienne Lecouvreur, one of the most important actresses of the Comédie–Française in the time of Voltaire, was indeed nearly poisoned by her rival in love. Scribe's famous play was a vehicle for Rachel, Bernhardt, and Duse, the greatest actresses of the later 19th century, and Adrienne's most affecting >aria, *Io son l'umile ancella*, expressing the humility of the great artist, is given substantial moral weight. The Princess is bad news, but Cilea does not find a characteristic tone for her; his forte is a natural and unpretentious lyricism, effective for being small-scale. It is not an opera that breaks fresh ground, but it uses the conventions with discretion – a poisoned-delirium final scene for Adrienne, an elevated tone in the love duet, a baritone lonely in love (Michonnet, the stage manager), a >parlato passage at a dramatic high point (the declamation of Phaedra's speech).

Overview: Overshadowed by more sensational operas at the turn of the century, *Adriana Lecouvreur* has never achieved great popularity. But, apart from other attractive features, it contains prime operatic material in the confrontation of two women who are rivals in love, inevitably bringing Ponchielli's **La Gioconda** to mind. It is also one of the few operas whose central character is a stage person, another in the select group being Puccini's **Tosca**. Strauss's **Capriccio** incorporates the important Comédie–Française actress Clairon, and his **Ariadne auf Naxos**, Hindemith's *Cardillac* and Janáček's **The Makropulos Affair** feature a prima donna.

Listening

CBS (UK) 79310
(US) M3-34588
New Philharmonia/Levine
(Scotto, Domingo, Milnes)

Umberto Giordano

Born: 28th August 1867/Foggia
Died: 12th November 1948/Milan

A >verismo composer of thirteen operas, Giordano is best known for *Andrea Chénier* and *Fedora*. He also wrote orchestral music, a ballet, and some chamber and piano music, but he is most notable as a composer with a strong sense of theatre.

ANDREA CHENIER

Four acts
Libretto: Luigi Illica
First performance: Milan 1896

Plot: A poet of independent outlook, André Chénier was at odds with the thoughtless cruelty of the ancien régime before 1789, and in 1794 he finds himself at odds with the conscious cruelty of the Reign of Terror. But, in love with Madeleine, he refuses the chance of leaving Paris in safety. This love becomes his death warrant; Madeleine is also loved by her former servant Gérard, now a man of political importance, who cannot brook Chénier's rivalry. After Madeleine

pleads with Gérard to save Chénier, he bravely attempts to discredit his own denunciation, but the Tribunal sends Chénier to the guillotine. Madeleine chooses to die with him; for these two death is welcome, because they will enter this new realm together.

The opera: Although the music is rarely memorable, Giordano lacking the lyrical flair to make use of most of his great opportunities, its natural language – a limited kind of >arioso – is sufficiently eloquent to express the emotions of a variety of characters at a crucial moment in history. Madeleine is Illica's invention, but Chénier was a poet, whose writing was the source for the Improvviso (*Un di all'azzurro spazio*) and *Come un bel di di maggio*, his two finest >arias; he becomes quite naturally an operatic tenor. Gérard is more mature both politically and emotionally, but as the baritone he is required to carry a touch of villainy. His awareness of it confirms him as the most interesting psychological portrait in the opera (*Un dí m'era di goia*). But this is an opera about a society: two societies – pre-Revolutionary France and France in the Reign of Terror. Besides incorporating representative music such as the Act I gavotte and, later, songs of the revolution (the Carmagnole and the Marseillaise), Giordano achieves for his characters and his settings a credibility that escapes many a more gifted composer.

Overview: Gérard's progression from angry humanist to compromised politician is all too real; Giordano adds to the work of Musorgsky (**Boris Godunov**) and Verdi (**Simon Boccanegra**) in depicting the inner experience which influences political behaviour. Yet at the end *Andrea Chénier* enters the very unpolitical territory of a greater opera, Wagner's **Tristan und Isolde**. Madeleine and André approach the guillotine quite clearly prepared for a >liebstod, their very words Wagnerian.

Listening

RCA (UK) RL 12046
(US) ARL 2046 4 ARK 3-2046
NPO/Levine
(Domingo, Scotto, Milnes)
1977

67

Ermanno Wolf-Ferrari

Born: 12th January 1876/Venice
Died: 21st January 1948/Venice

Wolf-Ferrari's works recreated the 18th-century Venetian comedy of Goldoni, but they were premiered with greatest success in Germany (his father was German). Also well-known: *I quatro rusteghil*, *Le donne curiose* and *I gioielli della Madonna*. Other operas were based on Molière and Shakespeare. He also composed instrumental music.

SUSANNA'S SECRET
Il segreto di Susanna

One act
Libretto: Enrico Golisciani
First performance: Munich 1909

Plot: With tobacco smoke in the air, Count Gil and Susanna, newly and blissfully married at the turn of the century, are at cross purposes. Gil suspects Susanna has a lover; she assumes he is angry over her secret vice. Once Gil discovers the truth, there is a touching reunion, and he starts smoking as well. Love and cigarettes have conquered all.

The opera: With smoking presented so attractively, this opera should carry a Government Health Warning. Rather as Wagner treats fire in **The Ring**, Wolf-Ferrari treats the smoke music with a definite personality, the flute spiralling upwards in ecstatic whirls, imitated occasionally by clarinet or violin. The score is a witty combination of bubbly 18th-century charm and luscious 19th-century orchestration, with some fine lyrical passages, such as the lovers' duet *Il dolce idillio*, Susanna's plea *Se v'offesi non volendo* and the particularly beautiful >Intermezzo, recalled at the end. Wagner is not far away in Susanna's monologue *Che palpiti*, nor Mozart equally in *Il dolce idillio*, but Wolf-Ferrari's musical language is too inventive and fundamentally attractive to be considered simply as pastiche.

Overview: In reaction against the over-heated drama of >verismo, composers such as Massenet, Strauss and Stravinsky created afresh in some of their works the style of the 18th century, or at least its spiritual idiom. Wolf-Ferrari was part of this trend, picking up the great >opera buffa tradition from Pergolesi onwards, and adding some 19th-century romance to the satire on human foibles.

Listening

CBS IM-36733 4
Philharmonia/Pritchard
(Scotto, Bruson)

Luigi Dallapiccola

Born: 3rd February 1904/Pisino, Istria
Died: 19th February 1975/Florence

Dallapiccola was a pioneer of >serialism in Italy. His other operas are based on Saint-Exupery's *Vol de nuit* (Flight to Arras) and Homer's *Odyssey* and he also wrote a ballet and film scores. As a fine concert pianist he publicised much contemporary music. Some of his own music was conceived in protest against the racist policies of the Fascists, and for a while he went underground during World War II.

IL PRIGIONIERO
The Prisoner

One act
Libretto: The composer, after Villiers de l'Isle Adam
First performance: Radio Audizioni Italiane 1949; Florence 1950

Plot: A mother describes her recurring dream that the tyrant Philip II threatens the imminent death of her son, already imprisoned and horribly tortured by the Spanish Inquisition for supporting the Flemish rebels. During her visit, her son describes how his gaoler's addressing him as 'brother' has restored his faith in life. We see the gaoler encouraging him – indirectly, with descriptions of the advances made by the rebels, and directly, with talk of hope and faith. Finding his cell door left open, the prisoner makes his perilous escape down a long tunnel, and finally reaches a huge garden open to the night sky. Ecstatic, he opens his arms to embrace all humanity – and finds himself embraced by the Grand Inquisitor, to

Mary Costa, Heinz Blankenburg and Michel Roux in *Susanna's Secret* (Glyndebourne 1958)

be led off to his death. Hope has been the final torture; the ultimate question-mark hovers over freedom.

The opera: *Il prigioniero* is linked with the earlier choruses *Canti di prigionia*. It was celebrated both as 'protest music' by a world emerging from Fascism and going almost immediately into the cold war, and as a technical achievement – the first important Italian opera composed entirely in the >twelve-tone system. Immensely powerful, it uses in its short compass a different vocal manner for each character, from the stark terror of the mother in the Prologue and the naturalistic emotions of the prisoner, to the insidious, seductive tones of the gaoler and the choral interludes expressing 'the crushing voice of the Inquisition'. The instrumentation, too, is clearly differentiated as in a >chamber opera, although the orchestra is a large one. The introduction to Scene 3 carries the same function as a >verismo >intermezzo, intensifying our knowledge of the prisoner's mood, his excitement deepening the sense of doom pervading the piece from the first three chords.

Overview: Although the mother–son relationship is implied as the first focus of the opera, it is the relationship of gaoler and gaoled which dominates, and through which the opera contemplates the political and philosophical aspects of freedom/loss of freedom. In other operas, an atmosphere of surveillance and terror is evoked to heighten the melodrama – explicitly in Ponchielli's **La Gioconda** and Puccini's **Tosca** and by implication in **Rigoletto** and Berg's **Wozzeck**; philosophically, only Beethoven's **Fidelio** really approaches the area confronted by Dallapiccola. Perhaps because of the demands of the compositional technique, few fully >serial, or twelve-tone, operas have been written; of these, Schoenberg's **Moses und Aron** shares the status of *Il prigioniero*, while Berg's **Lulu** leads the field in popularity.

Listening

Decca Headline HEAD10
NSO of Washington / Dorati
(Mazzieri, Barrera, Emile)

FRENCH OPERA

French opera has always had its own distinctive traditions; composers had to adapt their works to Parisian taste if they wanted to achieve success in this great cultural centre. Of course there had always been cross-fertilisation: in the 1750s Italian >opera buffa took Paris by storm, and at other stages both French >grand opera and >opéra comique left their mark on Europe. Over the years many Italians came to Paris – Lully, Cherubini, Spontini, Rossini, Bellini, Donizetti, Verdi – and several Germans – Gluck, Meyerbeer, Wagner, Offenbach, Weill. Some settled there, their output becoming part of the story of French opera. The tastes of 19th-century Parisian audiences are sometimes criticised because several of their favourite composers never achieved lasting international stature and are now largely neglected (Meyerbeer, Auber, Hérold, or Halévy). But to have the confidence to go your own sweet way is also an indication of cultural vitality, and Paris was nothing if not vital.

French opera amalgamated other popular theatre forms (ballets, pastorales, comédie-ballets and divertissements), including the magnificent classical drama, >spectacle and ballet being the high points. Lully's >tragédies lyriques established the form, and Rameau worked within it (giving music a more dominant role). The overriding principle was that all aspects of theatre art – music, drama, scenery, dance, effects – had to be balanced in a dramatically unified performance. The chorus had a high profile, and >recitatives alternated freely with more formal airs. Until the end of the 19th century the division between all-sung opera and opera with dialogue was quite clear: all-sung opera was to be found at l'Opéra, opera with spoken dialogue at the Opéra-Comique.

Growing out of popular parodies and stock comics, opéra comique only really got going after Pergolesi's La serva padrona had come to town. The French eagerly took up its new spontaneity and naturalness. They made the most of its opportunities for political propaganda and social comment, delighting in its dance rhythms and catchy melodies. Of the many composers who thrived in the world of opéra comique, the Belgian, Grétry, was the most popular.

Around this time Gluck decided he could put his reforms into practice in Paris, where the intellectual climate was sympathetic to them. In stripping opera of empty ornament, he created 'human' works of impressive dramatic power. He was criticised for his lack of spectacle, and his acclaimed simplicity certainly didn't enthrall all Paris, but his influence could still be felt later in Spontini and Berlioz.

Then came the Revolution, and after the austerity of Gluck and the charm of Grétry, spectacular action came back into vogue, showing the defiant spirit of France wrestling with a hostile Europe. Ordinary people were glorified, and comedy took second place to melodrama and stirring songs. Propaganda pieces, rescue stories and depictions of violent horror reflected the times. Cherubini and Méhul wrote some of the finest of these works.

Political statements remained important in the early 19th century: grand operas, often to librettos by Scribe, were packed with inflammatory epic struggles and noble principles. (One such work, Auber's La muette de Portici, apparently sparked off the 1830 Belgian revolution.) Audiences relished grand opera's impressive historical themes, its tableaux and striking effects – and above all the entanglement of individual passions with great crowds. The works of Auber and Rossini were followed by those of Meyerbeer and Halévy, and the culmination of this movement was Verdi's Don Carlos. Grand opera had become the meat of the Parisian diet. But there were soufflés and desserts, too – the opéra comiques of Boïeldieu and Hérold, and later the more ingratiating ones of Gounod and Thomas. In the end, just about the time that grand opera had had its day, the blatant onstage realism of Bizet's Carmen ensured that opéra comique could never be the same again.

Meanwhile the established vogue for Offenbach's iconoclastic comic operas and operettas pointed the direction in which lighter works were to go.

French opera remained active at the turn of the century with Massenet's sentimental love stories, Debussy's and Dukas's symbolist works, Ravel's one-off enchantments, Charpentier's new realism. One of its last individual statements came with Poulenc, whose operas offered something different. International audiences frequently rediscover the delights of the works that thrilled Paris. But while the great French tradition is kept alive with revivals, it pulses feebly on the contemporary scene.

George Shirley and Elisabeth Söderström as *Pelléas et Mélisande* (Royal Opera House 1969)

Jean-Baptiste Lully

Born: 28th November 1632/Florence
Died: 22nd March 1687/Paris

Lully went to Paris as a boy, and became the most significant musician of his era in France. He built up the standard of orchestral playing, wrote important church music, >pastorales, ballets and *comédies-ballets*. In his >*tragédies lyriques* he firmly established the specific pattern of French opera, with an important role for the chorus, for the dance and for >spectacle, yet great value accorded to the text – a pattern which endured for a century. Other celebrated operas include *Cadmus et Hermione*, *Alceste*, *Thésée*, *Atys*, *Phaëton*, *Amadis* and *Roland*.

Further reading: James Anthony – 'Lully' *The New Grove French Baroque Masters* (London 1986).

ARMIDE

Prologue and five acts
Libretto: Philippe Quinault
First performance: Paris 1686

Plot: In the Prologue, the allies Wisdom and Glory discuss their triumph over Love. Their hero Renaud is the single Crusader warrior able to withstand the charms of the beautiful Armide, a sorceress fighting for Hell against the Crusaders; she, however, is deeply troubled by her feelings for Renaud. Her helpers lure him to sleep in an enchanted garden, but she cannot bring herself to kill him – instead, she takes him to her palace, using her magic to make him love her. She also struggles to free herself of her own love for him. Eventually his fellow knights, finding him, remind him of Glory in battle, and he abandons Armide. Devastated, facing the perpetual torments of unrequited feeling, she destroys her palace, the cradle of their love.

The opera: Lully's >*tragédies lyriques* with Quinault were intended as a re-creation of Greek drama, a balance of music, libretto, dance and scenery. *Armide* was one of their finest achievements. The drama grows through Armide's struggles with her own feelings, the aid attempted by Hate, and the scenes between the lovers (only seen together in Act V, first amorous, then anguished) to its climax in Armide's cataclysmic reaction. The fluid, melodious >recitative is at its finest in the dramatic episodes where its flexibility allows sudden changes of mood: Armide's hesitant, confused monologue over the sleeping Renaud (end of Act II) was considered the jewel of French opera by Rameau. Other striking passages include Armide's troubled Act III monologue (*Ah! si la liberté*), the beautiful nature music which introduces Renaud to the enchanted garden, and the impressive orchestral *passacaille* in Act V, an early example of ballet being integrated naturally into the drama rather than superimposed on it.

Overview: As a tribute to Lully's *Armide*, Gluck set Quinault's libretto nearly a century later; Handel had incorporated the same theme in **Rinaldo** (=Renaud). The popular (and convenient) view of a man's love for a woman being the result of sorcery, an

entrapment, crops up frequently (Saint-Saëns's **Samson et Dalila**, Wagner's **Tannhäuser**, and Kundry's unsuccessful attempt, complete with magic garden, in Wagner's **Parsifal**); *Armide* presents it literally. There is also a significant connection with **Tristan und Isolde**, the turning point – Armide's capitulation as she stands poised to kill the sleeping Renaud – being paralleled between Wagner's lovers before the opera starts.

Listening

Erato STU 715302
Chapelle Royal/Herreweghe
(Yakar, Vandersteene, Borst)

Jean-Philippe Rameau

**Baptised: 25th September 1683/Dijon
Died: 12th September 1764/Paris**

Rameau's works most strongly rivalled, and indeed developed, Lully's heritage (the argument about which were

Jennifer Smith (centre) as Telaira in *Castor et Pollux* (English Bach Festival 1981)

superior occupied Parisian artistic circles for some time). He was an innovator in harmonic theory, and composed much valuable sacred and keyboard music. Because his theatre works – *opéra-ballets*, ballets, *comédies-ballet*, >*tragédies lyriques* and >*pastorales* – gave the purely musical elements greater prominence than they had previously held, he fell foul of the champions of Lully's style. His *tragédies lyriques* such as *Hippolyte et Aricie*, *Dardanus* and *Zoroastre* are highly regarded.

Further reading: Graham Sadler – 'Rameau' *The New Grove French Baroque Masters* (London 1986).

CASTOR ET POLLUX

**Five acts
Libretto: Pierre-Joseph Bernard
First performance: Paris 1737;
revised version Paris 1754**

Plot: The twins, Castor and Pollux, do not share the same father; Pollux, sired by Jupiter, was the King of Sparta. Both brothers love Telaira; but Pollux has given up his plans to marry her so as not to lose Castor. When Castor is killed defending Telaira from abduction, Pollux persuades Jupiter to let him become mortal, and sets out to take Castor's place in Hades. But Castor will only accept returning to life for a single day, in order to see Telaira. Moved by the brothers' mutual devotion, Jupiter grants each immortality with a place in the Zodiac.

The opera: The emotions represented in this opera are conveyed in pastel colours. Telaira's grief – in her air *Tristes apprêts* and in her fine exchange with Castor when he has returned from death – is particularly touching. Castor's poignant monologue in the Elysian fields (*Séjour de l'éternelle paix*) provides one of those moments of musical psychology when more is conveyed than is consciously expressed, while his final >*ariette* rejoices in sweet knowledge of Jupiter's goodness. While *Castor et Pollux* is not strikingly dramatic, Rameau's scheme of integrating a divertissement into each act generates vivid contrasts between the dances and the vocal music, the dances themselves marvellously diverse, often remarkable for their energy. There are also some beautiful choruses, notably the mournful *Que tout gémisse* at Castor's funeral and the appeal to Pollux by Hebe's attendants (*Qu'Hébé de fleurs toujours nouvelles*). The descent of Jupiter in the final act, to the strains of a flute, is conceived with exquisite restraint.

Overview: One senses in Rameau's >*tragédies lyriques*, particularly in *Castor et Pollux*, an anticipation of Gluck: with both composers dignity has musical value, with both the ceremonial is a source of expressive emotion. Even in details there are similarities – compare Castor's monologue as described above with Orestes's *Le calme rentre dans mon coeur* (**Iphigénie en Tauride**), or the dramatic placing of the *tombeau* at the start of the unrevised version with the opening of **Orfeo ed Euridice**. The central action – wresting a beloved soul from Hades, and offering oneself as substitute – is reflected in both *Orfeo* and **Alceste**. Pollux's generosity in conceding his

chosen Queen to Castor is shared by Titus in Mozart's **La clemenza di Tito**. And in another sense Rameau's operas look even further ahead: their seamless onward flow of >arioso-type >recitative connects Monteverdi with Wagner.

Listening

Christoph Willibald von Gluck

Gluck's work is Paris had a significant effect on the style of French opera. (For biographical information see entry in Italian section on page 20.)

Further Reading: Patricia Howard – *Gluck and the Birth of Modern Opera* (London 1963).

ALCESTE

Three acts
Libretto: F. L. G. Lebland du Roullet, after Ranieri da Calzabigi's Vienna version, after Euripides
First performance: Paris 1776

Plot: The people of Thessaly lament their lot as their beloved King Admetus lies dying. His wife, Alceste, leads prayers to Apollo, whose Oracle pronounces that for the king to live someone must undertake to die in his place. Alceste offers herself, and Admetus is restored to health. But when he hears of Alceste's forthcoming death he is distraught, and insists that he be the one to die. Alceste resolves the dispute by entering Hades, but Hercules, finding Admetus and the people quite crazed with grief, rescues her by force from the Gods of the Underworld. Apollo then appears, and restores the loving couple to their children and their people.

The opera: The Italian version of *Alceste* (Vienna 1767), Gluck's second great >reform opera, was, like **Orfeo**, reconceived for Paris. Unlike *Orfeo*, it is the French version which is more commonly performed today. The role of >deus ex machina is now shared by Hercules and Apollo; the >recitatives are in the flowing French style, accompanied by the orchestra. The first act is masterly, virtually a self-contained opera, ending with Alceste's extraordinary *Divinités du Styx*, part >aria, part invocation, never predictable. Throughout this act the chorus functions at a pitch of intense involvement. In the second act the crucial, affecting exchanges between Alceste and Admetus culminate in Alceste's lovely *Ah, malgré moi*. In the third act, as first Hercules and then Apollo take over, the pace steps up, virtually excluding the chorus. But it still allows Alceste some deeply expressive solos, notably her recitative and aria before the gates of Hades and, when Admetus joins her, the exquisite one-off *Vis pour garder*.

Overview: No composer's operas are more vulnerable than Gluck's; the statuesque dignity of his music cries out for performances of intense emotion and style. In the third act solos we begin to approach the >opere serie of Mozart; **Idomeneo** was five years away *Alceste*, like Gluck's own **Orfeo** but from a different standpoint, concerns itself with the inevitability of death. Its great central figure has to overcome the most human emotions in saving her husband from death; she does so, and triumphs. >Rescue opera, in manner worlds apart from Gluck, was soon to make realistic use of this symbolic process: Gluck's Alceste and Beethoven's Leonore (**Fidelio**) are sisters in spirit.

Listening

Orfeo S027823 F
CD: CO27823F

Bavarian Radio Orch./Baudo
(Norman, Gedda, Jordan)

IPHIGENIE EN TAURIDE
Iphigenia in Tauris

Four acts
Libretto: Nicolas-François Guillard and F. L. G. Lebland du Roullet, after Euripides
First performance: Paris 1779

Plot: The goddess Diana saved Iphigenia from being sacrificed by her father, Agamemnon, and brought her to Tauris as priestess of her cult among the barbarous Scythians. Unaware of this miracle, her mother Clytemnestra killed Agamemnon, and was killed in turn by Iphigenia's brother, Orestes. Now Iphigenia is forced by Thoas, King of the Scythians, to sacrifice all strangers, and when Orestes and his friend Pylades are driven to Tauris by a storm, Iphigenia, unaware of their identity, prepares reluctantly to kill them. Strangely drawn to Orestes, she offers him his freedom, but he, pursued by the Furies for matricide, wishes only to die, nor will he allow Pylades to die in his place. On the point of sacrificing Orestes, Iphigenia discovers his identity, and there is an ecstatic reunion. Thoas intervenes brutally, but Pylades brings rescue, and the battle between his Greeks and the Scythian army is stopped by Diana. She redeems Orestes from his guilt, and sends him back to Greece with Iphigenia.

The opera: It is not the action that makes the drama, but the inner feelings, expressed so lyrically and with such psychological perception. The initial storm continues in Iphigenia's anguished description of her dream; Orestes sings of calm returning to his heart, while the orchestra's agitated rhythm indicates his true state; the barbaric demands of Thoas are wrung from a tortured soul; Iphigenia conducts a funeral ceremony of heart-rending pathos for the brother she believes has died. Everything is integrated: the Priestesses share Iphigenia's emotions throughout, notably in their moving Act IV prayers to Diana, and the Scythians' ballet occurs naturally as a dance of savage jubilation. But a word of warning: any performance that has not grasped the purity of Gluck's language, where a few musical gestures are sufficient to evoke a world of feeling, leaves the music flat, the drama shallow. It is the music *between* the notes of the eloquently shaped melodies that carries both the true emotional immediacy of the friendship between Orestes and Pylades and the half-expressed vibrating awareness between the sister and the brother.

Overview: *Iphigénie en Tauride* was Gluck's last, and greatest, success, a synthesis of all that he had achieved in ridding opera of gratuitous musical effects and establishing an organic relation between the music and the drama. Beethoven was among its admirers, acknowledging Pylades's great Act III solo *Divinités de grandes âmes* in Florestan's dungeon scene; the whole development of Iphigenia's determination to rescue one of her prisoners, including the confrontation with Thoas, is echoed in Leonore (Beethoven's **Fidelio**). And the role of Gluck's orchestra, including its occasional 'alternative reading' of the singers' attitudes, became crucial to Wagner's entire method.

Listening

EMI IC 137 1731713 2
Paris Conservatoire Orch./Giulini
(Neway, Simoneau)

André Grétry

**Born: 10th/11th February 1741/Liège
Died: 24th September 1813/
Montmorency, Paris**

Grétry went to Paris as a young man. His many >opéra comiques (he wrote over sixty works for the stage) celebrated intimate, domestic and village scenes with graceful, natural melodies and orchestral colour. He also satirised contemporary musical fashion. Blondel's air in *Richard Coeur-de-lion* is widely regarded as a most important early instance of >leitmotiv.

Further Reading: David Charlton – *Grétry and the Growth of Opéra-comique* (Cambridge 1986).

RICHARD COEUR-DE-LION

**Three acts
Libretto: Michel Sedaine
First performance: Paris 1784**

Plot: Richard Coeur-de-lion, imprisoned in Europe, is being sought by both his beloved Countess Marguerite and his resourceful troubadour Blondel. Posing as a blind man, Blondel becomes go-between in the love of the local fortress governor and a young village woman, and tests the identity of the governor's secret prisoner by singing outside the fortress the love-song Richard once wrote for Marguerite. The prisoner proves he is indeed Richard by responding with the same song. With this song, Blondel makes himself known to Marguerite, and he and her men, using local help, storm the fortress to rescue Richard. Love and friendship are triumphant.

The opera: *Richard Coeur-de-lion* is a felicitous combination of light-hearted village life with great themes of loyalty and rescue. The deft characterisation is full of domestic charm. At first spoken dialogue predominates, but music is the natural medium for the gathering excitement, and the last scenes are a succession of peasant dances and choruses, battle music, marches and ensembles. Grétry moves easily between the music for the >trouser-role Antonio or the girlish Laurette and Blondel's stirring *O Richard! O mon roi!* or Richard's prison-song (*Si l'univers entier m'oublie*). Blondel's >romance (*Un fièvre brûlante*) runs like a thread throughout, linking all three main characters. Today the opera is most often called to mind when the old countess quotes from it in Tchaikovsky's **The Queen of Spades.**

Overview: Grétry's manner – call it relaxed formality – developed the

>opéra comique at a time when to be natural and spontaneous was much in vogue in France. The duet between Blondel and Laurette (*Un bandeau couvre les yeux*), an intimacy without any sexual overtones, is a prototype for the famous Papageno and Pamina duet in Mozart's **The Magic Flute**; Blondel himself is something of a Figaro character, combining heroism with humour. Village life, almost an end in

itself in other *paysanneries* of Grétry, became integral to the atmosphere in both Rossini's **William Tell** and Bellini's **La sonnambula** as well as affording a background to many a 19th-century operatic tragedy. But this engaging work was also part of the development of >rescue opera, and the similarities with Beethoven's **Fidelio** are interesting.

Luigi Cherubini

Born: 14th September 1760/ Florence
Died: 15th March 1842/Paris

Cherubini settled in Paris as a young man, and became a dominating figure in music education, opera and church music. A composer of striking personality, whose operas integrated music and drama to a greater extent than previously, he gives the orchestra considerable prominence. Beethoven ranked him higher than any other composer, and he was widely admired by the later Romantic composers, although he was in some senses a conservative. He wrote nearly forty works for the stage, mostly operas.

MEDEE

Three acts
Libretto: François-Benoit Hoffman, after Pierre Corneille, after Seneca
First performance: Paris 1797

Plot: As Dirce (Glauce in the Italian version) prepares to marry Jason, Medea, the wife Jason abandoned for the crimes she committed, comes to Colchis to plead her cause. Her crimes had aided Jason's heroic exploits, and she had saved his life in the process; she swears vengeance if rejected. But

Maria Callas in the title role of *Médée* at the Royal Opera House in 1958

77

Jason wants none of her; he threatens to kill her. King Creon, Dirce's father, exiles her, giving her only one day's grace, and Jason permits her to spend that day with her children, whom he has kept from her. Now Medea prepares her terrible revenge: she sends a poisoned robe as wedding-gift to Dirce, and she prepares to kill the children – at first unable to do it, she is galvanised by renewed thoughts of Jason. Then, proclaiming vengeance satisfied, she descends to suffer in Hell, while flames devour Colchis.

The opera: This remarkable work was restored to its full-length authentic form at the 1983 Buxton Festival, where the original spoken dialogue replaced the sung >recitatives added in the 19th century. It emerges as an opera of immense power. The fine characterisation of Jason, Creon and the lesser characters creates the context within which Medea's anguish is experienced, and she entirely dominates the opera: it is *her* drama. She is no monster, more a victim, in conflict with herself, driven to commit horrors equal to those inflicted on her. This sustained focus of psychological intensity, still rare in opera, is achieved with a score whose powerful forward thrust never flags; the impressive ensembles depicting Medea's public struggles maintain the driving quality of her magnificent monologues and her confrontations with Jason. There is a moment of genuine lyricism, dramatic for being so: Medea's moving pleas for one day's grace (*Eh bien, eh bien, je m'y soumets*).

Overview: *Médée* straddles two centuries: there is a line of austere dramatic intensity running from Gluck through Cherubini and Beethoven to Berlioz's **The Trojans** (and fascinating similarities in orchestral treatment of the great storms in *Médée* and *The Trojans*). Medea, her true nature distorted by her sense of outrage, still retains her clarity of vision; in this sense both Bellini's **Norma** (who teeters on the verge of a comparable infanticide) and Puccini's **Tosca** resemble her. So it is not surprising that the impetus for *Médée*'s rejoining the regular repertory was a 1953 revival in Italian for Maria Callas, incomparable in all these three roles.

Further reading: Max Loppert – *Medea Revealed* (The Listener 4.4.85, page 32); Basil Deane – *Cherubini* (London 1965).

Listening

Orizzonte AOCL 316001–3
La Scala/Votto
(Callas, Scotto, Picchi, Pirizzini)

Gasparo Spontini

Born: 14th November 1774/Maiolati
Died: 24th January 1851/Maiolati

A composer whose positions at various courts in Europe gave opportunities for performance of his operas, several of Spontini's works were widely successful in his lifetime. They are noted for the grandeur of their tableaux and processions, and – as with Gluck – the classical restraint of their large-scale emotions.

LA VESTALE
The Vestal Virgin

Three acts
Libretto: Etienne Jouy
First performance: Paris 1807

Plot: To gain the right to marry Julia, Licinius has won military honours for Rome – only to find that Julia, obeying her father's dying wish, has forsworn romantic love and become a Vestal Virgin. Her first duty is to crown Licinius with his victor's wreath, before spending the night guarding the sacred flame in the temple. Although it is blasphemy, Licinius comes to her there and they avow their love. The flame dies out: the goddess is angry. For this sacrilege the priests condemn Julia to be entombed alive, and Licinius musters a band of soldiers to rescue her. A sudden storm darkens the sky, a ball of fire strikes the altar and rekindles the sacred flame: the goddess has released Julia from her vows. She and Licinius can be united.

The opera: In his operas for Paris Spontini added >spectacle and effect to the noble simplicity of drama he inherited from Gluck. The scenes of the triumphal procession, the condemnation of Julia and the impending battle stopped by the darkness (not to mention the newly lit sacred fire illuminating the scene) enthralled the audiences of the Napoleonic era, with their developing taste for classical grandeur. In *La vestale*, personal, individual emotions are firmly welded into this large-scale approach without being swamped by it. So there is room for the fine line and intensity of Julia's *O des infortunes* within the impressive finale of Act II, whose increase in pace and density caused such excitement (it derived from >opera buffa, but was a novelty in >opera seria). Equally, each act starts 'small' and inflates gradually towards the climax unhampered by any flamboyance in its solo numbers, which make their point and move on. The best examples are Licinius's anguished entry at the start of Act III, or his *Les Dieux prendront pitié* (Act II). Even in Julia's extended Act II >scena (ending with the splendid *Impitoyables Dieux*), the drama continues to develop through (not after) her expression of feeling.

Overview: With *La vestale*, Spontini became a successful European composer, and he expanded his grand style with *Fernand Cortez* (1809) and *Olympie* (1819). The latter achieved enormous success in Berlin in 1821, yet within five weeks it was eclipsed by Weber's **Der Freischütz**. The Romantic age had left Spontini behind: in Bellini's **Norma** (1831), the next great opera where love invades the inner sanctum of chastity, religion is no longer accorded any importance, and the struggle is entirely in terms of personal emotion. But *La vestale* remained popular and was given a boost in a revival for Callas in 1955. It is usually sung in Italian translation.

Listening

Daniel Auber

Born: 29th January 1782/Caen
Died: 12th May 1871/Paris

A pupil of Cherubini, Auber was one of the 19th-century's leading composers of opera and >opéra comique (he wrote over forty). *La muette de Portici* helped establish French >grand opera – and a performance in Brussels sparked off the rioting for Belgian independence. *Fra Diavolo* has been the most lasting of his many opéra comiques.

FRA DIAVOLO

Three acts
Libretto: Eugène Scribe
First performance: Paris 1830

Plot: Lorenzo, an officer of the carabinieri too poor to marry Zerline, the innkeeper's daughter, is keen to catch the notorious bandit Fra Diavolo. An English couple, Milord and Milady Cockburn, arrive at the inn, having been robbed by Fra Diavolo's men. The bandit leader himself, disguised as an elegant Marquis, flirts with Milady, intending to steal her remaining jewels and money. Lorenzo returns, having fought the bandits and recovered the Cockburns' stolen jewels; in reward, they provide the money for Zerline to marry him. Late at night, the 'Marquis' is found near the ladies' bedrooms; his claim to be keeping an assignation leads to angry misunderstandings among the couples. But next morning Diavolo's henchmen accidentally give themselves away, Diavolo is captured, and everyone else lives happily ever after.

The opera: The music of this crisp, bright >opéra comique, almost entirely unsentimental, has an irresistible morning freshness. Nothing is especially memorable, yet the rhythmic jauntiness of the easy-going tunes is infectious. *Fra Diavolo* came at the peak of Auber's career (his last opéra-comique was written at the age of eighty-seven), and the sheer experience shown in the excellent Act I finale is impressive. The music never gets in the way of the action, yet the fun would be unthinkable without it. Bourgeois concerns with dowries and possessions, Romantic opera's obsession with horror, add to the comedy. Diavolo – an archetypal appealing rogue – strings everyone along; in his flirtation with Milady, his unscrupulous >Credo (Act III) and his superb reversal of the near-disaster in the inn (Act II) he invites us, with a wink, to mock the gullible and the vulnerable. The English couple's affectations are delightfully silly; their accent and their curses must have delighted the Parisians, no doubt already bored with tourists more than a century ago.

Overview: *Fra Diavolo*, Auber's answer to Rossini's **Count Ory**, had the Italian composer's manner without his inspiration. Its popularity throughout the 19th century (which the Laurel and Hardy film continued into the 20th century) was ensured by its rather tame ending, satisfying the requirements of bourgeois morality that the dashing hero should get his come-uppance – that naughtiness be enjoyed, yet kept safely in its place. This principle, ignored in Monteverdi's **The Coronation of Poppaea**, was already established in Mozart's **Don Giovanni** (Diavolo comes from the same stable as the Don), and dominated comedy long after the advent of Verdi and >verismo.

Listening

Fonit/Cetra LMA 3013
Martina Franca Festival Orch./Zedda
(Serra, Dupuy, Raffanti)

Gioacchino Rossini

An important composer for France in that his *Moïse et Pharaon* and *Guillaume Tell* helped establish French >grand opera, Rossini's Italian comic operas, followed by *Le Comte Ory*, virtually took over >opéra comique. (For biographical information see entry in Italian section on page 30.)

MOISE ET PHARAON

Four acts
Libretto: Luigi Balocchi and Etienne de Jouy, after Tottola
First performance: Paris 1827

Plot: In his efforts to gain freedom for the Israelites, their leader Moses invokes God's wrath on the Egyptians who have enslaved them. Each time a plague descends Pharaoh promises to let the Israelites go but when it is lifted, he vacillates. He is under pressure from his priests as well as his son, Aménophis, who is in love with Moses's niece, Anaï, and insists that she remain with him. Anaï, who loves Aménophis, is eventually inspired to escape with the Israelites, and they cross the Red Sea on miraculously dry land, reaching the shore safely just as the pursuing Egyptian army is engulfed in the returning waters.

The opera: *Moïse et Pharaon, ou Le passage de la Mer Rouge* was a revision for Paris of Rossini's earlier opera for Naples, *Mosè in Egitto*. Even when this Parisian version is performed in Italian translation, it is clearly a French >grand opera in conception, incorporating ballet and >spectacle, and shedding some of the vocal floridity of Rossini's Italian style. As everyone knew the story (and ten plagues might have stretched the resources even of the Paris Opéra), in the interests of drama Rossini's librettists needed only select enough disasters to keep up Moses's tug-of-war with the recalcitrant Pharaoh and to threaten Amenophis with the loss of his beloved. The chorus is fully employed, adding to the statuesque quality of the music, which develops a personal tone mainly in Anaï's more despairing solo utterances and in her duets with Aménophis. Moses is a powerful, dignified figure, very much a High Priest of the Israelites; his warmest music is reserved for his celebrated prayer to

God, taken up by all the Israelites, before the crossing.

Overview: Rossini only felt able to tackle his great **William Tell** after he had tested the waters with *Moïse* and other adaptations. The success of *Moïse*, much of it presented in massive static tableaux not far from oratorio in effect, influenced French grand opera. Of the two characters who move the drama forward, Anaï is the young woman torn between love and patriotism/religion so vividly depicted in Verdi (**Aida**, and Fenena in **Nabucco**); Moses is a stern spiritual leader, with touches of family feeling which slightly redeem his austerity.

Listening

Philips 6769 7654 081 3
Ambrosian Ch. Phil. Orch./Scimone
(Raimondi, Anderson, Nimsgern)

COUNT ORY
Le Comte Ory

Two acts
Libretto: Eugène Scribe and Charles Gaspard Delestre-Poirson
First performance: Paris 1828

Plot: Count Ory, who goes to great lengths to satisfy his whims, assails the virtue of Countess Adèle while her brother is away on a Crusade. His first ploy, to set up below her castle as a hermit with a good line in problem-solving, gets him as far as persuading her to fall in love – but he is unmasked. Undaunted, he makes use of an idea from his page, Isolier, who is himself in love with the Countess: to be accepted into her castle dressed as a nun fleeing from the wicked Count Ory. He does it in style, with thirteen followers similarly disguised. In the name of gratitude he presses his attentions on the Countess in the darkness, unaware that he is actually fondling Isolier, who has cracked his disguise and warned the Countess, and who is transmitting the Count's embraces to her on his own behalf. The lights come up when the Crusaders return, and Ory escapes, disgusted that *he* has been tricked.

The opera: Rossini, knowing his Paris audience, reduced solo vocal pyrotechnics by extending the writing for ensembles, and engineered an impressive >spectacle for the final moments. However, the original Rossini trademarks – jaunty, bouncy rhythmic patterns, the inimitable crescendo, a fresh, open lyrical style and witty, inventive orchestration – were all there, and >opéra comique was never the same again. For the wonderfully inventive Count, going is as much fun as arriving, if only because his brazen charades and his double meanings so hilariously expose the gullibility of the pious (note his brief ironic interpolations in the ensemble *Moi, je réclame*). Marvellous touches: the >a cappella response to the first unmasking (*O terreur, ô peine extrême*), the pizzicato accompaniment to Ory's henchman Raimbaud's patter >aria about his death-defying hunt for wine, the rapid switches of the 'nuns' from carousing to simpering prayers, the crafting of the final trio. It is a delicious send-up.

Overview: In the Count's improvisations, the inspiration of Count Almaviva (**The Barber of Seville**) is undimmed, although the romantic ardour has turned cynical. Auber's **Fra Diavolo** is equally brazen (Auber's opera was a notable spin-off from Rossini's), but for comparably funny dissimulations one must look to the women in Verdi's **Falstaff**.

Listening

HMV ROF 744
Glyndebourne Opera
1956

WILLIAM TELL
Guillaume Tell

Four acts
Libretto: Étienne de Jouy, Florent Bis, Armand Marrast, after Friedrich Schiller
First performance: Paris 1829

Plot: William Tell is working with wise old Melchthal to fire the Swiss with revolutionary fervour against the Habsburg tyrant, Gessler, but Melchthal's son, Arnold, is preoccupied with his love for Mathilde, the Habsburg princess. When Melchthal is killed by Gessler's soldiers, Arnold commits himself to the cause of Swiss independence. The men of the three cantons gather to rise in revolt at the signal – a lighted beacon. In Altdorf, centre of Gessler's power, Tell refuses to bow down to Gessler's hat on a pole; Gessler forces him to shoot an arrow at an apple placed on his son Jemmy's head. Seeing the courage of both father and son, the people become militant. Tell is taken by the soldiers, but Jemmy is saved by Mathilde, herself committed to independence for the Swiss. Jemmy lights the beacon – their own home; Tell kills Gessler and Arnold leads the capture of Altdorf. Switzerland is free.

The opera: This was Rossini's grandest >grand opera, history seen as epic events advancing through individual experiences. The intimacy between Tell, Jemmy and Tell's wife, the subordination of the love-relationship to the great undertaking, the friendships between the men, and their concern for Arnold on both the personal and the political level, are all part of this design. From the magnificent overture to the radiant final chorus it is the score of a mature master, with an endless variety of textures depicting the hunt, the army, the shepherds, the villagers' dancing, the storm. There are splendid solos for Mathilde and Arnold; the duet for Arnold and Tell and their trio with Walter are particularly fine. The foregathering of the three cantons, each with its own music, is thrilling; the ensembles are the heart of the drama throughout. Equally impressive is the famous scene of the shooting of the apple; Jemmy's sparky courage, Tell's terror that he might kill his son, his desperate abasement before Gessler and above all his words of advice to Jemmy (*Sois immobile*) are entirely unsentimental and deeply moving.

Overview: After *William Tell* Rossini was exhausted, and produced no more operas himself, but his achievement in balancing the political and the personal in grand opera would bear fruit in Verdi's **Simon Boccanegra** and Musorgsky's **Boris Godunov**, and

William Tell, his magnificent baritone creation, paved the way for Wagner's Hans Sachs (**Die Meistersinger**).

Listening

EMI SLS 970
Ambrosian Ch. Phil. Orch./Gardelli
(Bacquier, Caballé, Gedda, Taillon, Kovats)

Gaetano Donizetti

Donizetti's operas for Paris made a notable contribution to the development of opéra-comique and >grand opera. (For biographical information see entry in Italian section of page 35.)

THE DAUGHTER OF THE REGIMENT
La fille du régiment

Two acts
Libretto: Jules-Henri Vernoy de Saint-Georges and Jean François Alfred Bayard
First performance: Paris 1840

Plot: The 21st Regiment of Grenadiers have a 'daughter' – Marie, whom they brought up after finding her abandoned as a baby. Now she is their *vivandière*, supplying them with liquor and provisions. In their role of indulgent 'father', they accept her foreign suitor Tonio because she loves him – but he must join up if he wants to marry her. Marie's real mother, a Marquise, discovers her, takes her in hand, and arranges a marriage with a Duke. To escape this fate she, Tonio and the grenadiers spill the beans about her rough-and-ready life to the shocked guests at the solemnising of her marriage contract. Her mother is moved to bless her union with Tonio, and a regimental future is assured.

The opera: Donizetti wrote this >opéra comique in his own charming Italian style with a French tincture. Jaunty and sentimental in turn, it casts a humorous eye at the contrast between the restrictions of an aristocratic existence and the pleasures of a relaxed life in the army. The argument is heavily loaded in favour of military fun, particularly when Marie and the regimental leader keep turning a socially acceptable ballad into the regimental song, a stirring 'rataplan'. There is substantial beauty in the lyrical >*romanze* (*Il faut partir, Par le rang et par l'opulence, Pour me rapprocher de Marie*) and the scene when Tonio asks the regiment for Marie's hand (*Ah! mes amis*) can be a triumph for a good Donizetti tenor.

Overview: The 20th-century experience of war makes it a little harder than it was in the mid-19th to contemplate the charm of a regimental existence or the fun of battle, but military rhythms remain irresistible (which is why Berlioz worked the Rákóczy March into **The Damnation of Faust**) and the panoply of military life is sure-fire entertainment even when more realistically presented, as in Verdi's **The Force of Destiny**. Up to 1917 Paris celebrated Bastille Day at the Opéra-Comique with either Offenbach's *La fille du Tambour-Major* or this Donizetti work – what greater compliment could the French pay to an Italian composer?

Listening

Decca SET 372/3 K23 K22
CD: 414 520-2DH2
London OSA/5-1273
ROHCG/Bonynge
(Sutherland, Pavarotti, Sinclair)

LA FAVORITE
The Favourite

Four acts
Libretto: Alphonse Royer, Gustave Vaëz and Eugène Scribe, after François de Baculard d'Arnaud
First performance: Paris 1840

Plot: Fernand, a young novice at the monastery, has fallen in love with

Leonore, unaware that she is the King's mistress. The Superior, Balthasar, warns him against forsaking his spiritual path, but he seeks out his beloved, who returns his feelings. As a reward for heroism in battle, the King allows him to marry Leonore. But Fernand is ignorant of the King's link with her, let alone that the King had been stopped by Balthasar from divorcing the Queen and marrying Leonore himself. Leonore thinks Fernand knows the facts when they get married, and is appalled when, finding out the truth from the hostile courtiers, he abuses her dreadfully. He returns to the monastery, where she follows him, seeking his forgiveness. He is bitter, but cannot resist her. Exhausted, ill, exalted, she dies in his arms.

The opera: *La favorite* shows the developing depth and complexity of the operas Donizetti wrote after he left Naples for Paris. Unaccountably, an Italian translation is usually staged, despite inconsistencies in the plot, inappropriate matching of text and vocal line, and mutilating cuts. Certainly the 'feel' of Donizetti's music remains Italianate. But the conception is French; the standard performances in Italian are all wrong, although they cannot obscure the opera's many beauties. The fourth act is a superb mini-opera charged with inner feeling right from the brooding orchestral introduction to the final intense duet. Leonore's earlier *O mon Fernand* (*O mio Fernando*) shows the wide vocal and emotional range which appeals to dramatic mezzos; its nobility of manner infuses the whole score. This is the key to Fernand's famous *Ange si pur* (*Spirto gentil*), a fine example of Donizetti's way with the tenor voice. The warm, lyrical writing for King Alfonso suggests a confused human being rather than an operatic villain, despite the seething resentment of his courtiers.

Overview: Only five years after the unlikely dramatics of his **Lucia di Lammermoor**, in *La favorite* Donizetti shows a more real psychological insight. The conflict between sacred and profane love, already broached in Bellini's **Norma**, is touched on later in the century in **Samson et Dalila** (Saint-Saëns) and **Manon** (Massenet), and tackled substantially in **Parsifal**

83

(Wagner) and **The Force of Destiny** (Verdi). In the latter, Verdi's Leonora travels a spiritual road similar to Donizetti's Leonore, both women's lovers seeking peace for their wracked souls in a monastery. The thwarted love of Donizetti's King Alfonso, and his battle with the Church, are intensified with King Philip in Verdi's **Don Carlos**, whose Eboli has much in common with Leonore. But La favorite's real connection with these large-scale works of Verdi is in the broad scale of Donizetti's musical approach, and its unadorned expressiveness – positive aspects of the influence of Paris.

Further reading: Max Loppert – Lucrezia Borgia and La Favorite (Opera on Record 3, London 1984).

Listening

1   Pathé 1551-71
    (Reprint) Bourg DG41001-3
    Chorus and Orch./Ruhlmann
    (Lapeyrette, Lasalle, Albers)
    1910
2   Decca D96 D3 4 K96 K33
    London OSA/5-13113
    Teatro Communale, Bologna/Bonynge
    (Pavarotti, Cossotto, Bacquier)

Hector Berlioz

**Born: 11th December 1803/La Côte-St-André, Isère
Died: 8th March 1869/Paris**

Berlioz was perhaps the greatest of all French composers, particularly of ceremonial works, symphonies, concertos and opera, and a number of dramatic works that fall between those categories. He was a most individual composer, especially in his harmonic and melodic style and the quirky vitality of his rhythm, and a supreme orchestral colourist. He was an arch-Romantic when young, but many of his works have a Classical greatness. His first opera, Benvenuto Cellini, has recently gained in popularity.

Further reading: Hugh Macdonald – Berlioz (London 1982).

THE DAMNATION OF FAUST
La damnation de Faust

**Four parts
Text: Almire Gandonnière and the composer, after Johann Wolfgang von Goethe (including the translation by Gérard de Nerval)
First performance: Paris 1846**

Plot: The scholar Faust is melancholy; nothing lifts his weary spirit. When Mephistopheles appears, Faust jumps at his offer of experiencing life's delights. A crude sing-song in a wine-cellar disgusts him, but he is ecstatic after an enchanted sleep in which he dreams of the virginal Marguerite. There is a brief, intense love-scene in her bedroom, from which Faust is hurried away by Mephistopheles. Consumed with love, Marguerite unwittingly poisons her mother with sleeping-draughts while she prepares nightly for Faust's return, but it takes news of her pending execution to stir Faust. Desperate to save her, he signs the document Mephistopheles produces – and finds himself on a horrifying ride to Hell, condemned eternally to the flames, while Marguerite receives heaven's salvation.

The opera: It isn't an opera. Berlioz called it a légende dramatique, recognising that any staging would require much alteration. However, it remains popular in theatres as well as concert-halls. The potential greatness of Faust is embodied in several glorious Romantic addresses to nature, but he is undermined by lack of moral character. By contrast Marguerite's >arias (her 'Gothic song' and D'amour l'ardente flamme) are charged with the finest inner feeling. Mephistopheles, richly ironic, scorns his victim's self-indulgence; his own subtle range extends from the Song of the Flea, which caps Brander's vulgar Song of the Rat in the wine-cellar, to Voici des roses, part of the exquisite sequence (incorporating the well-known Ballet of the Sylphs) designed to ensnare Faust in passion for Marguerite. The choral element is strong and diverse, including

a hilarious send-up of sterile academicism in the Amen >fugue, and genuine contrapuntal brilliance at the end of Part Two. To a late 20th-century ear the Ride to the Abyss is still horrific, the Chorus of Demons less effective. It is a highly original work, full of Berliozian splendours of melody and orchestration.

Overview: Like Busoni in **Doktor Faust,** Berlioz gets far closer to the sweep and substance of Goethe's *Faust* than Gounod does. Partly operatically conceived, though not for the stage, *The Damnation of Faust* is nearest to Berlioz's own dramatic symphony, *Roméo et Juliette*, or his sacred trilogy, *L'enfance du Christ*, falling into the category of dramatic works such as Stravinsky's **Oedipus Rex** and Orff's *Carmina Burana* which may be given theatre or platform performances whatever their composers' intentions.

Listening

Philips 6703 042
CD: 416 395-2PH2
LSO/Davis
(Veasey, Gedda, Bastin)

THE TROJANS
Les troyens

Five acts
Libretto: The composer, after Virgil
First performance: Second part only, as The Trojans at Carthage, Paris 1863; complete, Karlsruhe 1890

Plot: After ten years of war, the Greeks retreat, leaving behind them a huge

wooden horse. Cassandra is full of foreboding, but, as always, her vision of doom is brushed aside amid the jubilation. Her brother Aeneas pronounces the horse sacred, and it is brought within the walls of the city. At night the Greeks hidden in its belly open the gates to their army, and begin to destroy Troy. A vision of the dead hero, Hector, urges Aeneas to found a great new empire in Italy. With his soldiers he saves the holy Trojan treasures and escapes, while Cassandra leads the women in an exalted suicide.

Dido, beloved queen of Carthage, is anxious that the city is vulnerable. She welcomes the Trojans, who help the Carthaginians repulse an invasion. Caught in a storm while hunting, Dido and Aeneas take refuge in a cave; there they consummate their love. But the Trojan destiny is known, and the god Mercury comes to remind Aeneas of it. Torn, but bowing to the inevitable, Aeneas departs precipitately. Dido, devastated, ceremonially burns relics of his sojourn, seeing in Hannibal her future avenger. To the horror of her people she stabs herself – only to picture Rome destroying Carthage, in her dying vision.

The opera: For all that Berlioz was an avant-garde composer *The Trojans* is a >number opera, with solos, ensembles and choruses, >recitative and >aria, clearly demarcated. No anachronism, this; Berlioz often preferred to distil his Romantic spirit in classical forms. The opera's forward movement is irresistible. Doom-laden Cassandra, a magnificent creation, is the pivot of the first two acts. Dido is a great queen, concerned even for the everyday life of her people. Her love relationship is given Berlioz's most inspired treatment, firstly in the symphonic interlude (the Royal Hunt and Storm) then in the glorious duet. She heaps scorn on Aeneas's claim that the gods demand his departure – 'Monster of piety!' – but laments that she has no child to remember him by. Her penultimate >scena (*Je vais mourir*) juxtaposes naked emotion with an exquisitely poised melodic line (*Adieu, fière cité*). Her final visions complement Cassandra's: 'immortal Rome' is constantly before our eyes, reinforced by the Trojans' march and the reiterated cries of *Italie!*, part of a design which encompasses both legend and history. Intimate, personal touches are there, too, in the silent blessing bestowed on Hector's son Astynax, and when Aeneas entrusts his son to Dido before going to fight for her; in the two sentinels gossiping about the good life in Carthage, or a young sailor falling asleep as he dreams of his childhood home (the haunting *Vallons sonore*).

Overview: Never performed in full during his lifetime, Berlioz's great opera on his beloved Virgil remained relatively neglected. In the spirit of Gluck, on the scale of Spontini and Meyerbeer, it balances epic events with revealing personal touches, as Rossini did in **William Tell** (the points of similarity between Aeneas and Arnold are not accidental). The theme of *Didone abbandonata* inspired many great works of art, Purcell's opera **Dido and Aeneas** being among the most notable; other legendary abandoned women – Medea (Cherubini's **Médée**), Armida (Gluck's *Armide*) – caught the imagination of composers in the same way.

Further reading: Ian Kemp – *Hector Berlioz: The Trojans* (Cambridge 1986).

Listening

Philips 6709 002/7699142 5
CD: 416 432-2PH4
ROHCG/Davis
(Veasey, Vickers, Lindholm)

BEATRICE ET BENEDICT

Two acts
Libretto: The composer, after Shakespeare
First performance: Baden-Baden 1862

Plot: While Hero and Claudio sigh ecstatically over their love, Beatrice and Benedict spar wittily, making a virtue of their mutual detestation and claiming they will never marry. Preparations for Hero and Claudio's nuptials are well under way (including the musical efforts supervised by the lovable, fussy old Somarone) when it occurs to the couple to trick Beatrice and Benedict by telling each that the other is hopelessly in love with him/her. With unexpectedly little resistance, these old enemies call a truce and get married.

The opera: Already in **The Trojans** Berlioz had used lines from Shakespeare's *The Merchant of Venice*; now he takes a single, major element from *Much Ado about Nothing* – love. Hero and Claudio are a little in love with love, and Berlioz cannot resist teasing Hero by ending her fine >aria (*Je vais le voir*) with an over-elaborate >cadenza in the earnest spirit of >opera seria. But in the glorious Nocturne that ends Act I, the composer acknowledges love's universal capacity to touch the spirit. Beatrice is more complex than Hero, encompassing a whole world of feeling in her magnificent >scena *Non! Que viens-je d'entendre?* (its melody *Il m'en souvient* shows Berlioz expressing the core of an emotion with a mere three or four notes). Her final scherzo with Benedict, heard earlier in the whirling notes of the overture, sums up this opera; it's full of laughter, warmth and tolerance. And cleverness – for we may sense Berlioz jibing at Somarone's inept attempts to produce a wedding-hymn and a drinking-song, yet he allows these oddities to achieve something of their desired effect.

Overview: Last operas are sometimes a climax of a composer's life's work, sometimes a heavenly postscript. Verdi's **Falstaff** and Monteverdi's **The Coronation of Poppaea** were both.

With Berlioz, the climax had been *The Trojans*, while *Béatrice et Bénédict*, his last major work, was an exquisite afterthought. He wrote it at a stage in his personal life and his career when he was feeling neither fulfilled nor happy. But there is a serenity in its music, and a sparkle, even when it hints at darker feelings below the surface; this is the poise achieved by Mozart in **The Marriage of Figaro** and **Così fan tutte**.

Listening

DG 2707 1302
Paris Opera/Barenboim
(Minton, Cotrubas, Domingo, Fischer-Dieskau)
1981

Ambroise Thomas

Born: 5th August 1811/Metz
Died: 12th February 1896/Paris

A composer of some twenty operas and >opéra comiques, Thomas was highly regarded in his time. He is now relatively neglected, though *Mignon* remains popular in France and, like *Hamlet*, is still performed elsewhere.

HAMLET

Five acts
Libretto: Jules Barbier and Michel Carré, after William Shakespeare
First performance: Paris 1868

Plot: Prince Hamlet is depressed at the death of his father and the hasty remarriage of his mother to his uncle Claudius, now King, but he and Ophelia, daughter of the Lord Chamberlain Polonius, reaffirm their love. When his father's ghost reveals that he was murdered by Claudius and the Queen (assisted by Polonius), Hamlet rejects

Ophelia, torments the King, and confronts the Queen. Claudius fears the judgment of God; Ophelia goes mad, drowning herself in a river. At her graveside the Ghost insists that Hamlet kill Claudius, and proclaims him King of Denmark. (Thomas later wrote an alternative ending: at Ophelia's graveside, Hamlet kills Claudius, and commits suicide.)

The opera: This slimmed-down version of Hamlet works on stage if one can wipe the original from one's mind. The most striking alteration is the inflation of Ophelia's mad scene: with the preceding ballet-divertissement it takes up the entire fourth act, and is by far the longest solo in the opera, even though Ophelia is a secondary, albeit important, character. But then the operatic heroine's mad scene was her greatest dramatic and vocal opportunity, and Thomas pulled out all the stops for this one, with even some evocative Lisztian >chromatic writing. The scene between the Queen and Hamlet could hardly fail to be dramatic, and particularly impressive is the first confrontation with the Ghost on the ramparts, leading to Hamlet's moving final lines *O lumière, o soleil*. The 'To be or not to be' soliloquy is an essay in mysterious atmosphere – Thomas's instrumentation was often original and interesting – and the gravediggers have a lugubrious drinking song worthy of *Alice in Wonderland*.

Overview: *Hamlet* confirmed Thomas's success at the Paris Opéra sixteen months after *Mignon* had gained great success at the Opéra-Comique, and Ophelia's mad scene joined the great gallery which included Elvira (Bellini's **I puritani**) and Donizetti's **Lucia di Lammermoor**. Compared with the depth of feeling between Azucena and Manrico in Verdi's **Il trovatore**, the mother–son relationship here is limited to one highly dramatic exchange, the version for opera stripping it of its psychological overtones in the original rather than achieving the kind of intensification so remarkable in Verdi.

Listening

Decca 410 184-1/4
Welsh National Opera Orch./Bonynge
(Milnes, Sutherland, Morris)

Giuseppe Verdi

(For biographical information see entry in Italian section on page 43.)

DON CARLOS

Five acts
Libretto: Joseph Méry and Camille du Locle
First performance: Paris 1867, revised Milan 1884, revised again Modena 1886

Plot: (It helps to make a diagram!) Don Carlos and Elisabeth of Valois fall in love, only to hear that Elisabeth must marry Carlos's father, King Philip II of Spain. Elisabeth sublimates her despair, becoming an honourable wife and Queen to Philip; Carlos, permanently anguished, hating his father, supports the people of Flanders, who are rebelling against Spanish oppression. His beloved friend, the Marquis of Posa, presses Carlos to become saviour of Flanders, and tries to persuade Philip to rule more humanely there. Although valuing Posa's friendship, Philip's hands are tied by the Inquisition, which condemns the Flemish 'heretics' and forces him to have Posa killed. Unloved by Elisabeth, Philip has taken her waiting-woman Eboli as his mistress. Eboli loves Carlos, but when she discovers his feelings for Elisabeth she assumes the couple are lovers and denounces them to Philip, who is furiously jealous. Then, remorseful, she rouses the people to protect Carlos from the consequences of his open defiance of his father. But Carlos is saved only by the awesome figure of his grandfather, Charles V, still alive.

The opera: *Don Carlos*, now usually given in Italian, was written in French, as a >grand opera combining spectacular crowd scenes full of 'action', political events, private and public tragedy. This is a strength and a weakness, and as performed in Verdi's 'composite' revision, sweeping from high point to high point, it lacks a sense of organic growth. The music justifies the dramatic overkill with huge ensembles and a series of individual show-stoppers for its five magnificent singing roles, like Philip's *Elle ne m'aime pas!* and Eboli's *O don fatal*, Posa's death scene and the superb brotherhood duet with Carlos, the tremendous confrontation between Philip and the Grand Inquisitor, the three scenes between Carlos and Elisabeth, Eboli's Song of the Veil. It is a score rich as plum cake.

Overview: Verdi hoped his 'theatre of ideas' would prove sufficiently exciting for its length to be ignored. A sprawling epic in the mould of Meyerbeer, its music was finer than any Meyerbeer opera, its drama tighter – and its psychology more realistic. Despite Carlos's inadequacies, his sworn brotherhood with the stronger Posa is never broken, unlike the friendships vaunted in **The Force of Destiny** or Bizet's **The Pearl Fishers**. Under challenge, Philip II holds on to his power, like **Simon Boccanegra**, but he is unloved. In the struggle in *Don Carlos* between the demands of Church, State and the individual heart, as in Donizetti's earlier **La favorite**, frail aspirations for love of a fellow human are doomed to fail.

Listening

DG 415 316-1GH4 4 415 316-4PH3
CD: 415 316-2GH4
La Scala/Abbado
(Domingo, Ricciarelli, Valentini-Terrani)

Charles Gounod

Born: 17th June 1818/Paris
Died: 18th October 1893/St Cloud

One of the most successful of opera composers, Gounod's operas are still performed frequently. *Mireille* is popular, but his real fame rests with the two operas (out of some twelve) covered here. His style left its mark on numerous important French composers. He also wrote church music and oratorios which were particularly appreciated in England.

Further reading: James Harding – *Gounod* (London 1973).

FAUST

Five acts
Libretto: Jules Barbier and Michel Carré, after Johann Wolfgang von Goethe
First performance: Paris 1859

Plot: To escape the barrenness of life, and inflamed by a vision of the chaste young Marguerite, old Faust commits his soul to Mephistopheles in exchange for youth and its sensual pleasures. Mephistopheles helps Faust to seduce Marguerite, but afterwards attempts to distract him, and thwarts her efforts to pray for grace. Eventually, yielding to Faust's urgings, he gives him the opportunity of saving Marguerite from execution for murdering her child. But although Marguerite's mind is wandering, she rejects Faust as a destroyer, and is accepted by the heaven to which she has continued to pray.

The opera: Enormously popular again after a mid-20th-century slump in its fortunes, *Faust* is a not untypical opera love story, with a spicy admixture of Satan and a touch of heavenly aspirations. Marguerite is the one character Gounod develops, balancing her meditative piety with her light-hearted vanity, her sense of honour with her need for love and her insistence on the right to feel as she did. The enchanting *Ah! je ris de me voir* is only a small part of the whole person, but so well done – sophisticated, psychologically apt on the surface, as with Faust's *Salut! demeure chaste et pure* and Mephistopheles's *Le veau d'or*. Equally impressive are several numbers barely central to the opera – Valentin's *Avant de quitter ces lieux* (the only generous sentiment from the heroine's yobbish brother), the delightful Easter Fair chorus (where the

voices are a rhythmic percussion for the orchestra's lilting waltz), and the famous Soldiers' Chorus. Perhaps the finest music is the brooding Introduction, showing Gounod's lifelong interest in the music of Bach.

Overview: Gounod brought to the Parisian stage a new and charming intimacy which, while retaining an element of >spectacle, left the >grand opera of Meyerbeer and Halévy behind. The sweetness of his lyricism belies the fact that Marguerite is, like Cherubini's **Médée**, the murderess of her child, or that Faust is an intense searcher after truth, and the connection with Goethe pales next to the settings by Berlioz and Busoni. In Siebel, Marguerite's gentle young admirer, Gounod created a >travesty role not dissimilar from Verdi's Oscar (**A Masked Ball**) which reaches back through Donizetti's Smeton (**Anna Bolena**) to Mozart's Cherubino himself (**The Marriage of Figaro**).

Listening

HMV SLS 5170 4 TC-SLS 5170
CD: CD57 47493-8
Angel SDLX CDCC 47492
Paris Opéra/Prêtre
(Freni, Domingo, Allen, Ghiaurov)
1979

ROMEO ET JULIETTE

Five acts
Libretto: Jules Barbier and Michel Carré, after William Shakespeare
First performance: Paris 1867

Plot: After a brief Prologue describing the age-long hatred between Capulets and Montagues, the Capulets' ball begins, in honour of Juliet's birthday. When Romeo, a Montague, enters masked, he is smitten by love for Juliet, and she for him. Later they exchange passionate vows on a balcony outside her bedroom, and the following morning they are married by Friar Laurence, who hopes in this way to reconcile the feuding families. Romeo's page initiates a fight with the Capulets

Dame Nellie Melba as Juliette in 1889 –
one of her most famous roles

which Romeo tries to stop, but then, to
avenge his friend Mercutio he kills
Tybalt, the leading Capulet. Banished
by the Duke, Romeo does not receive
Friar Laurence's message that Juliet, to
avoid being married to Count Paris, has
drunk a potion to simulate death.

Believing her dead, he goes to her
tomb, and takes poison – just before she
regains consciousness. Juliet stabs
herself, and they die together.

The opera: *Roméo et Juliette* is both
unaffectedly simple and stylish. There is
a preponderance of love-music, the
initial courtly exchange developing
through the fulness of feeling in Acts II
and IV to the fine, economical writing

of the final scene. Romeo is an ardent lover, his soliloquies at the start of the balcony and the tomb scenes being particularly beautiful. Juliet is interesting; behind her initial enchanting, wide-eyed *Ah! Je veux vivre* and her earnest directness about marriage with Romeo lies the sensitive woman who, in her last comment in Act I, has perceived the fateful significance of their love, and later confronts magnificently the terrors of drinking the potion. The highly charged moments as she 'dies' are a dramatic coup. Some striking pieces of orchestral writing – the 'dispute' music of the Introduction, and Mercutio's Queen Mab ballad – and the range of textures throughout, the judicious recurrence of the lovers' theme, plus the careful characterisation of lesser characters (note Stephano's delightful serenade, and Tybalt's bullish bellicosity) keep the score very much alive.

Overview: Compared with the settings by Bellini and Berlioz (the latter a dramatic symphony) Gounod's is the most conventional, allowing the Shakespeare play to dictate its shape, and leaning heavily on the love music, its outstanding element. But his alterations of the final scene create a very effective love-death, much in vogue after Wagner's **Tristan**.

Listening

HMV EX2701423 3
Capitole Toulouse/Plasson
(Malfitano, Kraus, Murray, Taillon)

Jacques Offenbach

Born: 20th June 1819/Cologne
Died: 5th October 1880/Paris

Offenbach went to Paris to study, and during the time of Napoleon III he established almost single-handed the satirical or comic operetta, with tremendous success. Working at a tremendous pace, he produced nearly eighty operettas cum >opéra comiques, as well as vaudevilles, ballets, dance music, cello music and songs. His international reputation was always high. He encouraged Johann Strauss in Vienna, and his work stimulated Sullivan in England. Operetta has since evolved into the musical and musical comedy.

Further reading: Alexander Faris – *Jacques Offenbach* (London 1980); James Harding – *Jacques Offenbach: A Biography* (London 1980).

ORPHEUS IN THE UNDERWORLD
Orphée aux enfers

Two acts (revised four acts)
Libretto: Hector Crémieux and Ludovic Halévy
First performance: Paris 1858, revised 1874

Plot: Orpheus and Eurydice are weary of one another, he concentrating on his violin playing (which she cannot bear), she on her affair with the shepherd Aristaeus, an earthly manifestation of Pluto, God of the Underworld. Things seem to work out perfectly when Eurydice, fatally bitten by a snake, has to leave for the Underworld. Public Opinion, however, requires that Orpheus rescue her, and Jupiter sanctions this, popping down to Hades himself to get an eyeful of the gorgeous Eurydice. Orpheus is instructed to take Eurydice back without turning round to see if she is following him. Unfortunately he obeys this ridiculous stricture, but Jupiter manages to put him off his stroke with a thunderbolt, and all ends happily as Pluto throws an Underworld party for his deliciously dead mistress and the visiting party of Gods.

The opera: Everyone has a good time deflating cherished ideals in this witty romp, which cocks a snook at society's complacency as much as at the reverence of the great legend itself (it helps to be familiar with Gluck's version, **Orfeo ed Euridice**, not merely to enjoy the quotation from *Che faro senza Euridice?*). Offenbach's melodic flair is always evident, and the familiar numbers are delightful in their proper setting, in particular the gods' attack on Jupiter for his earthly philanderings, John Styx's doleful reminiscences of his attractiveness before he died, and the glorious Can-Can, arguably the least macabre dance that Hell has ever known. The Overture is not by Offenbach – it was added by Carl Binder for the Vienna production in 1860.

Overview: *Orpheus* consolidated an interesting development in Parisian operetta: the establishment by Offenbach of his own theatre, the Bouffes Parisiens, in the mid-1850s (there was an eight-week London season in 1857). The repertory of the Bouffes included comic works by Adam, Delibes, Mozart and Rossini, younger composers being encouraged with a competition in which Bizet shared first prize for *Le Docteur Miracle*. In its first years Offenbach added numerous short comic works to the repertory, and he continued his enormous output long after, including three- and four-acters.

Listening

HMV SLS 5175
Angel SZX/4Z3X 3886
Capitole Toulouse/Plasson
(Sénéchal, Mesplé, Rhodes, Burles)

LA BELLE HELENE
Beautiful Helen

Three acts
Libretto: Henri Meilhac and Ludovic Halévy
First performance: Paris 1864

Plot: The goddess of love, Venus, has promised the most beautiful woman in the world to Paris, Prince of Troy – namely Helen, wife of King Menelaus of Sparta. Helen is agog: the hand of Fate threatens her virtue, and besides, she finds the young prince quite gorgeous. Her confidante, the High Priest Calchas, invokes the oracle to get rid of

Menelaus, leaving Helen free to accept Paris's attentions, but Menelaus returns early and sends Paris packing. Offended, Venus spreads the dread scourge of adultery throughout Greece. To calm the goddess and save the country, its leaders spell out Menelaus's patriotic duty: he must allow Paris to enjoy Helen's favours. Menelaus is reluctant. The High Priest of Venus arrives to offer a compromise: he will take Helen to make propitiatory sacrifices to the goddess. To the fury of the Greeks, he reveals as he leaves that he is Paris in disguise, and he is setting sail with Helen for Troy.

The opera: *La belle Hélène* began the run of Offenbach's greatest successes. Its intoxicating hedonism reflects the Second Empire, 'the hand of Fate' being doubtless as irresistible at Napoleon III's court as Helen finds it in Sparta. It is wonderfully irreverent: when the Kings start gambling, the High Priest is caught cheating – and accused of giving gamblers a bad name. When the Greek Kings lose the intelligence contest to Paris in disguise (a game of charades to find the word 'locomotive') they worry about losing to a 'shepherd'. The hilarious digs at conventional opera practice include a noble improvisation on the words *L'homme à la pomme*, a patriotic trio recalling Rossini's **William Tell**, a tragic Finale on the loss of Menelaus's honour – and a High Priest who yodels to get everybody happy. With tongue in cheek, Offenbach sets the chorus *Un vil seducteur* to an inappropriately lovely waltz. Although often zany, *La belle Hélène* is no romp, but a tightly constructed ironic comedy boasting fine lyrical moments such as Paris's Act I song, Helen's Invocation to Venus, and the Act II love duet.

Overview: *La belle Hélène* expands the approach of **Orpheus in the Underworld**. Greek myth and legend had always been source material for opera; Offenbach used it for poking fun at society and at opera itself. He might well have met with the approval of the early Florentine composers, who wanted to recreate Greek theatre in opera: in turning hallowed legends upside down, his method was closer to the wacky spirit of the Greek comedian Aristophanes than to the mainstream of operatic humour which had developed from the caricatures of the >commedia dell'arte.

Listening

EMI EX 27 01715 2
CD: CDS7 47157-8
Capitole Toulouse/Plasson
(Norman, Aler, Bacquier)
1984

LA PERICHOLE

Three acts
Libretto: Henri Meilhac and Ludovic Halévy
First performance: Paris 1868, revised 1874

Plot: We are in Lima, where, although the impecunious street-singers Périchole and Piquillo love each other, they cannot earn themselves the price of a square meal. The viceroy, Don Andres, takes a fancy to Périchole, offering her the position of lady-in-waiting to his dear departed wife ... but propriety demands that she be married. A husband must be found – and Piquillo, on the point of hanging himself over Périchole's sudden departure, is plied with drink to persuade him to marry the viceroy's new mistress. When he discovers at the palace that the lady is Périchole (who knew very well whom she was marrying) he makes such a jealous scene that he is condemned to a dungeon for recalcitrant husbands. Périchole contrives to escape with him by tying up the ever-eager Don Andres. Hunted throughout the town, the couple do an ingratiating street number about a king's mercy; Don Andres pardons them, and with the diamonds he has given Périchole, they need never starve again.

The opera: With this satire about a king's penchant for new mistresses, and the courtiers who provide them while feigning disapproval, Offenbach's topical allusions to the Emperor Napoleon III delighted the Parisians. In music of irresistible esprit and wit, he presents swiftly-changing situations, takes wholesale swipes at the foibles of humanity, and sends up operatic

conventions. Some of the casual silliness, such as Piquillo's reiteration of the last syllable of 'Espagnol', is inspired; the ensembles, notably the first act finale and the trio in the dungeon (*Je suis le joli geolier*), are among his best. But this opéra bouffe also shows deeper feeling: the artless charm of Périchole's letter to Piquillo explaining her departure is genuinely touching, and Piquillo's outburst in the palace, surely meant to ape all the violently indignant tenors of the century, takes the humour along an unexpectedly grim path in Act III.

Overview: With the end of the Second Empire in view, *La Périchole*'s cynical satire was more pointed, potentially more offensive, than the outrageous humour of Offenbach's own **Orpheus in the Underworld** or **La belle Hélène**. Its sentimental vein suggested hidden emotions in the characters; treated realistically, its main situation could well evoke Mozart's **Die Entführung** or Beethoven's **Fidelio**. The distance Offenbach still had to travel to a successful serious opera (**The Tales of Hoffmann**) was getting shorter.

Listening

HMV SLS/TCC-SLS 5276
CD: CDS7 47362-8
Angel DSBX/4X2X 3923
Capitole Toulouse/Plasson
(Berganza, Carreras, Bacquier)

THE TALES OF HOFFMANN
Les contes d'Hoffmann

Prologue, three acts, epilogue
Libretto: Jules Barbier, after Barbier and Michel Carré, after E.T.A. Hoffmann
First performance: Paris 1881

Plot: The poet Hoffmann's amatory escapades deflect him from his Muse, who therefore finds it necessary to keep guard over him in the earthly character of Nicklausse. In a beer cellar, Hoffmann relates three of his affairs, which all end in disaster – mainly through the malign offices of a single magically powerful enemy reappearing in the guises of Coppelius, Dapertutto and Dr Miracle. The women Hoffmann becomes involved with are contrasting aspects of his present love, the celebrated opera star, Stella – the mechanical doll Olympia, the cynical courtesan Giulietta, and the young singer Antonia. After telling his stories, the drunken Hoffmann rejects all promise of a fulfilling love; he will belong to his Muse alone.

The opera: Offenbach did not achieve his aim of seeing *Hoffmann* successfully staged at the Opéra-Comique before he died, nor could he complete the orchestration himself. Had he lived longer, there might have been fewer arbitary and insensitive alterations

Agnes Baltsa and Placido Domingo in *The Tales of Hoffmann* (Royal Opera House 1980)

made to the score; it has nonetheless survived as a work of genuine originality. Hoffmann the lover appears to be an anti-hero, a victim rather than an initiator. Yet his accumulated experiences give him substance, and once they are understood as an allegory of the artist seeking, but never gaining, complete fulfilment, it becomes clear that his life will be the source of his art. Into this ambitious design Offenbach poured all his skill, as in the wittily exquisite 'Doll Song' or the brilliant 'Ballad of Kleinzach'; he also created a language of lyrical beauty, particularly in the Antonia act. The single dramatically gratuitous item is the glorious Barcarolle duet, taken from an earlier operetta – but having it in *Hoffmann* ensures that it is heard frequently, and it is effective wherever it is placed.

Overview: *Hoffmann* joins an elite including Mozart's **The Magic Flute**,

Beethoven's **Fidelio** and Bizet's **Carmen** as one of the few popular operas whose use of spoken dialogue actually enhances its achievement. Earlier in the century the stories of Hoffmann had been source material for the darkest side of the Romantic imagination; properly presented, the spooky skills of Coppelius/ Dappertutto/Dr Miracle are more Satanic than all the Mephistophelianism Gounod could produce in **Faust**. After a life's career producing satirical operettas, Offenbach showed in his last work the serious side of his own imagination.

Listening

Decca SET 545-7/K109K32
CD: 417 363-2DH2
London OSA/5-13106
Suisse Romande Orch./Bonynge
(Sutherland, Domingo, Tourangeau)

Camille Saint-Saëns

Born: 9th October 1835/Paris
Died: 16th December 1921/Algiers

Saint-Saëns was an all-round composer of great importance in the second half of the 19th century with an impressive output of sonatas, chamber music, concertos and symphonies. A fine pianist and organist, an excellent writer (not only on music), he was an influential figure. He wrote thirteen operas, of which only *Samson et Dalila* achieved notable international success; it is still frequently performed.

SAMSON ET DALILA

Three acts
Libretto: Ferdinand Lemaire
First performance: Weimar 1877

Plot: Rousing the despairing Hebrews, Samson unleashes a successful revolt against the Philistines. The High Priest of Dagon demands that Delilah, the Philistine woman beloved by Samson, try again to discover the secret of Samson's strength. Delilah is willing – her love has always been a pretence, with vengeance its object. Although Samson's passion for Delilah runs counter to his God-given mission to lead his people, he is seduced by her into revealing the secret and captured. Blinded, he becomes an object of scorn to the newly victorious Philistines, and of horror to the Hebrews he has betrayed. During a celebration of the power of Dagon, Samson's anguished prayers to Jehovah are rewarded: with renewed strength, he pulls down the Temple on himself and the assembled Philistines.

The opera: *Samson et Dalila* was conceived initially as an oratorio, and the contrapuntal choral writing remains dense and impressive. It is presented clearly in a few great scenes, each leading to a huge climax, some providing the opportunity for splendid spectacle. The drama derives from the situation itself rather than from Saint-Saëns's treatment of it; the music for the main characters lacks complexity of characterisation, but is charged with intense dignity. Exotic elements are mainly reserved for the Philistines' Bacchanale, the writing for the Hebrews having a cathedral-liturgical quality. Material from Delilah's *Printemps qui commence* is woven like a >leitmotiv into the score, and her famous *Mon coeur s'ouvre a ta voix* is all the more beautiful in context, with Samson's ecstatic interpolations growing naturally from her sensuous melody. His conclusion to this song is the climax of the opera, for his true strength lay, of course, in never having given himself totally to Delilah; the long hair is virtually ignored, and his music shows us an inspirational leader rather than a strong man.

Overview: Compared with the convolutions of plot and character in the other popular Bible opera (Verdi's **Nabucco**), *Samson et Dalila* is simplicity itself, and neither work shares the intellectual approach of Schoenberg's **Moses und Aron**. At its core Saint-Saëns's opera explores the connection between love and patriotism. Samson is

95

less fortunate than Arnold in **William Tell**: Delilah polarises, rather than eases, his terrible conflict. Unlike Verdi's **Aida**, or Samson himself, her single concern is to exploit her lover's feelings to political advantage.

Further reading: James Harding – *Saint-Saëns and his Circle* (London 1965).

Listening

DG 413 297-1GX3
Orchestre de Paris/Barenboim
(Obraztsova, Domingo, Bruson)

Léo Delibes

Born: 21st February 1836/St Germain du Val
Died: 16th January 1891/Paris

A successful composer of operettas, operas and ballets (the latter including *Coppélia* and *Sylvia*), Delibes composed twenty-eight stage works in all. He was not an innovator, but is well regarded for his attractive style.

LAKME

Three acts
Libretto: Edmond Gondinet and Philippe Gille, after Pierre Loti
First performance: Paris 1883

Plot: Meaning no harm, Gerald, a British officer in India, breaks into the secret temple garden of the Brahmin priestess Lakmé and her father Nilakantha. He and Lakmé are deeply attracted to one another. Hoping Gerald will reveal himself so that the Indians may take revenge for this desecration, Nilakantha has Lakmé sing in the market place. The plan works and Gerald is stabbed, but the wound is not fatal, and Lakmé cures him in her forest refuge. While she is fetching sacred water which will seal their love forever, Gerald's fellow-officer persuades him to rejoin his

regiment. On her return Lakmé senses the change in Gerald, and bites a poisonous leaf before they drink the water; while Gerald reiterates his love, she dies, exalted.

The opera: Apart from certain numbers which anticipate the style of 20th-century romantic musicals, Delibes's music has an individual voice, only part of which derives from the mild exoticism of the score. Lakmé's *Pourquoi dans les grands bois*, its dreaminess heightened by the irregular line-lengths, or her languorous duet with her slave Mallika, are examples. A sense of proportion, coupled with striking warmth of melody, unifies the opera; the set pieces – the dances, the entractes, the military music, even the famous 'Bell Song' with its >coloratura display – are integrated within the drama. The surging activity in Act II satisfied the French appetite for >spectacle and excitement; the first and third acts are intimate, and intentionally small-scale. The lovers are touchingly ingenuous – this relationship is never consummated; by contrast, Nilakantha's feelings for his daughter could well be explained by 20th-century psychology.

Overview: Delibes, already famous for his ballets, gained great success with *Lakmé*. The theme of a Western officer disarmed by an oriental beauty who commits suicide when she loses his love – reappearing later in Puccini's **Madam Butterfly** – paralleled the growing fascination the East held for the French (and, unwittingly, the course of political events already unfolding). Nilakantha, a classic operatic father fiercely protecting the interests of his nation/religion, joins Amonasro (Verdi's **Aida**), Bajazet (Handel's **Tamerlano**), and Oroveso (Bellini's **Norma**). Certain details of the lovers' situation recall Wagner's **Tristan und Isolde**; certain features of the score, particularly the writing for the tenor and the treatment of the military music, recall Bizet's style in **Carmen**.

Listening

Decca SET 387/9
London OSA 1391
Monte Carlo Opera Orch./Bonynge
(Sutherland, Berbié, Vanzo)

Georges Bizet

Born: 25th October 1838/Paris
Died: 3rd June 1875/Bougival

Barely able to develop his tremendous
talent before his early death, Bizet
never lived to see the success of
Carmen, or of his incidental music for
L'arlésienne. His Symphony in C,
written when he was seventeen, is the
basis of one of Balanchine's most
delightful ballets for the New York City
Ballet; his suite for duet, *Jeux d'enfants*,
is part of the repertoire for many young
pianists.

Further reading: Winton Dean –
Georges Bizet: his Life and Work (3rd
edn, London 1975).

THE PEARL FISHERS
Les pêcheurs de perles

Three acts
Libretto: Michel Carré and Eugene
Cormon
First performance: Paris 1863

Plot: As youthful friends, Nadir and
Zurga swore not to pursue the love they
both felt for the beautiful priestess Leila.
Now Zurga has become king of a Hindu
community of pearl fishermen in
Ceylon. Nadir joins them, without telling
Zurga he once followed Leila just to be
near her. During the fishing season a
priestess comes to pray for the
fishermen; she must have no contact
with them. This year the priestess is
Leila. She and Nadir recognise one
another, and cannot resist meeting at
night; they are discovered and
prepared for execution. Zurga's
jealousy has overwhelmed his loyalty to
Nadir, but, discovering that Leila once
saved his own life, he acts fast: he
distracts the fisher folk by setting fire
to their tents, and frees the lovers. They
sail away, but Zurga remains, awaiting
death from the spreading flames.

The opera: None of the drastic
alterations made to *The Pearl Fishers*
over the years has improved its weak
libretto, but it has taken over a century
for the original version to be performed
again, and recorded. Despite its
artificiality of plot and character, the
opera has several fine passages, like
the brooding, languorous prelude, the
friends' celebrated duet *Au fond du
temple saint*, its theme haunting the
opera, and Nadir's expressive *Je crois
entendre encore*, worthy of Verdi.
Carmen-spotters will predict Micaela
in the writing for Leila, and hints of the
great final José/Carmen confrontation
in the dramatic exchange between
Leila and Zurga. Although 'exotic' colour
is daubed on rather than conceived as
part of the music, and the choruses lack
spontaneity, Leila's allure for Nadir (and
Zurga) brings a special quality of ardent
yearning to the score, which explains its
considerable appeal today.

Overview: Forbidden love held a
fascination for the middle and late 19th
century, so obsessed with
respectability. The shut-up priestess in
exotic, tragic tales such as *The Pearl
Fishers* and Delibes's **Lakmé** always
gave in to her passion for the man who
intruded; the wife in medieval stories
like **Tristan und Isolde** (Wagner) and
Pelléas et Mélisande (Debussy) did
the same, without the element of
titillation introduced by the breaking of
religious vows. When it happened to
Hindu priestesses in Ceylon or India,
the European bourgeoisie could enjoy
the thrill without worrying that
established values nearer home were
threatened.

Listening

EMI SLS 5113 4 TC-SLS 5113
Angel SXBL 3856 4 4X2X-3856
Paris Opera/Prêtre
(Cotrubas, Sarabia, Vanzo)
1977

CARMEN

Four acts
Libretto: Henri Meilhac and Ludovic
Halévy, after Prosper Mérimée
First performance: Paris 1875

Plot: José, a young soldier fresh from
the country, becomes involved with a

Sally Burgess in the title role of David Poutney's car-dump production of *Carmen* (English National Opera 1986)

gypsy woman, Carmen. Her feeling for him goes through various phases – flirtation, manipulation, possessiveness, irritation, and rejection. But José's passion is all-consuming, leading him to accept imprisonment, discard his sweetheart, Micaela, desert from the army, and join Carmen's gang of smugglers. Only news that his mother is ailing takes him from her, and when he returns, pleading to be taken back, she is already mistress of the triumphant toreador, Escamillo. José is now barely human, a creature destroyed by passion. But Carmen is indifferent to him; she will not be tied down, and she snaps her fingers at whatever life might bring, at hardship, at fear, at death. José makes the only statement left to him – he kills her.

The opera: *Carmen* has more popular numbers than any other opera (the Seguidilla, the Chanson bohème, the Flower Song, the Card >aria) including two which have become part of general culture – the Habanera and the Toreador Song. Strangely enough, it took a Viennese production to start

Carmen's international fame; France delayed years before accepting one of its greatest operas. The Parisian audiences were deaf to its beauty, shocked at the realism Bizet brought to the opera stage, disgusted at the orchestra's 'Wagnerian dominance'. Yet in form *Carmen* is a conventional >number opera, of an astounding melodic and rhythmic vitality, having little in common with Wagner apart from the judicious recurrence of one or two themes, and a richness of orchestration balanced by an economy that Wagner knew little of. >Spectacle, ballet, 'exotic' colour are all there, an organic part of the action; the spoken dialogues (too often missed out, in favour of >recitatives, which have nothing to do with Bizet) are a powerful necessity. Bizet's two protagonists are magnificently real in everything they sing, and they are characterised with unerring musical skill, the overtones of hysteria in José's high >tessitura contrasting with Carmen's vibrant, low sensuality. The José of the glorious Flower Song is the same man whose voice rises in anguish at having killed the Carmen he adores. The Carmen whose first careless words brush love aside is the same whose cards continually turn up death, the same who, faced with that death, defiantly asserts ier freedom. Micaela, a pure young woman of considerable character, and Escamillo, an arrogant show-stopper, are a necessary dramatic and musical contrast, but they have become irrelevant in the final stupendous confrontation.

Overview: *Carmen* is one of the select few truly great and truly popular operas. It has been reworked in several celebrated versions such as the Roland Petit ballet, the musical *Carmen Jones*, the orchestral Carmen Suite from Shchedrin's ballet version (popular in the Soviet Union), the Peter Brook theatre performances, and several films, including Rosi's with Julia Migenes Johnson and Placido Domingo. Its much-vaunted realism, a strong influence on >verismo, never takes over from the music – a balance the verismo composers could not maintain. Carmen herself, totally honest, is surely opera's first and greatest feminist heroine, making her own choices, and having nothing imposed on her. There are traces of this self-contained independence in Minnie (Puccini's **The Girl of the Golden West**), and permutations of it in Emilia Marty (Janáček's **The Makrupolos Affair**), but only in Carmen is it central to the character.

Further reading: *Carmen* (English National Opera Guide, London 1982).

Listening

1 HMV SLS 5021 4 TC-SLS 5021
French National Radio Orch./Beecham
(de Los Angeles, Gedda, Micheau)
2 Decca D11 D3/K11 K33
CD: 414 489-2DH3
London OSA/5-13115
London Philharmonic Orch./Solti
(Troyanos, Domingo, Van Dam, Te Kanawa)

Jules Massenet

Born: 12th May 1842/Montaud
Died: 13th August 1912/Paris

Massenet was the dominant French opera composer of the late 19th century,

whose work was successful all over Europe. As a teacher he influenced a whole generation of French composers. He wrote music in other genres, too – especially songs – but his fame rests on his nearly forty theatre works (including three ballets), the most notable after *Manon* and *Werther* being *Le Roi de Lahore*, *Hérodiade*, *Thaïs*, *La navarraise*, *Sapho*, *Le jongleur de Notre-Dame*, *Thérèse* and *Don Quichotte.*

Further reading: James Harding – *Massenet* (London 1970).

MANON

Five acts
Libretto: Henri Meilhac and Philippe Gille, after l'Abbé Prévost
First performance: Paris 1884

Plot: Manon Lescaut inspires passion without effort. While she is en route to a convent, elderly Guillot propositions her, but she uses his coach to elope instead with young Des Grieux. Loving him according to her rather shallow capacity, she abandons him for a wealthy friend of Lescaut (a cousin who exploits her attractiveness to his own advantage). Des Grieux takes holy orders in an attempt to forget Manon, but her return destroys his religious aspirations. Hoping to produce sufficient funds to keep Manon happy with him, Des Grieux is persuaded to gamble – and vengeful old Guillot denounces the couple to the police for cheating. Des Grieux's aristocratic father protects him, but Manon faces deportation with other women of ill repute. Des Grieux bribes a guard to allow him time with Manon, but she is now exhausted, and she dies in his arms.

The opera: With *Manon*, Massenet's melodic facility and his skill in evoking a variety of atmospheres were ideally suited to both the subject and its audience. In her charming >arias Manon's character – childishly self-indulgent, brittle, but without malice – is so well delineated that her moral failings gain a musical value. Des Grieux is equally self-indulgent, but his love for Manon is the centre of his world, and Massenet uses the ironies in their situation to dramatic effect throughout Act II. And Lescaut is well drawn, with a directness about his music which confirms him, like Manon, as wholly without malice.

Overview: Puccini inflates his *Manon* to tragic dimensions; Massenet is both more ingratiating and more knowing. In this and his numerous succeeding operas, his consistent involvement with The Feminine was derided in some quarters. With Manon, at least, he created a fully believable character, like Berg's **Lulu** an innocent victim of her own attractiveness, and no less self-involved. She is poles apart from her contemporary counterpart, **Carmen** (despite clear influences of Bizet on the writing for chorus in Massenet's excellent crowd scenes). The opera invites comparisons with Verdi's **La traviata** (in the father–son relationship as well as the circumstances of the lovers), and that composer's **The Force of Destiny** finds a faint echo in Des Grieux's thwarted attempt to sublimate his hopeless love in religion.

Further reading: *Manon* (English National Opera Guide, London 1984).

Listening

HMV SLS/TC-SLS 173141-3/5
Angel DSX/4X3X 3946
Capitole Toulouse/Plasson
(Cotrubas, Kraus, Quilico)

WERTHER

Four acts
Libretto: Edouard Blau, Paul Milliet and Georges Hartmann, after Johann Wolfgang von Goethe
First performance: Vienna 1892

Plot: For the sensitive young Werther, Charlotte, fully involved in bringing up her younger siblings, is a joyous affirmation of life. But Charlotte has promised to marry Albert, and she will not allow her feelings for Werther to divert her from her commitment.

Werther is unable to cope with her keeping him at arm's length, and he commits suicide; as he dies, Charlotte acknowledges her love for him. She is left feeling that she has caused the death of the man she really loves in trying to protect the husband whose anger she must now face.

The opera: *Werther* extended the enormous popularity Massenet had achieved in France with operas of intense human emotion divorced from any larger social issues. Both the domestic charm of Charlotte's family and the self-indulgent emotionalism of Werther, cloaked in Massenet's soft, lyrical style, were attractive for a comfortable audience to contemplate. Even the hysteria that leads Werther to commit suicide is given a thrusting, sobbing orchestral treatment that carries all but the cynical with it, and when, from Act III, we plunge into the understandable anguish of Charlotte herself, it is hard not to be warmed by the overheated emotions onstage. Massenet was an accomplished artist, producing a pliant melodic line and a lush sound that is never unlikeable; it is perhaps this fin de siècle sensuality whose period charm appeals to the harder-boiled audiences of today.

Overview: Goethe's hero of extreme sensibility created almost single-handed a new image for young men in the Romantic period; he has remained viable largely through the medium of opera, which specialises in young men of extreme sensibility. The fact that suicide is a social taboo, yet in opera the rate is high, suggests that this medium provides an outlet – perhaps a safety-valve – for our most intense emotions. But if we pull with Brünnhilde against the bourgeois principles of Fricka (Wagner's **The Valkyrie**), why do we identify with the predicament of Charlotte, who allows herself no such outlet? The answer lies possibly in our seeing her in the bosom of her family; ordinary family life is rare in opera, the more enviable when it occurs.

Listening

Philips 6769 4 7659 051
CD: 416 654-2PH2
ROHCG Orch./Davis
(Von Stade, Carreras, Allen, Buchanan)

Gustave Charpentier

Born: 25th June 1860/Dreuze, Moselle
Died: 18th February 1956/Paris

Charpentier wrote several operas and other dramatic works (almost all to his own librettos), none of which approached the success of his first opera, *Louise*.

LOUISE

Four acts
Libretto: The composer
First performance: Paris 1900

Plot: The daughter of upright working-class Parisians, Louise's home is torn apart by her love for Julien, a neighbouring poet. Her parents, anxious about Julien's way of life, are unwilling to let them marry, and Louise eventually leaves unannounced. She and Julien set up house in Montmartre, where their love flourishes, but when her beloved father falls ill she agrees to return to her parents if they permit her to leave later. Once she is home, they will not hear of her going back to Julien, but her longing makes her defiant, and in an excess of frustrated rage her father drives her out.

The opera: *Louise*, chosen to start the new century at the Opéra-Comique, is in many ways the representative turn-of-the-century opera. The love scene in the third act, with Louise's *Depuis le jour* signalling her new tone of inner fulfilment, develops its passionate climax through a philosophical exchange like Tristan and Isolde; the orchestral colour throughout has a ripeness that stems as much from Wagner as from Massenet. In the manner of late Verdi or Puccini, evocative >leitmotivs reiterate the mood of the lovers, Julien's clarion, Louise's dreamily tender, and a feature of the score is the repetition in different contexts of one character's statements by another. The central acts are carefully crafted, with the constant street-cries and sounds of the great city, the sharply observed seamstresses at work, the symbolic figure of the Noctambulist and the festive celebration of *la vie bohème*: Paris is hymned, given a mystical-romantic connection with the power of love. But the two outer acts mark Charpentier as an original, raising the work to the level of true music-drama – a warts-and-all picture of the tensions, the affections, the emotional blackmail of close family life.

Overview: The outer acts of *Louise* are more truly naturalistic than the Italian >verismo operas such as Mascagni's **Cavalleria rusticana** or Leoncavallo's **Pagliacci** without ever introducing their heighted dramatic effects. And while Charpentier's *bohème* is no less romanticised than Puccini's, he also shows through Louise's parents a disenchanted view of it which carries considerable truth. Such an opera inevitably treats the troubled relationship between Louise and her father more analytically than allowed by the epic approach to fathers and daughters in Handel's **Tamerlano**, Verdi's **Aida** or Wagner's **The Valkyrie**.

Listening

CBS 79302/M 3-34207
New Philharmonic Orch./Prêtre
(Cotrubas, Berbié, Domingo, Bacquier)

Claude Debussy

Born: 22nd August 1862/St Germain-en-Laye
Died: 25th March 1918/Paris

Debussy was one of the great innovators, whose single opera is not only his most important stage work but has proven as important as his many works in other fields. His treatment of harmony and texture is generally considered to have been seminal in the development of 20th-century music.

PELLEAS ET MELISANDE

Five acts
Libretto: Maurice Maeterlinck
First performance: Paris 1902

Plot: Golaud, a widower, returns to his grandfather's castle with a new wife, Mélisande. They were both lost in a forest when he found her. She and his young half-brother, Pelléas, are drawn to each other in a childlike relationship whose innocence obscures its deeper impulses. Golaud's suspicions, growing into maddened jealousy when he has questioned his little boy, Yniold, precipitate Pelléas and Mélisande into an ecstatic avowal of their feelings; Golaud comes upon them, and kills Pelléas. During the following days Mélisande gives birth to a little girl, but before Golaud can prove that her love with Pelléas was indeed 'guilty', she dies.

The opera: *Pelléas et Mélisande* is a remarkable embodiment of Debussy's aesthetic. All the myriad colours and textures of his orchestral palette are there, yet the music is entirely without superfluity, pared down to express the textual nuances, including its silences, without ever imposing itself. The singers' inflections may be described as musicalised speech: there is virtually no formal song, no chorus or ensemble. Longer phrases develop as the emotions of Golaud, and especially the young people, crystallise; generally, moments of intense feeling have been conveyed 'negatively', in a withdrawal of sound and weight. For this is an opera of shadows, of half-expressed feelings; Maeterlinck's symbolism is enhanced in Debussy's beautiful setting, as in the incredibly sensual scene when Pelléas plays with Mélisande's hair (compare Golaud's later treatment of it). But the composer's genius has created genuine characters as well. Probably the only untroubled person is the aged grandfather king, Arkel, deeply compassionate, wise and accepting. At

the other extreme, Golaud is wrung with unbearable anguish, alienated from the intimacy of Pelléas and Mélisande. And they? – they are in the end not children; she is a mysterious creature, who knows other lives and different truths, and it is Pelléas's sensitivity to this which brings their souls in touch.

Overview: Wagner's **Tristan und Isolde** tells a comparable tale, Verdi's **Otello** depicts an equally destructive jealousy, Poulenc's **Dialogues des Carmélites** approaches its text in a similar manner. Yet *Pelléas et Mélisande* stands alone in the repertory, unparalleled in purity and intensity. Not everyone responds to its enigmatic, becalmed atmosphere, but for those who do, Debussy's only opera opens up a whole world of inner feeling.

Further reading: Robert Orledge – *Debussy and the Theatre* (Cambridge 1982); *Pelléas & Mélisande* (English National Opera Guide 1982).

Listening

1 CBS M3 30119
ROHCG/Boulez
(Shirley, Söderström, McIntyre, Ward)
2 HMV SLS/TC-SLS 5172
Angel SZX 3885
Berlin Philharmonic Orch./Karajan
(Stilwell, Von Stade, Van Dam, Raimondi)

Maurice Ravel

Born: 7th March 1875/Ciboure, Basses Pyrénées
Died: 28th December 1937/Paris

Ravel is one of the most important French composers, and a highly individual craftsman. He was a brilliant orchestrator and writer for the keyboard, and an all-round composer of the highest order. His music is strongly characterised, each work evoking a specific world. He wrote only two operas.

Further reading: Roger Nichols – *Ravel* (London 1977).

L'HEURE ESPAGNOLE
The Spanish Hour

One act
Libretto: Franc-Nohain
First performance: Paris 1911

Plot: Married to Torquemada, an absent-minded clock-maker somewhat lacking in conjugal energy, Concepción is fretting for an affair. On Thursdays, when Torquemada's duties take him away, she hopes to use her time well: Gonzalve, an ardent poet, seems promising; even the fleshly Don Inigo might turn out acceptable. But Ramiro, a simple muleteer, is in the shop, waiting to have his watch fixed, and Concepción faces a logistics problem: how to get a lover unnoticed to her bedroom? She solves it by having the obliging Ramiro move two large grandfather clocks there in turn, each hiding a lover, but is frustrated both times – Gonzalve cannot advance beyond the poesifying stage, and Inigo cannot advance beyond the door of the clock, in which he is stuck fast. And now again the immensely strong Ramiro provides the solution to the problem – in person – while each would-be lover lands up buying 'his' grandfather clock from Torquemada.

The opera: *L'heure espagnole* is sheer delight. The libretto itself is very funny (you must follow a translation if you don't speak French), and Ravel has decked it out with waggish Spanishisms, deliquescent snatches of waltz, jazzy phrases in the bass – a veritable filing-system of musical witticisms. The introduction is a piece of wizardry, with its slightly crazy integration of chiming clocks, whirring mechanisms and chirruping cuckoos (an innuendo not lost on our heroine); the ending pokes fun at the statutory 18th-century address to the audience with some triumphant Habanera rhythm-play (raising the image of another woman who prefers to choose her own lovers than be chosen – **Carmen**). The five roles are sharply characterised, the most extravagant being Gonzalve, the most subtle Ramiro himself, full of laconic one-liners, but able to rise to the occasion when the time comes.

Overview: Here is another >opera buffa which casts an early 20th-century eye backwards, and in which the spirits of Pergolesi, Mozart and Donizetti may be heard chuckling. Musically it is superior to the most amusing of its contemporary rivals, such as **Susanna's Secret** (Wolf-Ferrari) or **Gianni Schicchi** (Puccini); no-one could better the sophistication and beauty of Ravel's orchestral textures or his glorious rhythms, his capacity to make the music funny even without words to help it along.

Listening

DG 2726 076
Paris Opéra/Maazel
(Berbié, Sénéchal, Bacquier,
Van Dam)

L'ENFANT ET LES SORTILEGES
The Child and the Spells

Two parts
Libretto: Sidonie-Gabrielle Colette
First performance: Monte Carlo 1925

Plot: Fed up with his mother, bored with his homework, the Child expresses his spleen in his customary way – by attacking his books, his pets, the furniture, even the wall-paper. But on this occasion the objects come to life, full of animosity towards him. Wretched, lonely, he can do nothing to redeem himself. His spirits rise when he finds himself in the garden, but its creatures have long resented his thoughtless cruelty, and they turn on him, eager to take revenge. A little squirrel is wounded in the fracas, and the Child, himself weak and battered, binds its paw. Realising that he, too, is wounded, the animals anxiously carry him towards the house, calling the word that he cried out earlier in his misery, and hymning his goodness as he, reviving, repeats it: *Maman!*

The opera: Brief though it is, Ravel and Colette cover a wide range of feeling and insight in this 'lyric fantasy', incorporating some deep-seated truths

103

about social behaviour as they explore the Child's unconscious. The two parts build to brilliant climaxes, the first involving the numbers (from arithmetic), the second the animals' anger; much of the score is a demonstration of exquisite 'chamber' orchestration. The passage with the garden sounds is pure magic; the ending, a touching little apotheosis. The vignettes are delightful, each character having a recognisable musical identity – a dance-form, a melodic type, or a specific combination of instruments. But the deeper moments give the opera its true quality. The Child's exchange with the Princess from his torn storybook, including his lonely lament when she sinks away, is particularly moving. Perhaps he learns most by discovering his insignificance in the eyes of an extemely articulate squirrel. Ravel's most sophisticated creativity is at work here, defining a whole world within small-scale parameters.

Overview: There are a few other operas with children at the centre – **Amahl and the Night Visitors** (Menotti), **Hansel und Gretel** (Humperdinck) – but *L'enfant et les sortilèges*, as a child's fantasy, is directly rewarding to both children and adults at their different levels. That its music was full of examples of Ravel's distinctive harmonies, colouring and melodic style did not prevent him from claiming that it was a mixture of Monteverdi, Massenet, Puccini, jazz and musical comedy!

Listening

HMV ASD/TCC-ASD 4167
Angel DS/4X5 37869
LSO/Previn
(Wyner, Augér, Berbié, Langridge,
Huttenlocher)

Francis Poulenc

Born: 7th January 1899/Paris
Died: 30th January 1963/Paris

A particularly important composer of
religious music and of songs, Poulenc

had a strong element of zany comedy
and pastiche of café music in his style.
He wrote film scores and incidental
music for plays, as well as several
ballets and a considerable amount of
choral and piano music.

Further reading: Roger Nichols –
'Poulenc' *The New Grove Twentieth-
Century French Masters* (London 1986).

LES MAMELLES DE TIRESIAS
The Breasts of Tiresias

Prologue and two acts
Libretto: Guillaume Apollinaire
First performance: Paris 1947

Plot: The Prologue announces a lesson
to popularise baby-making. Thérèse,
fed up, refuses to make any more
babies; she plans a worthwhile career,
gets rid of her breasts (two patriotically
coloured balloons which she pops), and
becomes hirsute. Calling herself
Tirésias, she ties up her husband in
woman's clothing, and galvanises the
local women to reject baby-making.
The husband decides to make babies
without the hindrance of a wife – and
produces 49,049, including several of
considerable accomplishment. A
fortune-teller, roped in to cope with the
consequences of overcrowding,
proclaims that the baby-makers shall
inherit the world. It is Thérèse, who has
returned to her husband and is now
looking forward to making more babies.

The opera: A post-war romp laughing
at the proclaimed need for population
increase, *The Breasts of Tiresias*
offended the conservatives with its
crazy style and its levity, even though
the composer was reinforcing their
view regarding the role of women. It
was Poulenc's first successful opera,
with a score full of characteristic
touches, including brief turns of lyrical
melody, some luminous orchestration,
and those almost imperceptible

Osbert Lancaster's set for the 1958
Aldeburgh production of *Les mamelles de
Tirésias*

switches to the serious and back again. Its general tone is iconoclastic and satiric, and pastiche is used with great flair, as in the comically appropriate dances (including a waltz, a Spanish dance, and a polka), an arch-conventional funeral scene, and some pompous choral admonitions to the audience. Journalists and nannies get a knocking; women's liberationists are treated as though comical, and the 'babies' are hilarious. Some of the funniest moments involve standing theatrical conventions on their head, as with the first curtain-fall, the babies in the orchestra pit, the fortune-teller's vocalisations into the auditorium, a fight between two indignant 'members of the audience', or the final admonition 'Make babies!' – all of which dissolve the barriers between audience, orchestra and stage.

Overview: This light, surrealist comedy perfectly expressed one aspect of Poulenc's talents, combining the rich vein of humour in Offenbach's best works with a post-Dada freedom of technique. It is sufficiently open to imaginative production styles to suggest points in common with Janáček's *The Excursions of Mr Brouček*, or even the wackier directorial approach to certain scenes in Mozart's **The Magic Flute** and Rossini's >opere buffe, but its atmosphere is really pure Gallic.

Listening

EMI 2C 061-12510
Opéra-Comique/Cluytens
(Duval, Giraudeau)
1953

DIALOGUES DES CARMELITES

Three acts
Libretto: Ernest Lavery, after Georges Bernanos
First performance: Milan 1957

Plot: In 1789 Blanche de la Force becomes a novice in a Carmelite Convent, seeking refuge from the terrors that everyday life holds for her. Morbidly concerned with her own lack of courage, she is guided by the ailing Prioress, who on her deathbed puts responsibility for Blanche on the sub-Prioress, Mother Marie. As the Reign of Terror threatens to destroy the convent, the strength and protection offered by Mother Marie, and the loving loyalty of young Sister Constance, sustain Blanche. But, terrified by the nuns' vow of martyrdom taken under Mother Marie's influence in the absence of the new Prioress, she runs away. Then she hears of the nuns' arrest: irresistibly drawn back, she comes to the scaffold as they are mounting it, singing, and – calm now – ascends it to die with them.

The opera: The martyrdom of the Carmelites of Compiègne in 1794 was written up by Mother Marie herself, who was away when the nuns were arrested; the opera's deeply moving last scene, with the singing of the *Salve Regina* and the *Veni Creator* at the guillotine, is a virtual replica of actual events. Mother Marie's *Relation* inspired Gertrude von le Fort's novella *The Last on the Scaffold*, on which Bernanos was asked to base the *Dialogues* for a film (eventually released in 1960). Completed before he died in 1948, it was soon published and staged. Poulenc followed Bernanos closely, simply pruning, and slightly rearranging some of the later scenes. His opera achieves dramatic conviction with painstaking fidelity to its text. While much of the nuns' conversation is metaphysical, there are vivid coups de théâtre, like the extraordinary death scene of the first Prioress. The characterisation of the nuns, especially the contrast between the heroic Mother Marie and the down-to-earth new Prioress, shifts the atmosphere constantly, with Blanche's fearfulness its central theme. In depicting this Poulenc uses a continuing lyrical >recitative; his music draws no attention to itself, even in the instrumental links between scenes.

Overview: Certain similarities of *Dialogues* to Debussy's **Pelléas et Mélisande** are often noted; both operas employ a vocal line which renders the text perfectly, with a discreet accompaniment to paint every utterance. With Puccini's **Suor**

Angelica, *Dialogues* shares only the interplay of female voices; their real subject matter is poles apart. Blanche's conquest of the terrors of death is more about sisterly love and loyalty than religious inspiration; the Trojan women in Berlioz's **The Trojans** show the same heroism, though theirs stems from euphoria.

Listening

EMI 2C 3585 065-3
Paris Opéra/Dervaux
(Crespin, Duval, Gorr, Berton, Depraz)
1957-8

LA VOIX HUMAINE
The Human Voice

One act
Libretto: play by Jean Cocteau
First performance: Paris 1959

Plot: A young woman, at the end of a five-year relationship with the man she still loves, has tried to commit suicide. She has been left alone so that she can receive her lover's promised telephone call. The practical difficulties of the phone-call (Cocteau's play was written in 1932: there are crossed lines, cut-off conversations, wrong numbers) are an outward manifestation of their difficulty in communicating. While talking freely, even amorously, confidentially, trying to protect him from a guilt we cannot be sure he feels, she is distraught, desperately trying to be calm. The telephone is her lifeline, a surrogate for her lover; when he ends the conversation it is like an execution for her.

The opera: The remarkable thing about this monodrama is that it is natural and convincing. One does not normally sing on the telephone: its effectiveness depends specifically on the unaccompanied spoken voice. Yet by pitching precisely every note, by *composing* every phrase, every inflection, the very silences, the composer has painted the familiar situation so that it lives. He has taken equal care over the instrumental colouring, meticulously creating out of the full orchestra an unassuming but effective partner for the single voice. The piece moves forward in brief units, some barely a bar or two. Poulenc finds among the woman's shifting states a rationale for several splashes of his characteristic sentimental lyricism, contrasting with the tense harmonies and textures which convey her true condition so sharply.

Overview: Although the style and the mood are so different, *La voix humaine* inevitably recalls Schoenberg's monodrama **Erwartung**. The single character in both is a woman teetering on the edge of the abyss after losing her lover. The fact that *Erwartung* dredges up the subconscious, whereas *La voix humaine* is painfully, articulately conscious, does not make the one a less devastating exploration of a persons' psyche than the other. The xylophone is not just illustrative of the telephone, it increases the tension, recalling its use in Act I of **Jenůfa** (Janáček). *La voix humaine* is a brilliant demonstration of the method used in Poulenc's own **Dialogues des Carmélites** and Debussy's **Pélleas et Mélisande** before it, where the vocal line is shaped by the natural inflections of the speaking voice.

Listening

EMI 2C 065-12052
Opéra-Comique/Prêtre
(Duval)
1959

BRITISH OPERA

There have been times when English Literature could with some justice have been called Irish Literature, but the misnomer persists. Equally, the tendency has been to call opera in Britain 'English opera', partly because its most visible development has been acted out in London, partly because of long-held assumptions. Most of the successful British composers have been English, yet several influential 18th- and 19th-century figures were Irish – Michael Kelly, Balfe, Wallace and Stanford. Then there was the vital and continuing infusion from Germany, starting with Handel and Pepusch and including Lampe, J. C. Bach, Weber, Benedict and Goehr. Later 20th-century developments have derived enormous strength from the success of national companies in Wales and Scotland, and the great and influential singers themselves have always been drawn from the entire country.

In the late 17th century, stage works by Purcell, to some extent influenced by French opera, promised well. But after Purcell's early death no strong native tradition developed to compare with that of Italy, France or Germany, or indeed Czechoslovakia and Russia, although in turn Eccles, Arne, Storace and Balfe kept the possibility alive. Reasons suggested have varied from

Britten's *Turn of The Screw*
(English National Opera 1979)

the supposed difficulty of setting the English language to music, to the absence in English of a sense of drama, and from the prurient 18th-century preference for Italian >castrati and French ballet dancers, to the popularity of early 18th-century ballad opera. Even after ballad opera (an important influence on the German >Singspiel) had lost ground in Britain, British use of opera as a medium for satire and spoof, like Lampe's *The Dragon of Wantley* (1737) or Arne's *Love in a Village* (1762) made it difficult for serious native works to get a foothold. In the 19th century the sentiment and fun of Gilbert and Sullivan operettas came to dominate the stage; dramatic music was reserved for oratorio. Nor did the folk-song revival in the first part of the 20th century produce a vital operatic idiom. It was only with the productive relationship of Britten

and Pears, and their English Opera Company founded after the Second World War, that British opera became internationally viable. Since then it has met other cultures on equal terms.

Deriving from the masque, early British opera usually incorporated spoken dialogue (Purcell's *Dido and Aeneas* was an exception), and the high standard of this dialogue has been maintained with the impressive literary quality of modern all-sung British opera. Now, towards the end of the century, questions are asked about the accessibility of a medium so heavily committed to allegory (Britten's church parables, and most of Tippett's operas) or music-theatre (Birtwistle). This is a genuine problem, not unique to Britain – it has to be confronted in opera the world over.

Henry Purcell

Born: 1659/London
Died: 21st November 1695/London

Britain's only great composer for 200
years, Purcell wrote scores of songs and
catches, anthems, services and odes,
and instrumental and solo harpsichord
music – an extraordinarily full output.
He provided incidental music for over
forty plays; for five more, now known as
semi-operas, he was able to add
masques and ceremonial music (these
include *The Indian Queen*, *The Fairy
Queen* and *King Arthur*). *Dido and
Aeneas*, Purcell's only full opera, was
the earliest opera in English – well
before Italian opera became
fashionable in London.

DIDO AND AENEAS

Three acts
Libretto: Nahum Tate, after Virgil
First performance: London 1689

Plot: Dido, Queen of Carthage, and
Aeneas, the Trojan hero, are in love,
although Dido knows that Aeneas plans
to rebuild the ruined Trojan kingdom
elsewhere. The prosperity of Dido's
empire, and her happiness, offends the
Sorceress and her witches, who decide
to undermine her relationship with
Aeneas and destroy Carthage.
Appearing in the guise of Mercury, the
Sorceress pretends to bring the gods'
message: Aeneas must forsake Dido
and proceed to fulfil his destiny. Grief-
stricken, he is half-ready to remain in
Carthage, but Dido, outraged that he
can have considered abandoning her,
sends him away – and dies, broken-
hearted.

The opera: *Dido and Aeneas* was
written to be performed by the 'young
gentlewomen' of a girls' boarding
school. Scored for strings only, it is not
excessively demanding either to play
or to sing. But to do justice to its subtle
beauties requires real artistry and skill.

The crucial role – Dido – is remarkable
in its intensity of emotion, less in the
florid passages than in the long-
breathed phrases of 'Ah, Belinda' and
the supremely expressive 'When I am
laid in earth', sung over a chromatically
descending >ground bass (a favourite
device in Purcell). Belinda, the Queen's
companion and her musical foil, has
sprightly charm and airy freshness;
'Fear no danger to ensue' is irresistible.
Aeneas is barely sketched, but a fine
singer can convey genuine grief at the
parting. The Sorceress is a figure of
supernatural spite rather than anything
cataclysmic, and there is a striking
cameo of a rollicking, cynical sailor.
Dance plays a substantial part in the
opera, and the chorus is important, often
repeating Belinda's solos as well as
commenting on the development of
events. In the Witches' scene (Act II) it
is in turn a laughing chorus and an echo
chorus, while at the end the plangent
'With drooping wings', is the very
embodiment of grief.

Overview: Purcell could spin an
>arioso as exquisite as anything in
Monteverdi (consider the >recitatives
of both Dido's >arias); his early death
was an immeasurable loss to British
opera, and *Dido and Aeneas* stood for
250 years as its lone pinnacle. With a
few brief strokes of consummate artistry
he created *Didone abbandonata*,
Woman Forsaken, whom Cherubini
(**Médée**), Berlioz (**The Trojans**) and
Puccini (**Madam Butterfly**) depicted in
full-length works. Perhaps the nearest
equivalent to Purcell's achievement,
albeit on a different scale, is Schubert's
famous lied, *Gretchen am Spinnrade*.

Further reading: Curtis Price (ed.) –
Henry Purcell: Dido and Aeneas
(Norton Critical Score 1987).

Listening

1 Chandos ABRD1034 4 ABTD1034
  CD: CHAN8306
  Taverner Players/Parrott
  (Kirkby, Nelson, D. Thomas)
  1982
2 Philips 416 299-1
  ECO/Leppard
  (Norman, McLaughlin, Allen, Kern)
  1985

John Gay

**Born: 16th September 1685/
Barnstaple
Died: 4th December 1732/London**

A poet and dramatist, Gay wrote the libretto for Handel's *Acis and Galatea*. He is most famous among musicians for inventing the ballad opera, where the characters and setting in *The Beggar's Opera* are given musical substance with popular tunes, a method as alive as anything in >opera buffa. But after *The Beggar's Opera* his works in this genre were undistinguished.

THE BEGGAR'S OPERA

**Three acts
Musical arrangements originally by
John Pepusch
Libretto: John Gay
First performance: London 1728**

Plot: Captain Macheath, a notorious highwayman, has promised himself to both Polly Peachum and Lucy Lockit. The fathers of the two women are confederates, running pimping and thieving rackets, and Lockit is also the Newgate Gaoler. Since Polly has secretly married Macheath, Peachum plans to get him hanged so that Polly will inherit the highwayman's fortune. Macheath, betrayed at a nostalgic reunion with some old flames, is gaoled. Persuading Lucy he is not married to Polly, he gets her to help him escape – only to be trapped again by Peachum and Lockit while with another old flame, and prepared for the gallows. Claimed by both women, hanging seems the only solution to his difficulties – yet suddenly he finds himself reprieved. And so he chooses Polly to be his lifetime wife – but asks her to keep their marriage secret. . . .

The opera: The conception is Gay's, and so, in large part, is the execution: Pepusch wrote the delightful overture, and the bass lines for the tunes (leaving scope for numerous later arrangements and settings). Gay was, for personal reasons, ready to lampoon the Government, and there was an easy second victim in the Italian opera and its declining fortunes. The third butt, giving the work its lasting popularity, was the double standards of a rampantly corrupt society (note Macheath's proud claim that, in despoiling so many virgins, he was provided a service, expanding the city's prostitute population). The work's success sparked off a continuing debate about its supposedly evil influence on public morals, and it was distinctly out of favour during the Victorian and Edwardian epoch, whose double standards were thoroughly entrenched. Gay's method was neither to nudge nor wink. He applied the sharpest irony of all, presenting the appalling behaviour of his low-life characters as the norm. There were sixty-nine attractive short numbers all more or less familiar at the time. They are linked by racy dialogue loaded with sexual innuendo, spoken by the most vivid rogues. The tunes themselves were often supremely inappropriate (the March from Handel's **Rinaldo** is sung by the chorus of highwaymen as they depart for business), a comic aspect lost on modern audiences who miss the topicality that brought the house down (such as the references to the Prime Minister's difficult choice between wife and mistress). But with a light touch, performances of *The Beggar's Opera* can still be richly rewarding.

Overview: Gay's ballad opera put a large nail in the coffin of Italian opera in England, although the two forms continued to co-exist for some time. More significantly, it blotted out any attempts to develop a more substantial home-grown product: English opera had to start all over again nearly two centuries later. Less vital spin-offs of *The Beggar's Opera* held the stage until mated with Offenbach to produce the Gilbert and Sullivan operettas (in both Gay and Offenbach, part of the joke lies in other composers' music being quoted out of context). Brecht and Weill devised a brilliantly successful updated version (**The Threepenny Opera**) – would Macheath have recognised himself as Mack the Knife? He would certainly have been interested in his re-emergence as Mozart's **Don Giovanni**, and intrigued to see himself played by Laurence Olivier in a film made in 1953.

Further reading: Oswald Doughty – *Introduction to The Beggar's Opera* (Dover, New York 1973).

Listening

Argo DP A5913
Argo Chamber Ensemble/Austin
(Noble, Prietto, Lipton, Jones)
1955

Carl Maria von Weber

Born: 18th/19th November 1786/Eutin, near Lübeck
Died: 5th June 1826/London

Weber played a crucial role in spreading the influence of the Romantic movement, by his conducting, his piano virtuosity and his critical writings as well as his compositions. Weber's operas tended to suffer from weak and undramatic librettos. Of the five main operas by which he is known *Der Freischütz* is by far his most important single work. His approach to tone colouring and to organic unity (including >leitmotiv) in his >grand operas, and the 'German-ness' of *Der Freischütz*, had a significant influence on Wagner. Other operas of note include *Abu Hassan*, a >Singspiel; *Die drei Pintos*, a comic opera completed by Mahler; and *Oberon*, recently emerged from neglect.

OBERON

Three acts
Libretto: James Robinson Planché, after Christoph Martin Wieland
First performance: London 1826

Plot: After a spat between Oberon, King of the Fairies, and his wife Titania,

Oberon vows not to be reconciled until two lovers prove their constancy under extreme duress. With a vested interest in finding such a pair, he and his servant Puck bring together Huon, a knight of Charlemagne, and Rezia, daughter of the Caliph of Baghdad. Deeply in love, this couple and their respective servants Sherasmin and Fatima are put through the kind of trouble that few marriages would survive, even before the 20th century: they undergo storm, shipwreck, enslavement, physical and sexual attacks, and separation. With the aid of a magic horn which renders the most hostile enemy helpless they land up intact at the court of Charlemagne – while in the fairy realm, marital bliss is re-established.

The opera: Weber took on *Oberon* because, being terminally ill, he wanted to earn as much as possible for his family (he died less than two months after the premiere). It was an English pantomime opera where costume and scenic effects (such as a Perforated Cavern on the Beach – *sic*) were almost more important than the music. The fatuous libretto involving stock characters and much stage business left little scope for an integrated score. But there are admirable numbers, like Oberon's 'Fatal oath!', Rezia's famous epic 'Ocean! though mighty monster', and the beautiful Mermaids' Song with its evocation of lapping waves. Most striking is the glorious overture, the very spirit of magic romanticism and exuberant chivalry, carried through into the sung material. Nowadays attempts to salvage the music require changes in the text, new libretti and updated stagings.

Overview: Weber's exquisite faery music, with the magic horn's misty Romantic glow, underpinned much of the finest orchestration of the 19th century, forging links with Mendelssohn and Berlioz. Rezia's and Oberon's numbers gave Wagner the model for larger-than-life characters such as the Dutchman, Wotan and Brünnhilde. But *Oberon* has most in common with Mozart's **The Magic Flute**. Both works show lovers put to the test, Rezia's touching >cavatina 'Mourn thou, poor heart' recalls Pamina's *Ach, ich fühl's*, and the magic horn duplicates the effect of the magic flute. The shenanigans in

Tunis reflect the kind of humour concerned with Islamic culture popular fifty years previously in Mozart's **Die Entführung aus dem Serail**, tapped also by Rossini in **The Italian Girl in Algiers**; there is even a quaint Turkish march for harem guards in the first act.

Listening

DG 419 038-IGX2 4 419 038-4GX2
Bavarian Radio Symphony Orch./Kubelik
(Nilsson, Domingo, Grobe, Prey, Hamari)
1971

William Walton

Born: 29th March 1902/Oldham
Died: 8th March 1983/Ischia, Bay of Naples

An all-round composer, Walton is noted for the choral work *Belshazzar's Feast*, his viola and violin concertos, the overture *Portsmouth Point*, the youthful work with the Sitwells (*Façade*) and his scores for Laurence Olivier's Shakespeare films. He wrote only two operas: *Troilus and Cressida*, which is considered theatrically effective but musically old-fashioned, and his romantic comedy *The Bear*.

Further reading: Frank Howes – *The Music of William Walton* (2nd edn, London 1974).

THE BEAR

One act
Libretto: Paul Dehn with the composer, after Anton Chekhov
First performance: Aldeburgh 1967

Plot: In the Russian provinces Madame Popova, a young widow, persists in mourning her husband – already dead over a year – by way of proving her devotion (although he had been an unrestrained philanderer). She will not go out, and sees no one. Into this

rarefied existence explodes an unpaid creditor, Smirnov, insistent that the husband's debt should be paid by the widow. Having no ready cash, she is in no position to pay; he, at the end of his tether, refuses to leave until paid. The hostilities become personal, insults are exchanged, and in an excess of outraged temper they prepare to fight a duel. At which point the creditor realises that he has fallen passionately in love with the widow, and her anger finally melts as she finds she loves him, too.

The opera: Chekhov's comedy provided a perfect basis for Walton's sense of fun. The poses taken up by the widow and the creditor – she with her mourning, he with his proclamations of imminent disaster – are exaggerated broadly. But this is merely the starting point: the score makes many sly points as it romps along, deliberately parodying the vocal excesses of operatic emotion in general, and the mannerisms of other composers in particular. Although the music tends to lurch from one style to another, these mannerisms serve the action perfectly. So it is difficult to stipulate at any time which composer is being sent up, and Walton deliberately tantalised both critics and music-lovers by refusing to disclose specific sources. It is more fun to enjoy the opera on the level of generalised parody than to try and pin down references as wide-ranging as Wagner, Weill, Schoenberg or Menotti. The set-pieces – Smirnov's 'Madame, je vous prie' and Popova's 'I was a constant, faithful wife' – offer marvellous opportunities for singers with the right flair and technique, who can maintain their characters' credibility and resist nudging the audience. And the build-up of mutual dislike leading to the duel is beautifully paced.

Overview: Like Offenbach, Walton occasionally makes perfectly 'straight' music sound funny when placed in an inappropriate setting. Perhaps because the work is a sexagenarian composer's in-joke initially produced for the Aldeburgh Festival, its more cunning parodies are veiled, more subtly integrated than in Britten's own parodistic passage in the last act of **A Midsummer Night's Dream**.

Julia Farron and Pirmin Trecu in *The Midsummer Marriage* (Royal Opera House 1955)

Listening

Chandos ABR1052
Melbourne SO/Cavdarski
(Harris, Yurisich)
1977

Michael Tippett

Born: 2nd January 1905/London

Only in middle age did Tippett gain the stature that has increased with the years, and ranks him with Britten as the great British composer of the middle and later 20th century. Among his several operas the most recent was *The Ice Break*; his oratorio *A Child of our*

Time was written at the start of World War II. He has composed several fine instrumental, orchestral and choral works, and his writings are testimony to his cultivated intellect.

Further reading: Ian Kemp – *Tippett: The Composer and His Music* (Oxford 1987); Eric Walter White – *Tippett and His Operas* (London 1980).

THE MIDSUMMER MARRIAGE

Three acts
Libretto: The composer
First performance: London 1955

The plot: It is midsummer, and various forces seem to threaten the marriage of Jenifer and Mark. The objections of Jenifer's father, King Fisher, impinge little upon the couple, and eventually he dies in the act of confronting them. It is Jenifer's search for truth, evoking a like response in Mark, which holds up the wedding, but ultimately saves it – a search that takes the couple, individually, through a progress towards self-knowledge, blending areas of experience connected with Athena and Dionysus and the Hindu deities. Parallel to this quest is the more prosaic progress of Bella and Jack, whose instincts and growing understanding protect them from the interfering power and mistrust that their boss King Fisher represents.

The opera: Behind its mystifying clutter, the allegory is simple enough: partners in an enduring relationship must integrate diverse elements within themselves to achieve a balance both personal and mutual. This balance, set up so carefully by Tippett the librettist, is undermined by Tippett the composer, in that he gives greater musical weight to a conventional equation of male = Dionysus and female = Athena. But the warm vibrancy of the music was a quality relatively new in English opera of the time, rendering the lack of intellectual follow-through or indeed of musical characterisation unimportant. Passages such as the lovely, fresh March (Act I), or the Ritual Dances (well-known in the concert hall) joyously affirm the inner pulse of life. The score is weakest in the sentimentalised exchange between Jack and Bella as they plan their homebody future, and Bella's bright reconstitution of herself as the attractive 'little woman'; it is finest in Jenifer's and Mark's now-lyrical, now-heroic expressions of doubt and new-discovered confidence.

Overview: There is a parallel in conception with Mozart's **The Magic Flute**. The two couples relate to Pamina and Tamino, Papageno and Papagena; bells and flute are early invoked, the false Queen of the Night becomes the false King Fisher of commerce and industry, and the guardians and priests of Mozart become ancient hallowed personages in Tippett (Sosostris, the prophetic medium, also recalls Wagner's Erda (**The Ring**) in her cryptic pronouncements). Compared with Mozart, or even with Stravinsky's **The Rake's Progress**, Tippett's hero

and heroine embark upon a less allusive, more conscious quest. But he fulfils his musical intention – to create 'images of abounding, generous and exuberant beauty'.

Listening

Philips 6703 027
Royal Opera House/C. Davis
(Remedios, Carlyle, Harwood, Burrows, Herincx)
1970

KING PRIAM

Three acts
Libretto: The composer, after Homer
First performance: Coventry 1962

Plot: Queen Hecuba of Troy dreams that her new-born child, Paris, will one day cause the death of his father, King Priam. Sent away to be killed, Paris is nurtured by a shepherd; when Priam accepts him back he is already a beautiful youth. After continually clashing with his brother, the great Hector, he travels – and returns with Helen, wife of the Greek king Menelaus. During the resultant war between Greeks and Trojans, Hector kills Patroclus, beloved friend of the Greek champion Achilles, and is killed in turn by Achilles. Anguished, Priam berates Paris, before going to plead with Achilles for his son's body. When Paris kills Achilles, it is too late for a true reconciliation with his father, but the old king acknowledges him again before they are both killed by the Greeks.

The opera: *King Priam* is a work of striking clarity. The plot advances with each crucial exchange between the main characters. In interludes between the scenes, a secondary set of characters with the function of a Greek Chorus comments on the action (this also allows for dramatic movement between Troy and the Greek camp). The viewpoints of the highly articulate women (each identified with a specific goddess) crystallise their husbands' experience. The atmosphere of the scenes is embodied in their instrumentation, with textures ranging through bright brass calls, the clatter of percussion, fragile, evocative solo guitar, scurrying piano and telling silences. Trojan jubilation at Patroclus's death is harshly interrupted by Achilles's ululating war-cry, a primitive bark echoed by the Greek soldiers and the fateful instrumental chords. In a score of consciously restricted lyricism the most powerful emotional expression is reserved for Priam, robbed by the death of his son Hector. The most intriguing theme relates to his rejection or acceptance of Paris, the son who will inadvertently destroy him.

Overview: For all its impressive musico-scenic effects, *King Priam's* incisive vocal declamation and textual intelligence combine to make it an opera of ideas, closer to works such as Busoni's **Doktor Faust** or Hindemith's **Mathis der Maler** than to the Romantic sweep of Berlioz's **The Trojans**. The limitations of choice and its implications, the nature of relationships: these and other themes, rather than common stylistic elements, are what relate it to Tippett's other operas. And its examination of the father-son relationship goes well beyond, for example, **Idomeneo** (Mozart), or **Don Carlos** (Verdi), hinting at Pfitzner's insight in **Palestrina**.

Listening

Decca D246D3 4 K246K33
London LDR 73006
London Sinfonietta/Atherton
(Tear, Allen, Palmer, Bailey, Minton, Langridge, Roberts, Harper)
1980

THE KNOT GARDEN

Three acts
Libretto: The composer
First performance: London 1970

Plot: Six people, partly directed by Mangus, an analyst, confront one another in a garden. Five are white; one is black. Each is in some sense unfulfilled, seeking the right direction. Thea has her gardening, away from her sexually predatory business-man husband, Faber. Faber is attracted to

their young ward, Flora, but ready to experiment with the musician Dov, whose relationship with Mel, his black lover, is fading. Thea's sister Denise is a freedom fighter physically twisted by torture. The cross-currents intensify to explosiveness. But some friendships are generated by mutual understanding, and, in using *The Tempest* for role-play, several of the characters find a potentially constructive resolution. Mel and Denise leave together, Flora and Dov each depart towards relative independence, and Thea and Faber are able to face one another creatively.

The opera: This score of concentrated strength yields little to the conception of opera as opulent or sensually appealing. The text is cryptic, the music tight, brilliantly coloured in hard tones. Nor do the various allusions to 'popular' music offer any concession: following Denise's >aria, whose 'operatic' virtuosity has an animal fierceness, the Act I finale deriving from the blues is an ensemble of startling power. In this context a lyrical stanza from Schubert's song-cycle *Die Schöne Müllerin*, quoted at one of the score's few moments of stillness when Dov conjures up a rose garden for Flora, is almost painfully sweet. The declamation is stylised, and exaggerated intervals tend to force the changes in the characters instead of allowing genuine growth or reorientation to emerge. But Thea's Act III contemplation stands out in relief, beautifully foreshadowing her approaching fulfilment, when she will untie the knot in her personal garden.

Overview: While Tippett's score builds on the austerity of **King Priam**, his theme reaches back to **The Midsummer Marriage**, with its ceremonial presentation of the quest for self-knowledge and integration as a prerequisite for mature living. *The Knot Garden* has been described as a modern variant of Mozart's **Così fan tutte** in that its characters dance a metaphorical Paul Jones before beginning again at the beginning. The link is informative but not illuminating, for relationships, rather than narrative situations, are the basis here. Yet it is a measure of his achievement that the roles, metaphors for cultural-emotional

types rather than individuals, are substantially characterised.

Further reading: John Steane – 'English Opera in the 20th century', in *Opera on Record 3*, ed. Blyth (London 1984).

Listening

Philips 6700 063
Royal Opera House/C. Davis
(Minton, Herincx, Gomez, Tear, Barstow, Carey, Hemsley)
1973

Benjamin Britten

**Born: 22nd November 1913/Lowestoft
Died: 4th December 1976/Aldeburgh**

Britten was responsible for putting British music on the international scene after World War II, particularly in the realm of opera. His work also included children's operas, a ballet, church parables, and incidental music for nearly twenty plays. He created a large body of songs for schoolchildren, to whom the *Young Person's Guide to the*

Britten and Eric Crozier with a model of the set for Peter Grimes (1945)

Orchestra is addressed, and arranged many folksongs. His vast output includes numerous choral works, of which the *War Requiem* is perhaps the most famous.

Further reading: Peter Evans – *The Music of Benjamin Britten* (London 1979).

PETER GRIMES

**Prologue and three acts
Libretto: Montagu Slater, after George Crabbe
First performance: London 1945**

Plot: The Suffolk fisherman Peter Grimes has been a virtual outcast since his little apprentice boy was lost at sea. Grimes's rough treatment of the boy had already attracted attention; now slander has done the rest. There is strong resistance to his taking on another apprentice, but Grimes and his friend Ellen plan to care properly for the new boy. Increasingly obsessed with earning enough to be able to marry Ellen, he loses his grip on reality, and when Ellen challenges him about manhandling the new boy he reacts wildly, undermined by her loss of belief in him. Apart from Ellen, Captain Balstrode and a few others, the villagers work themselves up into a righteous frenzy against Grimes. But he is in the grip of his obsession: he insists on going fishing, and his boy slips off the cliffside to his death. His plans in ruins, haunted by the deaths of the two boys, Grimes becomes deranged. Almost in a trance, he carries out Captain Balstrode's advice, and sinks his boat far out to sea, while the villagers, their lust for a scapegoat temporarily settled, move into the routine of a new day.

The opera: In *Peter Grimes* Britten created a powerful folk legend which centres on its anti-hero. The formal, chanting procedures of the coroner's inquest, the round sung in the pub ('Old Joe has gone fishing'), the hymns of the Sunday morning service, the thoughtful, compassionate Ellen and even the gossiping villagers (each distinctly characterised, though, when combined, a chorus of destructive self-righteousness) make up a kind of land-force whose more secure aspects attract Grimes. But the continuous presence of beach, sea and storm conjured up in the orchestral interludes are his true inner life, and those unforgettable unison strings starting the first Interlude, morning light shimmering and gulls crying, take us inside the character as in few other operas. Britten's sympathy for the outsider generates an ambiguity: Grimes *is* unthinkingly brutal to his apprentices, but he is also sensitive and indeed poetic, given to visionary lyrical utterances – note 'What harbour shelters peace' (end first scene), 'Now the Great Bear and Pleiades' (second scene), 'In dreams I've built some kindlier home' (Act II Scene 2). His anguished outcry 'And God have mercy upon me' after his break with Ellen becomes a >motif that haunts the opera. If Grimes is culpable, so are the malign villagers, and Britten spells this out in Grimes's final fragmented, unaccompanied interior monologue against the sound of the fog-horn and the villagers' ghostly cries of his name.

Overview: Grimes's madness is of a different order from that in a Romantic

opera by Donizetti, Bellini, Thomas (or, for that matter, Stravinsky's **Rake**): neither virtuoso, nor prettified, nor consciously theatrical. And it is different again from Handel's raging **Orlando**. Britten is in excellent company in treating madness as a natural psycho-musical development of the role: think of Musorgsky's **Boris**, Berg's **Wozzeck**. His focus shifts after *Peter Grimes* – in **The Turn of the Screw** and **Billy Budd** he is concerned more with the innocent victim than the perpetrator – but with this first mature opera he founded a thriving British tradition.

Further reading: Philip Brett – *Benjamin Britten: Peter Grimes* (Cambridge Opera Handbook 1983).

Listening
Philips 6769 014 4 7699 089
Royal Opera/Davis
(Vickers, Harper)
1978

THE RAPE OF LUCRETIA

Two acts
Libretto: Ronald Duncan, after André Obey
First performance: Glyndebourne 1946

Plot: The Etruscans rule Rome, and Roman resentment is endemic. In a camp outside the city, the generals Junius and Collatinus carouse with the Etruscan Prince, Tarquinius. Collatinus is the only Roman whose wife, Lucretia, is known to be faithful to her husband. Full of bitter jealousy, Junius plants the seed in Tarquinius's mind, and the rampant Prince, intent on self-gratification, rides back to Rome at night and requests hospitality from Lucretia. Later he creeps into her bedroom and demands that she submit to his desire for her; when she refuses, he rapes her at the point of a knife, and rides back to the camp. Now Junius alerts Collatinus to the danger; hastening to Rome, they are met by Lucretia, in mourning. She tells Collatinus what has happened – and stabs herself. Junius will make political capital out of this tragedy, to rouse the Romans against the Etruscans.

The opera: Written for small forces, *The Rape of Lucretia* is an ambitious conception, whose portentous philosophical framework around the action has been much criticised. The libretto places the rape in a Christian view of history conveyed by the Male and Female Chorus (who are also personally involved in the events). Its particular vision polarises supposed male-female differences; although this benefits both the dramatic and the musical structure and textures, it inevitably limits the work. Yet Britten makes the story compelling, strikingly so in the well-wrought partnership of Male Chorus and orchestra describing Tarquinius's ride to Rome, a metaphor for the rape to follow, or in Lucretia's infinitely poignant final appearance to greet Collatinus, accompanied by cor anglais and strings. The atmosphere of brooding, volcanic resentment in the opening scene is balanced with the earnest, pained Epilogue and, shining in between, Lucretia's lyrical purity.

Overview: Lucretia's poignant last entry echoes that of Andromache, Hector's widow, in Berlioz's **The Trojans**: bereavement is conveyed by 'dumb show', the orchestra speaking more eloquently than words. And when, unaware of the events of the previous night, Lucretia's maids collect flowers to greet Tarquinius, it recalls the extravagant delight shown by Puccini's **Madam Butterfly** and Suzuki as they prepare to welcome the sexually acquisitive Pinkerton: again, music lends itself to a dramatic irony more telling than words can convey. But while its Classical theme and its purely musical expressiveness link *Lucretia* with the great tradition, some of the fundamental themes in Britten's own operas are developed: purity ravaged, Christianity affirmed.

Listening

Decca SET 492
London OSA 1288
ECO/Britten
(Pears, Harper, Shirley-Quirk, Drake, Luxon, Baker)
1970

ALBERT HERRING

Three acts
Libretto: Eric Crozier after Guy de Maupassant
First performance: Glyndebourne 1947

Plot: The worthy dignitaries of Loxford are dismayed: they can find no candidate sufficiently virtuous to be crowned village May Queen. They feel compelled to choose a May King instead – modest young Albert Herring. But they are unaware that, while Albert has been too timid to venture out from under his stern mother's thumb, he does have fantasies of kissing a local lass or tasting a pint. And when his friends lace his lemonade with rum at the 'coronation' tea, Albert is emboldened to plunge into a night of drinking, fighting and womanising. His disappearance causes the deepest anxiety among all who have proclaimed him the moral pillar of the British Empire; his return, much the worse for wear, evokes their deepest outrage – although it wins him some respect from the local children. But Albert has asserted his independence, and there will be no turning back.

The opera: In the great comic tradition, *Albert Herring* mirrors an aspect of its culture. In 1947 Loxford was a recognisable village society, the class divisions razor-sharp, the smug assumptions not yet even decently disguised. The music subtly reinforces the personalities involved – the hortatory Lady Billows, the unctuous vicar, the repressed-romantic church school teacher and the limited police superintendent. Britten combines their distinct vocal styles particularly well, as in the final ensembles of the committee meeting and the coronation, or the mock-serious Threnody for the dead Albert. Albert's Act II monologue ('Help myself!') is a genuine dramatic >scena, whose scope suggests the significance of his gesture against those who try to keep him in the straitjacket of their own values. Callow youth confronting dominant mother had long been a theme fascinating to music-hall jokesters and Freudian psychoanalysts, a duality not lost on Britten, who makes

Mrs Herring a caricature but lines up Albert with none other than **Tristan**, linking the laced lemonade with the love potion in comically ironic musical quotations from Wagner.

Overview: Britten used several of the elements of *Albert Herring* in other operas: musical parody in **A Midsummer Night's Dream**, the menace of children's songs in **The Turn of the Screw**, the glorious sound of real children's voices in *Noye's Fludde* (and numerous other works), the incisive scoring of a chamber orchestra in **The Rape of Lucretia** and *The Turn of the*

Screw. Albert himself is a comic prototype of the ingenuous hero who discovers his strength and conquers figures of authority – the **Siegfried** of Loxford (see Wagner's **Ring**). His experience, prefigured in Donizetti's **L'elisir d'amore**, is the supreme operatic incarnation of the well-known nudge-and-wink line, 'We were so pissed!'

Listening

Decca SET 274-6
London OSA 1378
English Chamber Orchestra/Britten
(Fisher, Cantelo, Noble, Brannigan, Pears, Wilson)
1964

Basil Coleman's *Albert Herring* (Aldeburgh Foundation 1986)

BILLY BUDD

Two acts (originally four)
Libretto: E. M. Forster and Eric
Crozier, after Herman Melville
First performance: First version
London 1951; revised version BBC
1961

Plot: Old Captain Vere of the HMS Indomitable broods on the implications of an incident on his ship in 1797, during the wars against Revolutionary France. His sadistic, corrupt Master-at-Arms, Claggart, took against Billy Budd, a splendid young innocent whose healthy beauty and goodness shook Claggart's

equilibrium. Claggart accused Budd of mutiny, but the lad's stammer made it impossible for him to defend himself, and in frustrated outrage he struck Claggart a fatal blow. Vere believed in Billy's innocence but felt unable to save him from hanging even when Billy's demonstration of loyalty helped prevent a mutiny among the bitterly resentful sailors.

The opera: Britten sets Melville's superb short novel with economy and muscle, the male voices and striking harmonic conflict forging a concentrated unity, the large forces often reduced to a single note or a single instrumental colour. Billy's stammer is his 'fatal flaw', but clearly the brooding Claggart and the shining Billy are set for a head-on collision from the moment the brutal officer sizes Billy up as 'a beauty, a jewel . . . there are no more like him'. The Devil pits himself against God's image: Claggart is both repelled by Billy and drawn to him. Their confrontation is at the dramatic centre of the opera, but the real tragedy is Captain Vere's, paradoxically rendered ineffectual by his position as leader of a warship. There is a clear symbolic framework: 'Starry' Vere (truth) seeks illumination; Budd (young plant) is taken off a ship called The Rights of Man; HMS Indomitable is becalmed in mist until Billy fells Claggart. Life at sea is conveyed through vignettes of characters and incidents, naval fanfares and routine, the oppressive mist, and the preparation for battle. But the score is relatively abstract: the sea-shanty 'Heave away' is almost mystical; the men's mutinous mumbling at the moment of crisis is wordless. Claggart's monologue is sombre and narrow in range, both musically and psychologically, Billy's is joyous, unfettered; and when Billy is told that Vere cannot save him we hear a tortured orchestral interlude which shows Vere buckling to the demands of his position.

Overview: *Billy Budd* is Britten's most uncompromising embodiment, among all his operas, of the struggle between innocence and evil. The cheerful 'We're off to Samoa' recalls 'Old Joe has gone fishing' from **Peter Grimes**, and there are deeper parallels evoked by Britten's feeling for the sea: bleak and terrifying, in Davies's **The Lighthouse**; romantically turbulent in Wagner's **The Flying Dutchman**, luminous in Verdi's **Simon Boccanegra**.

Listening

Decca SET 379
London OSA 1390
LSO/Britten
(Glossop, Pears, Langdon)
1967

THE TURN OF THE SCREW

Prologue and two acts
Libretto: Myfanwy Piper, after Henry James
First performance: Venice 1954

Plot: A governess takes up a position of total responsibility for a young sister and brother, Flora and Miles, whose absent guardian is unconcerned. Both children appear to be good and sweet, yet Miles is expelled from his school. The governess becomes aware that two ghosts are preying on the children: the evil Peter Quint, once the guardian's valet, and the previous governess, Miss Jessel, whom he had debauched. As the governess tries to guard the children from the corruption around them, they become set against her. Eventually the housekeeper takes Flora away to the guardian; the governess, challenged by Miles, presses him to confront and thereby reject the relationship with Quint. It proves conclusive: the boy dies, spiritually torn apart.

The opera: Britten gives James's claustrophobic drama a tightly integrated chamber setting. Before each scene there is an orchestral variation of the twelve-note theme stated immediately after the Prologue. There are telling variants of crucial >motifs, such as the Governess's 'O why did I come?', the ghosts' 'The ceremony of innocence is drowned' and Miles's poignant song 'Malo, malo'. A gong announces the doleful Miss Jessel; Peter Quint, the single adult voice, is altogether more fully imagined, more alluring, with shining celesta accompaniment, melismatic lyricism, and light, exhilarating fantasies of dashing action. The beautiful natural setting depicted before Scene 4 becomes tarnished; the lake turns into 'the Dead Sea' that Flora almost crosses to Miss Jessel. The children's music – nursery rhymes, church-going hymn, Flora's lullaby, even Miles's Mozartean piano playing – develops sinister significance. As the governess gains in strength, her position becomes more ambiguous: she and Quint share musical material. At the end she sings in unknowing unison with Quint, her exalted words to Miles – 'Together we have destroyed him' – taking on a chilling irony as she realises that he is dead. Would Miles have been better left with Quint?

Christopher Renshaw's 1986 production of *A Midsummer Night's Dream*

Overview: With its orchestral episodes and its thematic symbolism *The Turn of the Screw* is one of Britten's most complex operatic structures, but – as with Berg's **Wozzeck** and **Lulu** – response does not depend on knowing its formal organisation. Quint's relationship with Miles goes further than Claggart's with **Billy Budd** or Aschenbach's with the Polish boy (**Death in Venice**). It is negative, corrupt – all these men, insofar as they engage with the beauty that draws them, destroy its innocence. More brutally explicit than any is Tarquin in **The Rape of Lucretia**. Britten chose superb texts for his operas; viewed together, they project a fear – his fear? – that to love innocent beauty leads to guilty corruption.

Further reading: Patricia Howard – *Benjamin Britten: The Turn of the Screw* (Cambridge Opera Handbook 1985).

Listening

Decca m GOM 560-1
Richmond m RS 65021
English Opera Group/Britten
(Pears, Vyvyan)
1955

A MIDSUMMER NIGHT'S DREAM

Three acts
Libretto: The composer and Peter Pears, after William Shakespeare
First performance: Aldeburgh 1960

Plot: In an Athenian forest Oberon and Tytania, King and Queen of the Fairies, are quarrelling. In pique, Oberon calls upon the services of his nimble assistant, Puck. With a magic juice he makes Tytania fall in love with the weaver, Bottom, who, through Puck's 'good offices', is temporarily sporting the head of an ass. Meanwhile Puck confuses the love problems of a quartet of young men and women, so that both Demetrius and Lysander, rivals for the love of Hermia, switch their allegiance to Helena, until Oberon rights matters between them and between himself

and Tytania. At the wedding of King Theseus and Queen Hippolyta, blessed by Tytania and Oberon, Demetrius and Helena, Lysander and Hermia, are also wed, and a play is performed with cavalier awkwardness by Bottom (now relatively proper-headed) and his colleagues.

The opera: There are two major simplifications in this adaptation of Shakespeare's comedy. Firstly, the forest is the setting for all the action until the final scene, so that the parallels between the fairy and human lovers become easily perceptible. Sleep and dream are evoked in some beautiful orchestral passages, especially the preludes to Acts II and III; other rewarding moments are the closing scenes of the first two acts, and Bottom's scene with the fairies. Secondly, the music for each group – fairies, lovers and 'mechanicals' – is distinctively characterised. As well as clarifying the plot, this creates a wide diversity of sound-textures, with the counter-tenor of Oberon and the speaking voice of Puck, the young boys' voices for the fairies and Tytania's ornamental vocal line, and the scenes with the rustics, their voices contrasted like wind instruments in >buffa chamber music. The rather contrived parody of their play and the succeeding dance presents another sound-world, sending up early 19th-century opera, with much ironic doffing of the cap to Bellini, Rossini and Verdi among others.

Overview: Apart from Mendelssohn's famous Incidental Music to the play, the same story served Purcell in his *Fairy Queen* and provided a point of reference for Weber's **Oberon**. For Britten it was a last 'big' opera before his change of style with the church parables, although he also used contrasted blocks of sound-textures as the structural basis of the *War Requiem*, first performed less than two years later.

Listening

Decca SET 338
London OSA 1385
LSO/Britten
(Deller, Harwood, Pears, Hemsley, Veasey, Harper, Brannigan)
1966

CURLEW RIVER

Church parable in one act
Libretto: William S. Plomer, after a
Japanese Noh play
First performance: Orford, near
Aldeburgh 1964

Plot: A group of medieval monks moves in procession, singing, to the performing area. Some lay brethren take up musical instruments, and the Abbot introduces the play:

Approaching the Curlew River that runs between the Eastern and Western lands, a Madwoman, source of some amusement to her fellow travellers, bewails the loss of her son, whom she seeks. The Ferryman reluctantly accepts her as a passenger. On the crossing, he tells of a boy, a slave he had ferried across a year previously, who was abandoned by his master to die on the far side. The boy's grave has become a shrine. The Madwoman

First performance of *Curlew River* at Orford Parish Church (Aldeburgh Foundation 1964)

weeps: it is her son. Taken to his tomb, she hears his voice accompanying pilgrims' prayers; the spirit of the boy appears, and comforts her, and she is freed from her madness.

The monks praise this sign of God's grace, and leave, singing.

The opera: Inspired by a Noh play in Tokyo, Britten reconceived its story as a medieval religious drama with a miracle, his first parable for church performance, starting and ending with a plainsong hymn. It marked a new direction in his music, with its sparing use of a few instruments exploiting their 'alien' sounds, freedom from regular metrical rhythm, and the highly stylised vocal manner of the actors: the Madwoman frequently sings her lines on a single note, ending with a slightly wailing glissando inflection, and there is significant use of glissando among the instruments. The characters (all male) wear masks, and employ a basic mime vocabulary; the setting is entirely unadorned, best in a church, but possible in any plain space where the audience can respond directly to this absorbing, deeply expressive work.

Overview: Britten wrote two later church parables, without quite recapturing *Curlew River*'s perfection. The use of non-naturalistic means for the actors – masks, stylised gesture, chanting chorus and soloists – bears superficial resemblance to Stravinsky's method in **Oedipus Rex**. But Britten was working within a different aesthetic – plain austerity rather than grand austerity. The Madwoman, for all that she is performed by a tenor in the all-male cast, is one of the few great mothers in the repertoire, with a quality of spiritual intensity much finer than Verdi's Azucena (**Il trovatore**). She parallels the Governess in Britten's **The Turn of the Screw**, with the difference that the Governess captures the body but loses the spirit of her (surrogate) child.

Listening

Decca SET 301
London OSA 1156
Instrumental Ensemble/Britten
(Pears, Shirley-Quirk, Blackburn, Drake)
1965

DEATH IN VENICE

Two acts
Libretto: Myfanwy Piper, after Thomas Mann
First performance: Snape Maltings 1973

Plot: An ageing Munich writer, famous for the formal perfection of his art but now dried-up (as his name, Aschenbach – brook of ashes – suggests), travels for refreshment of the soul to the warmth and beauty of Venice. At his hotel he falls in love with a Polish boy, the incarnation of Apollonian beauty, but can never bring himself to speak to him. As a cholera plague, hidden by the authorities, infests the city, so Aschenbach's hidden passion breaks down his reserves of intellectual or moral poise: Eros is brought into in his writing, Dionysus takes over from Apollo. He makes a pathetic attempt to look younger, he pursues the boy around Venice; with a fantasy of surviving alone with him he refrains from warning the boy's mother about the plague. On the day the family leaves, while the boy is still playing on the beach, Aschenbach dies.

The opera: Britten's last opera is an extraordinary work. Time and space are telescoped in cinematic continuity as Aschenbach moves from one scene to the next. It is a monothematic drama: most of the 'action' exists in the writer's interior monologue, his reflections accompanied by piano only. Thus his relationship with the boy is virtually never articulated outside his own mind, and the boy's own life is danced or mimed, never sung (his beach-games are transformed in Aschenbach's mind to mythological Greek contests). The boy's music is shining, other-worldly, evoked predominantly by pitched percussion. The other significant roles are manifestations of one composite character, half-menacing, comic or bizarre, a functionary of Aschenbach's fate – guide, host, ferryman and messenger of death. Venice is embodied in wonderfully poetic gondola music, ambiguous enough in its languor to suggest stagnant decay and oppressive heat. The tightly-knit score is built from brief >motifs, the intense concentration expunging any sentimental or conventionally tragic feeling. Yet after Aschenbach's death, as the beautiful music wells up in the strings and the sounds associated with the boy still glint in the air, the release from yearning suggests deepest fulfilment.

Overview: Like Hindemith's **Mathis der Maler** and Pfitzner's **Palestrina**, *Death in Venice* is concerned with the source and nature of the artist's inspiration. But this is Mann's theme rather than Britten's; the composer's concern, here viewed from the perspective of the ageing artist, is his abiding one of innocence and corruption. Thus it is no coincidence that his librettist is the same as for **The Turn of the Screw** (where Quint's shining music foreshadows the Polish boy's), or that at the end the boy walks

125

into the sea that brought forth **Peter Grimes** and **Billy Budd**.

Further reading: Donald Mitchell – *Benjamin Britten: Death in Venice* (Cambridge Opera Handbook 1987).

Listening

Decca SET 581
London OSA 13109
ECO/Bedford
(Pears, Shirley-Quirk)
1974

Harrison Birtwistle

Born: 15th July 1934/Accrington

Birtwistle has gained renown as the most significant British opera composer of the late 20th century, with *Punch and Judy*, *Down by the Greenwood Side*, *Yan Tan Tethera* and *The Mask of Orpheus*, as well as ballets and works of music-theatre. The use of tape features in several of his compositions, in particular the instrumental pieces. He has also composed choral, solo vocal and orchestral works.

Further reading: Michael Hall – *Harrison Birtwistle* (London 1985)

PUNCH AND JUDY

One act
Libretto: Stephen Pruslin
First performance: Aldeburgh 1968

Plot: Punch murders, successively, his baby and its mother Judy, the Doctor and the Lawyer who confront him, the Choregos who speaks the Prologue and commentary on the action and will speak the Epilogue, and the hangman. He engages in a word-game with each victim before leading him/her to the Altar of Murder, and ignores pleas from other victims who try to prevent him carrying out the intended crime. Alternating with these dark deeds, he rides his Horsey on a quest for Pretty Polly, whom he woos passionately, undeterred by her successive rejections of him for his crimes. At last Spring and Love take over; the gallows becomes a maypole, and Punch and Pretty Polly are united. The tragedy has become a comedy.

The opera: Birtwistle and Pruslin used the framework of the children's seaside show to present Punch as a myth through the medium of music theatre. The Chorus Gibbet, the Altar of Murder, Pretty Polly's pedestal, Choregos's booth, the appurtenances of Punch's quests are fixed points in the musical structure as well as the staging; so are the 'Passion Chorales', in which Choregos, with Judy, the Doctor and the Lawyer, comment on the preceding scenes in the manner of a Greek chorus. Pure singing and >sprechgesang alternate. Set-pieces – lullaby, quartet, love-duet, the recurring, >melodramas – form a pattern of fixed, recognisable units. But the overall work is kept flexible by the ingenuity of the conception, especially in Punch's Nightmare, where Judy becomes a Fortune-Teller and Polly a Witch (later, Choregos will double as the hangman), and a sinister wedding is enacted. Birtwistle's music, highly stylised, and for much of the time starkly violent, is remarkably expressive, full of inventive instrumental effects; rarely is percussion used with such freshness and refinement.

Overview: Pruslin himself has commented on the connection between Punch–Polly and Nero–Poppaea (Monteverdi's **The Coronation of Poppaea**). In both operas, the fullest lyricism is released by a triumphant love which gets rid of all (human) obstacles. Monteverdi's lovers have no qualms about the amorality of this process; Birtwistle's Polly actually withholds her love in protest against Punch's excesses, and they are brought together by an outside force – the principle of fertility. Monteverdi's protagonists are individually characterised, Birtwistle's exist mainly as manifestations of a myth drawn from medieval English knockabout comedy, whose re-enactment is still enjoyed by numerous children on holiday and by adults recalling their childhood.

Listening

Decca Headline HEAD 24
London Sinfonietta/Atherton
(Bryn-Julson, de Gaetani, Langridge, Roberts, Wilson-Johnson, Tomlinson)
1980

THE MASK OF ORPHEUS

Three acts
Libretto: Peter Zinovieff
First performance: London 1986

Plot: After Euridice has married Orpheus, Aristaeus the bee-keeper makes love to her, and in running from him she is killed by a water-snake. Determined to rescue her from death,

Harrison Birtwistle with his *Mask of Orpheus* at The English National Opera in 1986

Orpheus learns from the Oracle of the Dead how to proceed to the Underworld. In a dream he moves through the seventeen arches connecting life to death, overcoming all obstacles, but loses Euridice when he awakes, and hangs himself in despair. Other versions of his death are also enacted: he is killed by Zeus for revealing divine secrets, he is torn apart and eaten by the followers of Dionysus, and his skull, which has become an oracle, is silenced by the jealous Apollo.

The opera: The plot is not linear but cumulative, and the presentation is multi-dimensional. Time shifts continually, incidents are repeated, the past and the present are superimposed. Each of the three main characters is represented as person, as hero and as myth, enacted by singer, mime, and puppet-plus-singer respectively. The structural complexities do not hold back the flow, not even the six scenes, mimed to electronic music, which are interposed in the main action and relate to the myth of Dionysus. The electronic tapes, which took two years to prepare, include continuous auras (static sound spectra which resonate in the background) as well as transmutations of Apollo's occasional injunctions and Orpheus's harp. The harp dominates; its percussive, abrupt violence contradicts conventionally accepted interpretations of the myth, clearing a space for this opera's probing of original sources. The singing (one element among many) mingles lyrical outbursts with incantatory, dramatic or dream-like declamation; the climax that ends Act I is the more powerful for being the fullest vocal exchange till that point, and the strong onward impulse in Act II derives in part from a richer application of vocal resources as well as the more vivid instrumental colouring. The writing for the Oracle of the Dead is remarkable, compact and intensely dramatic: a reminder that much of the overall strength of *The Mask of Orpheus* derives from the conviction and skill applied to each component part.

Overview: The wild practices of the Dionysiac cult (best-known from Euripides's play *The Bacchae*) are central to Henze's **The Bassarids**.

Birtwistle's is the first important opera to pay attention to the relation between the Orphic and Dionysiac myths, adding substantially to the picture of Orpheus in Peri, Monteverdi and Gluck. It is unusually successful in welding late 20th-century techniques within an 'operatic' context. Triple representations of main characters are even more strikingly used in Stockhausen's **Donnerstag aus Licht**.

Peter Maxwell Davies

Born: 8th September 1934/ Manchester

A leading figure in the British music-theatre scene, Maxwell Davies has created many dramatic works (often for his own Pierrot Players, later The Fires of London), which include children's opera, ballets, masques, chamber opera and the full-scale opera *Taverner*. He has composed several works for the Festival in Orkney, his later output reflecting this involvement with and an involvement with Scotland in general. He has also written choral music (some for schoolchildren) and many vocal, orchestral and instrumental pieces.

Further reading: Paul Griffiths – *Peter Maxwell Davies* (London 1982).

THE LIGHTHOUSE

Prologue and one act
Libretto: The composer
First performance: Edinburgh 1980

Plot: At a Court of Enquiry three officers describe how they arrived at a lighthouse in winter to relieve its three keepers – and found it deserted. The mystery is never solved; the lighthouse is made automatic. But we see the keepers as they were, stormbound, waiting for the relief ship, at a breaking point of tension and mutual dislike: Arthur, a hypocritical Bible-thumper, the bluff, rough Blazes, and Sandy, trying to keep the peace. All three men have dark memories, tormenting ghosts, which call to them as the fog thickens outside. They hear the Cry of the Beast described by Arthur, its eyes blazing in the night, and they move out to defend themselves. When the three officers from the ship enter the lighthouse it is clear that they, too, have had to defend themselves – to the death. After they leave, the original keepers begin again a ghostly replaying of what has already been.

The opera: In this >chamber opera mystery thriller, the same singers play the keepers and the officers, and it is never clear how much is flashback or flash-forward, or whether we are seeing a ghost tale or a reconstruction. The language is naturalistic, the vocal line highly artificial; the singers have to cover a wide range and handle a very precise >sprechgesang. They are strikingly divergent characterisations, each with a wide emotional range, crystallised in a song: Blazes's a Satanic parody of music-hall, with banjo,

Sandy's a wistful parlour ballad to out-of-tune piano (it takes on an erotic meaning, when repeated in trio, that belies its seeming innocence), and Arthur's a long salvationist warning of the Beast to come. The dozen instrumentalists face a complex score demanding extreme virtuosity, ingeniously depicting the sounds of sea and storm and the inner storm of the characters, with eerie hallucinatory effects and orchestral shrieks as the foghorn sounds. The lighting is crucial to the piece's success.

Overview: Unlike Britten's all-too-real ghostly couple in **The Turn of the Screw**, the ghosts in *The Lighthouse* may well exist only in the over-heated minds of those who 'see' them. Like Britten in **Peter Grimes**, Davies evokes in his music a life bound up with the sea, here an actively threatening presence. These are clear connections with the British tradition. And by delineating each character through a song Davies calls to mind the prisoners in Janáček's **From the House of the Dead**, whose stories (not unlike Blazes's) define them for their comrades and the audience.

GERMAN OPERA

There had been splendid opera in Italy for two centuries, and in France for one, when German opera first made its mark with Mozart's great >Singspiels of the late 18th century. It then went on to produce the most enthralling >rescue opera (Beethoven's *Fidelio*), the incarnation of magic folk-tale Romanticism (Weber's *Der Freischütz*), and the ultimate expression of yearning love (Wagner's *Tristan und Isolde*). For many opera-goers Wagner's finest achievements are the peak of the entire opera repertoire. Yet German opera never stagnated, and out of the artistic and intellectual ferment before and after the first world war, when Italian and French opera were running out of steam, a set of German works was produced, standing among the greatest in the repertory. From this period date the achievements of Richard Strauss, Schoenberg, Zemlinsky, Busoni, Pfitzner, Berg, Weill and Hindemith.

German opera never had a continuing stream of masterpieces; its composers were free to use their creative initiative in exploring the medium afresh.

Although Beethoven, Weber and Wagner all took established models as their starting point, they forged works which blazed with individual genius –

works that were in the best sense unrepeatable. It is clear that German opera had no more than one towering figure at any one time, whereas French and Italian opera could often boast several. Then suddenly, in the space of a few years, came that spate of masterpieces from the composers mentioned earlier.

One tradition which developed in the late 18th century was the Singspiel. Influenced by the British ballad opera, sharing the naive charm of the French opéra comique, it remained at its core a homegrown genre. Its songs were not elaborate or formal; they were close to the simple lied of the common folk. The

André Serban's 1986 production of Beethoven's *Fidelio* for the Royal Opera House

most beloved of these Singspiels were written between 1766 and 1777 by Johann Adam Hiller; some of them, *Der Jagd* in particular, anticipated in their German-ness Weber's *Der Freischütz*, written nearly half a century later.

If, over a long period, a few crucial figures make up the story of German opera, was there any underlying link? Many of the greatest German works are by musicians who were not mainly opera composers, musicians more concerned with expressiveness than with their singers' vocal prowess. German opera has always appealed for its purely musical content – Wagner's operas are at least as remarkable for their >leitmotiv system, their harmonic language and their orchestral colour as for their vocal splendours.

In creating his 'truly German' opera in the early 19th century when Romanticism was at its most exciting, Weber had striven for a self-contained dramatic work that would amalgamate all other arts and give dramatic life to a new world; Wagner called it the >Gesamtkunstwerk. When bringing together similarly disparate elements, right from the beginnings of their opera the French had aimed at balance; now the Germans were seeking a passionate personal fusion. There was often an intellectual, aesthetic or moral concept helping to shape their works with an individual musical outlook. So when you hear a German opera, let it take your mind and your ear in equal measure.

Wolfgang Amadeus Mozart

(For biographical information see entry in Italian section on page 24.)

DIE ENTFÜHRUNG AUS DEM SERAIL
The Abduction from the Seraglio

Three acts
Libretto: Gottlob Stephanie after Christoph Friedrich Bretzner
First performance: Vienna 1782

Plot: Belmonte comes to Turkey in search of his beloved Constanze, whom pirates have sold into slavery along with her maid, Blonde, and Belmonte's servant, Pedrillo. He finds all three in the harem of the powerful Selim Pasha. Escape is urgently necessary, as the Pasha, in love with Constanze, is on the verge of forcing her to accept his attentions, while his overseer, Osmin – a nasty piece of work – has designs on Blonde. Following a plan to abduct the women, Pedrillo manages to get Osmin drunk, but Osmin catches the group as they are escaping, and they face dire consequences. Fortunately the Pasha shows an enlightened spirit, allowing all four to sail for home.

The opera: Although as a >Singspiel *Die Entführung* has a normal balance of spoken/sung material, and ample >buffa humour in Osmin's altercations with Blonde and Pedrillo, this rich score must have felt at times like >opera seria to contemporary audiences. Constanze's two >arias, stylistically contrasted, incorporate intense feeling, Belmonte's hardly less so, although he sings nothing as brilliant as her *Martern aller Arten*. The salacious Osmin, initially conceived as a secondary comic, plays a significant role in many ensembles, and his buffa anger is

characterised well beyond the conventional. Pedrillo signals the start of the abduction with an exquisite song, strangely prophetic of early 19th-century Romanticism, suggesting hidden depths in the character. The Pasha is a non-singing role, challenging the actor's subtlety to express passion, cruelty and wisdom in a dramatically static work whose real life is all in the music.

Overview: In Mozart's later Singspiel, **The Magic Flute**, this mix of high seriousness and earthy comedy would be repeated to greater effect, as well as forming an important ingredient in his intervening operas. Here he also courted popularity with the exotic element, responding to a local fascination for things Turkish. The story echoes those of opera seria – a demanding tyrant, a lover potentially sacrificed, a woman of independent and noble spirit; later, Rossini's **The Italian Girl in Algiers** would extract hilarious comedy from it. The embryo of **Così fan tutte** may be seen in the fine Act II finale which deals with the men's unpleasant suspicions that, if the women have been unfaithful to them, the goods are cheapened, and Sarastro (*The Magic Flute*) is implicit in the enlightened ruler, Selim Pasha.

Further reading: Thomas Baumann – *W. A. Mozart: The Abduction from the Seraglio* (Cambridge Opera Handbook 1987).

Listening

Deutsche Grammophon 2740 203 (3) 2709 051
Dresden State Orch./Böhm
(Augér, Grist, Schreier)
1974

THE MAGIC FLUTE
Die Zauberflöte

Two Acts
Libretto: Emanuel Schikaneder
First performance: Vienna 1791

Plot: Tamino, on a quest to rescue the Queen of the Night's daughter, Pamina, from the clutches of the evil Sarastro,

The David Hockney set for Glyndebourne's 1978 production of *The Magic Flute*

learns a higher truth: Sarastro is profoundly good, and, guided by him through a series of trials both physical and symbolic, Tamino and Pamina gain the light of knowledge. Their friend, Papageno, unable or unwilling to learn in the same way, achieves domestic happiness with his Papagena. The starry power of the Queen of the Night, and the menace of the slave Monostatos, both of whom are blind to the values of Sarastro's kingdom, is destroyed.

The opera: This >Singspiel is one of the glories of the operatic stage, accessible to children – and adults – of all ages. On one level it is a parable containing hidden symbols – like the recurrence of the number three, or the austere tone sounded by the Men in Armour – for the Freemasons, suffering religious persecution. On another level *The Magic Flute* is also a pantomime, mingling fairy-tale elements, musical instruments of potent magic, clowning, sudden appearances and disappearances, goodies and baddies (and we learn that first impressions may be deceptive). It contains typical >buffa elements, including slapstick humour and delightful street music. Above all it shows the human quest for enlightenment in a world which can be confusing and contradictory. In this sense the music of each of the three 'novices', is often intensely personal, – it characterises an aspect of Everyone. Tamino and Pamina, with their different areas of sensitivity, must combine in attaining spiritual harmony, while

Papageno has different needs as Common Man (Common Woman, his Papagena, doesn't get much of a look-in). Possibly best beloved in this wonderful score are Papageno's delightful birdcatcher song, Pamina's heart-breakingly beautiful *Ach, ich fühl's*, and their duet *Bei Männern*, surely the most natural act of friendship in opera. Sarastro's warm, deep music (all too often dragged) parries the crystalline brilliance of the Queen of the Night; the simplicity of the three boys and the pronouncements of the priests undercut the operatic nature of the Queen of the Night's three ladies; the magic instruments make their own enchanting contribution, in contrast with the eerie hollowness of the flute and drums during the trials. Mozart's universal genius is demonstrated to perfection in this unpretentious work. Who else could open Heaven in just eight bars of the lovers' *Tamino/Pamina mein! O welch ein Glück!*?

Overview: Far more than Mozart's **Die Entführung**, *The Magic Flute* brought the Singspiel to an entirely new level. It has never been bettered. Always immensely popular, it has received some highly imaginative productions (one being the memorable Ingmar Bergman film), only the finest able to balance the philosophical earnestness with the comedy, the fantasy, the drama and the sheer beauty of the music.

Further reading: Brigid Brophy – *Mozart The Dramatist* (London 1964).

Listening

1 HMV SLS 5223 4 TCC-SLS5223
   Bavarian Radio Symph. Orch./Haitink

133

(Popp, Gruberová, Lindner, Jerusalem,
Brendel, Bracht)
1980

2 Philips 411 459–1PH3 4 411 459-4PH2
CD: 411 459-2PH3
Dresden Staatskapelle/C. Davis
(M. Price, Serra, Schreier)

Ludwig van Beethoven

Baptised: 17th December 1770/Bonn
Died: 26th March 1827/Vienna

As one of the greatest figures in all
music, and its most popular, Beethoven
composed many symphonies,
concertos, string quartets, piano
sonatas, overtures and works of
chamber music. His output of vocal
music was comparatively small: one
opera, a wonderful Missa Solemnis,
some fine songs (including the first real
song cycle), and a few other notable
choral works. Perhaps he is best known
for the Ode to Joy from his Choral
(Ninth) Symphony (he was the first to
employ voice in symphonic music). All
his major choral works are considered
extremely demanding for the voice.

Further reading: Joseph Kerman and
Alan Tyson – *The New Grove
Beethoven* (London 1982).

FIDELIO

Two acts
**Libretto: Joseph Sonnleithner after
Jean Nicolas Bouilly**
**First performance: Vienna 1805,
revised 1806, revised 1814**

Plot: Leonore suspects that her
husband, Florestan, has been
incarcerated by the prison governor
Pizarro for fearlessly attacking tyranny.
Disguised as a youth, Fidelio, she is
taken on as gaoler's assistant, and
overhears Pizarro instructing the gaoler

to prepare a grave in the dungeon of
a secret prisoner, whom he wants out
of the way before the Minister of State's
visit. Leonore determines to rescue the
prisoner, even if he is not Florestan. At
her instigation, the other prisoners are
allowed briefly to enjoy the sunshine in
the prison yard. At last allowed to help
in the secret prisoner's dungeon, she
gives a little bread and wine to the half-
starved prisoner: it is indeed her
husband. With an immense effort she
hides her feelings, and, when Pizarro
comes down to gloat over his victim
before killing him, she reveals her
identity, threatening Pizarro with a gun.
The Minister is announced; Pizarro is
exposed, and the husband and wife are
reunited.

The opera: Although its greatness as a
music drama is universally accepted,
Fidelio is often criticised for the stiffness
of its early scenes, and the demands
made on the singers in the later ones.
But Beethoven works within parameters
rarely used by opera composers. Some
of the early numbers certainly lack
white-hot inspiration, but they establish
a frame of complacent domesticity out
of which extraordinary qualities 'burst,
to illumine our tempestuous day'
(Shelley). There is a foretaste of the
wonders to come in the quartet (*Mir ist
so wunderbar*), and, step by step,
Leonore draws us into a drama whose
power to involve us is unparalleled in
opera. Through her every utterance,
charged with desperate courage, we
experience love, loyalty, and the
striving for freedom from tyranny. Her
part in the trio *Gut, Söhnchen, gut*
intensifies the growing gap between
her concerns and those of the others, so
that we are ready for Pizarro, with his
stark, half-controlled mutterings, as the
force of evil she will have to confront.
In her own tremendous >aria and the
Prisoners' Chorus we are in realms that
only Beethoven occupied, and this level
continues in Act II right through
Florestan's magnificent >scena, the
whole dungeon scene, the heart-
stopping climax and the finale. The
spoken dialogue is crucial, a few telling
lines preparing in each case for the
intense medium of music; and in the
dungeon the >melodrama, does more
to depict the horror than any scenic
designer could. At the symbolic giving
of the bread and the wine the music

attains a true warmth of spirit; from Pizarro's entrance the drama is almost unendurable until the pent-up emotion can be released in the exalted duet and the great finale.

Overview: *Fidelio*, Beethoven's only opera and technically a >Singspiel, was based on an earlier libretto drawn from a true incident during the French Revolution. It is the greatest >rescue opera, and the first great drama in German opera. Beethoven transmuted his theme into a statement about human values – including marital love – that has enriched our culture. *Fidelio* transcends its own medium: it is one of the signal works of Western art.

Listening

HMV SLS 5006 4 TC-SLS 5006
Angel SCL 3625
Philarmonia/Klemperer
(Ludwig, Vickers, Berry, Frick)
1961

Carl Maria von Weber

(For biographical information see entry in British section on page 112.)

DER FREISCHÜTZ
The Freeshooter

Three acts
Libretto: Friedrich Kind, after Johann August Apel and Friedrich Laun
First performance: Berlin 1821

Plot: Max hopes to win the hand of Agathe, the Chief forester's daughter, at the approaching shooting trial, but he has recently been unable to maintain his celebrated marksmanship. Kaspar, a hunter who has sold himself to the Devil (Samiel, the Great Huntsman), hopes to postpone the date on which Samiel will

claim him, by offering him another soul. To this end he persuades the depressed Max to join him in the dread Wolf's Glen, where they cast the devil-enchanted bullets which never miss their mark. Mindful of Agathe's loving admonitions, Max saves himself from Samiel by making the sign of the Cross, and at the shooting trial his final 'free' shot is directed by Samiel to kill Kaspar, whose time is up. Once it is known that Max has risked trafficking with the Devil he faces banishment, but a Hermit who has been watching over the young couple recommends rather that he be allowed to marry Agathe after a year's probation. The gentleness of God is hymned at the end.

The opera: *Der Freischütz* exploded upon the German music scene as though a match had been put to dry tinder: never did an opera so completely fulfil the needs of its time and place. The German forest, still a place of folklore and folksong, was the cradle of an awakening culture. For this huntsman's tale of dark pagan superstition threatening village piety, Weber created music which became universally known – the Bohemian waltz, the bridesmaids' chorus, the huntsman's chorus, the scene in the Wolf's Glen, Max's *Durch die Wälder* and Agathe's >aria *Leise, leise* (which was actually incorporated into church services). The carefree young Aennchen, Agathe's cousin, pointed the delights of the >Singspiel in contrast with the more operatic Agathe, their first scene together showing them engaged in practical domestic activities. The overture is a magnificent structure, a tone poem in which the moods of nature are evoked by superb orchestral colouring. The extraordinary Wolf's Glen scene crystallises German Romanticism; its weird chorus, melodrama, stage effects and chanting, not to mention the chilling effect of Samiel's speaking and snatches of significant music from previous scenes, are welded together in Weber's own magic brew.

Overview: By adding the colours of Romantic imagination to the Singspiel with echoes of Beethoven's **Fidelio**, Weber established German opera at a stroke. His model inspired countless others, including Marschner's **Hans**

Heiling; his use of >leitmotiv was an inspiration for Wagner. The core of the story is a rustic version of the Faust legend, whose opportunities for terrifying effects were also relished by Berlioz, that other great orchestrator, in **The Damnation of Faust**.

Listening

EMI 1C 183 30171-3
Berlin Phil./Keilberth
(Grümmer, Otto, Schock, Kohn, Prey)
1959

Heinrich Marschner

Born: 16th August 1795/Zittau
Died: 14th December 1861/Hanover

A significant figure in the development of German romantic opera, Marschner is now generally considered a half-way house from Weber to Wagner, despite his contemporary reputation. He composed some twenty-five stage works – ballets, incidental music, >Singspiels, pageants, comic and romantic operas. Among these latter were his finest efforts to create unified works of art for the stage – *Der Vampyr*, *Der Templer und die Jüdin*, and *Hans Heiling*. He wrote a great deal of other vocal music (including a notable output for male-voice choir) as well as instrumental works.

HANS HEILING

Prelude and three acts
Libretto: Eduard Devrient, after Karl Theodor Körner
First performance: Berlin 1833

Plot: The half-mortal gnome king Hans Heiling wants to give up his underground throne for love of Anna, a mortal woman, against the wishes of his mother, the Queen of the Spirits. Anna herself is torn: she is in love with the hunter Konrad, but Heiling threatens her with vengeance if she betrays her vow to him. And while Anna's mother wants her to marry the wealthy Heiling, his own mother – the Queen of the Spirits – warns Anna of doom unless she rejects him. When Anna opts for Konrad and reveals that Heiling is an earth spirit, Heiling is furious. Finally acknowledging the futility of pursuing a mortal woman, he and his gnomes attack Anna's wedding party until his mother appears and calls him back to his rightful domain.

The opera: *Hans Heiling* is at first sight pure German Romantic >Singspiel, full of horn calls and hunting atmosphere, simple village life, sinister magic and dark forests. But Marschner could put aside the self-contained numbers typical of Singspiel for >through-composed groupings of solos, duets, larger ensembles and choruses (the Prelude is a celebrated example). His writing is classically restrained, impressive in depicting Anna's inner distress (*Wehe mir*), and in the superbly evocative >melodrama (Act II Scene 2) spoken by Anna's mother when anxious about her daughter's whereabouts. There are >opera seria aspects to Heiling, who misuses his power but is not fundamentally a villain, and to the Queen, who resolves the final conflict as >deus ex machina. But it is clear from the Queen's relationship with her son (a psychological metaphor), from his own duality, and from the anguish of the gnome as one of the rejected 'other' people, that in subject matter this opera anticipates the future.

Overview: There are interesting links to be made with Wagner: pleading with Wotan in **The Valkyrie**, Brünnhilde, uses a melody from the Queen's Act II >aria; **The Flying Dutchman** – like Heiling, half-spirit and half-mortal – stands to lose more if betrayed by a young woman; the gnomes/dwarves who threaten the village in Marschner threaten the world in Wagner's **Rhinegold**; Konrad's sword, shattered by Heiling, will become Nothung in **The Ring**. A more significant link is the relative strength of the drama, and Marschner's propensity for larger continuous sections rather than compartmentalised numbers. The Bohemian folktales, original sources for the libretto, reappear in Dvořák's **Rusalka**.

Otto Nicolai

Born: 9th June 1810/Königsberg
Died: 11th May 1849/Berlin

Nicolai was a fine conductor with a particularly important role in the history of opera and concerts in Vienna. He wrote five operas, of which *The Merry Wives of Windsor*, an example of early romantic operà, was his most popular.

THE MERRY WIVES OF WINDSOR
Die lustigen Weiber von Windsor

Three acts
Libretto: Herman Salomon
Mosenthal, after William
Shakespeare
First performance: Berlin 1849

Plot: Fat, elderly Sir John Falstaff propositions two wealthy Windsor wives in identical letters. Frau Fluth, whose husband is excessively jealous, and Frau Reich, in dispute with hers as to whom their daughter Anna should marry, plan to punish both Falstaff and Herr Fluth. Frau Fluth makes two assignations with the old rogue, both interrupted as her husband searches for her 'lover'. To escape him the first time, Falstaff is dumped in the River Thames with the soiled linen; the second time, he is disguised as an old gossip, and gets thrashed. Fluth goes to great lengths to confirm his wife's infidelity; finding himself mistaken, he joins the women in luring Falstaff to Windsor Forest to be attacked by 'woodland sprites'. On this occasion, Anna eludes her parents and her other suitors for the man of her choice, Fenton – and it all ends amicably.

The opera: The Merry Wives is a straightforward account of the Falstaff story; its appeal lies in its easy-going manner (belying the excellent technique of the composer), an Italianate charm that sits comfortably on the bourgeois characters. Apart from the attractive overture and the final chorus, there is little music of particular distinction, but Nicolai makes up in verve for what he lacks in melodic inspiration, and the change of instrumental texture for the love scene is a felicitous touch. The comedy tends towards slapstick, with much lusty laughter over Falstaff's physical discomfiture, all of which requires an inventive conductor, and inventive singer-comedians to match.

Overview: The list of other composers who have set the Shakespeare original (*The Merry Wives of Windsor*, with a bit of plundering from the *Henry IV* plays) is impressive: Dittersdorf, Salieri, Mercadante, Verdi, Holst and Vaughan Williams. Nicolai's version inevitably pales beside the wonderful Verdi setting, much as Paisiello's **The Barber of Seville** suffers next to Rossini's. But for a Germany looking for a home-grown comic product it fitted the bill, and it is still reckoned to be a masterpiece of Romantic bourgeois comedy.

Friedrich von Flotow

Born: 26th April 1812/Teutendorf,
near Neu-Sanitz, Mecklenburg-
Schwerin
Died: 24th January 1883/Darmstadt

A prolific composer with a flair for well-crafted music of graceful charm, Flotow wrote nearly thirty operas as well as several ballet scores and the incidental music for stage plays. His two most successful works – *Alessandro Stradella* and *Martha* – were written within three years of one another in a career that spanned over forty years.

MARTHA

Four acts
Libretto: Friedrich Wilhelm Riese,
after the ballet by Vernoy de Saint-
Georges
First performance: Vienna 1847

Plot: In the time of Queen Anne, Lady Harriet, jaded with life at court, offers herself for hire as a serving-girl with her companion Nancy at Richmond Fair. A prosperous farmer, Plunkett, and Lionel, his foster-brother, hire 'Martha' and 'Julia', who find that their little diversion has bound them to live and work for a year on Plunkett's farm. Worse, they and the farmers are attracted to one another, but as the difference in social position makes romantic developments impossible, they escape. Lionel and Harriet pine for each other, but chance meetings in Richmond Park lead to misunderstandings and resentment, compounded when Harriet proposes marriage once Lionel has turned out to be the Earl of Derby. It takes a full-scale reconstruction of the servant-hiring scene at the Fair to lift the young man's morbid depression and bring both couples happily together.

The opera: A mixture of Italianate >arias and >Singspiel ditties, *Martha* is like >opéra-comique without spoken dialogue. Its humour rests on a joke in poor taste – aristocrats slumming, with little regard for the feelings or rights of those they dupe. Yet there is a freshness about the music which masks both the unconscious cynicism of the plot and its well-worn comic/romantic situations. Flotow's writing for chorus and ensemble is inventive and eminently singable, and with Harriet and Lionel he showed real flair; their music is always appealing, even affecting. The ballad *The Last Rose of Summer*, a happy inclusion, is well integrated into the score, and Lionel's famous *Ach, so fromm*, a lovely aria, has a fine, clean line (heard in Italian translation as '*M'appari*', it gained the nickname 'Emma Parry', an hilarious reference to the tenor's 'Italianate' vocal style – try it!).

Overview: *Martha* has lasted particularly well, although its considerable popularity in 19th-century England is only partly due to its rather dubious 'English' setting, more to the recurrence of *The Last Rose of Summer* in a tuneful score. With its mixture of styles, its patter music for chorus and its light-hearted treatment of emotional disorder, it also pleased the audiences who had responded to Rossini, the same audience that would take Gilbert and Sullivan's operettas to their hearts.

Listening

Eurodisc 25422
Bavarian State Opera/Wallberg
(Popp, Jerusalem)
1977

Richard Wagner

Born: 22nd May 1813/Leipzig
Died: 13th February 1883/Venice

Wagner's operas form almost his entire significant output. After *Rienzi*, a >grand opera, *The Flying Dutchman*, *Tannhäuser* and *Lohengrin* are German Romantic operas, followed by *The Ring* cycle and *Tristan und Isolde* (music dramas), a comedy (*Die Meistersinger*) and the religiose *Parsifal*. His operas, many of them among the longest in the repertory (the Ring cycle probably being opera's most extensive conception), call for singers of power and stamina, a vast orchestra, and ambitious staging. In the later works, particularly *Tristan und Isolde*, his musical language seemed to take chromatic harmony about as far as it could go, paving the way for younger composers to introduce other harmonic idioms. His use of >leitmotiv became the skeleton and the flesh of his music, so thoroughly applied as to overshadow the use of leitmotivs by any other composers, helping to give the orchestra relatively greater weight than the voice. His theories about staging, and the importance of drama vis-à-vis music have remained of signal importance.

Further reading: Ernest Newman – *The Life of Richard Wagner* (repr. Cambridge 1976); Carl Dahlhaus – *Richard Wagner's Music Dramas* (Eng. trans. Cambridge 1979); Richard Wagner – *My Life* (Eng. trans. Cambridge 1983).

RIENZI

Five acts
Libretto: The composer, after Edward Bulwer Lytton and Mary Russell Mitford
First performance: Dresden 1842

Plot: Rienzi, Tribune of the Roman people, finds the rival patrician families of Orsini and Colonna fighting in the course of abducting his sister, Irene, and forces them to stay within the law. The patricians plot against him, are thwarted, and sentenced to death. Colonna's son Adriano, in love with Irene, torn between loyalty to father and class and Rienzi's vision of freedom for all, persuades Rienzi to forgive the patricians – who promptly mobilise an army to march on Rome. Rienzi leads the defending army, and Orsini and Colonna are killed. Adriano now throws in his lot with a group of malcontents, whose cause is well served when Rienzi is excommunicated. Only Irene remains loyal to Rienzi, despite Adriano's urgings that she abandon him. When Rienzi addresses the people, they stone him and set fire to the Capitol. Adriano, in a last effort to save Irene, perishes with the brother and sister whose power he has undermined.

The opera: *Rienzi* is >grand opera in the Spontini manner, studded with processions, marches, battles, hymns, noble proclaimings, prolonged ensembles and a large-scale ballet/pantomine. It is well done – the ensembles are actually singable, every procession has its own musical character, there are trumpet calls and tolling bells. Much of the writing is fresh and incisive, individuality showing in the musical muscle of the conspiracy scene, the fine declamatory style of Adriano's *Ha, meine Liebe*, and above all Rienzi's celebrated Act V prayer,

anticipated in the overture, with its beautiful >motif. But the grandeur and constant excitement rarely touch the deeper feelings. Adriano, a >trouser role, is reminiscent of an >opera seria hero: the pattern of his vacillations maintains the continuity between the first part (Rienzi's triumph) and the last (Rienzi's downfall). The work's real emotional and vocal weight is given to Rienzi's passionate love of the people, and Irene's loyalty to him. These are themes Wagner would develop in future works; here, while they show political and moral substance (as in Rienzi's splendid denunciation of the greedy, parasitic and self-indulgent nobles). They are not enough to sustain five long acts.

Overview: In *Rienzi*, written in vain for Paris, Adriano's situation recalls Arnold's in **William Tell** (Rossini). Beethoven's Leonore (**Fidelio**) was an unmistakeable influence on Adriano's *Gerechter Gott*. Wagner's processional treatment of chorus is retained to great effect in **Tannhäuser**, and Irene's nobility foreshadows Elsa (**Lohengrin**) – but few people seeing *Rienzi* would have predicted that **The Flying Dutchman** was just around the corner.

Further reading: John Deathridge – *Wagner's Rienzi* (Oxford 1977).

Listening

EMI 1C 193 0277 6/80
Dresden State Opera/Hollreiser
(Kollo, Wennberg, Martin)
1976

THE FLYING DUTCHMAN
Der fliegende Holländer

Three acts
Libretto: The composer, after Heinrich Heine
First performance: Dresden 1843

Plot: The Dutchman, a legendary figure, has been condemned to sail the seas for eternity until redeemed by the constancy of a woman. He is allowed to land once every seven years to seek this woman. He yearns for death: after one more sojourn on the land he faces eternal damnation on the seas. Since hearing this legend, Senta, daugher of a ship's captain, has felt alienated from her life, and from Erik, her betrothed. When her father brings home a strange ship's captain she accepts marriage with him, sensing his identity, and pledges her devotion. But the stranger overhears Erik pleading with her, and assuming she loves Erik after all he sets sail in despair, having confirmed that he is the Flying Dutchman. But Senta, crying out her love, hurls herself after him into the sea. His ship sinks, and she and he, transfigured, rise up to heaven.

The opera: In inflating this slim story into a grand Romantic opera, Wagner has diluted its central drama: the gripping tale gains little from Erik's unrequited feelings, or Senta's prosaic father, Daland. Musically it is equally uneven: the famous overture starts with striking ideas, but dissipates their

The chorus in Mike Ashman's production of *The Flying Dutchman* (Royal Opera House 1986)

forceful energy in lesser material. Yet the work demonstrates powerful orginality. The obsessed Senta is a magnificent operatic character – a true bride-of-the-soul for the haunted Dutchman: his Act I narration and, above all, her ballad (the crux of the whole opera) evoke an intense imaginative world, weakened in their uninspired duet but reaffirmed in the climactic exchanges of the final scene. The music of sea and storm, the sailors' chantings and the Steersman's Song make for vivid 'local colour'; the well-known Spinning Chorus establishes the busy, fussy life from which Senta breaks free. The recurring phrases connected with the Dutchman, and with the Redemption represented by Senta, are not yet >leitmotivs – they do not create the texture of the music – but in their potency they dominate Wagner's conception, giving it the sense of a whole.

Overview: *The Flying Dutchman* is very much a German Romantic opera: Marschner's **Hans Heiling** was the model for the Dutchman, and the Spinning Chorus is a large-scale piece deriving from Agathe's first scene with Aennchen in Weber's **Der Freischütz**. The Steersman's Song would reappear in **The Trojans** (Berlioz). But Wagner's

operas are most interesting compared with one another – and Senta, the pure woman required to sacrifice herself unconditionally to redeem the blighted man, is a favourite Wagnerian theme, reappearing in **Tannhäuser**, **Lohengrin**, and **The Twilight of the Gods**.

Listening

Philips 416 300-1PH 4 416 300-4PH2
CD: 416 300-2PH3
Bayreuth Festival/Nelsson
(Balslev, Estes)
1985

TANNHÄUSER

Three acts
Libretto: The composer
First performance: Dresden 1845, revised Paris 1861

Plot: Tannhäuser, a minstrel knight, has spent a year in thrall to Venus, goddess of love. To celebrate his return to the Wartburg, the minstrels set up a Song Contest, where he is reunited with Elisabeth, his former love. Wolfram

hymns chaste love; in answer, Tannhäuser sings of erotic passion. Only Elisabeth's heart-broken intervention prevents the knights killing him for this cruel insult. He makes a pilgrimage to Rome to seek absolution, but the Pope pronounces that he cannot be redeemed, any more than the Papal staff might sprout leaves. Wretched, he returns greedy for Venus again – but is saved when reminded of Elisabeth, who after praying daily for him has abandoned hope of his return, and died. At her hearse, asking her spirit to pray for him, Tannhäuser dies – as pilgrims bring news that the Pope's staff has bloomed with green leaves.

The opera: Wagner modified the score of Act I to provide the ballet required for Paris, but *Tannhäuser* remains an essentially German work, combining two legends, the redemption of Tannhäuser and the medieval tale of Heinrich von Ofterdingen at the Song Contest. It is particularly accessible as a 'popular' opera, with its beautiful Pilgrims' Chorus, the processional march before the Song Contest, Elisabeth's ringing *Dich, teure Halle* and Wolfram's song to the evening star (Act III), not to mention the splendid overture. In the battle for Tannhäuser's soul, the attractions of profane love which possesses (Venus) and heavenly love which redeems (Elisabeth, aided by the noble-spirited Wolfram) are clearly demarcated in music of contrasting styles. Where Venus offers sensual delights, and curses Tannhäuser for leaving her, Elisabeth makes her poignant plea to the angry knights, *Ich fleh' für ihn* – and, as with Solomon's Judgment, the claimant who is less possessive gains the victory.

Overview: *Tannhäuser* is interesting more for itself than as a pointer to what Wagner would do later, in the music dramas. Yet two single passages were the seed of greater things to come: the young shepherd on the Wartburg who pipes and sings unaccompanied would reappear at a crucial stage in **Tristan**; and the manner of Tannhäuser's Act III 'Rome narrative', no >aria but a long-breathed free declamation with a dramatic life of its own, would become the very core of works such as **The Valkyrie** or **Tristan und Isolde** where Wagner shed conventional forms.

141

Listening

Decca SET506 4 K80K43
CD: 414 581-2DH2
VPO/Solti
(Kollo, Dernesch, Ludwig)
1971

LOHENGRIN

Three acts
Libretto: The composer
First performance: Weimar 1850

Plot: Elsa is accused of murdering her
younger brother, Godfrey, heir to the
throne, by the regent Frederick and his
wife Ortrud who seek the throne for
themselves. A knight in shining armour
appears, in a boat drawn by a swan, to
champion Elsa's innocence. He will
marry her, if she swears not to ask his
name or origins. She swears; Frederick
is defeated. But the sorceress Ortrud
works subtly to persuade Elsa to break
her vow, and she puts the forbidden
questions to her husband. Sadly he
reveals that he is Lohengrin, Knight of
the Grail; once known, he must leave.
Ortrud triumphs further: she announces
that the waiting swan is Godfrey,
bewitched by her, never to return to
Elsa. Lohengrin prays; the swan
becomes Godfrey again – but Elsa falls
dead as Lohengrin sails off.

The opera: Although *Lohengrin*
remains a Romantic opera, with a
strong, conventional choral element
(wonderfully vivid in building up the
knight's arrival), the elaborate set of
>leitmotivs used to label characters
and ideas would later become the very
basis of the music dramas starting with
The Ring cycle. To ensure that the main
characters embody the principles they
represent, Wagner aimed at a contrast
in their styles, foregoing dramatic
realism. Inevitably, the villainous Ortrud
is the most interesting, especially in her
powerful Act II scene with Frederick
and then Elsa; a sorceress invoking old,
pagan Gods, her evil energy partly
defeats Lohengrin. The fragile beauty of
the Prelude is extended into Elsa's dream
(Act I) and her song of love's happiness
(Act II); rapt, rapturous, exalted, she

represents the vulnerability of the Grail,
for Lohengrin shows always a deep
inner conviction, most radiant in his Act
III narrative. The two most famous
numbers – the Bridal Chorus and the
Prelude to Act III – are somewhat
outside the musical feeling of the opera.

Overview: Spotting similarities among
Wagner's operas is a fascinating game:
the Prelude to *Lohengrin* anticipates
that of **Parsifal**; Elsa's Dream evokes
Brünnhilde's or Isolde's great moments;
Lohengrin's Farewell occasionally
suggests Wotan's. Other resonances
place Wagner amongst his peers. The
first bars of Verdi's strings-only Prelude
to **La traviata** strikingly resemble the
Lohengrin Prelude. The Forbidden
Questions and their dread
consequences – in Wagner a supreme
statement of male ego – were put to
effective dramatic use by Puccini in
Turandot and Bartók in **Duke
Bluebeard**. Elsa is a prototype of the
ecstatic Wagnerian heroine who
subjugates herself to her Glorious Man,
a flower to be crushed underfoot, a
stream to travel alongside his path.
Whatever might Wagner have thought
of Bizet's **Carmen**?

Listening

EMI EX290955-3 4 EX290955-5
VPO/Kempe
(Thomas, Grümmer, Ludwig, Fischer-
Dieskau)
1962/3

TRISTAN UND ISOLDE

Three acts
**Libretto: The composer, after
Gottfried von Strassburg**
First performance: Munich 1865

Plot: Isolde's lover was killed by the
Cornish knight, Tristan. Subsequently
she found Tristan wounded and
helpless, but, strangely unable to kill
him, cured him instead. Now, as though
none of this has happened, he has
forced her to sail from her native
Ireland to marry old King Mark of
Cornwall. Brooding angrily, she
determines that they should both die,
and sends for him. He is also wretched,

and welcomes the death potion prepared by Isolde's servant, Brangäne – but it is a love potion, and their unspoken passion for one another is suddenly released, just as they are welcomed joyously in Cornwall. Nightly, fearing the harsh reality of the day, Tristan and Isolde pursue their secret relationship. But a malign knight, Melot, warns King Mark, and the lovers are discovered together. Mark is deeply grieved: Tristan lets Melot wound him, and is taken by his faithful servant Kurvenal to Brittany, where he waits in torment for Isolde to come again. At last she comes, he dies in her arms – and when King Mark arrives, full of understanding and forgiveness, Isolde dies, in mystical union with her beloved.

The opera: In embodying the lovers' yearning for fulfilment, Wagner took >chromaticism so far that most contemporary singers or orchestral musicians could not cope with it (after numerous rehearsals, the first production was abandoned as impossible). The two main roles are exhausting but deeply rewarding, their spiritual intensity creating music of incomparable sensual beauty. *Tristan's* >leitmotivs evoke psychological states or atmosphere; the very first phrases of the Prelude conjure up the Romantic urge towards night, a dark world of imagination and passion, giving way to a bleak daytime element in the Sailor's wistful song. The ecstasy of consummation proving temporary, the Act III Prelude is charged with tragic frustration, reflected in the strange piping of the Shepherd. Tristan, in delirious agony from his festering wound, has to accept his own guilt in forging their great love before he can die. The tremendous series of monologues in which he does this is the real climax of the opera, although when at the end Isolde expresses the triumphant fulfilment of their love in death, her >liebestod, her music reaches the level of the sublime.

Overview: *Tristan* could be described as a medieval tale of little action and much inner drama, in which two lovers die and an ageing husband is left grieving. All this is true of **Pelléas et Mélisande**; it is method that makes the difference between the two scores, for Wagner was a putter-inner, Debussy a taker-outer. Debussy pares away almost everything to expose the deepest recesses of the unconscious; Wagner conveys his lovers' sexual-mystic passion with the richest possible materials. *Tristan's* musical language was epoch-making – Mahler, Strauss and Schoenberg internalised it; a host of composers imitated it.

Listening

EMI EX290684-3 4 EX290684-9
CD: CDS7 47322-8
Angel CD: CDCD47321
Philharmonia/Furtwängler
(Flagstad, Suthaus)

DIE MEISTERSINGER VON NURNBERG
The Mastersingers of Nuremberg

Three acts
Libretto: The composer
First performance: Munich 1868

Plot: Pogner, a member of the Guild of Mastersingers, offers marriage to his daughter Eva as the prize in a song-contest at Nuremberg's St John's Day festival. The knight Walther is determined to win Eva, but at an early preliminary trial before the Guild his song is condemned as lacking regard for the rules. Of the Mastersingers only the cobbler Hans Sachs recognises in Walther a new, creative spirit worth fostering. Although Sachs, a widower, has himself considered wooing Eva, he assists the young lovers by grooming Walther to qualify as a Mastersinger. Another member of the Guild, Beckmesser, who has ambitions to win Eva, steals Walther's song, assuming it is by Sachs – but his performance of it is a travesty. Walther, demonstrating its true worth as a Mastersong, receives the plaudits of the Mastersingers and the people, and Eva's hand.

The opera: In contrast with **Tristan**, *Die Meistersinger* is mainly >diatonic, affirming the freshness and clarity of daytime (especially the morning) against the confusion of night-time.

143

>Chromaticism is used mainly for the profound feelings of Hans Sachs, beautifully conveyed in the Prelude to Act III (the core of the opera) and in his monologue musings. Though tinged with sentiment, the intimate scenes of Act III are the finest in the opera, displaying the different facets of Sachs's humanity, and culminating in the lovely quintet. Next to Sachs, who really existed, Walther cuts a curiously old-fashioned figure. His songs are supposed to be unfettered by 'tradition', yet in their warm lyricism they are readily accessible, hardly 'modern'. Wagner makes much of the people's instinctive response to true art, which leads him to a xenophobic hymning of pure German music which, although acceptable to his local audience, is inappropriate to the warm, reasonable voice of Sachs. There is the same loss of balance in his grotesque caricature of Beckmesser. The poor chap never has a chance: Wagner simply puts him in the stocks to sling mud at him (doubtless with great satisfaction, as he is supposed to represent Wagner's enemy, the famous critic Hanslick).

Overview: *Die Meistersinger*, Wagner's only important 'happy' work, is sometimes considered the equal of the indisputably great comedies, **Figaro** and **Falstaff**. Yet, especially in its portrayal of small-town life, it has more in common with Nicolai's **The Merry Wives of Windsor**, although its score is much more rewarding. The overture is one of those which are vastly popular on the concert platform, and the quintet shares the still magic of the quartet in **Fidelio** and the final trio in **Der Rosenkavalier**. Hans Sachs is Wagner's best-loved character; Beckmesser is a figure of ridicule deriving from the Rossini grotesques. A small point: the relationship between Sachs and his apprentice David puts the behaviour of Britten's **Peter Grimes** in context, reminding us that the apprentice was his master's property, however unpalatable that may appear without *Die Meistersinger*'s jocularity or sentiment.

Listening

1 EMI m RLS 740 4 TC-RLS 740
Berlin State Opera/Kempe
(Frantz, Schock, Grümmer)
1956

2 DG 2713 011 4 3378 068
CD: 415 278-2GH4
German Opera Orch./Jochum
(Fischer-Dieskau, Ligendza, Domingo)
1975

THE NIBELUNGS' RING – THE RHINEGOLD Der Ring des Nibelungen – Das Rheingold

Four scenes
Libretto: The composer
First performance: Munich 1869

Plot: The Nibelung dwarf Alberich steals wondrous gold from the River Rhine; forswearing love, he has it fashioned into a ring of immense power, with which he plans to rule the world. Enslaving the other dwarves, he builds up a glorious treasure, and gets his brother Mime to make the Tarnhelm, a helmet whose wearer can change shape and identity instantaneously. The god Wotan has contracted with the giants, Fasolt and Fafner, to help build Valhalla, a glorious fortress from which the gods will rule. Fricka, Wotan's wife, is sceptical of his methods, especially as the giants believe their payment will be Freia, goddess of eternal youth, without whom the gods will lose their immortality. Loge, god of fire, tells Wotan of the Nibelung hoard; they descend to Niebelheim and capture Alberich. To go free Alberich must hand over his entire treasure, and he bitterly curses the ring: it will always give misery to its possessor. Now from Wotan the giants demand enough treasure to hide Freia from their view, including the Tarnhelm and the ring – and Fafner immediately kills Fasolt for the ring. Wotan had reluctantly accepted a warning from Erda, the Earth Mother, against the ring; now he sees the power of Alberich's curse. As the gods enter Valhalla, the Rhine maidens bewail the loss of the Rhinegold.

The opera: *The Rhinegold*, the 'preliminary evening' before the three operas in The Ring cycle, presents the

Wotan and Loge from *The Rhinegold*
(Welsh National Opera 1983)

mythological protagonists whose
concerns generate the later human
drama. Alberich always forswore love
for greed and power; it was natural for
him to want the ring, and for Wotan to
prevent his regaining it. But Wotan
never intended to return it to the Rhine
maidens, and after his false dealings
with the giants, he used it to ransom the
gods' immortality. Wotan is the most
complex personality in the cycle: he
has sought absolute power by trickery
and bargaining; finding it unattainable
he manoeuvres desperately to maintain
the balance of good and evil. The
Rhinegold's ceremonial declamatory
exchanges and vivid scene-painting
contain the source of what is to come
musically, and right from the opera's
extraordinary 'pre-music', where the
music seems to well up from the very

core of the earth, it is fascinating to
trace the >leitmotivs which make up
the very substance of the entire cycle.

Overview: No other important opera
exists, either musically or dramatically,
in terms of its successors rather than
itself. And as the story of Siegfried
originates in the machinations of gods,
giants and dwarves, *The Rhinegold*
contains no human characters at all,
whereas most opera, concerned with
humans, only occasionally lets in a god
as >deus ex machina.

Listening

Decca 414 101 1DH3 4 414 101-4DH2
CD: 414 101-2DH3
London 414 101-1LH3 4 414 101-4LH2
CD: 414 101-2LH3
VPO/Solti
(Flagstad, London, Svanholm)
1958

THE NIBELUNGS' RING
– THE VALKYRIE
Der Ring des Nibelungen
– Die Walküre

Three acts
Libretto: The composer
First performance: Munich 1870

Plot: A young man, weaponless, gains refuge in Hunding's house. The stranger and Hunding's wife, Sieglinde, deeply drawn to one another, discover they are twins. Naming him Siegmund, she shows him a sword stuck fast in a tree, which he wrests free before they rush away, passionately in love. These two are the god Wotan's children; he is shaping their destiny, and he orders his great Valkyrie daughter, Brünnhilde, to protect Siegmund in the forthcoming battle with Hunding. But Fricka, goddess of marriage, insists on justice for Hunding against the incestuous adulterers, and Wotan, his plan in ruins, must now command Brünnhilde to protect Hunding. Brünnhilde understands Wotan's innermost feelings; sorrowfully telling Siegmund that he will die, she is so moved by his love for Sieglinde that she decides after all to protect him in the fight – but Wotan shatters his sword and he is killed. Announcing that Sieglinde will give birth to Siegfried, Brünnhilde helps her escape with the pieces of the sword. Now Brünnhilde faces Wotan's punishment for disobeying him; she can no longer be a Valkyrie, and will be woken from a deep sleep by the first man who sees her. But, kissing her farewell, Wotan agrees to her request: that the rock where she sleeps be surrounded with fire so that only the bravest hero can discover her.

The opera: The warmest, most human of the four operas in the Ring cycle, *The Valkyrie* prepares us for the story of **Siegfried** and his discovery of Brünnhilde. Yet nothing in **The Rhinegold** prepares the audience for the blooming of its >leitmotivs into the lyrical outpouring of awakening love that is *The Valkyrie's* Act I. Neither in the third act of Siegfried, nor in **Tristan**, did Wagner achieve such clear,

uncluttered writing, so little tortuous discussion, and such grateful parts for his singers. And in Act III he gives to Sieglinde the single most beautiful phrase in the cycle – *O hehrstes Wunder! Heilige Maid! The Valkyrie* also sets the stage for the downfall of Wotan. In the first act, his plans are in the ascendant; by the time he says farewell to his beloved Valkyrie daughter he has lost the initiative, and become a genuinely sympathetic character. More than the laboured spectacle of the Ride Valkyries, or the oddly unfierce fire shimmering around Brünnhilde's rock, it is Wagner's insight into the intensity of human feeling to make this opera memorable.

Overview: *The Valkyrie* approaches Verdi's **Otello** or Wagner's own **Tristan und Isolde** as one of the great operas of romantic love even though this element takes up barely half the opera. It also conveys beautifully the deep-rooted love of daughter and father at a more epic level than Handel's **Tamerlano** or Verdi's **Simon Boccanegra**.

Listening

1 Philips CD: 412 478-2PH4
  Bayreuth Festival Orch./Böhm
  (Nilsson, Rysanek, King, Adam)
  1967
2 Decca 414 105-1DH 4 414 105-4DH4
  CD: 414 105-2DH4
  London 414 105-1LH4
  CD: 414 105-2LH4
  VPO/Solti
  (Nilsson, Crespin, King, Hotter)
  1965

THE NIBELUNGS' RING
– SIEGFRIED
Der Ring des Nibelungen
– Siegfried

Three acts
Libretto: The composer
First performance: Bayreuth 1876

Plot: Sieglinde has died giving birth to Siegfried; the dwarf Mime has brought him up. Mime is deeply frustrated; he is unable to weld the pieces of the shattered sword, Nothung, with which he hopes Siegfried will take the ring from the giant-turned-dragon, Fafner. Siegfried, who knows no fear, forges Nothung, and kills Fafner without much ado. After tasting the dragon's blood by chance, he can understand the song of a bird who tells him to take from Fafner's hoard only the ring and the magic Tarnhelm; undirected by the gods, ignorant of the ring's power, he need not fear Alberich's curse on its possessor. Mime clearly intends to drug and kill him, so Siegfried, who has always loathed him, kills him instead. Led by the bird, he approaches a rock encircled by fire. Wotan confronts him – but the God's spear, which once shattered Nothung, is now shattered in turn. Passing through the fire to the summit, Siegfried finds Brünnhilde asleep. When he realises she is a woman – the first he has ever seen – he is consumed with fear. But he wakes her – and she, as his passion becomes white-hot, is drawn with him into an entirely new condition: radiant love.

The opera: In this myth the young hero tames a bear, forges an invincible sword, blows a silver horn, kills a dragon, talks to a bird, walks through a fire, and wakes a sleeping beauty with a kiss. But *Siegfried* is partly a pre-Freudian allegory, during which time moves swiftly, unnoticed. It is a boy, curious about his origins and his future, who plays in the forest, and kills Fafner with the confidence of the young. An aggressive adolescent brushes Wotan aside; an anxious, ardent youth greets Brünnhilde. It is hard not to feel a sneaking sympathy for Mime, and we sense Wotan's baffled anger at the gracelessness of his grandson, but as a lover Siegfried becomes sensitive. The opera may well seem static, being a series of duologues, yet with a good >heldentenor the forging of Nothung is a magnificent climax to Act I, and in Act II the magical episode of the forest murmurs, including Siegfried's by-play with his makeshift pipe, is, as it should be, enchanting. Most extraordinary is the third act, each of its scenes attaining a new plane, the concentrated tension of the previous exchanges in the subterranean cave and at the foot of the mountain opening out on the summit

into a love-duet which is one of the glories of operatic music.

Overview: With Mime, as with Beckmesser in **Die Meistersinger**, the singer has possibilities for a >buffa interpretation harking back through Verdi's Melitone (**The Force of Destiny**) to Rossini's grotesques. And this huge opera recalls another tale of magic talismans and fearful trials through which lovers prove their worth – Mozart's **Magic Flute**.

Listening

1 Philips CD: 412 483-2PH4
  Bayreuth Festival Orch./Böhm
  (Nilsson, Windgassen, Wohlfahrt, Adam)
  1966
2 Decca 414 L110 1DH4 4 414 110-4DH4
  CD: 414 110-2DH4
  London 414 110–1LH4 4 414 110–4LH4
  CD: 414 110-2LH4
  VPO/Solti
  (Nilsson, Windgassen, Stolze, Hotter)

THE NIBELUNGS' RING – THE TWILIGHT OF THE GODS
Der Ring des Nibelungen – Götterdämmerung

Prologue and three acts
Libretto: The composer
First performance: Bayreuth 1876

Plot: The Norns, daughters of Mother Earth, finish telling their story of the fate of the world, for humans have taken control of their own destiny. The gods wait only for the ring to be returned to the Rhine so that the world will be saved from evil. The process starts when Siegfried, giving Brünnhilde the ring as a pledge, embarks on a quest for further glory. Alberich's son, Hagen, plotting to regain the ring, has made a plan with his half-brother and -sister Gunther and Gutrune; Gutrune drugs Siegfried so that he falls in love with her, forgetting Brünnhilde, and undertakes to win Gunther a glorious woman. Brünnhilde has just rejected the plea of

The Twilight of the Gods at the Royal
Opera House in 1913

her Valkyrie sister, Waltraute, that she
return her lover's ring to the Rhine,
when Siegfried appears, transformed
into Gunther's likeness by the
Tarnhelm. He wrests the ring from
Brünnhilde, not recognising her, and
abducts her as Gunther's bride.
Brünnhilde openly accuses Siegfried of
betraying her; with Hagen and Gunther,
she swears vengeance. On a hunt,
encouraged by Hagen, Siegfried recalls
how he came to love Brünnhilde – and
Hagen thrusts his spear into the one
vulnerable part of the hero's body, his
back. Hagen also kills Gunther – but
when he goes to take the ring,
Siegfried's hand rises to stop him. Then
Brünnhilde takes command: from the
Rhine maidens she has learnt the whole
process which her self-sacrifice, an
independent act, will complete.
Wearing the ring, she rides onto
Siegfried's funeral pyre. The flames
roar up; the Rhine overflows. Plunging
forward to grab the ring, Hagen is
drowned by the Rhine maidens, who
retrieve the ring from Brünnhilde's
ashes. The world is redeemed – and the
fire, reaching the heavens, consumes
the gods in Valhalla.

The opera: *The Twilight of The Gods*
is the culmination of the Ring cycle and
its longest opera. It is a tale of humans,
constantly informed by the myths and

legends of the three previous operas.
These are retold by the Norns, by
Waltraute, by Alberich, and by
Siegfried. They are also alive in the
>leitmotivs running throughout the
cycle, which evoke associations with
Alberich's curse, the Sword, Wotan's
farewell to Brünnhilde, Siegfried and
Brünnhilde's love, and so on. No key is
needed; brief, vivid, pictorial, the
leitmotivs actually make the operas
more accessible, not least the
orchestral interludes such as Siegfried's
Rhine Journey and the magnificent
Funeral March. Everything in *The
Twilight of The Gods* is therefore
charged with significance in relation to
the whole, including the conventional
set-pieces (Siegfried and Gunther's
blood-brotherhood duet, a chorus of
Gunther's vassals, and the vengeance
trio), the early love-music, and the long
crescendo of intensity from Siegfried's
rapturous dying vision of Brünnhilde to
her enthralling Immolation Scene.

Overview: Otello also presents a great
love relationship destroyed by an arch-
villain; the heroine of **The Trojans** also
dies on a funeral pyre. Rather than be
linked with Verdi or Berlioz, Wagner
would doubtless prefer a connection
with Beethoven, but their difference in
outlook was too great. At the end of
Fidelio, the villain's machinations are
thwarted by the courage of the heroine,
and the lovers can go home together –
something quite unthinkable in any

Wagner opera apart from **Die Meistersinger**.

Further reading: Curt von Westernhagen – *The Forging of the 'Ring'* (Eng. trans. Cambridge 1979).

Listening

1 Philips CD: 412 488-2PN4
   Bayreuth Festival Orch./Böhm
   (Nilsson, Windgassen, Stewart)
   1967
2 Decca 414 115-4DH
   CD: 414 115-2DH4
   London 414 115-1LH 4 414 115-4LH
   CD: 414 115-2LH4
   VPO/Solti
   (Nilsson, Windgassen, Hotter)
   1964

PARSIFAL

Three acts
Libretto: The composer, after Wolfram von Eschenbach
First performance: Bayreuth 1882

Plot: The youth Parsifal stumbles upon a holy order of knights, whose regenerating rituals centre on the Holy Grail. Amfortas, King of the Grail, is in perpetual agony: diverted by sexual contact with a beautiful woman, he lost the Holy Spear to an evil magician, Klingsor, who used it to inflict on Amfortas a wound which bleeds afresh on contact with the Grail. Not even Kundry, a strange, wild woman, can find a balm to assuage the agony. Only a pure innocent who has learnt compassion can bring Amfortas salvation. Ever hopeful, the old knight Gurnemanz brings Parsifal to the ceremony where the Grail is revealed, but although Parsifal feels intensely for Amfortas, he understands nothing. Leaving, he comes to the seductive flower garden of a magic castle. A beautiful woman – Kundry, transformed by Klingsor's spell – starts to seduce him, as she once did Amfortas, but her kiss reawakens in him Amfortas's agony; he rejects her, and she curses him. Klingsor flings the Spear at him; catching it, he makes the sign of the Cross, and the castle and its garden disappear. Delayed many years by Kundry's curse, he brings the Spear back to the Knights on a Good Friday, finding the order much weakened. Kundry, accursed since laughing at Christ on the Cross, is now serene, wishing only to serve. With the Spear, Parsifal heals Amfortas and becomes King of the Grail: Kundry, redeemed, can die at last.

The opera: Wagner called *Parsifal* a Festival Play for the Consecration of the Stage. Certainly it is less an opera than a stage ceremony: in place of action and character there is a slow, ritual acting out of the conflict between sacred and profane love. Its design is based on a simple symmetry – both outer acts start with Nature and move towards the Grail: the middle act shows the inner battle between temptation and renunciation. Wagner was always a master of theatrical effect, and there is no lack of spectacle here, although the splendour of the Grail ceremony has worn better than the Magic Garden. The seamless score is clearly set out, with >diatonic passages of mystical beauty for what is deemed good, and intense >chromaticism for the torments of Amfortas and Kundry. This mixture of pagan, Christian and medieval symbolism may seem like plain mumbo-jumbo, it won't matter – *Parsifal* stands or falls by its music.

Overview: In his last opera, Wagner's all-male higher world, full of sensual mysticism, grants Kundry no genuine role: her sexual aspect is accursed, her capacity to serve is gratuitous; once these have played their part in the story, she is made redundant. (How much more mature was Mozart, who was half Wagner's age when he wrote his unpretentious **The Magic Flute**, where hero and heroine together learn to rule the kingdom of goodness.) Yet somehow, Parsifal will produce a son, called **Lohengrin**, the hero of a much earlier Wagner opera. It took the full thirty years after *Lohengrin* for Wagner to expand his initial ideas into *Parsifal*, a conscious summation of his life's work, where art and religion become one. All the operas in between prepare us for it, especially the theme of renunciation which recurs with Wotan (**The Ring**), **Tristan**, and Hans Sachs (**Die Meistersinger**).

Further reading: Lucy Beckett – *Richard Wagner: Parsifal* (Cambridge Opera Handbook 1981).

Listening

Decca SET
CD: 417 143-2DH4
VPO/Solti
(Kollo, Hotter, Frick, Ludwig, Fischer-Dieskau)
1972

Johann Strauss

Born: 25th October 1825/Vienna
Died: 3rd June 1899/Vienna

Johann Strauss ('The Waltz King'), composer of waltzes, was inspired by Offenbach to write several Viennese operettas. *Die Fledermaus* is the greatest of its type and has become a staple of the opera repertory. *The Gypsy Baron*, *A Night in Venice*, and *Wiener Blut* have also been popular; the Hungarian element in the first of these initiated the kind of operetta taken up by Lehár and others.

DIE FLEDERMAUS
The Bat

Three acts
Libretto: Carl Haffner and Richard Genée, after Henri Meilhac and Ludovic Halévy
First performance: Vienna 1874

Plot: Eisenstein once manoeuvred his friend Falke into walking alone through Vienna dressed as a bat, and now Falke wants 'the bat's revenge'. Knowing that Eisenstein has to spend a few days in prison (a result of his own bellicosity and his lawyer's muddling), he arranges an elaborate practical joke to expose his philandering. He invites Eisenstein to attend the jaded Prince Orlofsky's party as a French nobleman, before going to prison. Others at the party are

another 'French nobleman' (the prison governor, Frank); a masked Hungarian countess (Eisenstein's wife, Rosalinde) and an actress (Rosalinde's chambermaid, Adele). With the help of champagne, Falke's plan works splendidly: Eisenstein flirts with the 'countess' before he and Frank, drunk and unaware of one another's identity, leave together for prison – where Adele pursues Frank, with whom she has formed a creative relationship. After identities have been sorted out, an unplanned complication arises: after Eisenstein had left Rosalinde 'for prison' earlier, her former suitor, the singer Alfred, had turned up to woo her, only to be imprisoned in her husband's place. When Eisenstein plays the outraged husband over Alfred's visit, Rosalinde parries with the news that she had been the masked Countess. Eisenstein has been exposed, but there is liberal forgiveness – and champagne – all round.

The opera: The third act is often the Achilles heel of an operetta; here dialogue overburdens it. Despite this drawback, *Die Fledermaus* has an unusually good libretto (largely Genée's work), and is an irresistible celebration of the Viennese waltz and other popular dances. The Overture's promise of riches to come is fulfilled time and time again. It is not only that Strauss produced many melodies – and what melodies! – but that they are appropriate, and cleverly characterised. The mock tragic trio *So muss allein ich bleiben* would be beautiful in any context; here it is offset by each character's irrepressible delight at the secret prospect of an evening to remember (*O je, o je, wie rührt mich dies*) – a dramatic, as well as a melodic, inspiration. Alfred is the classic unstoppable tenor (great fun for the singer) whose drinking song includes what must be opera's most seductive phrase (*Glücklich ist, wie vergisst*) – it certainly works on Rosalinde, who joins in. And to conclude the lovely *Brüderlein* in Act II, there is the woozy *Duidu, duidu*, doubtless what the angels sing in heaven when they're tipsy. Other memorable moments include the joyous 'vengeance' trio when Eisenstein is exposed in Act III, Orlofsky's two numbers and Rosalinde's csárdás (both particularly vulnerable to 'operatic' oversinging, Orlofsky's less so when cast, against tradition, with a male), and the two concluding choruses, *Ha, welch ein Fest* (Act II) and *Champagner hat's verschüldet* (Act III). Choose your own favourites.

Overview: *Die Fledermaus* is traditional New Year's Eve fare at many opera houses, where Orlofsky's party becomes the excuse for singers' guest appearances. This indulgence can distract from the work's verve and pace; so can the speaking part of the gaoler, Frosch, when played to the hilt by a beloved stage personality. Yet indulgence is the basis of Viennese operetta – it is so knowing, mixing sparkle with *gemütlich* charm rather than the mordant wit or zany satire of the French. And the cynicism in *Die Fledermaus* protects it from sentimentality – a safeguard that fell away in the many works it inspired. Offenbach could be proud that his own splendid output was the impetus for such a masterpiece.

Listening

1 Preiser PR135035/6
Vienna State Opera/Krauss
(Patzak, Gueden, Dermota, Lipp, S. Wagner)
1950
2 DG 2707 088 4 3370 009
CD: 415 646-2GH2
Bavarian State Opera/C. Kleiber
(Prey, Varady, Kollo, Popp, Kusche, Weikl, Rebroff)
1976

Engelbert Humperdinck

Born: 1st September 1854/Siegburg, near Bonn
Died: 27th September 1921/ Neustrelitz

Humperdinck assisted Wagner in the preparation of *Parsifal* at Bayreuth, and later became a teacher and a music critic. *Hansel and Gretel*, his first opera, gained lasting success; of his later compositions *Königskinder* was the most notable. His incidental music, mainly for Max Reinhardt's productions of plays by Shakespeare and other great dramatists, is of considerable interest. He also wrote many songs and choral works.

HANSEL AND GRETEL

Three acts
Libretto: Adelheid Wette, after the brothers Grimm
First performance: Weimar 1893

Plot: Too hungry to work, Hansel and Gretel are sent to the forest to forage for strawberries. Finding themselves lost, they say their prayers, and the Sandman puts them to sleep. After a beautiful dream they wake to see a house made of cake and sweets, and are nibbling at it when a witch emerges; she casts a spell over them, puts Hansel in a cage for fattening up, and smacks her lips over the plump Gretel. The children show remarkable presence of mind under these trying conditions, cottoning on to the Witch's plans for cooking Gretel, learning a crucial spell and eventually pushing her into the oven. It burns fiercely and explodes, freeing a troop of ginger-bread children. Hansel and Gretel's parents discover their children at last, and the Witch has become a huge gingerbread cake.

The opera: An enchanging mixture of children's singing games and lush Wagnerian harmonies and textures, *Hansel and Gretel* sparked off a vogue in fairy operas, and remains the most popular of them all. The music in childlike/folk idiom (of which *Brüderchen, komm tanz' mit mir* is the most famous) runs throughout the opera. The Witch, characterised as spritely rather than really frightening, has a particularly wacky number of this type (*Hurr hopp hopp hopp*); she is no match for the two children, her spells being merely 'Hocus pocus'. Of the music treated in a Wagnerian manner, the children sing only the Evening Prayer (it is taken up in the Overture and in the Dream Pantomime that ends the second act); the authentic Wagnerian tone of the mother's early monologue is never really developed, and it is left to the purely orchestral passages to do the Wagnerian service compulsory in the 1890s.

Overview: Humperdinck's famous opera started as a play with incidental music that he and his sister wrote for her children. His forest in *Hansel and Gretel* retains some of the fairy magic which Mendelssohn or Weber conjured up so wonderfully (in their overtures to *A Midsummer Night's Dream* and **Oberon**, respectively), but it has become a domesticated, friendly place, where you can converse with birds (shades of **Siegfried**), and the Sandman and the Dew-Fairy come and go. For Hansel and Gretel themselves, full of superstitious tales about bears or witches abducting children, it would still have had the fearful elements we encounter in Weber's **Der Freischütz**. The forest remained central to the German psyche long enough for Schoenberg to draw on it for a very different purpose in **Erwartung**.

Listening

Decca D131D2 4 K131K222
CD: 421 111-2DH2
London CD: 421 111-2LH2
VPO/Solti
(Popp, Hamari)
1978

Richard Strauss

Born: 11th June 1864/Munich
Died: 8th September 1949/Garmisch-Partenkirchen

Richard Strauss was famous early for his brilliant orchestral tone-poems and then his shocking operas. Six of the operas were written with Hugo von Hofmannsthal; it is one of opera's great composer-librettist relationships (others are Mozart-da Ponte and Verdi-Boito). He composed fifteen operas,

many choral and orchestral works, and beautiful lieder.

SALOME

One act
Libretto: text after Oscar Wilde
First performance: Dresden 1905

Plot: King Herod of Judea is obsessed with Salome, the nubile daughter of his wife Herodias. The girl, irritated and jaded, is herself powerfully stirred by the voice of the imprisoned prophet, Jokanaan (John the Baptist). She persuades Narraboth, a guard helplessly in love with her, to bring Jokanaan up from his dungeon – and finds she wants him, fascinated by the whiteness of his body and the strength of his inner conviction, even more by his total rejection of her. Narraboth, stabbing himself in extreme jealousy, falls between them, unnoticed; Jokanaan descends to continue his pronouncements from his dungeon. With his disputatious followers, Herod comes outside; getting no response from Salome, he swears to reward her if she will dance for him. After doing the Dance of the Seven Veils she demands as her prize Jokanaan's head on a silver platter – a request that terrifies the superstitious king. Once she possesses the head she continues her seduction, alternately brooding and triumphant, sinking into ecstasy as she kisses its mouth – until Herod, appalled, has her killed.

The opera: Strauss's setting of *Salome* shocked its first audiences, for he had heightened the mood of restless decadence, and brought Salome's obsessed eroticism almost too close for comfort by mixing into it the harmonies of Wagner's exalted love scenes. The score's conscious modernism, with its extreme dissonance, fragmented cries and exaggerated textures, can sound dated, and the waltzy lilt and modal 'exotica' of Salome's dance do not carry adequate dramatic weight. The music is well characterised (except for the oddly ineffectual Herodias), in particular the crowded, jangling lines of dialogue, and the rock-like >diatonic utterances of Jokanaan's open brass

>motifs, heard to the end in intermittent dialogue with Salome's snaky twists of music. But the brilliant, vivid orchestration tends to outweigh the voices, which adds to the difficulty of finding a singer able to meet the vocal challenge and also convey Salome's sullied, innocent amorality.

Overview: Strauss never recovered from the sensation he caused with *Salome*, the public rejecting his apparent conservatism in the operas following the slightly less sensational **Elektra**. In fact, though no longer avant garde, he continued to develop, the sonorities and sheer craftsmanship in operas like **Arabella** and **Capriccio** being further advanced than all the fin de siècle theatricality of *Salome*. Salome herself has an almost unconscious sexual allure with the destructiveness of a monster – a combination of the nastier aspects of Berg's **Lulu** and Puccini's **Turandot**.

Listening

HMV SLS 5139 4 TC-SLS 5139
Angel SBLX 3848
VPO/Karajan
(Behrens, Baltsa, Böhm, Van Dam)
1977

ELEKTRA

One act
Libretto: Hugo von Hofmannsthal, after his adaptation of Sophocles
First performance: Dresden 1909

Plot: Queen Klytemnestra has killed her husband Agamemnon and married her accomplice Aegisthus. Haunted by fear of retribution, she has sent her son, Orestes, into exile; her daughters, Elektra and Chrysothemis, are treated no better than servants. Chrysothemis passionately wants a normal life, with children, away from the dark misery of the palace; Elektra is totally obsessed with thoughts of avenging her father. After a night of particular terror and misery, Klytemnestra confides in Elektra, who then flaunts before her hated mother the prospect of Orestes's

murderous revenge. When two strangers report that Orestes is dead, Elektra tries desperately to persuade the fearful Chrysothemis to join her in avenging their father, and then determines to do it herself. But one stranger reveals himself as Orestes; after an emotional reunion with his sister he kills his mother, then Aegisthus. Elektra, in a transport of triumphant ecstasy, drops dead.

The opera: Much is made of the advanced harmonic language of *Elektra*, whose stark dissonance, accentuated in the vast orchestra, underpinned the grim horrors in Strauss and Hofmannsthal's first collaboration, especially its central confrontation between the grotesque, ravaged Queen and her powerful daughter. Yet a large part of the glory of *Elektra* lies in the main character's exalted outpourings of warm human emotion in a non-dissonant style couched in the Wagnerian idiom. Most notable in her hymn of welcome to Orestes, it is woven into important earlier passages, such as her opening monologue to her father's spirit, and her passionate attempt to embrace Chrysothemis as a partner in vengeance. Add to these her lament for her purportedly dead brother, her sad explanation of her loss of youthful charm and Chrysothemis's anguished expression of yearning for a wholesome existence, and *Elektra* reveals itself as a tale of the persistence of the human spirit and the tragic limits of its endurance.

Overview: *Elektra* was the farthest Strauss could go along the road opened up by **Salome**, and so it stands in striking contrast to its successor, **Der Rosenkavalier**. Yet there is also a link: having created in Elektra, Chrysothemis and Klytemnestra three of the finest female singing/acting roles in the repertory, Strauss added three more in *Der Rosenkavalier* and continued in this vein (although the two in **Arabella** are a very different pair of sisters).

Listening

Acanta m DE 23073
Hamburg State Opera/Jochum
(Schlüter, Kupper, Hammer)
1943 reissued

DER ROSENKAVALIER
The Knight of the Rose

Three acts
Libretto: Hugo von Hofmannsthal
First performance: Dresden 1911

Plot: In mid-18th-century Vienna, the beautiful Marschallin is just approaching young middle age. Her current lover, the impulsive seventeen-year-old Count Oktavian, adores her. During an early morning visit from her country cousin, Baron Ochs, the Marschallin suggests that Oktavian act as emissary in presenting the silver rose later that day to Ochs's intended, young Sophie Faninal. Oktavian and Sophie fall in love, and Ochs's own clumsy arrogance destroys any chance of a positive response from the eager, romantic girl. He soothes himself with the thought of his coming assignation at an inn with the Marschallin's fresh-faced young servant, Mariandel. 'Mariandel' is really Oktavian: in disguise to avoid compromising the Marschallin, 'she' had attracted the Baron's interest during his visit; the assignation will compromise Ochs in front of Sophie's father, Faninal, leaving Sophie free for Oktavian. Faninal is indeed sufficiently outraged to put an end to the Baron's hope of marrying into this *nouveau riche* family, and the way

is already clear for Oktavian when the Marschallin appears. Always gracious, and wise in the ways of love, she makes it easy for the ecstatic young lovers.

The opera: The rich, lustrous sound of the prelude (the love-making of the Marschallin and Oktavian) and the lovers' banter which opens the opera serves notice that in *Der Rosenkavalier* Strauss and Hofmannsthal had created a romantic opera, using gloriously anachronistic music (the waltz came in a century after the period portrayed) with a wry sophistication very representative of the early 20th century This complex conception, which also incorporates >buffa comedy, has elicited criticisms of over-elaboration and long-windedness – minor characters abound, the setting in each act is meticulously built up, and every sentiment is fully expressed. The best character is the boorish Baron Ochs, who is perfectly believable when not vulgarised in performance; his self-indulgent >Credo (the waltz *Mit mir*) is an inspiration. having Oktavian as a >trouser-role creates many opportunities for female vocal textures, 'his' final trio with Sophie and the Marschallin bringing the music to a ravishing peak. It is not equalled by the young lovers' duet, with its overtones of

Jessye Norman in the title role of *Ariadne auf Naxos* at the Royal Opera House in 1985

The Magic Flute, but then those who lose out – the Baron and the Marschallin – interest us more.

Overview: Written in the looming shadow of the end of the civilisation it celebrates, *Der Rosenkavalier* is said to be the last great romantic opera (**Ariadne, Arabella** and **Capriccio** all make use of nostalgic Viennese or Parisian settings, but they are more modern works on a smaller scale). Inevitably, the characters in *Rosenkavalier* are seen to reflect some of their predecessors, particularly in Mozart's **The Marriage of Figaro** – Oktavian is certainly a development of Cherubino, and some see a touch of the Countess Almaviva in the Marschallin. But Baron Ochs, for all that he continues a long line of >buffo comics, is an original on the scale of Verdi's **Falstaff**.

Further reading: Alan Jefferson – *Richard Strauss: Der Rosenkavalier* (Cambridge Opera Handbook 1985).

Listening

Decca SET 418 4 K3N23
CD: 414 493-2DH3
London OSA 1435
CD: 414 493-2LH3
Vienna State Opera/Solti
(Crespin, Minton, Donath, Jungwirth)
1969

ARIADNE AUF NAXOS
Ariadne on Naxos

Prologue and one act
Libretto: Hugo von Hofmannsthal
First performance: Stuttgart 1912 (without Prologue); Vienna 1916 (revised with Prologue)

Plot: Hired to entertain a rich man's guests, the singers of a new >opera seria ('Ariadne') and the dancers of a >commedia dell'arte entertainment are told to save time by combining their performances so that the evening's firework display will not be delayed. *Ariadne*'s Composer is indignant at this vulgarising of his work, although he is momentarily softened by the charms of the dancer, Zerbinetta, who is more

pragmatic about the change of plans. In the performance Ariadne, heart-broken that her lover Theseus has abandoned her on Naxos, yearns for death; Zerbinetta, Arlecchino and their fellows from commedia dell'arte dance and flirt to distract her, pointing out that there is always another Godlike male around the corner. And indeed, when the god Bacchus appears, although at first Ariadne welcomes him as the messenger of Death, and he assumes she is a siren, they fulfil one another's dreams of love, and depart to live eternally among the stars.

The opera: *Ariadne* originally formed a double bill with a Molière comedy, but the coupling was not a success, and Strauss and Hofmannsthal created the bustling Prologue instead. It gives a rationale for the mingling of commedia dell'arte and opera seria, extends Zerbinetta's part, and adds the delightful >trouser role character of the Composer, which has proven particularly popular among singers. Mainly because the Composer has some faintly ridiculous moments, the Prologue does not really prepare us for the earnest, poetic tone of the opera itself, where we are plunged into Ariadne's grief-stricken longing for death, Bacchus's triumphant escape from the sorceress Circe, and the metaphysical exchanges leading to the lovers' apotheosis. Yet the beauty of the music makes this sudden shift acceptable. Using a small chamber orchestra, Strauss has adopted a neo-classic manner, with clearly-defined >recitative and ensemble; in this texture alternately light and glowing or richly sensuous, the voice is always dominant. Zerbinetta's >scena demands lyrical warmth as well as superb >coloratura, the part of Ariadne exploits the full soprano range superbly, and Bacchus is a splendid tenor, rare for Strauss.

Overview: *Ariadne* contrives to evoke both the >*tragédies lyriques* of Lully and the exalted harmonies of Wagner's **Siegfried** and Brünnhilde – with Mozart just around the corner. It is Strauss's first chamber opera, a striking contrast to its prececessor, **Der Rosenkavalier**, notwithstanding that work's nostalgia for the 18th century. Smiling at an earlier age yet taking it seriously, *Ariadne* was a first step towards Stravinsky's **The Rake's Progress**.

Listening

EMI SLS 936
Dresden State Orch./Kempe
(Zylis-Gara, Geszty, Janowitz)
1968

DIE FRAU OHNE SCHATTEN
The Woman Without a Shadow

Three acts
Libretto: Hugo von Hofmannsthal
First performance: Vienna 1919

Plot: On the basis that a woman who casts no shadow does not want children, the Empress – daughter of Keikobad, master of the shadowless spirit-world – must gain a shadow so that she can bear children, or the Emperor will be turned to stone. She and her Nurse, who has demonic powers, descend to the chaotic world of ordinary people; they become servants to Barak the Dyer's wife, who is prepared to sell her shadow because children would aggravate her wretched existence. Barak is a hard-working, loving human who yearns for children but has little understanding of his wife's needs; when she tells him that she has sold her shadow, he attempts to kill her. The Empress recognises that the loss of the wife's shadow will bring further pain to Barak; if she can't save her husband without taking a shadow from a human, she is prepared to die. Keikobad, perceiving that she has learnt insight and compassion from her sojourn, grants her a shadow, and she and the Emperor join the springtime world of humans. The Dyer's wife, recognising her fundamental love for Barak, has her shadow restored. The unborn children of both couples rejoice.

The opera: This has never been an opera for everyone's stomach; the allegory all too often loses its fairy-tale-cum-Arabian Nights charm in elaborate moralising (and the narrow assumption

about woman's role, rooted in its main symbol, does not endear it to a new generation). Hofmannsthal wanted music as light as Mozart's in **The Magic Flute**, yet Strauss produced one of his most intense dramatic post-Wagnerian scores, with – once again – three magnificent soaring roles for female singer/actors. Much of the music is immediately accessible, such as the beautiful orchestral interludes connected with the Emperor (Act II) and the Empress's confrontation with her father (Act III), or the Act III duet for Barak and his wife. The Empress's refusal to compromise is a tremendous climax. And what a challenge the opera offers to scenic and lighting designers!

Overview: Like Sarastro in **The Magic Flute**, Keikobad (who never appears) puts the two couples through trials, ensuring that their developing humanity does not go unrewarded. But in giving symbolic substance to a moral Utopia, *Die Frau ohne Schatten* is closer to Wagner's **Parsifal**, although it advocates a more practical, arguably more wholesome, way of life than is provided for in the mythology of the Wagner opera. The relationship of Barak and his wife at the point when murder is threatened has overtones of Zemlinsky's **A Florentine Tragedy**, produced two years earlier.

Listening

DG 415 473-1GH3 4 415 473-4GH3
CD: 415 473-2GH3
VPO/Böhm
(Rysanek, Nilsson, King, Hesse, Berry)
1977

INTERMEZZO

Two acts
Libretto: The composer
First performance: Dresden 1924

Plot: As usual, Robert and Christine Storch are bickering while he – a celebrated composer and conductor – prepares to leave for a two-month stint in Vienna. Left alone, Christine finds a convenient companion in young Baron Lummer, until faced with his designs on her finances. She is then shocked to intercept a telegram for her husband from a woman of doubtful virtue, which suggests an established relationship between them; she instantly seeks divorce. Hearing from her in Vienna, Robert is appalled, until his similarly-named colleague, Herr Stroh, reveals that the telegram had been intended for him. Stroh hastens to visit Christine to explain the misunderstanding, but when Robert returns home he finds Christine still suspicious, and only his show of temper humbles her into accepting a genuine reconciliation.

The opera: *Intermezzo* incorporates every kind of dialogue-setting, from the most lyrical outpouring through various kinds of >recitative to >sprechgesang and ordinary speech, with expressive orchestral interludes between the scenes. Marital arguments about trivia, disputes with the servants, an all-male card game of skat interlaced with gossip, make up a deliberately prosaic picture. For such a consciously crafted score the overall effect is remarkably natural, and all the roles are brilliantly characterised. The odious Christine is self-deceiving and entirely self-centred, while Robert, notwithstanding his warm reasonableness, casually dismisses her more worthwhile aspirations. The single moments when each waxes lyrical about the other hardly dispel the impression of a rather unpleasant couple, and the infantile ending emphatically dates the piece. Since its initial success derived from its autobiographical content, while its innovations in word-setting went largely unrecognised, there is some irony in a modern-day assessment which reverses that view.

Overview: Closest to *Intermezzo* in Strauss's technical mastery are his other naturalistic settings of dialogue, the Prologue of **Ariadne auf Naxos**, and the 'conversation-piece' **Capriccio**. Christine's grateful submission to her husband's lordly anger is echoed in **Die Frau ohne Schatten**; it forms the denouement of Zemlinsky's **A Florentine Tragedy** and Puccini's **Turandot**. In showing independent-minded Woman irresistibly attracted to a gutsy male assertion of dominance just when women were struggling against their social and political fetters, these works serve as a discouraging

reminder that opera is all too often the most conservative of the arts.

Listening

EMI SLS 5204
Bavarian Radio Symphony Orch./Sawallisch
(Popp, Fischer-Dieskau)
1980

ARABELLA

Three acts
Libretto: Hugo von Hofmannsthal, after his own short story
First performance: Dresden 1933

Plot: The down-at-heel Waldner family desperately need an advantageous marriage for their daughter, Arabella, who must choose from among her suitors before the Viennese Cabbies' Ball is over – yet she still hopes to meet 'the right man'. Her sister, Zdenka, made to masquerade as a boy because 'bringing out' two girls would be too expensive, has to hide her feelings for Matteo, Arabella's still-ardent rejected suitor. When the wealthy Croatian landowner, Mandryka, arrives, he and Arabella recognise in one another the ideal partner. At the ball, while Arabella bids farewell to her other suitors, Mandryka overhears Zdenka handing the distraught Matteo the key 'to Arabella's bedroom', in fact her own bedroom, where she gives herself to him in darkness. Mandryka accuses Arabella of playing him false. When Zdenka appears, clearly a woman, all is explained – and the remorseful Mandryka willingly accepts Arabella's ceremonial gesture of love.

The opera: The libretto was finished when Hofmannsthal died, but only the first act had been properly reworked, and Strauss's refusal to alter Acts II and III left some awkward 'bumps' – the gratuitous appearance of Fiakermilli, mascot of the Viennese cabbies, or the clumsy overhearing which produces all the misunderstandings. But the subtleties of character and motive, the believable material anxieties, and the loyalty of the sisters add real substance to the libretto. Strauss uses intensely

157

agitated music, weaving into it themes of pure lyrical warmth associated with 'Der Richtige' (the right man), the lovers' deep mutual regard, and the staircase down which Arabella descends at the end in one of opera's supreme, charged moments.

Overview: Viennese life is also portrayed in Strauss and Hofmannsthal's earlier **Der Rosenkavalier** and Johann Strauss's **Die Fledermaus**; in all three works the waltz has some significance (least in *Arabella*), and in all three there are >trouser roles, although Zdenka is actually a female character. For both *Rosenkavalier* (the overture) and *Arabella* (Act III) Strauss wrote a magnificent orchestral prelude depicting sexual ecstasy (taken even further in Shostakovich's **Lady Macbeth of Mtsensk**). Other comparisons between them only heighten the contrasts; where *Rosenkavalier* revels in its voluptuous post-Wagnerian score, *Arabella's* orchestral texture is beautifully pointed and refined, its romantic nostalgia much more wry. The echoes of Mozart's **Figaro** here would not be lost on *Arabella's* creators: the warm understanding between Arabella and Zdenka, so far apart in personality, evokes the Countess and Susanna, while Arabella's inner grace at the end is a variant of the Countess's sublime words of forgiveness.

Further reading: Nicholas John ed. – *Arabella* (ENO/Royal Opera guide no. 30)

Listening

EMI SLS5220
Angel SCX3917
Bavarian State Opera/Sawallisch
(Varady, Fischer-Dieskau, Donath)
1981

CAPRICCIO

One act
Libretto: Clemens Krauss
First performance: Munich 1942

Plot: Near Paris, late 1700s – the time of Gluck's opera 'reforms'. The poet

Olivier and the musician Flamand are both in love with the Countess, while she cannot choose one over the other, any more than she can decide whether words or music are the higher artistic truth. For the great theatre director La Roche, music and poetry are subservient to the director's art. His description of the performance he is planning for the Countess's birthday gives rise to a suggestion, happily accepted, that Olivier and Flamand collaborate on an opera about the day's events. The Countess knows that her choice between poetry and music, Olivier and Flamand, will decide the way this new opera is to end. Yet to choose one would mean to lose the other . . .

The opera: The Countess muses long and beautifully, smiling as she leaves the stage: she cannot answer the question. Strauss's 'conversation piece', an aesthetic argument given human significance by the Countess's relationship with her adoring suitors, is full of the most graceful knowing winks for connoisseurs. The beautiful overture – a string sextet whose themes flow through the opera – has been composed by Flamand for the Countess, and she is listening to it as the curtain rises. There are allusions, both musical and verbal, to valued composers of the period, including Gluck and his rival Piccinni; a sonnet by Ronsard runs through the work, and the celebrated Comédie Française actress Clairon appears. There are 18th-century dances performed to contemporary instruments. Two singers 'in the Italian style – great grief in a gay melody' – scoff cakes and wine, and worry about their fee. La Roche defends his plans for celebrating the Countess's birthday in what is virtually a classical dramatic >scena. The most arch device is the characters' decision to write an opera about the events that are taking place: will that be the opera we are watching? Yet *Capriccio* is anything but artificial. It is a distillation of Strauss's most lyrical style – warm, gracious, seemingly effortless.

Overview: Aspects of *Capriccio* are hinted at in the earlier **Ariadne auf Naxos** (the aesthetic arguments, the character of the Composer), and its intimate dialogue and small scale link

it with Strauss's other 'conversation piece', **Intermezzo**. The old composer called it his testament, and wrote no more operas after it. As a 'heavenly postscript' to his operatic output, its love games carrying no rancour and its serene wit masking a consummate technique, it stands alongside Verdi's **Falstaff** and Berlioz's **Béatrice et Bénédict**.

Listening

DG 2721 188
Bavarian Radio Symph. Orch./Böhm
(Janowitz, Fischer-Dieskau, Schreier, Prey, Ridderbusch, Troyanos)
1972

Ferruccio Busoni

Born: 1st April 1866/Empoli, Tuscany
Died: 27th July 1924/Berlin

Busoni was a brilliant all-round performing and creative musician. He

Thomas Allen as *Doktor Faust* in David Pountney's production for the English National Opera in 1986

combined his Italian and his German parentage to fruitful advantage in his operas, *Die Brautwahl*, *Arlecchino*, *Turandot* and *Doktor Faust*. He was the greatest pianist of his time, and an equally great teacher/writer; he also championed important new orchestral music. He has not been popularly appreciated but acquaintance with his music is rewarding.

DOKTOR FAUST

Six tableaux
Libretto: The composer, after 16th-century puppet play
First performance: Dresden 1925

Plot: The master teacher, Faust, contracts with Mephistopheles to receive 'riches, power, fame . . . freedom, genius' in exchange for his soul becoming forfeit to Hell.

159

Mephistopheles protects Faust from the brother of a woman he has ruined, and gets rid of Faust's creditors. Faust elopes with the Duchess of Parma after performing magic feats at her wedding, but abandons her when she falls pregnant. When Mephistopheles conjures up Helen of Troy and Faust finds he cannot hold her in his arms, he acknowledges that he has been over-ambitious. The Duchess, now apparently destitute, gives him their dead child, charging him to use well the time remaining, but Faust's attempts to redeem himself with good deeds are thwarted by Mephistopheles. Just before midnight, defiant of both God and the Devil, he lays the dead child on the ground, enjoining it to use his life-force for improving the lot of humankind. As he dies, a youth rises up and bears a blossoming branch into the night.

The opera: Busoni's *Faust* was completed from his notes after he died by his student, Jarnach. Both score and libretto are a masterly demonstration of economical writing, beautifully put together. Not a note, not a word, is wasted, and the final scene fuses the visual, the musical and the philosophical aspects of the theatrical experience at a level rarely reached by more popular composers of opera. In the two Prologues in which Mephistopheles (a brilliant high tenor) entraps Faust, and in the Interlude with the brother, Mephistopheles establishes Faust's new status quo. In the three Scenes following, he hovers nearby, but it is Faust who initiates the action and adventure, and whose independent thinking gives considerable intellectual substance to the work. The music of the orchestral preludes and >intermezzi is sparing of gesture and clear of line; there is a lyrical classical spirit within its confident modernism.

Overview: Berlioz's **Damnation of Faust** is epic, picaresque, sensually involved with Nature: Gounod's **Faust** is an attractive, well-told tale. Neither approaches the philosophical significance of Busoni's opera, or even its dramatic vitality (superseded in Mozart's Faustian **Don Giovanni**). Both Busoni's opera and Hindemith's **Mathis der Maler** deal with the search for the 'right way'; they are modern tonal

works, incorporating an almost Baroque polyphony, which further the long tradition without distorting or parodying it. But while Hindemith's opera is basically realistic, Busoni's is a symbolic fantasy; his hero, striving to extend his creative genius, reaches beyond the accepted alternatives of damnation or redemption.

Listening

DG 2740 273
Bavarian Radio Symph./Leitner
(Fischer-Dieskau, Cochran)
1970

Hans Pfitzner

Born: 5th May 1869/Moscow
Died: 22nd May 1949/Salzburg

A much honoured composer, pianist, conductor and teacher, Pfitzner was an important polemicist on musical aesthetics and theory and a great admirer of Wagner. Of his several stage works (music dramas, incidental music, and operas), few of which were successful outside Germany, *Palestrina* is by far the most important.

PALESTRINA

Three acts
Libretto: The composer
First performance: Munich 1917

Plot: Palestrina, Rome's renowned 16th-century composer, has lost his inspiration since his wife's death. His loving, ingenuous son is not attuned to his inner life, and in the changing world of the late 16th century his gifted pupil, Silla, is attracted to the modernists. At the Council of Trent, convened to resolve differences within the Church, Cardinal Borromeo strives to save polyphonic music, considered too complex for the common people the Church is wooing. He commissions a

Mass from Palestrina, whose clarity within the established medium will prove a pattern for future church music. Feeling unequal to the task, Palestrina declines, unflurried by Borromeo's fury – and then, supported by mystical communion with the great masters of old, the invisible presence of his dead wife and numerous angels, he composes a Mass. When Borromeo's agents put him in prison in a crass attempt to force inspiration from him, his son ransoms him with this Mass; it is acclaimed as the signal work of its time. To Palestrina, the glowing praise even of the Pope and the remorseful Borromeo is incidental; he is concerned above all to continue to serve God.

The opera: Although the lengthy first act is undramatic and lacks rhythmic impetus, the machinations at the Council of Trent (Act II) and the emotions of the last act flesh out the conflicts. It is a persuasive, moving work. Pfitzner quotes the real Palestrina's Pope Marcellus Mass, and his own sound-world – making use when necessary of all the richness of Wagnerian harmony and textures, yet fundamentally, chaste, earnest, >diatonic – compares in some ways with Palestrina's, its open intervals and interweaving of flowing melodic lines creating a radiant texture. The >leitmotivs reflect the mood of the drama rather than dictating it (those associated with Palestrina's wife and with his artistic aspirations are particularly beautiful). The most sustained expressive writing is reserved for the Preludes which establish each act's mood of outer or inner 'reality', and the magnificent orchestral climax to Act I.

Overview: The touching father-son relationship shows a mature, wry insight missing in Verdi's **Don Carlos** or Wagner's **The Valkyrie**. The crucial theme – the freedom and responsibility of the artist of integrity – is shared by several major German operas after Wagner's **Die Meistersinger**, in particular Hindemith's **Mathis der Maler**, with which Palestrina has numerous points in common. The Council scene is a virtuoso demonstration of how to handle a huge ensemble on stage, in the tradition of Verdi and Musorgsky.

Listening

DGG 2711 013
Bavarian Radio Symph. Orch./Kubelik
(Gedda, Fischer-Dieskau, Sassbender)

Franz Lehár

Born: 30th April 1870/Komárom
Died: 24th October 1948/Ischl

Lehár was the most important composer of operettas in the early 20th century. He crowned his career with an operetta (*Giuditta*), of such stature that it was staged by an opera-house. Yet *The Merry Widow* – purely an operetta – has gained the same acceptance without trying to be anything but itself.

THE MERRY WIDOW
Die lustige Witwe

Three acts
Libretto: Viktor Léon and Leo Stein, after Henri Meilhac
First performance: Vienna 1905

Plot: The Pontevedrian Ambassador in Paris instructs his secretary, Danilo, to marry Hanna Glawari as a patriotic duty to keep her late husband's enormous wealth in Pontevedrian hands. Danilo has been in love with Hanna for some time, but prefers to avoid marriage, although he is prepared to see that no-one else gets her. The Ambassador's wife, Valencienne, is having some difficulty keeping her ardent lover Camille at arm's length. She pushes Camille in Hanna's direction – and Hanna plays along, to arouse Danilo's jealousy. Thus Danilo is impelled to declare his love for Hanna – while Valencienne and Camille will maintain their frustrating liaison.

The opera: *The Merry Widow* seems the epitome of what operetta is about – tuneful, escapist entertainment full of

Nigel Douglas's production of *The Merry Widow* (Sadlers Wells 1985)

singing strings and clashing cymbals evoking a glamorous never-never world where the only problem is the current state of the current flirtation. Its determination to remain on the surface can become wearisome – yet the love-plots, slight as they are, never seem heartless, for (unusually in operetta) they derive from realistic situations. And Lehár's operetta is treated with considerable respect by musicologists. The reason is not its few social-topical references – although one chorus, *Damenwahl* (Ladies' Choice), is built up on the theme of women's suffrage – but, quite simply, the superb quality of the music, in turn seductive, nostalgic, elegant, and rousing. The languorous waltzes are beautifully integrated into the score, the choruses are irresistible, the melodies substantial, much enjoyed by opera singers. Even excluding Hanna's exquisite *Vilja, o Vilja*, what other work has so large a clutch of memorable numbers? It is sheer joy to make fresh contact with Camille's

lovely *Sieh dort den kleinen Pavillon*, the two wonderful waltzes *O kommet doch, o kommt, ihr Ballsirenen* and *Lippen schweigen*, Danilo's hilarious *O Vaterland*, and *Ja, das Studium der Weiber ist schwer*, surely the most catchy chorus of all time.

Overview: Like Offenbach, Lehár later set his sights on more serious stage works, and his last work, *Giuditta*, represents for him what **The Tales of Hoffmann** did for Offenbach. Both composers flourished on the eve of a cataclysm – but although Offenbach could spin a beautiful tune, his earlier work derived its enormous success from its satirical or irreverent wit and its topicality – Parisian virtues; whereas Lehár's popularity was based on the beauty of music which turned aside from social comment – Viennese failings?

Listening

HMV SLS823 4 TC-SLS823
CD: CDS7 47178-8
Angel SBL 3630

CD: CDCB 47177
Philharmonia/Matačič
(Schwarzkopf, Waechter, Steffek, Gedda)
1962

Alexander von Zemlinsky

Born: 14th October 1872/Vienna
Died: 15th March 1942/Larchmont, New York

Zemlinsky, a Viennese composer and conductor, worked with Schoenberg to champion new music. He is noted for the adaptability of his compositional style, which altered according to its subject matter and, sometimes, within it. He wrote eight operas, incidental music, and a ballet, as well as finely crafted orchestral, chamber and vocal works. *Es war einmal* and several of his

---

liberated by the experience, sexually alive to one another perhaps for the first time. From the extended prelude, meant to suggest a love-scene between Bianca and the Prince, the music has a power of its own, swirling lyrically, menacing, constantly suggesting more as it rearranges and develops its web of >leitmotivs – it is that heavy, restless sound of 20th-century angst familiar from Mahler and the earlier works of Schoenberg.

Overview: Comparisons with Puccini's **Il tabarro** are inevitable. In both operas we find the older husband forced to dissimulate, the gleaming young lover, the beautiful wife hungry for passion. But Puccini the Italian and Zemlinsky the Jewish Viennese were different musical animals, and Puccini, who had earlier considered setting the Wilde text, would have given it a very different feel: where his one-acter is a stark statement of a classic situation, full of naturalistic touches in a realistic setting, Zemlinsky's is symbolic, ambiguous, more narrowly focused and closer in spirit to Bartók's **Duke Bluebeard's Castle** or Schoenberg's **Erwartung**.

Listening

Schwann VMS 1626
CD: CD11626
Berlin Radio SO/Albrecht
(Soffel, Riegel, Sarabia)
1984

THE BIRTHDAY OF THE INFANTA
Der Zwerg (The Dwarf)

One act
Libretto: Georg C. Klaren, after Oscar Wilde, revised by Adolf Dresen
First performance: Cologne 1922

Plot: A hideous, misshapen Dwarf has been captured in the forest as a birthday present for the Infanta (Spanish Princess). She is delighted with her new toy, especially when he develops a passion for her and enjoys being her gallant, romantic knight, unaware of how he looks. Her maid tries

in vain to protect the Dwarf from discovering that he is an object of horrified amusement. Left alone while the Infanta is dancing, the Dwarf stands in front of a mirror, and gradually grasps that the monster he sees is himself. In an agony of shock and distress, he begs the Infanta for some show of feeling, but she cannot understand, and when he dies of a broken heart, she goes off to continue dancing, stipulating that her next toy should not have a heart.

The opera: During most of the work, instrumental intensity is reserved for the Dwarf's innocently voluptuous yearnings. It is appropriate that his earliest music is only mildly grotesque, while the spoilt, protected Infanta is presented with sugary cool formality: he has the beautiful nature, hers is stunted and incomplete. Zemlinsky makes us consider the implications of conventional concepts of beauty and ugliness, and the harsh cruelty and exclusiveness behind a tasteful, courtly façade where 'correct' behaviour is taken for granted. He uses the discussion between the Dwarf and the maid, and the Dwarf's prolonged process of recognition, to articulate the difficulty of knowing oneself (*Der lügt!* – 'it's lying!' – screams the Dwarf at the image in the mirror). The text is predominant until the denouement, when the shrieking of the Dwarf is only one strand of the expressionist cataclysm let loose by his terrible discovery. It is a remarkable piece of music drama, only becoming known some fifty years after the Nazi ban on all of Zemlinsky's music.

Overview: Beyond the Beauty and the Beast theme lies the wider issue: the reality behind the appearance, touched on in such widely contrasting works as **The Magic Flute** (Mozart), **Arabella** (Strauss), **Albert Herring** (Britten) and Zemlinsky's own **A Florentine Tragedy**. The Dwarf sharpens our perspective on Verdi's **Rigoletto** and Leoncavallo's Tonio (**Pagliacci**), but where their souls are as twisted as their bodies, the Dwarf's soul is warm and loving. Zemlinsky, always responsive to the music of his contemporaries, reflects in his score Ravel's cut-glass formality for the Infanta and some of Schoenberg's distorted expressiveness for the Dwarf.

Listening

Schwann VMS 1626
CD: CD11626
RSO Berlin/Albrecht
(Nielsen, Riegel)
1984

Arnold Schoenberg

**Born: 13th September 1874/Vienna
Died: 13th July 1951/Los Angeles, California**

After producing superb music in the late-19th century manner Schoenberg became one of the great prophet-revolutionaries of the 20th century. He was at the head of the group known as the Second Viennese School which included Weber and Berg, leading the move to atonal and then to >twelve –tone composition through his example, his teaching and his writings. He produced important music in all genres; of his few operas *Erwartung* is by far the most popular, while *Moses und Aron* has taken longer to be understood.

Further reading: H. H. Stuckenschmidt – *Arnold Schoenberg* (Eng. trans. London 1977); Arnold Schoenberg – *Style and Idea* (London 1975).

ERWARTUNG
Expectation

**One act
Libretto: Marie Pappenheim
First performance: Prague 1924
(composed 1909)**

Plot: A woman searches in a forest, now dark, now moonlit, for her lover, who has not come to her for some time. Her sensations in the forest terrify her; throughout she talks to her lover, to herself. She stumbles across a tree trunk, later across a dead body – her lover. To it she expresses her longing and her ecstasy, her jealousy, her anger and her compassion. As day breaks, and she faces the loneliness of her life without her lover, she wanders off, living again the search for his presence, his kiss.

The opera: This famous half-hour monodrama marked Schoenberg's move into expressionist drama as the vehicle for his changing style of composition. The style is atonal, freely dissonant – without reference to a point of harmonic rest (a doh or a tonic chord). It is deliberately exaggerated in its intensity, the voice leaping and plunging over wide intervals or reined in to an equally expressive monotone, occasionally half-speaking and half-singing (>sprechgesang or >sprechstimme). The music demands the most acute listening, for there is virtually no thematic unity – in effect, nothing is repeated, although the powerful atmosphere created by orchestral colouring and text imposes a sense of unity. For all its complexity, it is no surprise that Schoenberg composed it in a mere seventeen days, for its hallucinatory, obsessive quality suggests another dimension of creative power. As a drama *Erwartung* is riveting, functioning on the level of dream (nightmare) and inner dialogue; it is generally supposed that the woman has killed her lover, or that she is demented – who knows what is real, or if anything at all exists? Ultimately this woman's spirit is deeply affirmative, transfiguring itself beyond the violence of fear and jealousy to forgive her lover his infidelity and imagine he is before her, alive.

Overview: Schoenberg followed *Erwartung* with *Die glückliche Hand* and *Pierrot lunaire* (the last-named not an opera, but often staged), and opera would never be the same again. Berg's **Wozzeck** is a full-scale development of the mood and method initiated in *Erwartung*, which is also reflected in Zemlinsky's **A Florentine Tragedy** and Bartók's **Duke Bluebeard's Castle.** Schoenberg's monodrama is very much of its time, along with the dream theories of Freud and the stream-of-consciousness technique in the work of novelists such as Joyce and Woolf; its librettist was related to 'Anna O', whose case history marked the start of psychoanalysis in Vienna. As a piece of theatre focusing on the psychological anguish of a single character, it is echoed in Poulenc's **La voix humaine**.

Listening

Decca SXDL7509 4 KSXDC7509
CD: 417 348-2LH2
London CD: 417 348-2LH2
VPO/Dohnányi
(Silja)
1979

MOSES UND ARON

Three acts (Act III not composed)
Libretto: The composer, after the
Bible (Exodus and Numbers)
First performance: Hamburg 1954
(concert); Zurich 1957 (staged)

Plot: The Lord appoints Moses as his prophet to the people of Israel, who are slaves in Egypt. Since Moses lacks eloquence, his brother Aaron will speak for him. But Aaron does not fully realise that he must offer no concrete images of God to cling to, God being infinite and inconceivable, so he uses common miracles to convince the people of God's power, and to rally rebellion against Pharaoh. Then, with Moses away on the Mountain of Revelation (Sinai), Aaron allows the people a golden calf as an image of God. Restless, lacking guidance, they revive pagan practices round the golden calf. When Moses returns with the tablets of God's law, he destroys both the calf and the tablets as images. Seeing the people follow a pillar of fire, he breaks down in despair at the impossibility of communicating to them the Idea of God. However, he shows Aaron the terrible limitations of what has been imposed unwittingly on the people, and Aaron, himself unable to exist without such limitations, dies. Moses proclaims the only goal: unity with God.

The opera: Schoenberg composed Acts I and II in 1930–32, as a climax in two related processes: his return to

Judaism and with it, Zionism, and his artistic expression of the search for communion with God. After several attempts to compose Act III he eventually suggested it be spoken. This is less drastic a solution than it sounds, since pitched speaking (>sprechgesang) is already a vital part of the score in the voice of God in the burning bush and in the whispering in the Interlude between the first two acts, as well as in the role of Moses. (In Biblical terms, Moses stammers, so in practical terms he lacks eloquence, and therefore in operatic terms, apart from one crucial outburst, he does not sing.) The singing is not born of the 19th-century tradition: even its intense lyricism is an unfamiliar language, whose melodic beauty, heightened by remarkable instrumental colouring, is strikingly different from Mozart's or Verdi's, and the choir is given far more importance. But the dramatic power of the score is in the great tradition – a leaner, less compromising, contemporary grand opera, complete with >spectacle, dance and great themes. Typically of Schoenberg, the famous orgy round the golden calf is carefully structured, each section containing its own drama and marking a crucial stage in the loss of religious integrity.

Overview: A 20th-century masterpiece, Schoenberg's last opera is a supreme demonstration of the flexibility and variety of music that can be generated in serial composition, heading a select group which includes Schoenberg's own *Von heute auf morgen*, Berg's **Lulu**, Zimmerman's **Die Soldaten** and Dallapiccola's **The Prisoner**. For all that there is a philosophical theme at its centre, the opera takes an epic approach to the movement and beliefs of a people, an approach it shares with Berlioz's **The Trojans** and Musorgsky's **Boris Godunov**

Further reading: Karl H. Wörner – *Schoenberg's 'Moses und Aron'* (New York 1964).

Listening

Decca 414 264-1DH2
CD: 414 264-2DH2
London 414 264-1LH2

CD: 414 264-2LH2
Chicago SO/Solti
(Bonney, Zikai, Langridge, Mazura)
1984

Alban Berg

Born: 9th February 1885/Vienna
Died: 24th December 1935/Vienna

A composer of the Second Viennese School, Berg's two operas are signal and highly successful 20th-century works of great dramatic flair, their partially-serial (*Wozzeck*) and wholly serial (*Lulu*) elements wrought into scores of beauty and nervosity. He is considered the most accessible of the serial composers, lyricism being a

A scene from Peter Hall's production of *Moses und Aron* for the Royal Opera House in 1965

marked feature of his work. Among the important items in his relatively small output are songs, orchestral pieces and a violin concerto.

WOZZECK

Three acts
Libretto: The composer, after Georg Büchner
First performance: Berlin 1925

Plot: Wozzeck, a poor, innocuous soldier, is considered fair game for general abuse. He submits himself to a manic Doctor's dehumanising dietary experiments, and serves his surreal Captain, to scrape together some money for his common-law wife Marie and their child. On these two – his family – he pours out all his compassion and protective love, until he discovers that Marie is having an affair with the bullish Drum-Major, who beats him up. As Wozzeck gradually loses his grip, his

friends show no real concern, and the Doctor and the Captain continue to view him as a 'case'. Maddened by Marie's betrayal, and unaware of her remorse, he stabs her one evening in a forest, and later, returning half-crazed to the scene, drowns himself in a pool. In the morning the child trots along with some older children to stare at the body of his mother, freshly discovered.

The opera: *Wozzeck* is a brilliant expressionist drama, an intricately organised composition, a powerful musical experience, an eloquent socialist gesture, a fascinating psychological case-history. Having seen a production of Büchner's play, Berg's obsession with it was nurtured during the war when his own experiences increased his identification with the central character. The work's atmosphere of paranoia generates a mounting horror, underlined in the orchestra with a naked note B after the murder (all the more arresting in this dissonant, substantially atonal score), and given climactic expression in the orchestral interlude after the drowning. Although much of the vocal line is continuous >sprechgesang, the style is widely varied; the scenes are linked by brief orchestral interludes, and Berg embeds several self-contained musical items, often horribly distorted, in the dramatic action (folksong, lullaby, march, ländler, waltz, scurrilous song, children's song, and so on). Of the individual characters' >motifs, Wozzeck's *Wir arme Leut* ('we wretched folk') becomes the motto for a work whose impact is inescapable.

Overview: *Wozzeck* shares much of the atmosphere and organisation of other great 20th-century operas while retaining a quality specifically its own. Like Debussy's **Pelléas et Mélisande** and Poulenc's **Dialogues des Carmélites** it is very much a sung play, but the brooding hysteria of its musical textures takes it closer to Strauss's early operas, and the forest of its blood-red moon is host also to the woman in Schoenberg's **Erwartung**. In **Madam Butterfly**, too, a child as mute witness heightens our horror at the experience of its parents, but Berg's final scene is the more chilling for being entirely without Puccini's sentimentality.

Listening

DG 413 804-1GG2
German Opera Orch./Böhm
(Fischer-Dieskau, Lear)
1965

LULU

**Prologue and three acts (Act III completed by Friedrich Cerha)
Libretto: The composer, after Frank Wedekind
First performance: Acts I and II, Zurich 1937; with Act III completed, Paris 1979**

Plot: Since childhood Lulu has been an object of the desire that makes people abandon any other aspirations, or impels them to incorporate her into their lives. She survives by exploiting those who exploit her, looking ahead the minute they are destroyed. Her first 'Daddy', the old asthmatic Schigolch, still hangs around. Her 'respectable' lover Dr Schön sets her up in short-lived marriages until she forces him to marry her. Driven half-crazy by the admirers who circle round her, he tries to make her kill herself; she shoots him in panic, and is imprisoned. Countess Geschwitz, who loves Lulu entirely unselfishly, takes her place in prison, and Lulu escapes to Paris with Schön's besotted son, Alwa. There, surrounded by shady characters, blackmailed as a fugitive from justice, she again evades the police. Penniless in London with Alwa, Schigolch and the Countess, she becomes a prostitute. One client kills Alwa; another – Jack the Ripper – kills Lulu and the Countess. Only Schigolch survives – offstage.

The opera: When Berg died, the third act was clearly sketched, but circumstances prevented a full realisation until the 1970s. *Lulu's* sordid rise-and-fall tale of corruption and cynicism is presented with an almost laconic realism. Yet the score mingles radiant lyricism and dark late-Romantic beauty with violent dissonance, and the heightened declamation of >sprechgesang with naturalistic straight-talk. Berg's sensitivity to colour, his capacity for finding the sublime in the prosaic, is intensely alive. There is humour, too – even farce in Act II when Dr Schön's home becomes a hive of admirers. But the last scene confirms that Lulu and those who love her unconditionally are victims. To familiar material eloquently suggesting Lulu's tragic, debased, need for affection, she brings in three clients, representing her three husbands – Dr Schön effectively killing her in the persona of Jack the Ripper, leaving the dying Geschwitz to utter the most cosmic expression of love Lulu ever evoked. The score, incorporating contemporary jazz material, is a series of self-contained forms (such as a sonata, and a theme and variations) which help characterise the roles, and are felt subliminally even if not clearly perceived. The orchestral interludes include, at the opera's middle-point, a passage of superb film music (intended to accompany a silent film which telescopes Lulu's experiences after being arrested); in general the orchestra must perform feats of virtuosity equal to that of the singers, whose vocal line can be cruelly demanding. The Five Symphonic Pieces from *Lulu*, with soprano, is more commonly heard in the concert hall before the opera itself became better known.

Overview: *Lulu* is one of the 20th-century masterpieces. More advanced in its use of >serial technique than **Wozzeck**, and less obviously connected with expressionism, its extraordinary musical complexity never saps its theatrical vitality. The uncompromising realism of its subject matter goes far further than in any >verismo work, marking the extreme distance travelled since the earliest operas, and dating the representations of comparable heroines such as Bizet's **Carmen** or the **Manon** operas (Massenet or Puccini). A warning: it would be a mistake to superimpose anything of Pabst's film *Pandora's Box* on Berg's opera: the two works share only their common source and its theme, not their interpretation of Wedekind's plays.

Listening

DG 2740 213 4 3378 086
DG (US) 2711 024 4 3378 086

CD: 415 489-2GH
Paris Opera/Boulez
(Stratas, Mazura, Riegel, Blankenheim, Minton)
1979

Paul Hindemith

Born: 16th November 1895/Hanau
Died: 28th December 1963/Frankfurt am Main

Very much an all-round musician, both as composer, solo performer, conductor, teacher and writer, Hindemith was particularly influential before and after the Second World War. His seven operas, his film scores, ballets, and various other stage works, are a relatively small part of his vast output in all genres.

MATHIS DER MALER
Mathis the Painter

Seven tableaux
Libretto: The composer
First performance: Zurich 1938

Plot: (It is an imaginary re-creation of incidents in the life of the 16th-century artist, Mathias Grünewald.) During the Peasants' Revolt of 1525, Mathis is so affected by the people's suffering that he can no longer paint. His feeling is less political than humanitarian: just as he instinctively saves the peasants' leader and his daughter Regina from the government army, so he protects a Duchess from the vengeful mob. But he takes leave of those closest to him – his intense friend Ursula, and his beloved patron, Cardinal Albrecht – and joins the peasants. Regina's father is killed when the peasants' army is routed; while caring for her, Mathis has a Vision – the Temptation of St Antony and his conversation with St Paul the Hermit (which he painted on the great Isenheim Altarpiece) – and is persuaded that his contribution to the people will be to express himself in his art. Feverishly, he resumes his artistic endeavours until, drained, he packs up his implements and leaves his home, to die where he is unknown.

The opera: In *Mathis der Maler* Hindemith faced the crucial issue for many German artists in the 1930s (and emphasised his commitment to tonal music while it was unfashionable). The people Mathis is close to and others he has known appear in his allegorical Vision, offering alternatives to his inescapable destiny as an artist, but he rejects them, withdraws from political activity, and pours his human experiences into his art. Without writing 'authentic' contemporary music, Hindemith has created a brilliant tapestry of the times, cleverly evoking through choral exchanges the conflict between Lutherans and Roman Catholics; there are also plainsong, traditional folk-song and hymn. The only non-historical character, Regina, is especially convincing, whether describing the ravages of war or her dead father's stare; she sings the most lyrical music, apart from the orchestral prelude and interlude and the Vision itself, all incorporated into Hindemith's magnificent *Mathis der Maler* symphony.

Overview: In showing a 16th-century painter engaging with men and women of varied conviction, Hindemith fleshed out the themes of the modern artist – the limits on political involvement, the politicisation of art, the extent to which a work of art remains connected with its creator. This last is alluded to in Strauss's **Capriccio**; Wagner in **Die Meistersinger** and Pfitzner in **Palestrina** dwell on the moral influence of art. Direct or implied investigations of the artist's moral position appear in operas such as Hindemith's *Cardillac* and *Die Harmonie der Welt*, Davies's *Taverner* and Henze's *Elegy for Young Lovers*, the most profound being Schoenberg's **Moses und Aron**.

Listening

EMI 1C 165 03515/7
Bavarian Radio Symphony Orch./Kubelik
(Fischer-Dieskau, Feldhoff, King)
1978

Kurt Weill

Born: 2nd March 1900/Dessau
Died: 3rd April 1950/New York

Weill is an interesting, controversial figure, whose career and approach to composition changed dramatically with his flight from Nazi Germany via Paris to the US. At first the rising star of music theatre in the Germany of the 1920s and early 1930s, particularly in his collaborations with Brecht, he became a respected composer of American musicals which are among the finest and most creative works of their type. He wrote some fifteen stage works in each period, as well as a number of other vocal works.

THE THREEPENNY OPERA
Die Dreigroschenoper

Prologue and eight scenes
Libretto: Bertolt Brecht, after John Gay
First performance: Berlin 1928

Plot: Mack the Knife, the notorious London criminal, marries Polly, daughter of Mr Peachum and chief attraction of his business, (a begging racket). Hoping to get his hands on his son-in-law's fortune, Peachum denounces Mack to the police, and he and his wife bribe Pirate Jenny, whose pimp Mack the Knife had once been, to betray his ex-lover. The Chief of Police, Tiger Brown, is reluctant to unsettle his profitable financial arrangements with Mack, but Peachum prevails by threatening to get all the beggars in London to disrupt a forthcoming Coronation. In prison, Mack is forced to choose between Polly and Lucy, Tiger Brown's daughter. Opting for the latter enables him to escape, only to be betrayed again by Jenny and faced with the gallows. But for the sake of a happy ending, Mack is reprieved – and granted an annual income, a castle, and a peerage.

The opera: Brecht and Weill's setting of Gay's **The Beggar's Opera** caused a sensation in Germany, with its bitter, ironic comedy directed against the 'respectable' classes who uphold the corrupt monopolies of government and big business. The effect was all the stronger for eschewing pathos until the very last verses (added in 1930), *Und man siehet die im Lichte/Die im Dunkeln sieht man nicht* (And you see the ones in brightness/Those in darkness you don't see) – although pathos is not entirely absent in Jenny's vengeful vision of her ship coming in (originally written for Polly). In ridiculing opera's conventions – the earnest Baroque overture, the ferocious prima donna duet between Lucy and Polly, Lucy's Jealousy >aria, the >deus ex machina bringing the reprieve and the idiotic chorus that follows – Weill was challenging his audience's values, even creating a new audience. He had incorporated elements of popular music into previous scores; here he devised a series of ballads which were spare and singable. In these songs, whose intensely refined harmonic and instrumental accompaniments range from sweetly luminous textures to those of grating dissonance, every turn of phrase or shift of colour tells.

Overview: Although the Nazis attempted to destroy the work's existence, it is now more popular than its 18th-century model. Its highly original style (with its peculiarly European transmutation of jazz) has become almost a cliché in evoking the mood and atmosphere of the Weimar Republic, and the grotesque realism of The Ballad of Mack the Knife has been somewhat sentimentalised by its general popularity. Weill and Brecht employed a similar approach in *Happy End*, and enlarged its scope in **The Rise and Fall of the City of Mahagonny**. There is a small-orchestra suite, *Kleine Dreigroschenmusik*, arranged by Weill.

Further reading: Rodney Milnes – 'The Stage Works of Weill', in *Opera on Record 3* (ed. Alan Blyth, London 1984).

Listening

1 CBS (UK) 78279 4 40-78279
(US) Y2-32977
Radio Free Berlin Dance Orch./Brückner-
Rüggeberg
(Neuse, Trenck-Trebitsch, Hesterberg, Schellow, Von Koczian, Lenya, Wolffberg) 1958
2 CBS (UK) 61138
(US) PS 34326
New York Shakespeare Festival/Silverman (Brocksmith, Alexander, Wilson, Julia, Kava, Greene, Browne) 1976

THE RISE AND FALL OF THE CITY OF MAHAGONNY Aufstieg und Fall der Stadt Mahagonny

Three acts
Libretto: Berthold Brecht
First performance: Leipzig 1930

Plot: Three criminals set up a pleasure-city in the desert, which attracts the prostitute Jenny and the miners Jimmy, Jake, Bill and Joe. Jimmy buys Jenny into a tenuous love affair, but still finds the pleasures of the city unsatisfying. When a hurricane threatens Mahagonny with destruction he calls for the end of all restrictions. The hurricane neatly bypasses the city, which transforms itself into a temple of excess – eating, sex, fighting and drinking – retaining only one restriction: you must be able to pay. Jake dies of over-eating; Joe is killed fighting – and Jimmy, who had put all his money on Joe for old time's sake, is broke. Unable to pay for the rounds of drinks he orders, and deserted by both Jenny and Bill, he is tried and executed. God won't condemn Mahagonny – it is already a living Hell.

The opera: Brecht mistrusted the kind of theatre which tickles your emotions and leaves you comfortably fulfilled. So this collaboration with Weill (based on their earlier *Mahagonny Songspiel*), deliberately upsets its audience's expectations; it is an anti-opera, parodying the conventions of the medium as it satirises 20th-century capitalism and its underlying cruelty. Its most memorable tune – *Oh, Moon of*

Alabama – pretends to be a Broadway ballad, its *Benares-Song* is a lament about the city's poor supply of whiskey, lovers and telephones; in what is effectively an Act I Finale, while everyone is anticipating the hurricane, Weill mixes operatic ensemble elements with a Lutheran-type chorale and Jimmy's paean to personal gratification ('As you make your bed, so you lie on it'). Jazz and cabaret influences dominate the score, giving it that sour ironic quality that has become for later generations *the* sound of the Weimar Republic, but which at the time was the focus of vicious efforts to 'purify' state-subsidised theatre of elements unacceptable to Nazism.

Overview: Brecht and Weill's political opera was a courageous gesture in a Europe where the groundswell of fascism was soon to become a raging flood. Shortly afterwards Blitzstein in the United States and, many years later, Nono in Italy made specific anti-capitalist statements (in *The Cradle Will Rock* and *Intolleranza* respectively). But, while unique in their musical style, the Brecht-Weill collaborations are also among those operas which cock a snook at the complacent guardians of received thinking, operas such as Mozart's **The Marriage of Figaro**, Offenbach's *The Grand-Duchess of Gerolstein*, or Henze's *Der junge Lord*.

Listening

CBS 77341
NDR Orch./Brückner-Rüggeberg
(Lenya, Litz, Saverbaum)
1958

Bernd-Alois Zimmermann

Born: 20th March 1918/Bliesheim
Died: 10th August 1970/Königsdort

Known at first as an avant-garde composer, Zimmerman became increasingly individual in his approach.

His music was mostly unpublished in his lifetime. *Die Soldaten* is his sole opera, an example of the 'pluralism' represented in his compositions (at its simplest, the term means that they work on many levels and incorporate quotations of other composers' works).

DIE SOLDATEN
The Soldiers

Four acts
Libretto: The composer, after Jakob Michael Reinhold Lenz
First performance: Cologne 1965

Plot: Marie Wesener, engaged to cloth merchant Stolzius, is wooed assiduously by Baron Desportes, an army officer. Her father, protective at first, soon encourages Marie to accept this chance of marrying into the nobility. Desportes seduces Marie, but begins to find her a nuisance, and gets his friend, Captain Mary, to take over. Stolzius, joining the Captain's services, watches helpless as Marie becomes the plaything of bored officers. Marie persists in writing to Desportes, and he tricks her into meeting one of his servants, who rapes her. Crushed finally, she becomes a street-walker, unaware that Stolzius has avenged her by poisoning Desportes as well as himself. A passer-by whom she approaches reluctantly gives her money – without recognising her as his own daughter.

The opera: Marie sinks into the abyss, and the soldiers' identification of sexual lust with power is strongly emphasised; it is a stark drama. And there are other factors that make *Die Soldaten* a contemporary theatre director's dream. It is a visual embodiment of Zimmermann's pluralism, superimposing events occurring at 'different' times (Time being simultaneous), and juxtaposing diverse media (including film, acoustic and electronic sound, pre-recorded tape, dance, and mime). The most striking music includes the Act II >Intermezzo (combining Bach chorales, the Dies Irae plainsong, and onstage marches in different tempi), and, before the final insistent drumrolls, the sound montage which concertinas the agonised yells of the rape victim with high jazz trumpet. The women's trio ending Act III is a moment of luminous music, but there are long passages of loudly rumbling, tearing sound, where the voices intone a serially organised vocal line almost perversely far from the inflections of natural speech. Zimmermann was more interested in construction than in his characters, and so it is in the orchestral interludes that he reveals his full range of colours and textures.

Overview: The lying tenor seducer, Desportes, embodies within himself the Duke of Mantua (Verdi's **Rigoletto**), Pinkerton (Puccini's **Madam Butterfly**), and countless others. *Die Soldaten* is sometimes hailed as the most important German opera since Berg's **Wozzeck**. Certainly the works have subject matter and atmosphere in common: Stolzius and Wozzeck, both officers' servants, are cheated of their love; both Maries are seduced by cocky officers; both armies dehumanise their personnel, who dehumanise others in turn. But while *Wozzeck* is also a complex piece of organisation, its music gives flesh to its characters; in *Die Soldaten*, the characters live more through what they do than through what they sing.

Listening

Heliodor Wergo 2729001
Cologne Opera/Gielen
(Kelemen, Gabry, Nicolai, de Ridder)

Hans Werner Henze

Born: 1st July 1926/Gütersloh

Henze has produced many ballets, radio operas, operas, film scores and incidental music. He is noted for his use and development of traditional musical forms and contemporary techniques (serialism in particular) as well as his socialist commitment. His music is in general more accessible than that of

other late 20th-century composers of equivalent standing.

Further reading: Hans Werner Henze – *Music and Politics: Collected Writings 1953–1981* (London 1982).

THE BASSARIDS (Followers of Dionysus)

One act (full-length opera without breaks)
Libretto: W. H. Auden and Chester Kallman, after Euripides
First performance: Salzburg 1966

Plot: Pentheus, the young king of Thebes, is intent on stifling the new cult of Dionysus. Dionysus's dead mother, Semele, and Pentheus's mother, Agave, were sisters; Agave and others in her family do not accept that Semele's lover was the god Zeus, hence they reject the cult. But Dionysus lures the Thebans, including Agave, to the groves of Mount Cytheron, where they give themselves to ecstatic worship. Pentheus, ignoring his mother's rapture and his old nurse's warnings, proscribes the cult with imprisonment and torture. Among those rounded up is a Stranger (Dionysus in disguise), whom he interrogates. Repelled and fascinated by what he perceives of the cult, he goes to Mount Cytheron, disguised as a woman, to learn more. There, in a trance, the followers of Dionysus hunt him as a spy, and led by Agave they tear him to pieces. Later, all disclaim guilt except Agave; as she goes into exile she warns Dionysus that the gods will not last forever. Dionysus has Thebes burnt; his mother, Semele, joins him on Olympus.

The opera: Henze's score is impressive in juggling rationality and sensuousness without ever being simplistic. Pentheus and Agave, controlled and compelling, are contrasted with the vibrant warmth of the Dionysiac Voice and the chorus, and the free, ecstatic >arioso adopted by Agave after first being on Mount Cytheron. As he faces death, Pentheus realises that he, too, has been worshipping a god, by making a cult of himself; he expresses this with disturbing eloquence. No less disturbing is Dionysus's final speech, glorying in vengeance. Agave, having unknowingly wrenched the head off her own son, is rocked with grief over the wretched remains of his body – and the full ensemble sung before her lament is deeply moving. Henze drops his rich orchestral palette for the crucial >recitatives, where he might use a bassoon accompaniment, or harp punctuation. The most striking contrast in texture comes with the quasi-18th century >Intermezzo, which reflects Pentheus's distorted view of the Dionysiac cult.

Overview: Henze's Pentheus is destroyed because he cannot integrate instinct with intellect. Tippett's **The Midsummer Marriage** resolves a similar dilemma optimistically (both composers' scores were remarkable in their times for positive lyrical beauty); Britten's **Death in Venice** turns it into an artist's struggle within himself. 20th-century settings of Greek myth and drama vary greatly in approach: contrast The Bassarids, full of naturalistic emotion, with Stravinsky's stylised **Oedipus Rex**, or Birtwistle's forbidding **The Mask of Orpheus** with Strauss's ingratiating **Ariadne auf Naxos**.

Karlheinz Stockhausen

Born: 22nd August 1928/Burg Mödrath

Stockhausen is a remarkably prolific avant-garde composer who has consistently created new methods, forms and manners for music (often demonstrating with his own performing group, and supporting his theories in his writings). He has extended the principles of >serialism to electronic music and used 'open' form where the performers determine much of the shape the music takes. Donnerstag aus Licht is a new conception, part of a projected cycle of seven operas.

DONNERSTAG aus LICHT
Thursday, from the Light cycle

Three acts, a greeting and a farewell
Libretto: The composer
First complete stage performance: Milan 1981

Plot: Coming to Earth among humans as part of his great experiment of Creation, the angel Michael's relatively happy youth becomes poisoned by family troubles. After attempting suicide his mother is committed to an asylum, where she is later killed by a doctor; his father is shot dead in battle. Michael forges a constructive link with the half-human Moon-Eve, and passes the entrance examination for the High School of Music. He then travels around the earth and becomes familiar with various cultures. Returning to Heaven, where he is hymned in a Festival and receives various symbolic gifts from Eve, he has to deal with Lucifer's obstructive behaviour. Eventually he has a vision of seven months that make up his life, seeing himself as an intermediary between the Humanity he loves, and God.

The opera: It took several years to complete the various sections that make up Donnerstag. It is a many-layered composition, the simplest part being the fanfare greeting and farewell (performed from the balcony of the opera-house, and surrounding rooftops). The first part – Michael's Youth – is clearly autobiographical and nearest to conventional theatre. Already in that section the technique of superimposition of voices and multiple representations of individual characters (as singer, dancer and instrumentalist) takes root, creating fascinating interplay, and it is developed throughout the opera. Lucifer is both Michael's earth-father and his cynical devil-opposite in heaven, Eve takes many forms – mother, seducer, companion, guardian angel, affirmation of Heaven. In Michael's Journey (Act II), Michael is predominantly a trumpeter, whose form of communication with the

Michael Bogdanov's 1985 production of
Donnerstag aus Licht

Moon-Eve/basset horn player is purely
musical; he also 'converses' with
musicians of other cultures.
Stockhausen's dedicated team involved
in the performance of *Donnerstag*
includes various people close to him,
able to respond to his demands for
improvisation and remarkable
virtuosity. Stockhausen's soundscape is
richly complex; it includes magnetic
tape, choir, full orchestra and onstage
soloists, using speech, declamation,
song, whispers, chant, tongue-clicks
and hand-claps, with ancient Hebrew
texts, popular song, military songs and
children's songs. Dance, gesture and
lighting are active elements in the work,
precisely determined by the composer.
None of this vast and sophisticated
complexity is an obstacle to an
instinctive enjoyment of *Donnerstag*'s
beauty, drama and humour until it
arrives at the dense mysticism of Vision,
the final part, which overwhelms with
the sense of an important personal
mission.

Overview: The medium of opera has
clearly become valuable to

Stockhausen, and he makes full use of
it for his purposes. Narrower in
compass, Birtwistle's **Mask of Orpheus**
is equally bold in exploring opera's
infinite possibilities; the contrast in
personality of the two composers, and
their view of themselves, naturally
makes for very different results.
Stockhausen's untrammelled vision,
creating new forms of opera theatre
rather than working within its
conventional limits, places him
alongside Wagner: the *Licht* cycle is
really the >*gesamtkunstwerk* of the
end of the 20th century, just as **The Ring**
was the most elaborate conception
produced in the 19th. One of its
dominant themes – the mother-son
relationship – is deliberately explored,
in ways that illuminate earlier operas
like **Il trovatore** (Verdi), **Hamlet**
(Thomas), and **The Bassarids** anthem.

Listening

DGG 2740 272
WDR Cologne, NOS Hilversum, DGG in
IRCAM Paris/Stockhausen and Eotvos
(Rosness, M. Stockhausen (trumpet),
Meriweather, Stephens (basset horn), Holle,
Tezak)
1981

175

CENTRAL AND NORTHERN EUROPEAN OPERA

There is clearly little common musical ground between the works of Nielsen, Sallinen, Bartók and the Czech composers, but there is one interesting link. For centuries Denmark had to struggle against both Swedish and German domination, while Finland has had to preserve its culture from the Swedes and the Russians. In both northern countries homegrown opera asserted some degree of national independence, just as it did for the Hungarians and the Czechs. The Danes were producing national opera in the 1840s, the Finns at the start of the 20th century. Nielsen's *Maskarade* (1906) is the one Danish opera to achieve international popularity; Finnish opera has gained international attention in recent decades through Merikanto's *Juha* (first staged in 1963) and then through the works of Sallinen. It is too soon to judge how substantial Sallinen's contribution to world opera might be, but it is already an exciting new element.

Hungary was the poor relation in the Austro-Hungarian empire, its language and music subordinated to German. Ferenc Erkel was determined to establish a true national style, and his *Hunyadi László* (1844) was the most important step forward, while with *Bánk Bán* (1861) he made his mark internationally. In the late 19th century, Bartók and Kodály launched their researches into genuine folk music. It was still virtually unknown by its own people, and so-called gypsy music was really a debased sub-class for café musicians. Bartók so internalised the melodic shapes and inflections of the heritage he uncovered that his *Duke Bluebeard's Castle* (1918), a work of the European symbolist tradition, stood out as a truly Hungarian opera. By the time Kodály produced his delightful *Háry János* (1926), a celebration of a much-loved folk-character, the point had been made.

But it is the Czechs whose works have proven most important in the repertory. The story of Czech opera is a battle-cry. For centuries the sovereignty of the people of Bohemia was undermined by their German neighbours. Then with the national movements of Europe, the independent Czech spirit again began

stirring, and in 1859, while Austria was losing its hegemony in Europe, the use of Czech as the medium of education

David Pountney's production of *Rusalka* (English National Opera 1986)

made its first official advances. Although Smetana hoped to be conductor of opera at Prague's new (1862) Provisional Theatre, he was passed over, a casualty of the continuing struggle for leadership of the patriotic movement. When eventually given the position in 1866, he set about building an impressive repertoire of international and Czech works. In the face of continual criticism, he was supported by Dvořák and Fibich, amongst others. His own *The Bartered Bride* had just been performed; for the laying of the stone for the new National Theatre he wrote *Dalibor* (1868) and for its opening he produced *Libuše* (1881). Other landmarks in the advance of Czech opera were Dvořák's *The Cunning Peasant* (1878) and Fibich's *Šárka* (1897).

Janáček was Moravian, not Bohemian, his melodic language close to Moravian folk music and tied to the Czech language. In 1916, once *Jenůfa* had been recognised both nationally and internationally, he was encouraged to produce the famous series of magnificent works through which he became one of the towering figures in all opera. Although Martinů did not carve a similar niche for himself, his very cosmopolitanism added a new dimension to mid-20th-century Czech opera.

For the rest of the world, Czech opera is Smetana, Dvořák, Janáček and Martinů; Hungarian opera is Erkel, Bartók and Kodály, Danish opera is Nielsen, and Finnish opera is Sallinen. Far from the centres of power and influence, these composers are evidence of the vitality of their own cultures. It is our loss not to be familiar with the many other composers who have nourished this vitality.

Bedřich Smetana

Born: 2nd March 1824/Litomyšl
Died: 12th May 1884/Prague

A founder of Czech national music, Smetana composed eight operas and the famous cycle of six symphonic poems *Ma vlast* (My Fatherland). There are many other famous choral, orchestral and chamber pieces (of which the best known is the string quartet *From My Life*), as well as songs and piano music. Other operas not dealt with here include *Libuše* and *The Kiss*, and the comic operas *The Two Widows*, *The Secret* and *The Devil's Wall*. Several of these were written after the composer had become totally deaf.

Further reading: John Clapham – *Smetana* (London 1972).

THE BARTERED BRIDE
Prodaná nevěsta

Three acts
Libretto: Karel Sabina
First performance: Prague 1866, revised 1870

Plot: The happiness of young Jeník and Mařenka is threatened when the matchmaker Kecal arranges with Mařenka's parents that she should marry Vašek, the gawky son of Mícha and Háta, wealthy land owners. But Jeník is himself Mícha's son by an earlier marriage, who had left his father's house because of the hostility of his stepmother whose identity is unknown. By contracting to give up Mařenka 'for Mícha's son', Jeník earns three hundred guilders from Kecal – and then reveals that Mařenka, heartbroken at being bartered for money, can still choose him as her husband according to the terms of the contract. Kecal is left out of pocket, his reputation in shreds, and the stepmother still has her bumbling son Vašek on her hands (unless he becomes a permanent member of the

travelling circus then visiting), but everyone else is happy that true love, reinforced by peasant cunning, has triumphed.

The opera: Smetana raised the flag of Czech opera with *The Bartered Bride*: of his many operas popular in his homeland, this is the one that achieved international renown. The simplest of stories, it is brimming over with sunshine, an expression of Bohemian folk life in song and dance. The polka at the end of Act I, the drinking song and the *furiant* which open Act II, and the comedians' dance in Act III, with the villagers' opening chorus and the comedians' duet *Milostné zvířátko*, have enriched Czech folk culture as much as they have drawn on it. Smetana's comic style is in the 18th-century Italian tradition – his handling of the materialistic Kecal is light, witty, and economical, and even Vašek's stammer makes for playful rhythms. There is no malice or vulgarity; all situations are resolved with a cheerful laugh. Yet when the mood darkens with Mařenka's distress at Jeník's seeming cynicism, the passionate lyricism of her >aria *Ten lásky sen* confirms the hints from the lovers' first scene together that Smetana is also a Romantic. And note the warmth of a minor character like Mařenka's mother, or the delightful vignettes in the comedians' scene. The consistency of the musical invention as well as its high points warrant Martinů's view of this opera as 'a work of human felicity'.

Overview: As a village comedy *The Bartered Bride* gives the world of Donizetti's **L'elisir d'amore** a sharper perspective, and Kecal's patter style recalls such comic Rossini creations as Dr Bartolo (**The Barber of Seville**). But the constant lightness of touch, rhythmic vitality and melodic richness underline a companionship announced with the first energetic rhythms of the famous overture – the Mozart of **The Marriage of Figaro**.

Listening

1 Supraphon 1116 3511-3
Czech Philharmonic/Košler
(Beňačková, Dvorský, Novák, Kopp)
1981
2 EMI 1C 149 30967/9 (in German)
Bamberg SO/Kempe
(Lorengar, Wunderlich, Frick)

DALIBOR

Three acts
Libretto: Josef Wenzig and Ervín Špindler
First performance: Prague 1868

Plot: Milada denounces the knight Dalibor to the king for murdering her brother. But Dalibor is a champion of liberty and justice; his crime was an act of revenge for the killing of his beloved friend, Zdeněk. During Dalibor's trial Milada realizes this, and falls in love with the brave knight, but he is imprisoned. Disguised as a youth to help the gaoler Beneš, she makes contact with Dalibor to plan his escape. When the plan is partly discovered, the king, fearing treason, reluctantly agrees to have Dalibor killed. Milada leads Dalibor's supporters in an attempt to rescue him, but she is fatally wounded. Having lost the two people he loves most, Dalibor allows himself to be killed.

The opera: The premiere of *Dalibor* was the climax of the stone-laying ceremony for the foundations of the new National Theatre, and in the opera Smetana associates music with Czech aspirations for freedom and justice. Dalibor, a legendary, Quixotic, 15th-century hero, shows the finest feelings of love and performs feats of arms for the right reasons only. The gaoler says 'I know no Czech who would not love music'; Zdeněk was a musician; Dalibor consoles himself in prison with a fiddle, and uses it to signal that he is escaping (the plan fails partly because a string breaks). Smetana's spacious, mellifluous score has the quality of a pageant, its scenes static, its tone exalted. It is at its most poetic in Milada's early >scena describing her brother's death. Dominating all is the Dalibor theme, a rising scale with a falling tail, which changes according to the mood of the scene. Entirely different from Wagner's >leitmotiv method, it is supposed to be the first use of thematic transformation in opera.

Overview: Beethoven's **Fidelio** hovers in the background (Milada's impressive Act II >aria specifically echoes Leonore's great '*Abscheulicher!*') but the type of drama in *Fidelio*, linking psychological states with action, makes it a very different work. There is an obvious link with Grétry's **Richard Coeur-de-lion**, which also uses music as the signal for its hero's escape. Also close to it is Verdi's **Aida**, pageant-like in parts and associated with an event of national importance (but not, like *Dalibor*, setting out to glorify national traits). Both operas are relatively conventional in manner, and in both a major element in the drama shows a highly-placed woman striving to stop the state machinery she had set in motion to destroy a man she loves.

Listening

Supraphon 112 0241-3
Prague National Orch./Krombholc
(Přibyl, Horáček, Kniplová, Svobodová-Janků)
1967

Antonín Dvořák

Born: 8th September 1841/Nelahozeves
Died: 1st May 1904/Prague

The best-known Czech composer, Dvořák is famous for his cello concerto and his symphonies (especially From the New World). His Slavonic Dances for piano duet are popular favourites, and his substantial output of chamber music includes the well-known Dumky Trio. There are particularly beautiful songs, as well as sacred and secular choral works. Of his other eleven operas, which have not been successful outside Czechoslovakia, *The Devil and Kate* is the most popular.

RUSALKA

Three acts
Libretto: Jaroslav Kvapil
First performance: Prague 1901

Plot: Rusalka is a naiad of the lake, who for love of a Prince persuades a witch

(Ježibaba) to change her into a human even though this means she will become mute. The Prince, who returns her love, arranges to marry her, but becomes uneasy at her lack of warm human passion; just before the wedding he allows a foreign princess to lure him temporarily from Rusalka. Broken-hearted, she flees back to her father, the Water-Sprite – but to regain a naiad's existence she must draw blood by killing the Prince, and this she will not do. The Prince's yearning for Rusalka, now almost a sickness, leads him to the lake; there she kisses him, and he dies, redeemed at last – but she, a half-creature, must forever lure humans to their doom.

The opera: Dvořák gives spacious lyrical expression to his love of woods, water and moonshine and their imaginary spirits; the opera's real 'action' is elaborated in the pure orchestral passages in the manner of a symphonic tone poem. The two most interesting >motifs – a beautiful melody associated with Rusalka's feelings, and a menacing reiteration in the bass – dominate the music, their continuing transformations an orchestral counter-balance to much lovely vocal writing (Rusalka's invocation to the moon is sometimes heard in recitals). Although the Nature-creatures and the irritable Ježibaba generate the musical vitality of the opera, fine singers can make something of the Prince and the Foreign Princess, and of the Prince's fussy, protective gamekeeper, a delightful folk character. Modern productions have emphasised the psychological overtones of Kvapil's fairy-tale, whose lovers invite doom by crossing over into one another's world; the closing scene, where Rusalka cures and kills the ecstatic Prince with her kiss, is arguably more Freud than fantasy.

Overview: Dvořák's theme-transformations may recall his countryman, Smetana, but it is clear that Ježibaba and Humperdinck's Witch (**Hansel and Gretel**) learnt their spells at the same International School of Sorcery. The unmissable influence is Wagner's, and not only in the >leitmotivs: the opening scene verges on (unconscious) parody of **The Rhinegold** Scene 1; both Brünnhilde

and Rusalka lose their special powers for love of a mortal, and the Prince's love-sickness, resolved in death in the arms of his beloved, parallels **Tristan**. For all that, it is the special lyrical beauty of Dvořák's writing which has created *Rusalka*'s success.

Listening

Supraphon 1116 3641/43 ZA
CD: C37-7201/3
Czech Philharmonic/Neumann
(Beňačková, Novák, Drobková, Soukupová, Ochman)
1983

Leoš Janáček

Born: 3rd July 1854/Hukvaldy
Died: 12th August 1928/Ostrava

The most important Czech composer of the early 20th century, Janáček's operas rank with the greatest, and as a group they are, along with Mozart's, the most consistently fine in the medium. *Osud* (Fate) and *The Excursions of Mr Brouček*, not included here, are noteworthy, and his late Glagolitic Mass is particularly impressive. There is a small, valuable output of orchestral, piano and chamber music (including the string quartet Intimate Letters). He also made a crucial contribution in the field of Moravian folk music.

Further reading: Jaroslav Vogel – *Leos Janáček* (London 1962).

JENŮFA
Její pastorkyňa

Three acts
Libretto: The composer, after Gabriela Preissová
First performance: Brno 1904; revised version Prague 1916

Plot: Unknown to anyone but her lover Števa, Jenůfa is pregnant. Her step-

Philip Langridge, Evá Randová and
Gabriela Beňačková in *Jenůfa* (1986)

mother the Kostelnička (Sacristan),
much respected in the village, insists on
a year's delay before the light-weight
Števa can marry her. But Števa's half-
brother Laca, who has always loved
Jenůfa, knifes her cheek in frustrated
jealousy. Hidden by the Kostelnička,
she bears a healthy, lovable baby – but
as Števa will no longer marry her now
that she is disfigured, the Kostelnička
turns to the remorseful Laca. To ensure
an honourable future for Jenůfa, the
Kostelnička tells him the baby is dead
– and drowns it. Jenůfa, who thinks that
the baby died while she was ill,
gratefully prepares to marry Laca – but
the baby is found. Laca defends Jenůfa
from the villagers' threats, and the
Kostelnička, who has been wasting

away in torment, reveals the truth.
Understanding that she acted from love,
Jenůfa forgives her, her own soul
opening out to the deep love that Laca
offers her.

The opera: With *Jenůfa* Janáček found
his true voice, and it is still his most
popular opera. The marks of greatness
are already there – the tense >ostinati,
the insistence of a particular instrument
(the xylophone in Act I is
extraordinary), the raw orchestral
colouring transformed swiftly to radiant
warmth, the unerring sense of dramatic
timing. The emotions are bare,
expressed naturally, without
melodrama or sentimentality. Two outer
acts are set in the context of village life;
the middle act is 'inner' indeed, a series
of heart-rending monologues and
exchanges. Wrongly played, the

Kostelnička is a monster; in fact she is a complex figure with substantial, if conflicting, motivations for what she does. Her attempt by every possible means to bring Števa to accept Jenůfa and their child is a marvel of musical characterisation, self-abasement mingled with deepest compassion; her decision to murder the child, accompanied by vivid, inventive instrumental movement, is the high point of the drama. Laca is the one male character in Janáček's operas possessed of genuine insight and a capacity to grow. Jenůfa herself, insecure during pregnancy, is tense and anxious; in the second and third acts she is shown as a loving mother and daughter, still crushed by her experiences. Her growth towards affirmation of life is the great theme of the opera; having expected nothing for herself, her radiance at finding love on a level of moral understanding approaching her own brings about a magnificent, exalted conclusion. Janáček himself had lost his little son four years before starting work on *Jenůfa*, and his grown-up daughter died after a long illness during the final stages of its composition; the optimism of the ending suggests a strong inner life.

Overview: Largely because he adapted *Jenůfa* directly from Preissová's play rather than from a prepared libretto with conventionally symmetrical verse, the natural 'feel' of Janáček's declamation sets him apart from Smetana and Dvořák despite the Czech (Moravian) setting. The opera's main female characters are unusual in *both* standing among opera's great mothers: Jenůfa's Act II >scene with its intense maternal concerns places her alongside Cherubini's **Médée** and Bellini's **Norma**. The Kostelnička, like Strauss's Klytemnestra (**Elektra**), is one of the most rewarding dramatic character roles in the repertoire.

Further reading: *Jenůfa* (English National Opera Guide 1985).

Listening

VPO/Mackerras
(Ochman, Dvorský, Söderström, Randová)
1982

KÁŤA KABANOVÁ

Three acts
Libretto: The composer, after
Aleksandr Nikolaevich Ostrovsky
First performance: Brno 1921

Plot: Katya, sensitive and impulsive, is the wife of a merchant, Tichon Kabanov, in a small town on the Volga. They are dominated by his mother, the vile Kabanicha, ultra-respectable and devoid of warmth. When Tichon goes away Katya, encouraged by her sister-in-law, succumbs to a cultivated Moscow youth, Boris, himself under the thumb of an unpleasant uncle. She does not commit adultery lightly, and once Tichon returns her morbid guilt puts her on the rack. In a public shelter during a thunderstorm she confesses her sin; then, after a poignant farewell with Boris, who is sent to Siberia for his part in the affair, she leaps into the Volga and drowns. Kabanicha is unmoved; only her son and her public role matter.

The opera: *Káťa Kabanová* was the first flowering of Janáček's extraordinary late operatic output. **Jenůfa** had at last gained international success; furthermore, Janáček had fallen in love with a young married woman who became his Muse without returning his feelings. The opera is an intense excursion into a trapped woman's passion in a claustrophobic environment. Each of Katya's monologues enlarges our view of her, and challenges the singer in the range and complexity of its expressiveness. Her sensitivity is felt even when she is not singing, for her music – foreshadowed in Janáček's unusually rich, full overture – pervades the score. In opposition, Kabanicha's music, assertive and angular, reinforces the score's disruptive switches of tone and menacing drumbeats. The folk-songs and prosaic >recitative of Katya's sister-in-law and her lover set off Katya's and Boris's exalted lines.

Decca D267D3 4 K267K33
CD: 414 483-2DH2
London LDR 73009
CD: 414 483-2LH2

Although there are no ensembles, Janáček brilliantly establishes the naked feelings of several characters simultaneously, especially in Tichon's departure scene, during Katya's confession, and in the laconic responses to her suicide. The lovers' emotions are encapsulated in an instrumental passage of utmost beauty as they stand, silent, during their last embrace.

Overview: Katya's situation parallels Katerina Ismailova's (Shostakovich's **Lady Macbeth of the Mtsensk District**), but the women are as different as their music. Where Katerina kills, Katya worries and confesses – and although they both jump into the river at the end, Katya's suicide has nothing of defiance in it. In Janáček's *Káťa*, as in **The Makropulos Affair**, only the central person is fully developed – other characters are sketched – and in his most successful operas apart from **From the House of the Dead** he has, like Richard Strauss, enriched the repertoire with superb roles for women.

Further reading: John Tyrrell – *Leoš Janáček: Káťa Kabanová* (Cambridge Opera Handbook 1982); *Káťa Kabanová* (English National Opera Guide 1985).

Listening

Decca D 51D2 4 K5122
London OSA 12116 4 OSA 5-12116
VPO/Mackerras
(Söderström, Kniplová, Dvorský)
1976

THE CUNNING LITTLE VIXEN
Příhody Lišky Bystroušky

Three acts
Libretto: The composer, after Rudolf Tesnohlidek
First performance: Brno 1924

Plot: The Gamekeeper, drowsing in the forest, catches a beautiful little vixen as a pet. At his home she rules the roost, and then escapes; for years afterwards he tries to recapture her without success. In the forest she dislodges a badger and takes over his burrow, and then is courted by a handsome fox, with whom she has many cubs. Aiming to steal the goods from a young poacher's basket, she incurs his wrath and gets shot. The Gamekeeper, old now, drowses one day in the forest and encounters a vixen cub, the image of his former pet – but this one he doesn't capture.

The opera: The antics of forest creatures and the way they impinge on humans, an unlikely subject for operatic treatment, become here a wonderful opera. The animals (mostly sung by children or adult female voices) behave with quaint and comic anthropomorphic charm, but Janáček is never sentimental. The vixen herself is quite splendid: she is attractive to all, bites when tormented, reveals feminist tendencies and political acumen, escapes with brazen bravery, displays a sharp, insulting tongue, is courted, rears a family, and is killed for her cocky cunning. Sexuality is presented with unaffected wholesomeness – the vixen symbolises a feminine allure for the Priest, the Schoolmaster and the Gamekeeper, frequently connected in their minds with Terynka, a woman on whom they pin their fantasies (the poacher, Harasta, both kills the vixen and marries Terynka). Like the vixen, the Gamekeeper is a portrait in depth, his final stream-of-consciousness in the forest a moving affirmation of the life-cycle (it was played at Janáček's funeral). The integration of humanity and nature pulses through this glorious score, in the fully worked-out orchestral preludes and interludes, the creatures' dances, the folk-songs and, above all, in Janáček's vocal line, natural enough to cope with every manner of expression.

Overview: In Wagner's **Siegfried** the Woodbird converses prettily with Siegfried; the bird's dramatic function is to advance the action connected with the hero, after which it no longer really exists. In Ravel's **L'enfant et les sortilèges**, the pets and garden creatures are mainly portrayed as filling the Child's world. In Janáček's opera, the inner life of the forest is no less self-contained than the human life in contact with it, nor are the forest creatures a metaphor for human experiences. Ever renewed, all life is the experience, in a ripe world which incorporates us all. What a testimony from a seventy-year-old composer!

Further reading: Essay by John Tyrrell accompanying the recording below.

Listening

Decca D257D2 4 K257K22
CD: 417 129-2DH2
London LDR72010 4 0SA5-72010
VPO/Mackerras
(Jedlička, Popp, Randová)
1981

THE MAKROPULOS AFFAIR
Věc Makropulos

Three acts
Libretto: The composer, after Karel Čapek
First performance: Brno 1926

Plot: Emilia Marty, a famous and beautiful singer, tells of a will crucial to the century-old case of Gregor versus Prus, which suggests that Gregor had been Prus's illegitimate son by a singer, Ellian MacGregor. Emilia eventually gets hold of the Greek document attached to this will, in exchange for which she allows Prus's descendant to make love to her – her only concession to the extreme passion she arouses in those around her, whom she insults and exploits. Finally forced to explain herself fully, her strange history becomes clear: originally Elina Makropulos, born 1585, she consumed an elixir giving her over 300 years of life. Since then she has lived under different names, all with the initials E.M., and her feeling for people and indeed the value of living itself has atrophied. The Greek document is the recipe for the elixir, but once she has it she realises she no longer wants to live, and she dies as it is burnt.

The opera: Despite its supposedly non-operatic subject matter Janáček made a superb music drama out of Čapek's

play. We first see Emilia Marty/Elina Makropulos as almost comically absurd, making intimate personal comments about people who have been dead for centuries. Gradually the destruction sown by her beauty and coldness becomes apparent. When she is cornered she becomes grotesque, even pathetic, judged by 'ordinary' values. But as she finally begins to die, and she articulates the loneliness of her meaningless existence, she emerges as a figure of immense tragedy. The power and beauty of this final scene make it one of Janáček's greatest passages and one of the most eloquent in all opera. It is the climax to a striking score of concentrated intensity. The opera's forward impulse, right from the churning overture, is at no stage modified by song-forms or self-contained scenes (although in orchestral colour at least, Emilia's reminiscences with her former lover, old Hauk, recalling a Spanish interlude when she was Eugenia Montez, stand apart). Janáček finds a natural declamation perfectly adapted to the terse, nerve-jangling drama.

Overview: Like old Schigolch in Berg's **Lulu**, Hauk is an almost surreal character. But Elina, the opera's unique figure, dominates *Makropulos*; other characters take on dramatic life only in relation to herself. This is unusual partly because the traditions of Italian opera (which shaped opera in general) would not support one singer's predominance, partly because powerful personalities seem more vivid beside their foils. **Madam Butterfly** (Puccini) and **Médée** (Cherubini) come nearest to defining their operas as Elina Makropulos does, with the emotional concentration carried almost entirely by them alone.

Further reading: Essay by John Tyrrell in booklet accompanying the Decca recording below.

Listening

1 Decca D144D2 4 K144K22
London OSA 12116 4 OSA 5-12116
VPO/Mackerras
(Söderström, Dvorský, Zítek, Jedlička, Blachut)
1978
2 Supraphon 50811-2
CBS (US) B 2 C 167

Prague National Theatre Opera/Gregor
(Prylová, Žídek, Kočí, Berman, Karpíšek)
1967

FROM THE HOUSE OF THE DEAD
Z mrtvého domu

Three acts
Libretto: The composer, after Fyodor Dostoyevsky
First performance: Brno 1930

Plot: In a Siberian prison camp in the mid-19th century there is little action, and much talk. A newly-arrived political prisoner, Petrovich, irritates the Commandant and is flogged. He forms a touching, loving friendship with the young boy Alyeya. Two plays are performed on a feast day. Various prisoners hold the floor with tales of their crimes and their punishment: Luka and Shashkin describe their encounters with police or prison officers, while both Skuratov and Shishkov recall violent, jealous murders. Violence tends to explode among the prisoners, too – there are fights, Alyeya is attacked, Shishkov curses Luka, who has just died, recognising him as his rival in his story. The Old Prisoner yearns for his family, and shows compassion for the dead man. Petrovich is released, while the camp mascot, an injured eagle now healed, flies to its freedom. Work goes on.

The opera: *From the House of the Dead* was the last fruit of a remarkable burst of creativity in old age. The subject matter may not at first appear effective for the medium, yet for many this is Janáček's greatest opera. Not that he attempts to transform it into anything conventionally more acceptable, leaving it virtually plotless, sung almost entirely by male voices, its most vivid dramatic action contained in narration. Its strength lies in its truth, its intensity, and its humanity – almost as though these brutalised men, when they have told their stories without disguising their passion and their guilt, have in some perverse way regained their dignity, that 'spark of God' which the composer

perceived in each one. And so there are moments of sweetest lyricism in this score, and a tonal framework around its abrasive dissonances which include the sounds of work and punishment in the camp – and individual prisoners sound more natural and human when singing as a chorus. In the extraordinary centrepiece, an 'opera' and a pantomime, the orchestra takes over with a 'popular' tone appropriate to the setting. With its long introduction, the opera is notably eloquent throughout.

Overview: There is an inevitable comparison with Beethoven's **Fidelio**, although in the earlier work there is a striving towards life outside the prison, whereas the camp is really a way of life for Janáček's prisoners. Both operas are heart-rending in depicting the yearning for freedom, which was achieved fully in *Fidelio*, but only by proxy in *From the House of the Dead* (Petrovich's discharge, and the eagle's flight, to the men's cries of 'Freedom, dear freedom!'). Janáček's opera is his darkest, neither sentimental nor tragic: it is realistic – and poetic.

Further reading: Essay by John Tyrrell accompanying the recording below.

Listening

Decca D224D2 4 K224K22
London LDR10036
VPO/Mackerras
(Jedlička, Zahradníček, Zítek, Žídek)
1981

Carl Nielsen

Born: 9th June 1865/Sortelung
Died: 2nd October 1931/Copenhagen

The leading Danish composer of his time, Nielsen broke away from the Romantic style and opened the modern era in Danish music. His symphonies and solo wind concertos are internationally known, but he wrote in all genres, producing a substantial output of choral and solo vocal music (the latter including an important group of popular songs). *Saul og David* and *Maskarade* gave him pre-eminence in Scandinavian opera, and his writings were equally influential.

MASKARADE

Three acts
Libretto: Vilhelm Andersen, after
Ludvig Holberg
First performance: Copenhagen 1906

Plot: Copenhagen, 1723. The popular practice of attending the masquerade is condemned by upstanding citizen Jeronimus, the more when his son Leander meets a young woman at a masquerade and decides to marry her. But Leander is betrothed to Mr Leonard's daughter, who shows her father the same filial resistance, for the same reason. The fathers insist that the planned marriage take place. Forbidden to leave the house, Leander slips out with his manservant, Henrik, to meet his new beloved at the masquerade. Jeronimus pursues him there in a mask, and commits a little indiscretion of his own. When it is found that Jeronimus's wife Magdelone and Leonard have been flirting, this is overlooked, for Leander's new sweetheart is revealed as Leonard's daughter, his intended all along.

The opera: In 1724 when Holberg's play was first performed, the masquerade had just been banned, for it apparently undermined class distinction, and behind masks people could drop their day-to-day mask – respectability. The enchanting overture shows Nielsen as a liberal clearly in favour of their continuing. His crisp, witty writing, playing with 18th-century conventions, is brimming with dance rhythms and simple, singable tunes. The central character is Henrik, who pokes fun at accepted attitudes, parodies the Italianate style of the lovers' duet, and makes the final 'lights-up' appeal for applause. Act I shows true >buffo humour in the exchanges between Jeronimus and Henrik, and Leonard and Jeronimus, in Jeronimus's disapproving >aria and Magdelone's dance scene. Jeronimus's servant Arv, if not played

for laughs, is a gem, in particular his Act II Mozartean ditty, and the lovely Dance of the Cockerels (Act III) is an amusing piece of orchestration. But several features relate also to the 20th century: the beautiful Prelude to Act II expresses a richer lyrical warmth than much of Leander's love music, and when in Act II Jeronimus assumes proprietorship of that familiar package, patriotism/morality/law-and-order, Nielsen neatly exposes his pompous pretensions.

Overview: The sheer healthy geniality of Nielsen's music, markedly different from Richard Strauss's fin de siècle evocations of the 18th century (**Der Rosenkavalier** and **Ariadne auf Naxos**), ensures that *Maskarade* is not mere pastiche. Nielsen's score, in the great tradition, shares the exuberance of Verdi's **Falstaff**, and the speed and lightness of Pergolesi. Henrik challenges Rossini's Figaro (**The Barber of Seville**), and Jeronimus and Leonard, those triumphant characterisations, are natural successors to the Doctors Bartolo and Basilio (in Mozart's and Rossini's Beaumarchais operas) without ever recalling their bite or spite.

Listening

Unicorn Records RHS 350/2
(Dansk Musik Antologi)
Danish Radio Symph/Frandsen
(Hansen, Landy, Schmidt Johansen, Sörensen, Bastian, Brödersen)
1977

Béla Bartók

Born: 25th March 1881/
Nagyszentmiklós
Died: 26th September 1945/New York

As with Debussy, and Beethoven before him, opera was the sphere of music Bartók was least involved in, and he produced only one. He was a strikingly individual composer of piano, chamber and choral music, with a number of important orchestral compositions.

There are also two ballets, of which *The Miraculous Mandarin*, part-pantomime, is one of his greatest works. His enthnomusicological research (much of it with Kodály) was of enormous influence.

DUKE BLUEBEARD'S CASTLE
A Kékszakállú herceg vára

Prologue and one act
Libretto: Béla Balázs
First performance: Budapest 1918

Plot: Judith elopes with Bluebeard on her wedding day and they come to his castle. It is dark and oppressive inside; loving him passionately, she wants to let in light and air. There are seven doors set in the walls; she unlocks the first three, and Bluebeard encourages her to open the fourth and fifth. In turn they reveal Bluebeard's torture chamber, his armoury, his treasure-store, his secret garden, and his vast domain. Each opened door lets in more light, but there is blood everywhere. Resisting Bluebeard's attempts to deflect her, Judith asks questions about his rumoured previous wives, and insists on opening the sixth door – to find a lake of tears. Finally, demanding the truth, she unlocks the seventh door, and three women emerge silently – Bluebeard's wives. As they return to their existence behind it, Bluebeard arrays Judith in a crushingly heavy mantle, jewels and crown. She too goes through the seventh door, Bluebeard's best-loved, but now part of his past – and darkness closes in.

The opera: With *Bluebeard* Bartók was freeing himself (and Hungarian music) from German domination, developing his own harmonic language and drawing on folk-song patterns for his word-setting. The result is a score of stark individuality, with a particular kind of muscle in its Impressionist colours. The vocal line, shaped by natural speech, gains force from the strong short first syllables of Hungarian words.

Aural and visual elements, equally powerful, are put to the use of potent symbolism. Ritual feeling is built up by brooding >ostinati in the orchestra, obsessive repetitions by both characters, and the device of the seven doors, each as it opens letting in new light, new colour, new music, new fears, with an almost unbearable climax at the fifth door. There are many possible interpretations (the spoken prologue, too often omitted, emphasises this); certainly the castle represents Bluebeard's inner life, Judith invades it too fully, and he murders her symbolically at the end. The emphasis on Bluebeard's terrible loneliness, rather than his cruelty, increases as Judith moves towards the point of no return. Her fate is inevitable – coming from outside she cannot possibly grasp the depth of his darkness.

Overview: Dukas's Bluebeard opera, *Ariane et Barbe-bleue*, was based on a text by Maeterlinck, and a Maeterlinck text was the basis for Debussy's **Pelléas et Mélisande**. *Pelléas* was a strong influence on *Bluebeard* in many ways – its harmonies, its colours, its symbolism, its word-setting. In both works light is threatened by almost tangible darkness. The fairy-tale, ritual element is ominous in *Bluebeard*, both comic and dramatic in **Turandot** (Puccini), and glamorous in Wagner's **Lohengrin**, another opera where a man demands total trust from a woman who has reason to challenge him.

Listening

Hungaroton SLPD 12254
CD: HCD12254
Hungarian State Opera/Ferencsik
(Nesterenko, Obraztsova)
1982

Bohuslav Martinů

Born: 8th December 1890/Polička
Died: 28th August 1959/Liestal

A leading Czech composer of the mid-20th century, Martinů's vast output included chamber, choral and orchestral works as well as twelve ballets and sixteen operas. Most of his adult life was spent outside his home country.

Further reading: Brian Large – *Martinů* (London 1975).

JULIETTA

Three acts
Libretto: The composer, after Georges Neveux
First performance: Prague 1938

Plot: Michel seeks Julietta in a bewildering town whose people, with no memory of their own, bully or pay others to hear their reminiscences. He finds Julietta just as he remembers her from a visit three years previously, and tries to recall with her the substance of their previous contact – but she prefers romantic fantasies of travel in Spain, and rushes off in anger. Thwarted, he shoots her as she flees, but then forgets her as well as his reason for coming, even when she reappears. Finding himself in the Central Bureau of Dreams, he overhears the wishes of other clients. Since many of these centre on a woman called Julietta, he begins to recall his own dream – and now he cannot tear himself away from the sound of Julietta's voice, which becomes more real and more desirable than the grey day-to-day life he knows. He will remain forever in the dreamworld; his dream starts all over again.

The opera: The action in *Julietta* is circular, allusive, bizarre; even the Bureau of Dreams, although it explains the first two acts, has a surreal quality of its own. The symbolism is suggested rather than clearly rooted: is Michel wholly inside his dream, or can he exercise a choice about remaining there? As with most dream-experiences, these exaggerate reality, with scenes of charm and humour switching to confusion and terror. Accordingly, Martinů has created a mosaic of styles. Michel's relationship with Julietta combines warm romantic nostalgia with the sentimentality of her

picture postcard reminiscences. The townspeople are amusingly differentiated in vocal writing; the visitors to the Bureau generate contrasting orchestral contexts. Accompanied by a wash of solo piano, two old people reaffirm their past identity through the kindly 'Grandpa Youth'; to a slow, sad *moto perpetuo*, a blind beggar pleads for a chance to enjoy the printed fantasies he sells; a matter-of-fact railway engineer reminds himself of his dead daughter while the orchestra makes his tragedy palpable.

Overview: Ravel's **L'enfant et les sortilèges** treats the child's fantasy as reality, so that it becomes an innocent tale; Poulenc's **Les mamelles de Tirésias** makes a zany comedy out of wish-fulfilment. In **The Lighthouse**, Davies merges fantasy and reality, past and present, within strictly limited parameters. In *Julietta* Martinů suggests contradictory planes of experience without any apparent formal structure, yet rather than becoming incoherent, his score gains substance and focus. It is an unusual and fascinating achievement.

Listening

Supraphon 50 611/3
Prague National Theatre/Krombholc
(Žídek, Tauberová)
1964

THE GREEK PASSION
Řecké pašije

Four acts
Libretto: The composer, after Nikos Kazantzakis
First performance: Zurich 1961

Plot: At Eastertime in a Greek mountain village, two events take place: the roles are allotted for the following Easter's Passion play, and a group of refugees arrives, starving, driven from their homes by the Turks. In dealing with the refugees, the local villagers gradually take on the identity of their roles in the Passion play. The Priest and the Elders reject the refugees, who attempt to rebuild their lives on a barren mountainside nearby. Manolios (Christ), growing in purity of soul, is drawn to preaching on their behalf, rousing the villagers in the name of Christ's humanity. His three friends (the Apostles) and Katerina (the Magdalene) find spiritual fulfilment in upholding his cause, the Priest excommunicates him and a jealous villager (Judas) kills him. At the end the refugees take up their wanderings again.

The opera: Martinů wrote *The Greek Passion* while he was fighting cancer in his last years. The sense of Greek life is as strong in the music as the exiled composer's feeling for his Czech homeland. But it would be a mistake to look for local colour here. Even with its roots in a realistic story, the Passion is played out at a symbolic level, with the two choruses (one for the villagers, one for the refugees) adding a ritual intensity to the fabric of the drama. Martinů's orchestral writing, the accompaniment and the interpolations, both heightens and comments on the text – he worked with Kazantzakis on the adaptation, and was deeply concerned not to distract from the lines themselves. The vocal style is declamatory and flexible, with brief lyrical moments, notably a starving villager's wordless death-moans, Katerina's exalted play on the word 'sister', and some of the lines of the Apostles (particularly those of Yannakos). The real lyricism is cumulative, as in Manolios's exalted confession before he is killed, the choral writing, or the sublime, hopeful music that ends each of the four acts.

Overview: While the spiritual growth of Manolios in no way parallels Blanche's movement towards martyrdom in **Dialogues des Carmélites**, both works share an intense Christian experience, and a faithfulness to the text rare in opera. Using flesh-and-blood characters to re-enact the Passion, Martinů's opera also depicts the pressures of village life with all the force of Janáček's **Jenůfa** or Britten's **Peter Grimes**.

Listening

Supraphon 11163611/2 4 3611/2
Brno State Philharmonic Orch./Mackerras (Mitchison, Field, Tomlinson)
1981

Arwel Huw Morgan (Ladas) and Richard Morton (Yannakos) in *The Greek Passion* (Welsh National Opera 1984)

Aulis Sallinen

Born: 9th April 1935/Salmi

Finland's leading composer in the late 20th century, Sallinen had already made a reputation as an orchestral and chamber music composer before he wrote his first opera, *The Horseman*. With both subsequent operas he has gained in stature, not least because each has proven to be entirely different from what was expected.

THE RED LINE
Punainen viiva

Two acts
Libretto: The composer, after Ilmari Kianto
First performance: Helsinki 1978

Plot: 1907, the harsh Finnish backwoods. A crofter couple struggles desperately to survive. Nature is cruel: when the winter snows are ended, a marauding bear takes their livestock. The villagers and the church give them no support; their growing children are their only hope. But change is abroad: elections, the chance of a new life from socialism. They attend meetings, read the newspaper, and mark their vote with a red line. Then they wait for their lives to change. By the time news comes, their children have died, and barking dogs have scented the waking bear. Topi goes to fight it and is killed, a red line of blood at his throat. Riika stands alone – but a young birch tree is in green leaf.

The opera: Sallinen encapsulates the thwarted lives of these people in music hewn from deep insight into the realities of poverty and despair. Nothing is more poetic than Riika's lonely monologue (Scene 2), nor more poignant than her later description, against plangent string textures, of how she has endlessly cleared the death-like snow from the ski trail for the expected bringer of good tidings.

Although the prevailing tone is bleak, each scene creates a different colour, as in the beautiful traditional Finnish chorus sung against those determined to overthrow the 'rotten old pines' and make a new order with their own rallying song. And there is the couple's ferocious bickering, Riika's warm, ripe description of her youth on a prosperous farm, the complacent church organ in Topi's nightmare vision of the Church Rejecting, the pedlar's fine ballad, the political tracts spoken like a sermon, the uncompromising agitator, the festive excursion to vote, the lullaby sung over Riika's dead children. Sallinen makes entirely original use of single percussive sounds in a work whose silences are as telling as the shattering orchestral passage after the discovery of the children's death. The chorus is a crucial element throughout.

Overview: Sallinen made so strong an impression with *The Red Line*, which depicts a crucial episode in Finnish history, that there was disappointment over his change of style for **The King Goes Forth to France**. Although poverty and loss also affect the communities of **The Greek Passion** (Martinů) and **Porgy and Bess**, in the latter work Gershwin's instantly appealing, life-affirming music takes

Michael Melbye in the 1987 production of *The King Goes Forth to France* (Royal Opera House)

some of the sting out of the suffering it portrays. The truth is at its starkest in *The Red Line*.

Further reading: Essay by Erkki Arni accompanying recording below.

Listening

Finlandia Records FA 102 LP3
Finnish National Opera/Kamu
(Hynninen, Valjakka)
1980

THE KING GOES FORTH TO FRANCE
Kuningas lähtee Ranskaan

Three acts
Libretto: Paavo Haavikko with the composer
First performance: Savonlinna 1984

Plot: With a new Ice Age threatening to submerge modern England, the Prince assumes power as King. He marches with his Prime Minister, his army, his people and his four potential wives (two Carolines and two Annes) across the frozen English Channel to France. Time moves backwards: at Crécy he wins a battle, and then moves North to besiege Calais, to the frustration of an English archer, whom he punishes cruelly. By this time he has married a German princess and pawned her to finance his campaigns (upsetting The Caroline with the Thick Mane, who is becoming mentally unhinged). He decides he loves The Nice Caroline; after he takes Calais, she will accompany him to Paris, to new conquest, the sun and the wine. And yet – as they depart, the storm and the gale get worse.

The opera: *The King Goes Forth to France* is a political/historical allegory, in which the horror of modern war and the age-old subjugation of women are handled with rumbustious wit. It mingles farcical situations and positive good humour with trenchant comment about power, bureaucracy, and other forces undermining civilisation. While Schubert's *Marche militaire* is invoked to hilarious effect, the music for The Caroline with the Thick Mane gently parodies the sentimental-lyrical mad scenes of Bellini/Donizetti to touching effect. Never mawkish, The Nice Caroline affirms old-fashioned social and musical values; the Prime Minister's clipped phrases and the fatuous heroics of the English Archer are clever characterisations, and the King splendidly incorporates lyrical, comic and dramatic elements.

Overview: Much has been made of the influences manifest in the score (Shostakovich, Prokofiev, Weill, amongst others). If these have helped make Sallinen's music approachable, then they are simply the sources of his greatest strength. As an allegorical fantasy-satire the opera may evoke Rimsky-Korsakov's **The Golden Cockerel** although it boasts a more inventive score; as an epic, Prokofiev's *War and Peace*, and Poulenc's **Les mamelles de Tirésias** for its sport with naturalistic conventions. But it goes farther than these, nor does it repeat the combination of socialism and >verismo in the composer's earlier **The Red Line**. *The King Goes Forth* forges a genre of its own, and the sheer theatrical flair and melodic conviction of this rich, multi-layered work displays an identifiable personality such as Stravinsky maintained throughout his famous shifts of style.

RUSSIAN OPERA

I **n terms of Western tastes, the history of Russian opera spans the thirty-five year period between the first performances of Musorgsky's *Boris Godunov* (1874) and Rimsky-Korsakov's *The Golden Cockerel* (1909). Obviously there is more to it than that.**

In the reign of Catherine the Great (late 18th century), visitors such as Cimarosa or Paisiello left their mark on the native musicians (just as Berlioz's sojourns would influence the nationalist composers of the later 19th century). But in reaction to these cosmopolitan composers producing works in their own languages, composers like Sokolovsky and Fomin started writing in Russian. The most popular were part-spoken, part-sung comedies of village life – a kind of local >Singspiel. Since that time Russian opera has been at its most vital when depicting the common people, a vitality due partly to the use of folk-song (however awkward its

early, 'Westernised' settings). Other favourite themes – historical drama and fairy tale – would yield rich fruit in the great days that followed.

Up to the age of six, Glinka imbibed Russian folksong, Orthodox chant and the sound of the church bells almost exclusively, and it was reflected in his *A Life for the Tsar* (1836) and *Ruslan and Lyudmila* (1842). A self-taught musician, he is now regarded as the father of Russian opera, the source for nationalist heroism, fantasy-humour, the use of folk music and exotic orchestral colour. Writing after Glinka, Dargomizhsky developed a word-setting that followed the natural

Anthony Roder in the title role of
Stravinsky's *Oedipus Rex* (Opera North
1987)

inflections of the Russian language,
which culminated in his *The Stone
Guest* (1872). This kind of 'melodic
>recitative' stimulated Musorgsky's
own efforts, magnificently fulfilled in
Boris Godunov.

It is important to note that Glinka was
self-taught, for 'proper' training had to
be Western training, and the amateur
or even part-time composers tended to
be nationalists, interested in Russian
subject matter and the use of folk
material. (Tchaikovsky, who applied
folk elements only when they were
called for in the libretto, but whose
characteristic Russian lyricism
pervaded his music, did not fit into this
picture). When part-timers like Borodin
and Musorgsky left their works
unfinished or unorchestrated, those who
took on the job of completion tended to
iron out supposed inelegancies which
were often truly individual, Russian

elements. Rimsky-Korsakov was the
main culprit in committing this
'revisionism', but since he was loyal
enough to take on his colleagues' work,
criticism must be tempered with
gratitude. The vitality and originality of
Musorgsky's *Boris Godunov* or
Borodin's *Prince Igor* were missing in
Rimsky-Korsakov's own operas. His
fantasy-comedies, remarkable mainly
for their glittering colours, led in their
turn to the satires of Shostakovich and
Prokofiev, and before Stravinsky
embarked on his unique journey
through different styles he produced a
fairy-tale opera, *The Nightingale*, in the
same mould.

Since the 1930s, when Stalin and his
colleagues killed off the wonderful
upsurge of artistic creativity unleashed
by the 1917 Revolution, most new
Russian operas have been virtually
unknown outside the Soviet Union, and
there is no audience for the socialist-
realist works of the mid-century.
Interest has increased in Shostakovich's
Lady Macbeth of the Mtsensk District
and some of the Prokofiev operas
(notably *The Gambler, The Fiery Angel*
and *War and Peace*). But Western
opera houses still await a regeneration
of Russian opera.

Mikhail Glinka

Born: 1st June 1804/Novospasskoye
Died: 12th February 1857/Berlin

Glinka is generally regarded as the
founder of the Russian nationalist school
of composers. *A Life for the Tsar*
(originally named *Ivan Susanin*) and
Ruslan and Lyudmila, the second
Spanish Overture and the orchestral
piece *Kamarinskaya* were works which
particularly influenced the major
Russian composers. Glinka was also a
prolific song-writer, as well as
producing orchestral and instrumental
works.

Further reading: David Brown –
*Mikhail Glinka: A Biographical and
Critical Study* (London 1974).

RUSLAN AND LYUDMILA

Five acts
**Libretto: Valerian Shirkov, Nestor
Kukolnik, N. Markevich,
M. Gedeonov, after Alexander
Pushkin**
First performance: St Petersburg 1842

Plot: In Kiev the Princess Lyudmila has
chosen Ruslan over her other suitors
Farlaf and Ratmir, but during her
betrothal celebration she is secretly
abducted by the dwarf Chernomor. All
three suitors set off to rescue her. Farlaf
meets the wicked witch Naina and is
promised her help. Ruslan meets the
Finn, a magician hostile to Naina, who
encourages him in an heroic exploit
which wins him a magic sword. Naina's
beautiful maidens entrap Ruslan and
Ratmir but the Finn frees them, to the
relief of Ratmir's previous love
Gorislava, who is pursuing him.
Lyudmila has resisted Chernomor's
blandishments, but in an enchanted
garden he casts a spell of sleep over
her, and when Ruslan defeats him and
rescues her, she does not awake.
Although she is abducted by Naina on

Farlaf's behalf, once in Kiev Farlaf
cannot wake her. It takes Ruslan to do
so with a magic ring from the very
helpful Finn – and the interrupted
celebrations are resumed.

The opera: Despite a flabby,
unbalanced libretto and a disjointed
score, *Ruslan and Lyudmila* remains
popular in Russia. The plums include
the dashing overture, the Act I canon
following Lyudmila's abduction,
Ruslan's beautiful *O polye, polye* (Act
II), the chorus of the Persian women, the
Oriental Dances for Chernomor. The
two magical nasties and Farlaf, Naina's
>buffa stooge, are comical in their
villainy. Vivid choruses and dances, and
fairy-tale magic and horror touched up
with chromaticism, create a splendid
spectacle. Colour is important: the
whole-tone scale (making its first
appearance in European music) sets
Chernomor apart from the >diatonic
Ruslan, an Oriental atmosphere clings
to Ratmir (the use of a contralto works
well here), and an archaic solemnity
surrounds the bards and their
prophecies. Although the Finn does the
real work of resue, Ruslan certainly
sounds heroic. Only Lyudmila's
>coloratura is out of place – it is almost
perversely Italianate.

Overview: The opera set a distinctive
pattern for Russian composers to follow.
Borodin's Polovtsian dances (**Prince
Igor**), the March from Prokofiev's **The
Love for Three Oranges**, the satire of
the quest in **The Golden Cockerel**
(Rimsky-Korsakov), Musorgsky's
solemn choruses in **Boris Godunov**, not
to mention any magical and grotesque
elements in these and other works – all
are foreshadowed here. There are
wider connections too. The enchanted
garden appeared earlier in Lully's
Armide and Handel's **Orlando**;
Wagner used it in **Parsifal**; the magic
ring, and a magic sword wrung forth by
noble exploit, appear in **The Valkyrie**.
But *Ruslan and Lyudmila* remains
quintessentially Russian.

Listening

Le Chant du Monde/Melodiya LDX 78681/84
Bolshoi Opera/Simonov
(Nesterenko, Roudenko, Maslennikov,
Sinyavskaya)
1970s

Alexander Borodin

**Born: 12th November 1833/
St Petersburg
Died: 27th February 1887/
St Petersburg**

A brilliant academic in the field of chemistry, Borodin's teaching and research were of considerable importance. As a musician he was really a part-timer, yet he produced symphonies, chamber music, piano music and songs. Much of his work has been edited, orchestrated and even completed by other musicians. *Prince Igor* is the most important; its composition was a feature of his life for eighteen years.

PRINCE IGOR
Knyaz Igor

**Four acts
Libretto: The composer, from a
scenario by Vladimir Stasov after a
Russian chronicle
First performance: St Petersburg 1890**

Plot: Despite auguries of doom, the Russian Prince Igor takes his troops into battle against the Polovtsian invaders, leaving his wife Yaroslavna and her brother Prince Galitzky in command of the capital city, Putivl. Galitzky, a libertine, keeps a house dedicated to lust and drunkenness, and Yaroslavna can barely restrain him. The campaign proves a disaster for the Russians, and Igor is imprisoned with his son Vladimir by the Khan, Konchak. The Khan's daughter and Vladimir fall in love, and when Igor escapes, Vladimir hesitates; he is caught – but allowed to marry Konchakovna. Igor returns to Putivl, where he and Yaroslavna bring new hope to the beleaguered Russians.

The opera: *Prince Igor* is the most impressive part-time composition to reach the stage. Although Borodin spent eighteen years working on it, it had to be completed and partly orchestrated by Rimsky-Korsakov and Glazunov (Act III remained so sketchy that it is often omitted, despite containing important dramatic elements). Written piecemeal, the opera is no aesthetic trail-blazer. Yet it has considerable personality, balancing two cultures, one local and one 'exotic', whose leaders, both impressive, are as different as their music. The Polovtsian Dances (incorporating chorus) with which the open-hearted Khan keeps his royal prisoner entertained are languorous, shimmering, barbaric in turn – a glorious set-piece, made even more famous by the musical *Kismet*. Borodin's lyrical flair is abundantly expressed in Yaroslavna's two >arias (Acts I and IV), and in the series of fine numbers in Act II – the song of the Polovtsian maiden, Konchakovna's and Vladimir's >cavatinas, their duet and, best of all, Igor's solo, an expression of his great spirit. Prince Galitzky's irresistibly self-indulgent >credo and the Khan's two numbers are effective character-pieces; broad comedy is provided by the two drunken deserters, Eroshka and Skula, who hastily switch their support back to Igor just in time to save their skins.

Overview: *Prince Igor* combines conventional operatic writing of some distinction with the kind of nationalist sentiments which endeared it to its local audiences. The young lovers coping with the conflict of loyalties is a classic situation familiar from several famous operas (take your pick – **Idomeneo**, **William Tell**, **Nabucco**, **Aida**), but the Khan is an interesting development of Mozart's Osmin (**Die Entführung aus dem Serail**), and the two funny-men deserters a broad echo of the escaped priests in **Boris Godunov**. The conflict between Russian and 'Oriental' music was foreshadowed in Glinka's **Ruslan and Lyudmila**.

Listening

EMI/Pathé Marconi CAN 176-8
Sofia National Opera/Semkov
(Christoff, Chekerlisky, Wiener, Todorov, Penkova)
1966

Modest Musorgsky

Born: 21st March 1839/Karevo
Died: 28th March 1881/St Petersburg

A major Russian composer of the late 19th century, Musorgsky responded strongly to the language and spirit of his people. The solo piano suite (later orchestrated) *Pictures at an Exhibition* and the orchestral *St John's Night on the Bare Mountain* have brought him popularity, but it was in his songs and his operas that he showed his greatest originality. Apart from the two included here there are also *Salammbô* and *Sorochintsy Fair*. Much of this work was edited and 'improved' by his colleagues; it had been left unfinished after an early death brought on by consistently heavy drinking.

Further reading: M. D. Calvocoressi – *Musorgsky* (London 1974).

BORIS GODUNOV

Prologue and four acts
Libretto: The composer after Alexander Pushkin and Nicolai Karamzin
First performance: St Petersburg 1874

Plot: The sufferings of the Russian people, which trouble the reign of Tsar Boris Godunov, are widely attributed to his murder of the child prince and rightful heir, Dmitri. Boris, who loves his own children, is haunted by the crime, and the most powerful noble, Prince Shuisky, uses it against him. Disaffected elements rally around Grigory, a Pretender to the Throne, who calls himself Dmitri and gains credibility from being the same age as the murdered Prince. After a sensational escape from Russia, Grigory/Dmitri rallies Poles and Lithuanians to his cause, including the Jesuit Rangoni who fosters Dmitri's love for the beautiful Polish aristocrat Marina in order to

The Bolshoi Theatre's *Boris Godunov* (1987)

restore Roman Catholicism to Russia. Even before Boris dies in terrible physical and spiritual agony, Dmitri has the support of Shuisky. As his motley army advances through the forest to Moscow, a Holy Idiot bewails the fate of the Russian people.

The opera: Well-intentioned composers' large-scale alterations to the opera have led to productions and recordings which rarely do justice to Musorgsky's intentions, watering down its strengths and its individuality. *Boris Godunov* is a >grand opera without spacious theatricality: the function of Musorgsky's music was to convey the stark emotions of his main characters against the vast canvas of the Russian people itself, and although he does not eschew lyricism, or even the full-blooded romantic duet between Dmitri and Marina, his natural medium is a wholly flexible dramatic >recitative, occasionally approximating speech. The touching exchanges between Boris's children and their Nurse, the robust drinking of the errant monk Varlaam and the eagerness of the Innkeeper for company, and above all the sad, confused truths uttered by that very Russian character, the Holy Idiot, are no less alive than the 'false' Dmitri's vanity, Marina's ambition, or Boris's tortured mental state. National colour is not only embodied in the wonderful series of folksongs and quasi-folksongs sung by individual characters: it is etched in every magnificent chorus, whether made up of women, priests, boys, vagabonds or a random crowd.

Overview: Although Boris makes substantial appearances in only two scenes, his burning presence dominates the drama no less than Verdi's **Macbeth**, another king virtually destroyed by the visions conjured out of his own guilt. But while the suffering of the Scottish people is directly related to Macbeth's regicide, Musorgsky shows us that the suffering of the Russian people continues, whatever the complexities of government – a point made even more strongly in his own **Khovanshchina**. Standing in total contrast is his skilful use of children's songs in little Prince Fyodor's carefree

scene – a new element later taken up
by Berg (**Wozzeck**) and given
significance in several works by Britten.

Further reading: *Boris Godunov –*
(English National Opera Guide 1982).

Listening

1 (1872 version)
  Philips 412 281-1PH3
  CD: 412 281-2PH3
  Bolshoi Theatre/Fedoseyev
  (Verdernikov, Sokolov, Matorin, Rakov,
  Eizen, Arkhipova)
  1978–1980
2 (Lloyd-Jones edition)
  HMV Angel SLS 1000
  Angel SX 3844 (US)
  Polish National Radio Symphony/Semkow
  (Talvela, Gedda, Mroz, Kinasz, Hiolski,
  Baniewicz, Haugland)
  1977

KHOVANSHCHINA
(The) Khovansky
Goings-on

Five acts
**Libretto: The composer (with
Vladimir Stasov, after historical
sources)**
First performance: St Petersburg 1886

Plot: On the eve of young Peter the
Great's assumption of power, Moscow is
torn between rival leaders – either the
Regent, Prince Galitsin, and the leading
Boyars (nobles), or Ivan Khovansky and
his son Andrey, supported by their
personal army, the feared Streltsi. The
Khovanskys safeguard a fundamentalist
religious sect, the Old Believers, whose
leader Dosifei fears for his cause. Ivan,

politically sophisticated, poses as a father figure; Andrey is a brutal creature of unbridled violence, sufficiently motivated by the desire for self-gratification to attack his discarded lover, Martha (Marfa), for thwarting his rape of a young foreign woman. Martha, an Old Believer, makes prophecies which prove accurate when a break-away group of Boyars, led by Shakloviti, supports Tsar Peter: Galitsin is exiled, Ivan Khovansky is assassinated, and the Old Believers, rather than be persecuted by the new regime, commit mass suicide. Among them is Andrey Khovansky. He has no choice but to die with Martha – who still loves him – rather than at the hands of the Tsar's guards.

The opera: Unfinished by Musorgsky, *Khovanshchina* has been much changed through illustrious composers' efforts to complete it. Musorgsky left a confused plot with much of the action poorly motivated. Although Ivan Khovansky works well portrayed as a rough-hewn, self-made man, and although the Streltsi are brownshirts to the life and the scribe is a clever vignette, most of the characters remain undeveloped. But the glories of Musorgsky's particular genius are undimmed. The opening Prelude is exquisitely lyrical; there are some impressive solo numbers (Shakloviti's brooding on the fate of Russia, and Martha's folk song – both Act III – and Dosifei's final prayer). Galitsin's departure for exile and the concluding music of Acts III and V are all deeply expressive. The choral treatment of the Old Believers, derived from their liturgy, invests them with a special beauty and dignity, and the concentration of folk songs to entertain Ivan Khovansky is irresistible (especially *Gaiduk, gaiduchok*) – the more ironic when mocked by Shakloviti, his assassin.

Overview: *Khovanshchina* is an epic: the Old Believers mounting their funeral pyre evoke the suicide of the Trojan women in opera's greatest epic, Berlioz's **The Trojans**. As in **Boris Godunov**, Musorgsky drew inspiration from death, exile, partial madness, martyrdom – and politics. What these works show of the intertwining of personal and political ambition (revealed also in Verdi's **Simon Boccanegra**), and the suffering of the common people from the power games of their rulers, rings true even more urgently today.

The curtain created by A. Golovin for *Eugene Onegin* at the Kirov Theatre, Leningrad in 1926

Listening

Le Chant du Monde LDX78590/3
Bolshoi Theatre/Khaikin
(Krivchenya, Pyavko, Maslennikov,
Nechipailo, Ognivtsev, Arkhipova)
1974

Pyotr Tchaikovsky

Born: 7th May 1840/Kamsko-Votkinsk
Died: 6th November 1893/ St Petersburg

One of the great Romantic composers of the later 19th century, Tchaikovsky's music has become embedded in the consciousness of millions of music-lovers. Of his many operas, only *The Queen of Spades* and *Eugene Onegin* are regularly included in the repertory, although *Iolanta*, *The Maid of Orleans*, *Vakula the Smith* and *Mazeppa* are also performed. His ballets are the backbone of the repertoire (The *Sleeping Beauty*, *The Nutcracker* and *Swan Lake*), as well as his symphonies, overtures and concertos in the concert hall. He also wrote choral and chamber music, and a considerable number of beautiful songs.

Further reading: David Brown – *Tchaikovsky: A Biographical and Critical Study* (London 1978).

EUGENE ONEGIN
Evgeny Onyegin

Three acts
Libretto: Konstantin Shilovsky and the composer, after Alexander Pushkin
First performance: Moscow 1879

Plot: Tatiana, intense and sensitive, is consumed with ardour for Eugene Onegin, the friend of her sister Olga's fiancé, Lensky. In a letter to Onegin she pours out all her feelings, but is met only with patronising kindness – he is fundamentally jaded and cynical. At a ball, Lensky's over-reaction to Onegin's dancing with Olga leads to a duel between them: Lensky sees it as the end of his youthful dreams, and indeed he is killed by his friend. Onegin travels abroad, but returns to Russia still haunted by what he has done. Meeting Tatiana, now married to Prince Gremin, he falls hopelessly in love with her, and writes to her as she once had to him. Although acknowledging her love for him, Tatiana stands by her marriage, and sends him away.

The opera: Tchaikovsky called this opera 'lyric scenes', and it is his lyricism which carries all before it. There is a remarkable homogeneity of tone: a descending group of four notes, first heard in the brief prelude, is the impetus for much of the melodic writing (including Tatiana's magnificent Letter Scene, Lensky's >aria before the duel and Tatiana's first distraught response to Onegin's declaration of love) as well as some of the more intimate moments, most notably Tatiana's touching exchange with her Nurse. As Tchaikovsky deepens his involvement with the main characters, the opera loses the rare Chekhovian atmosphere of the opening scene, which incorporates so many different strands with a natural ease: the warm respect shown for the older women, the glorious folksongs of the peasants, the nostalgic view of an harmonious routine ('Habit is a gift sent from Heaven to replace happiness') – all as 'Russian' in their own way as the personal dramas of Tatiana, Lensky and Onegin. The balls in Acts II and III give opportunities for a fine Waltz and Polonaise respectively, although their conventional splendour interferes with the opera's organic feeling.

Overview: *Eugene Onegin* has always been Tchaikovsky's most popular opera, its intense emotionalism a harbinger of his two famous last symphonies. Yet given that Onegin appears cruelly cold and bored almost until the end, he is one of the most difficult roles in opera to bring alive. The hero of Massenet's **Werther** is an amalgam of Lensky and the

199

transformed Onegin of the final act, its heroine Charlotte forced into the same situation as Tatiana, and Massenet's emotionalism is no less intense than Tchaikovsky's – but he just cannot match those memorable melodies.

Listening

Parlophone m PMA 1050-2
Bruno m BR 23001-3L
Bolshoi Theatre/Khaikin
(Vishnevskaya, Belov, Lemeshev)
1956

THE QUEEN OF SPADES
Pikovaya dama

Three acts
Libretto: Modest Tchaikovsky and the composer, after Alexander Pushkin
First performance: St Petersburg 1890

Plot: St Petersburg, late 18th century. The young officer Herman is too poor to gamble (although he watches obsessively) nor can he pursue his love for Lisa, an aristocrat. When he learns that Lisa's grandmother, the old Countess, had once by dubious means gained the secret of the winning cards, he senses the pull of Fate, and becomes bolder. Lisa responds to his passion, even giving him the key to her house. Taking his opportunity, he demands the secret from the old lady. She is speechless with horror, and when Herman threatens her with a gun, she drops dead. Now Lisa believes he has pursued her only to get access to her grandmother, and sends him away. When, months later, she tries to rejoin Herman, the Countess's ghost has just revealed the secret to him, and he has no more thoughts for Lisa. She flings herself into the river, and Herman rushes off to gamble maniacally. He keeps winning until, challenged by Lisa's ex-fiancé, he loses with the queen of spades. Mocked by another vision of the Countess, he stabs himself, and dies.

The opera: Tchaikovsky and his brother made fundamental changes to Pushkin's story, developing the love-interest and the melodrama to make it

more conventionally effective as an opera. This diluted the Satanic aspect of the Herman/Countess/cards axis, although the music reinforces any macabre elements, and left an ambiguity about Herman's reaction to the break with Lisa. The crowded scenes tend to distract from the drama. But the main exchanges between the lovers, their solos, and the Countess's ruminations about the good old days in Paris (including a full quote from Grétry's **Richard Coeur-de-lion**) share an emotional power and melodic richness in the true Tchaikovsky mould, and the Bedroom Scene reaches a high level of dramatic intensity. The orchestral images of Hell, or of Nature made angry by the unholy gambler, contain a vivid imaginative force.

Overview: While not a fully developed character, the Countess is worth cherishing as one of opera's very few interesting old women. She and Herman are incarnations of the belief that a gambler's soul has been sold to the devil: in death they are no closer to redemption than Mozart's **Don Giovanni**. 18th-century pastiche, a favourite Tchaikovsky touch – there is a charming song in **Eugene Onegin** – is substantially represented by the Act II >pastorale. The boys' mock-soldiers' chorus in the first scene is as delightful as its equivalent in **Carmen**.

Listening

HMV SLS 5005
Musical Heritage Society MHS 3865-8
Bolshoi Theatre/Khaikin
(Andzhaparidze, Mazurok, Levko, Arkhipova)
1967

Nikolay Rimsky-Korsakov

Born: 18th March 1844/Tikhvin
Died: 21st June 1908/St Petersburg

An influential composer, teacher, and musicologist, Rimsky-Korsakov devoted much time to editing his colleagues' works, as well as producing a great number of his own in all genres. Best known for his symphonic suite *Sheherazade* and his opera *The Golden Cockerel*, he wrote some fifteen other operas including *The Snow Maiden*, *Mozart and Salieri*, *The Tale of Tsar Saltan*, and *Legend of the Invisible City of Kitezh*.

Further reading: Nikolay Rimsky-Korsakov – *My Musical Life* (London 1974).

THE GOLDEN COCKEREL
Zolotoy petushok

Prologue, three acts, epilogue
Libretto: Vladimir Belsky, after
Alexander Pushkin
First performance: Moscow 1909

Plot: Old King Dodon, seeking advice in coping with enemy invasions, receives from the Astrologer a golden Cockerel which can warn him of approaching danger. He promises the Astrologer any reward he wants. Summoned by the Cockerel to war, the King finds himself doing battle with the beauty of the Queen of Shemakhan. He returns with her to his city in a triumphal wedding procession. When the Astrologer demands as his reward the Queen herself, the outraged King kills him, and is killed in turn by the angry Cockerel. In the Epilogue, the Astrologer claims that only the Queen and himself were real.

The opera: The allegory which forms the plot has never been explained satisfactorily. But Rimsky-Korsakov wrote the opera during the reign of Tsar Nicholas II, and the censors certainly recognised its satiric intent. Dodon is foolish to start with, concerned primarily with food and sleep; when he meets the Queen, he becomes idiotic. As a ruler, he reneges on promises, and bends the law to suit himself – a thoroughly unappetising character. Apart from the pomposity associated with the King and his equally foolish

courtiers, the score is dominated by the themes of the Cockerel (a brass alarm call), the Queen (a descending chromatic phrase) and the Astrologer (staccato notes outlining two contrasting chords). With these Rimsky-Korsakov, a famous orchestral colourist, works his instrumental magic, further showing his scene-painting capacity in two other passages – the mountain gorge music opening Act II, and the wedding procession in Act III.

Overview: *The Golden Cockerel* displays a decorative charm which may not sustain the interest of those who respond to more substantial music. Deriving from Glinka's **Ruslan and Lyudmila**, its exotic, fantasy aspect in turn influenced Stravinsky's *The Nightingale*, and its combination of fantasy and satire foreshadowed Prokofiev's **The Love for Three Oranges**, although the younger composer's score is more biting. The opera remains popular, as does the arrangement for orchestral suite, but to make the satire strike home (since Nicholas II himself is no longer with us) it would need an ingenious director to place it in a modern setting.

Listening

Le Chant du Monde LDX78011
Moscow Radio/Kovalyov and Akulov
(Korolyov, Kadinskaya, Pishchaev)
1962

Igor Stravinsky

Born: 17th June 1882/Oranienbaum
Died: 6th April 1971/New York

One of the most important composers of the 20th century, Stravinsky is famous for his magnificent Dyagilev ballets with their original approach to rhythm and harmony. During the war he turned to small-scale music-theatre pieces, and then while in France to his great neo-classical works. Up to this period he also composed a number of 'Russian' works. During his last years, spent in America, when he produced *The*

Rake's Progress, he incorporated the >serial technique into his writing. There are twenty-one dramatic works (ballet, opera, >melodrama and inbetween), those with voice including *The Nightingale, Renard, Pulcinella, Mavra, The Wedding, Oedipus Rex, The Rake's Progress* and *The Flood*. He wrote a number of important choral and orchestral works, solo vocal, instrumental and piano pieces.

OEDIPUS REX
King Oedipus

Two acts
Libretto: Jean Cocteau, after Sophocles
First performance: Paris 1927 (concert version); Vienna 1928 (staged)

Plot: The oracle pronounces: only when King Laius's murderer is ejected from Thebes will the plague cease. King Oedipus moves to root out the culprit, and by degrees it becomes apparent not only that he himself is the murderer but that Laius was his father. When he came to Thebes he had married the widowed Queen, Jocasta, unaware that she was his mother. Jocasta, suspecting the truth and unable to prevent its being revealed, hangs herself; Oedipus stabs out his eyes with the pin from her dress, and is sent from the city by his loving, sorrowing subjects.

The opera: More than any other, the story of Oedipus throbs with the dramatic rhythm of inexorable destiny. Stravinsky sets it as an opera oratorio using a Latin translation to emphasise its monumental, objectified character, with >ostinato (constantly repeated patterns) dominating the music. The most immediate theatrical impact comes not from the fixed expression (masks) and ritual manner of the characters and chorus, but from its striking, almost shocking contrast with the modern-dress Speaker's free, personal use of the audience's own language in narrating the events. Oedipus and Jocasta adopt a florid, flaunting vocal manner, displaying their arrogant complacency and symbolising

their half-conscious deviousness; Oedipus's speech is later stripped bare as he faces the terrifying truth. Towards the end the Chorus abandons its passive, reflecting role to articulate the agonies of the King and Queen, its compassion expressed in luminous textures as it helps Oedipus depart. The overall drama is conveyed without any pretence at naturalism, but the horror and pity behind the restraint are almost palpable, intensified by Stravinsky's instrumentation at its most refined and its most telling.

Overview: Orff's medium in *Carmina Burana* was Latin, fitted to a festive, sensual atmosphere. In *Oedipus Rex* Stravinsky chose Latin for its 'lofty dignity'; he saw it as 'a medium not dead but turned to stone'. Where living language's natural inflections suggested the appropriate musical line to Debussy and Poulenc or exaggerations of it to Schoenberg and Berg, Stravinsky rejoiced in the freedom to treat the syllables as neutral units for word-setting. Nothing could be further from the highly coloured emotions of Strauss's **Elektra**: Stravinsky's view of Greek tragedy is restrained, depersonalised. In its neo-classic austerity Stravinsky was recreating opera's earliest aesthetic, embodied in the **Euridice** of Peri; in its neo-Baroque grandeur there lay something of Handel's oratorios – and something, too, of the Russian Orthodox Church, which the composer rejoined in 1926.

Listening

CBS (UK) 72131
Washington Opera Society/Stravinsky
(Verrett, Shirley, Reardon)
1962

Sergey Prokofiev

Born: 23rd April 1891/Sontsovka, Ekaterinoslav
Died: 5th March 1953/Moscow

With Stravinsky and Shostakovich, Prokofiev is one of the three great 20th-century Russian composers, his music displaying both passionate lyricism and witty irony. A fine pianist, he made a notable contribution to piano literature; there are also songs, chamber and instrumental works, and important orchestral pieces including the well-known concertos for piano and for violin. Other famous works include the cantata *Alexander Nevsky*, adapted from his film score, and the perennial favourite *Peter and the Wolf*, the ballet *Romeo and Juliet* (one of eight), and the suite *Lieutenant Kije*, written as a film score. He wrote a dozen or so operas, of which *The Gambler*, *The Fiery Angel* and *War and Peace* are best known after *The Love for Three Oranges*. Having gone to live in the United States and France after the Revolution, he returned to the Soviet Union in the late 1930s, where he had to navigate Stalin's official policies on musical aesthetics.

Truffaldino and the Prince from *The Love for Three Oranges* (Sadlers Wells 1963)

THE LOVE FOR THREE ORANGES
Lyubov k tryom apelsinam

Prologue and four acts
Libretto: The composer, after Gozzi
First performance: Chicago 1921 (in French); Leningrad 1926

Plot: The King of Clubs is trying to equip his hypochondriac son to succeed him. Working to undermine him are both the Prime Minister and the King's niece (who intend to rule together), various rascally little devils and the wicked sorceress, Fata Morgana. Supporting the King are Tchelio, a sorcerer temporarily rendered powerless, and the clown Truffaldino. When, as his first achievement, Truffaldino gets the

depressed Prince to laugh, the thwarted Fata Morgana curses him with an unbridled love for three oranges. Off he sets with Truffaldino to seek them, and after surviving great dangers – mostly deriving from spanners thrown in the works by the aforementioned schemers, who are ultimately routed – he returns with Ninetta, the only princess to have survived transformation from her existence as an orange. She will be his future queen.

The opera: Prokofiev's manner in *The Love for Three Oranges* is mostly anti-Romantic and non-lyrical, the declamation ranging from stylised ritual chants to free >recitative. The delightful mock-pompous March – by far the opera's catchiest tune, famous from the Orchestral Suite – is frequently heard; it is characteristic of the score – spiky, colourful, rhythmically playful and slightly grotesque. There are riotous interruptions by various partisan choruses, wonderful wailing and moaning by whoever happens to be in trouble, and the lightest of impassioned outbursts from the Prince as an earnest lover. Prokofiev's most popular opera, a typically Russian comic fantasy incorporating fairy-tale sorcerers, villains, and heroes, adds several >commedia dell'arte characters and some well-aimed satirical commentary on the nature of theatre and its stock types and themes (not to mention the rather nutty oranges). Clearly it lends itself to extravagant productions, the visual element being enormously important – almost more so than the music, whose prime function is to heighten the sense of fun.

Overview: The Don Quixote/Sancho Panza quest undertaken by the Prince and Truffaldino parodies Mozart's **The Magic Flute** (Tamino and Papageno), and the commedia dell'arte characters, closer to their role in the 'straight' theatre than in Strauss's **Ariadne auf Naxos**, bear an uncanny resemblance to Leoncavallo's play within a play in **Pagliacci**. The card game which Tchelio loses to Fata Morgana occurs in Stravinsky's **The Rake's Progress**, while the comical choruses' double role – now commenting, now participating – are recalled by Ping, Pang and Pong in **Turandot**, another opera inspired by Gozzi.

Listening

Le Chant du Monde LDX 78311/2
USSR Radio Orch./Dalgat
(Rybinsky, Makhov, Rashkovets, Yelnikov, Poliakova)
1970s

Dmitry Shostakovich

Born: 25th September 1906/ St Petersburg
Died: 9th August 1975/Moscow

For many Shostakovich is the greatest 20th-century Russian composer. His output was extensive, including some important piano music, songs and choral music, orchestral works, thirty-six film scores, incidental music for over ten plays and several ballets, the operas *The Nose* and *Lady Macbeth*, a musical comedy, and an orchestration of *Tea for Two*. He had to face official cultural disapproval in the thirties both with *Lady Macbeth* and again in the late forties with his colleagues.

Further reading: Eric Roseberry – *Shostakovich: his Life and Times* (London 1981).

LADY MACBETH OF THE MTSENSK DISTRICT
Ledi Makbet Mtsenskovo uyezda

Four acts
Libretto: The composer and A. Preys, after Nikolai Leskov
First performance: Leningrad 1934; revised version Moscow 1963

Plot: For Katerina Izmailova, life as a rich merchant's wife is crushingly boring, until she is possessed by the sexual and romantic excitement of her new relationship with Sergey, a labourer. When her father-in-law discovers the affair and flogs Sergey cruelly, Katerina poisons the old man; and when her husband finds out, she and Sergey kill him. During their subsequent wedding a drunken peasant discovers the husband's body, and tells the police: Katerina and Sergey end up marching with other convicts through Siberia. Becoming irritated with Katerina, Sergey pursues a young convict, Sonyetka. In despair, Katerina pushes Sonyetka into the river, and jumps in after her – and as the women drown, the convicts march on.

The opera: The opera has been called 'a stunning piece of Russian >verismo' and its lurid melodrama, dominated by arbitrary violence, is indeed shocking. There are crude extremes of loudness and dissonance, abrupt galloping rhythms, sudden unison blasts of brass. But there is also the exquisite line of Katerina's monologues, that immobile outcry of barren loneliness in Act I, or her final Expressionist vision of the black, cold waves. Most striking are her avid moans of hunger, '*Tseluy, tseluy, tseluy menya*' (Kiss, kiss, kiss me) after strangling her husband, and the subsequent statement heavy with meaning, 'Now you are my husband'. This is a convincing aspect of the opera – love has become a drug, blocking out Katerina's horror at the murders it unleashes – whereas her connection with Shakespeare's Lady Macbeth is conventionally melodramatic she feels haunted by the presence of her victims. Stalin claimed to be disgusted by the 'chaotic' music, and the opera, condemned as neurotic and bourgois, was effectively banned in the USSR for twenty-five years. The revised version, renamed *Katerina Izmailova*, came well after Stalin's death. Perhaps he had been irked by the loony, grinning policemen of Act III, as hungry for action as Katerina was for love; more likely he could not stomach the orchestra's blatant frenzy in expressing the sexual act between the lovers.

Overview: Orchestral depictions of sexual intercourse range in tone from ecstasy to 'acceptable' violence – from Wagner's **Tristan und Isolde** (Act II), one works up the scale through Strauss's **Rosenkavalier** introduction, his **Salome** finale, the prelude to Act III of **Arabella**, to the symbolic Calaf/**Turandot** kiss in Puccini's opera, so brutish and so without sensuality. In *Lady Macbeth*, once labelled 'pornophony' by an American magazine, sexual passion brings an awakening to new life and the abandoning of all moral constraints; in this sense it stands alone.

Listening

EMI SLS 5157
London Phil./Rostropovich
(Vishnevskaya, Gedda, Petkov)
1979

AMERICAN OPERA

Well into the 20th century American operas were too dependent on Italian or German models to make any lasting impact, especially as the opera-going public had ready access to the great originals themselves. It seemed that a fresh idiom would have to be found for the Great American Opera.

In fact the stimulus came from an unlikely quarter. Operettas and musicals offered American composers scope for the drive and vitality that their society produced in abundance. The two great names were Jerome Kern and George Gershwin. Kern's *Show Boat* (1927) is regarded by some as an early quasi-opera in-the-style-of-a-musical; Gershwin's *Porgy and Bess* (1935) is of greater significance, not as a Negro folk opera but as an American one. Blending Black music, jazz and ballads with Gershwin's own inimitable melodic feel, it mirrored familiar musical elements in American life, and showed would-be opera composers that their source was all around them. In later decades, Leonard Bernstein and Stephen Sondheim revealed their flair for taking the idiom of the musical right into operatic territory.

The rise of Nazism and the start of World War II intensified the flow of notable composers out of Europe. Prokofiev had already been and gone, but the arrival of Schoenberg, Weill, Hindemith, Stravinsky and Bartók implies the injection of fresh talent. Yet of these only Weill made the United States his *cultural* home, his contribution to both the musical and opera extending the possibilities opened up in his own earlier works.

And so, as far as American opera is concerned, it was the homegrown composers who proved more fruitful. several of Marc Blitzstein's works, spanning the late 1920s to the early 1960s, incorporate parody and jazz elements; in *Regina* (1949) he followed the same principle as Gershwin and Weill, blending several styles, and producing a truly American opera. The same could not be said of Gian-Carlo Menotti and Virgil Thomson, who were roughly contemporaneous with Blitzstein. Thomson's links with post-World War I France were reflected in his conscious modernity: his two operas stand alone in the American output, but as a *cul-de-sac* rather than a possible highway. The Italian–American Menotti

represents the dead end of a long and well-worked path, for all that he popularised opera on Broadway, the heartland of the musical. Along with the more conservative Barber, his fundamentally unoriginal use of European models has robbed his operas of stature after giving them an initial measure of respectability. Douglas Moore was notable for the American-ness of his subject matter and his flexible use of an American musical idiom; time will tell whether the music is sufficiently substantial to carry American opera into the future. By contrast Philip Glass has reached a fresh audience and created considerable interest. In his minimalist works since the 1960s, the concept of opera is stretched wide, but it risks being stretched too thin as well.

These composers, by creating many works that are good in their own terms, suggest that no single Great American Opera need ever be written. Perhaps it is simply a matter of valueing what exists and striving for more, rather than seeking to recreate the European successes of yesteryear.

Willard White and Cynthia Hayman in the title roles of *Porgy and Bess* (Glyndebourne 1986)

Igor Stravinsky

By the time of *The Rake's Progress*, his longest opera and his first in English, Stravinsky was more cosmopolitan than Russian. But he was a United States citizen, he had been inspired by the Hogarth paintings in Chicago, and his librettist was an American poet. Because of this tenuous connection *The Rake's Progress* has been included in this section. (For biographical information see entry in Russian section on page 201.)

THE RAKE'S PROGRESS

Three acts
Libretto: W. H. Auden and Chester Kallman, after engravings by Hogarth
First performance: Venice 1951

Plot: Tom Rakewell leaves his country sweetheart Anne Truelove to spend his inheritance in the city, guided by the servant of his wishes, Nick Shadow. Starting at a brothel, he descends the primrose path by stages, finally becoming a bankrupt. He marries Baba the Turk, a grotesque sideshow with a long black beard, but finds her prosaic prattle unbearable – and when Anne comes seeking Tom, Baba generously persuades her that Tom still loves her. In a graveyard Nick Shadow reveals himself as the devil, ready to claim Tom's soul, but offers Tom a sporting chance to redeem himself by guessing three cards. Trusting in thoughts of Anne, Tom guesses correctly. Cheated, Nick turns him insane: Tom believes he is Adonis waiting for his Venus in springtime. Anne, his Venus, comes to him in the madhouse where Tom shows her his profound gratitude and love, and she blesses him. But after she leaves, he dies of a broken heart. The moral is proclaimed: the Devil finds work for the idle.

The opera: One of Stravinsky's finest and most popular neo-Classical works, *The Rake's Progress* is an 18th-century-type >number opera, complete with harpsichord for >recitatives, small orchestra, and neat divisions of solo, ensemble and chorus. Its vocal manner, however, is almost perversely atypical, most commonly a zig-zag line removed from any attempt to 'express' the text, which points the comedy as clearly as Hogarth's series of paintings that inspired it. The atmosphere becomes grim in the graveyard (with a change of function for the harpsichord), and deeply moving during Anne and Tom's reunion as Venus and Adonis with the wonderful sequence of his plea for forgiveness, their duet and her lullaby. Mozart and Donizetti, amongst others, are recalled in the lyrical high points standing out from the work's ironic context, such as Tom's >aria in the brothel, Anne's great Act I >scena, the Act II trio when Anne discovers Tom is married, and, later, her crucial exchange with Baba. Baba's cunning characterisation in both her florid and her patter styles suggests Rossini.

Overview: The similarities with Mozart's **Don Giovanni** are external – the graveyard confrontation with the Devil, the Epilogue sung with the house lights up. But the Faust theme, and the myth of Venus and Adonis, actually underpin the tale. *The Rake's Progress* is like Busoni's **Doktor Faust**, an intellectually conceived progression toward the hour of reckoning and the thwarting of the Devil's plan, which gives birth to a new spirit. It is the last great neo-Classic opera to join the repertory. (But its card game is used for a parallel purpose in a full-blooded late-Romantic opera – Puccini's **Girl of the Golden West**.)

Further reading: Paul Griffiths – *Igor Stravinsky: The Rake's Progress* (Cambridge Opera Handbook 1982).

Listening

CBS (UK) 77304
(US) M3S-710
Royal Phil./Stravinsky
(Raskin, Young, Reardon)
1964

Douglas Moore

Born: 10th August 1893/Cutchogue, New York
Died: 25th July 1969/Greenpoint, New York

Moore composed ten operas, several of which are on big American themes. This has placed him firmly among those who worked to produce an American operatic idiom. His most successful

works are *The Devil and Daniel Webster*, *Carrie Nation*, and *The Ballad of Baby Doe*. He has written incidental music, documentary film-tracks, and popular songs as well as instrumental and vocal pieces which also reflect his American heritage.

THE BALLAD OF BABY DOE

Two acts
Libretto: John Latouche
First performance: Central City, Colorado 1956; revised New York 1958

Plot: Leadville, Colorado, 1880. Horace Tabor, now wealthy and powerful from his silver mining, has been supported through the hard early years by his wife, Augusta. But he and Elizabeth 'Baby' Doe, a miner's wife, form a deep attachment leading to marriage. Although fabulously rich, they are excluded from political position or social acceptance. When silver threatens to collapse, Horace rejects Augusta's warning to sell the 'Matchless' silver mine, defiantly sinking all his other assets into it. But he loses heavily. He campaigns for the Presidential candidate William J. Bryant on the 'Free Silver' issue, but after Bryant's defeat penury forces him to become a common labourer. Augusta is too hurt to offer help; only Baby's devotion sustains him. After his death she remains beside the Matchless Mine, deserted by her children, till she dies thirty-six years later.

The opera: Moore's opera is a factual account of a love affair at an important point in American economic history. Its diverse scenes of American life (boisterous miners on a night out, a society wedding, a Presidential campaign rally) include splendid traditional music. The successful solos are popular forms, like Baby's sentimental ballad 'Willow, where we met together' (complete with out-of-tune piano), or her touching lullaby at the end. Among the better dramatic monologues, Horace's 'Turn tail and run, then' vibrates with powerful anger – it is his strength and his weakness that he thinks always in terms of Big Gestures – and Augusta's final acknowledgement of love and hurt is convincing. In Baby's letter scene, her 'silver >aria' at the wedding and her 'The fine ladies walk' she is idealised through Horace's childlike need for 'the little woman', with decorative high notes but little substance. Despite her mettle she has no musical character, barely reflecting the emotional experience of the American dream turning into the American nightmare. With laboured, portentous >recitative, Moore strains for 'operatic' effect rather than accepting his natural bent towards the lighter form of musical theatre so impressive in the final scene.

Overview: Unlike Blitzstein in **Regina**, Moore does not find the tang and rhythm of American dialogue; his sense of place and time is embodied in the variety of musical styles he brings to life. Rather than portray the effect of economic and political change on its main characters, as in Sallinen's **The Red Line**, *The Ballad of Baby Doe* uses major events as background colour for an investigation of the love triangle.

Listening

DG 2709 061
New York City Opera/Buckley
(Sills, Cassel, Bible)
1959

Virgil Thomson

Born: 25th November 1896/Kansas City

A well-known writer and critic, Thomson is one of the doyens of American composers despite having been something of an *enfant terrible*. His relationships with Satie and Gertrude Stein were of crucial importance in his career. Apart from the two Stein operas his other significant work was *Lord Byron*. His music is too diverse in style to be categorised; his output has been considerable, including film scores, ballets and incidental music, as well as numerous choral and solo vocal, instrumental and orchestral, pieces.

Further reading: Kathleen Hoover and John Cage – *Virgil Thomson* (New York).

FOUR SAINTS IN THREE ACTS

Prologue and four acts
Libretto: Gertrude Stein (scenario by Maurice Grosser)
First performance: Hartford, Connecticut, 1934

Plot: In Spain the Saints Teresa and Ignatius, and the imaginary Saints Chavez and Settlement, discourse and disport themselves with several other saints in a generally sunny and lyrical picture of an innocent existence. There are dances, a vision of the Holy Ghost, and a procession. A Compere and Commere comment on the tableaux of the saints and engage in their own discourse.

The opera: Stein's text, all word-play and cryptic inner logic, suggests no obvious scenes or action; rather than connecting with it, the activities Grosser devised go side-by-side as a series of almost-events (it depends on the production how much is made concrete). St Teresa, represented by two singers, converses with herself, and with St Ignatius (a fanciful connection; they never knew each other); she is seen painting eggs, holding a dove, cradling a baby, caught in an attitude of ecstasy; Ignatius serenades her with guitar, presents her with flowers, and so on. As the action becomes more particularised its surreal humour increases: there is a love-scene between Compere and Commere, whom the saints toast, and Teresa sees a Heavenly Vision through a telescope, which Ignatius won't let her keep. Thomson's music, poker-faced and pleasant, frames the rhythms and cadences of Stein's text, with lilting inflections which fall into familiar childlike patterns and just occasionally, gently, evoke both folk-dance and popular dance. The prelude to Act III, a rare passage of eloquence, depicts vividly and with melting sentimentality a sense of homespun, wholesome American life (in this act, later, there is also a suggestion of Spanish musical colour). The tone of the work can be determined by the production; it could equally present sublime innocence at play, or tongue-in-cheek waggishness – like the music of Satie, an early influence, it is equivocal, but always elegant, as it exploits the charm of the prosaic.

Overview: The success and notoriety of the initial production, and the standing of both Thomson and Stein, have contributed towards the reputation of *Four Saints* as a senior American opera. It is really a piece of music theatre deriving from the Paris of the twenties, with roots in the work of Satie and Cocteau. Its ability to use elementary patterns with sophistication, and to generate a substantial atmosphere with insubstantial means, puts it in the advance-guard for Philip Glass's minimalist opera **Akhnaten**.

Listening

Nonesuch 7599-79035-1
Orchestra of Our Time/Thome
(Allen, Matthews, Thompson, Dale, Quivar, Brown, Bradley)
1982

THE MOTHER OF US ALL

Prologue and three acts
Libretto: Gertrude Stein (scenario by Maurice Grosser)
First performance: New York 1947

Plot: Susan B. Anthony, who worked for abolition of slavery and for women's suffrage, is shown at home with her companion Anne, and engaged in conversation and dispute with other American political luminaries from epochs earlier and later than her own. Woven around this theme and independent of it are the conversations and relationships of other typical American characters.

The opera: Less extreme than **Four Saints in Three Acts**, *The Mother of Us All* is not music-theatre but a homespun American folk opera. Thomson evokes an idyllic way of life whose characters' acceptance of one another allows for harmonious discussion, suggesting the possibility of political change. The later orchestral suite, a set of musical pictures of American life, adds to the opera itself, which blends sprightly band music, nursery-rhymes, waltzes and hymns – open-air stuff – with engaging comedy (such as the pompous chorus of the VIPs or the way in which people assembled for a marriage allow a conversation to distract them from their main purpose). Compared with *Four Saints in Three Acts* the score of *The Mother of Us All* is substantial (Susan B.'s monologues are the nearest Thomson gets in either opera to writing an >aria). The text is less elliptical, its meaning far more accessible, particularly concerning Susan B.'s aspirations and her experience of the methods men use to silence or trivialise her efforts.

Overview: The musical and textual personality of *The Mother of Us All* retains the studied charm and inconsequential manner of *Four Saints in Three Acts*. So it stands in striking contrast to the works of Thomson's

Mignon Dunn as Susan B. Anthony aboard the 'Ship of State' in *The Mother of Us All* (Santa Fe Opera 1976)

contemporary, Blitzstein – its use of American subject-matter and musical traditions makes a comparable contribution to the body of home-grown opera. It also incidentally offers a brief operatic view of Daniel Webster, here Susan B. Anthony's sparring partner, the hero of Douglas Moore's *The Devil and Daniel Webster*.

Listening

New World Records NW 288/289
Sante Fe Opera/Leppard
(Dunn)
1977

George Gershwin

Born: 26th September 1898/Brooklyn, New York
Died: 11th July 1937/Hollywood, California

A composer of highly successful musicals and popular songs, Gershwin is now acknowledged as one of the great pioneers who incorporated American jazz and folk elements into major classical structures. His best-known works are *Rhapsody in Blue*, *An American in Paris*, and *Porgy and Bess*. There was also an earlier, unsuccessful jazz opera (*Blue Monday Blues*) and a piano concerto. Selections from his own solo piano versions of his songs have become a favourite concert item.

Further reading: Ira Gershwin – *Lyrics on Several Occasions* (New York 1959).

PORGY AND BESS

Three acts
Libretto: Ira Gershwin and Du Bose Heyward
First performance: Boston 1935

Plot: Catfish Row is a poverty-stricken black district of Charleston on the coast of South Carolina. There are God-fearing folk, there is gambling, and much inbetween. After killing Robbins in a gambling fight, Crown runs off; he will come back for his woman Bess when the coast is clear. Bess takes refuge with the crippled Porgy, finding a warm, loving relationship which she is loth to give up even when Crown reasserts his hold over her. In the inevitable confrontation, Porgy manages to strangle Crown. Although he is not under suspicion, he is taken away to identify the body – and Bess, told that Porgy will be imprisoned for life, is persuaded by the drug-dealer Sporting Life to leave with him for New York. When Porgy returns a week later, he sets off in his goat-cart to find her.

The opera: The 'highlights' approach to *Porgy and Bess* crippled interest in the opera as a whole, but in the later 20th century there have been full-scale productions and recordings. As in most great operas, the music defines the drama with a vivid, deeply felt reality. Melodic beauty and dramatic sweep triumphed over criticism of the technical limitations such as the repetitive orchestral fill-ins. Gershwin cleverly avoids a true overture with the Jasbo Brown blues on the piano, but he has given Porgy a recurring >motif in the orchestra. The story, of its period in presenting black people as 'characters', is a morality tale, with Bess choosing between male representations of what is noble and what is degraded in her. She is faced with the almost supernatural courage and aggression of Crown (he twice survives a murderous hurricane, and devilishly interrupts communal prayer with his phallic paean to 'A red-headed woman'), the compassion of Porgy, and Sporting Life's evil. Contrast the different plea she makes to each of her men, the simple 'I loves you, Porgy – don' let him take me' with the tortured, ambiguous 'What you want wid Bess? She's gettin' ole now' to Crown. Sporting Life is sinuously corrupt in 'It ain't necessarily so', triumphant in 'There's a boat dat's leavin' soon for New York'. 'Operatic' music comes with the highest and lowest points of Bess's relationship with Porgy (the supremely beautiful 'Bess, you is my woman now' and Porgy's 'Oh, Bess, oh where's my Bess?') and Porgy's dramatic defiance of the low-flying buzzard, symbol of trouble and death.

The other famous numbers are part of the mosaic of life in Catfish Row – street cries, a wake ('My man's gone now'), a lullaby ('Summertime'), spirituals, a worksong, prayers, festive celebration ('Oh, I can't sit down'), and happy, jaunty songs ('A woman is a sometime thing', and Porgy's 'I got plenty o' nuttin'' with banjo). Only the strangely truncated finale, 'Oh Lawd, I'm on my way', falls short of the finest expression in this magnificently integrated score.

Overview: In *Porgy and Bess* Gershwin treated the vernacular with the easy alternation of song, freely pitched speech and straight >recitative found in later works combining elements of opera and the musical, such as Blitzstein's **Regina** and Bernstein's **West Side Story** (the music for the fight between Robbins and Crown foreshadows the famous clash between the rival gangs in Bernstein's work). *Porgy and Bess*'s brief vignettes of white racism are still sickeningly real, but its claims to being a folk opera, a true representation of black people, have dwindled under late 20th-century perceptions, although the Gershwin Estate have wisely instructed that all productions use black singers only. Whatever the verdict on this aspect of the work, it stands now simply as the first great American opera.

Listening

Decca SET 609 4 K3Q28
London OSA13116 4 0SA5-13116
CD: 414 559-2DH3
Cleveland Orch./Maazel
(White, Boatwright, Mitchell, Hendricks, Clemmons, Quivar, Thompson)
1976

Kurt Weill

During his years in the US Weill internalised American idioms and produced many musicals, the most successful being *Lady in the Dark*. *Street Scene* is regarded as his main American opera, but several of his other American works pioneered the

incorporation of 'serious' elements into Broadway shows. Although political events in South Africa swiftly overtook *Lost in the Stars* (based on Alan Paton's *Cry the Beloved Country*), the score has great beauty. (For biographical information see entry in German section on page 170.)

STREET SCENE

Two acts
Libretto: Elmer Rice and Langston Hughes, after Elmer Rice
First performance: New York 1947

Plot: The inhabitants of a poor New York apartment house live as much outside the building as inside it. Children play, people gossip, the janitor muses, a woman is about to have a baby, high school girls bring their graduation diplomas home, Anna Maurrant sings to her little boy, Willy. Both Anna and her daughter Rose want something more from life: Rose's aspirations are shared by her sensitive friend Sam, and Anna's are partly fulfilled by an affair with her neighbour Mr Sankey. Anna's husband Frank, finding his wife in bed with Mr Sankey, shoots them both, and is taken off for trial and execution. Rose decides she will go away – not under the wing of Harry Easter, who has had designs on her for some time, but to be her own person.

The opera: *Street Scene* is a tale of passionate individual yearnings set in a typical New York locale. Neither the individual nor the communal aspect predominates: Weill includes children's singing games along with Anna's expansive quasi-Puccini >aria 'Somehow I could never believe', the pliant melody of Sam's 'Lonely house' with the block-like choral ensemble of 'The woman who lived up there'. Frank Maurrant's broken 'I loved her, too' involves the entire community in the terrible experience. The result is what Weill himself called 'a real blending of drama and music', now known as a Broadway opera. Occasionally sentimental words and music weaken the work, most markedly in Rose and

Sam's 'We'll go away together', Rose's 'What good would the moon be?' and their final duet. But jazz and blues enhance the musical landscape – note the orchestral introduction, the janitor's fine 'I got a marble and a star' and Easter's knowing 'Wouldn't you like to be on Broadway?' And there is parody in a viciously comical duet for two nursemaids and in the contributions of an operatic trio of gossiping women.

Overview: Gershwin's **Porgy and Bess** is echoed in the opening numbers (and Harry Easter is a cool city version of Sporting Life). But *Street Scene* is specifically New York, rather than American; in its own way it does for New York what Charpentier's **Louise** did for Paris. Like the later **West Side Story** (Bernstein) it brings out one kind of street life. It combines elements of the musical with opera, harnessing original American idioms like jazz and blues to a classical conception – a whole new genre in which Gershwin, Blitzstein, Weill and Bernstein have created the supreme examples.

Marc Blitzstein

Born: 2nd March 1905/Philadelphia, Pennsylvania
Died: 22nd January 1964/Fort-de-France

An important figure both before and after World War II, Blitzstein's consistent socialist commitment found notable expression in *The Cradle Will Rock*, which was, with *Regina*, the most memorable of some twenty dramatic works (including ballets, operas and musicals). He wrote several film scores, and incidental music for nine stage classics whose authors include Shakespeare, Jonson, Büchner, Shaw, and Hellman. He is regarded as a pioneer of American vernacular speech-setting; his feel for a comprehensive range of musical styles, a gift he shared with Kurt Weill, blazed the trail for the blend of opera and musical taken up by Bernstein, Loesser and Sondheim.

REGINA

Prologue and three acts
Libretto: The composer, after Lillian Hellman
First performance: New York 1949

Plot: Alabama, 1900. The Hubbard siblings – Regina, Ben and Oscar – are poised for a big business coup. Although she knows her husband Horace's heart condition is fatal, Regina dispatches her daughter Alexandra (Zan) to fetch him from hospital in Baltimore, determined not to lose her part of the deal. But Horace is wise to Regina's selfish manipulations, and refuses to put up the money. When her brothers get Oscar's son Leo to steal it from Horace they reckon without Regina. Having deliberately provoked a fatal heart attack in her husband, she threatens her brothers with prison unless they give her a 75 per cent stake in the expected profits. Yet Regina does not win every battle: Zan, refusing to be caged like Oscar's wife, her beloved aunt Birdie, proves a match for her mother and leaves home.

The opera: Blitzstein incorporates all kinds of popular American music, from sentimental ballads and ironic crooning to folk spirituals and early ragtime, or the home-spun quartet 'Make a quiet day'. The shifts in style, never imposed, are born out of the situation. The title role should be a tour de force; Regina must cope with high operatic declamation, an aggressive Broadway show-stopper, a seductive >Credo, and some exhilarating, rattling >recitative. Birdie is finely characterised, with an emotional >scena which she reveals the full measure of her misery. Vocalising (without words) is used impressively in Leo's self-congratulatory 'Deedle doodle' and the maidservant's keening over Horace's death. In Blitzstein's compelling finales, naturalistic or symbolic exchanges clash against choral outbursts. Threading through it all is speech, heightened speech, pitched speech, even 19th-century >melodrama: it is not simply the absence of singing, but the appropriate medium at specific moments.

Overview: Some critics of radical artists who move away from doctrinaire positions question their right to develop, and it has been is claimed that in *Regina* Blitzstein softened his commitment to the constructive social insights of *The Cradle Will Rock* or *No for an Answer*. Yet *Regina*'s point about the destructive effect of financial power on the warmer human emotions comes over loud and clear (as an allegory, it partly anticipates Tippett's **The Midsummer Marriage**). He was as alert as Weill (**Street Scene** and *Down in the Valley*) to the value of accessible American music, as courageous as Gershwin (**Porgy and Bess**) to the operatic possibilities of the American vernacular.

Listening

Columbia/Odyssey Y3 35236
New York City Opera/Krachmalnik
(Lewis, Carron, Brice, Hecht, Irving, Renan, Strine)

Samuel Barber

Born: 9th March 1910/West Chester, Pennsylvania
Died: 23rd January 1981/New York

A much-honoured composer with a Romantic musical style, his famous Adagio for Strings (from his own string quartet) tends to overshadow his successful opera *Vanessa*, solo concertos, orchestral and choral works and songs.

ANTONY AND CLEOPATRA

Three acts
Libretto: Franco Zeffirelli, after William Shakespeare, revised by Gian Carlo Menotti
First performance: New York 1966

Plot: The Roman general Antony, deeply involved with Cleopatra, Queen of Egypt, returns to Rome to heal his growing rift with Octavius Caesar, and marries Octavius's sister to cement the reconciliation. Cleopatra is devastated, but Antony has a vision of her which impels him to return to Egypt. Defeated in the subsequent naval battle with Caesar, he upbraids Cleopatra for her fleet's desertion and her apparent readiness to deal with the victor. He is told that she has died; he falls on his sword and is taken to her monument: she is still alive, and he dies in her arms. Rather than be paraded as a slave in Rome, Cleopatra chooses suicide and the hope of reunion with her beloved Antony.

The opera: After the failure of the first production, which opened the new Metropolitan Opera house at the Lincoln Center, *Antony and Cleopatra* was extensively revised, and it has become better known through concert performances of Cleopatra's death scene preceded by specially composed funeral music. Despite being an accomplished work of lyrical appeal, it lacks an inner life. The libretto is a scissors-and-paste job of Shakespeare's play, and is occasionally difficult to follow. As though seeking an idiom which eludes him, Barber employs a declamatory vocal manner without much muscle, mainly set against portentous string writing. Yet the orchestral extensions of each scene are eloquent, and there are vivid contrasts between the musical spectra of Egypt and Rome – the one sensuous, the other military and formal. Perhaps because the superficially 'operatic' romanticism of Barber's conception falls far short of the drama of Shakespeare's most complex pair of lovers, the love duet (added in the revision) and Cleopatra's recurring >motif ('My man of men') do not carry the emotional weight required of them, whereas the simple death scene of Eros, Antony's attendant, is more affecting. The spare instrumentation of the first part of Antony's own death scene heralds the convincing, elegiac tone of the final section.

Overview: As Barber intimated with reference to Verdi/Boito's great **Otello**, Shakespeare is not easy to set; his words are too rich, too allusive for the sweep on which so much opera depends. Since the inflated Zeffirelli production, reminiscent of a Hollywood spectacular, was widely blamed for the opera's initial failure, it will be interesting to see whether the fresher production it has since received will rate it higher in public and critical favour.

Listening

New World Records NW 322/323/324
Spoleto Festival Orchestra/Badea
(Hinds, Wells)
1983

Gian Carlo Menotti

Born: 7th July 1911/Cadegliano

An Italian-born composer, Menotti studied and lived in the United States. His major works, technically very accomplished, were cleverly adapted to the taste of his contemporary American public, which reinforced rather than negated their turn-of-the-

Régine Crespin (right) in *The Medium*
(Opera Company of Philadelphia 1986)

century Italian opera flavour. He has been highly successful, educating a generation of wary New Yorkers to take opera with sugar on the spoon, with emphasis on the voice and on dramatic effect. He was responsive to new challenges, writing operas for radio and for television, and operas for children. Other notable works include *Amelia Goes to the Ball*, *The Saint of Bleecker Street* and *Help, Help, the Globolinks!*. He composed several instrumental works, including concertos.

Further reading: Robert Tricoire – *Gian Carlo Menotti* (Paris 1966).

THE MEDIUM

Two acts
Libretto: The composer
First performance: New York 1946

Plot: At Madame Flora's fraudulent seances her daughter Monica acts as the ghost, imitating the voices or laughter of long-dead children; the mute gypsy boy, Toby, manipulates wires to make the table move. Madame Flora ill-treats Toby, but cannot hold back his loving relationship with Monica. Feeling a cold hand touch her throat during a seance, her confidence in the non-existence of the spirit world is undermined. She drives away her clients, who still insist that they have been in touch with their dead. Trying to find out if it was Toby who had touched her – who else? – she coaxes and tortures him, but he refuses to give a sign. Drunk, terrified, haunted now by the very voices and visions with which she exploited her clients, she mistakes Toby for a ghost, and shoots him. Desperate, mad, she asks the dead boy – 'Was it you?'

The opera: *The Medium*'s great success on Broadway may be an indication of its strengths and its failings as an opera. It is undeniably gripping, highly charged, and highly coloured in treatment. Dissonance and orchestral 'effects' alternate continually with sentimental-lyrical phrases, as for instance when Madame Flora (Baba) intersperses her cries of horror with

broken phrases of 'O black swan, where has your lover gone' (a song of no discernible significance). Speech is frequently employed for dramatic impact. The 'children' are portrayed as either nubile or infantile according to how this will best serve the dramatic moment. And in case Baba's genuine problem with the undead is insufficiently terrifying, Menotti has her recall various apocalyptic horrors, presumably of the Second World War in Europe. His melodramatic methods have brought Menotti considerable criticism, and the work has dated fast, yet it remains effective, and provides a set of juicy roles.

Overview: Not unlike Puccini's >verismo operas in approach, but without the musical substance to be accounted for a true opera, *The Medium* is really an old-fashioned melodrama set in a quasi-operatic manner, and works rather better in a theatre than an opera-house. In this sense it reverses roles with Bernstein's works (*Trouble in Tahiti*, **Candide** or **West Side Story**) which have received attention from opera companies. Menotti illustrates Weill's principles about reaching out to a popular audience, but *The Medium* lacks the integrity of **Street Scene** or *Lost in the Stars*.

Listening

CBS MS 7387
Opera Society of Washington/Mester
(Resnik, Blegen)
1969

THE TELEPHONE

One act
Libretto: The composer
First performance: New York 1947

Plot: With a train to catch, Ben wants to declare his love for Lucy so as to make a proposal of marriage, but he is thwarted by Lucy's thoroughgoing involvement with the telephone calls she receives and makes. There is a full-scale conversation with Margaret, a ferocious argument with George and a subsequent unburdening to Pamela, interspersed with taking a call from someone who has dialled the wrong number, and a somewhat gratuitous time-check. Ben makes an ineffective attempt to put paid to the telephone's activity, but he is eventually able to declare himself, and be accepted – on the telephone.

The opera: This comic vignette, a curtain-raiser for **The Medium**, was labelled >opera buffa. There is an 18th-century spirit about much of the music, with its pointed woodwind and pizzicato interpolations, small-scale lyricism, and chatty >recitative. The colloquial word-setting is skilful, the telephone calls creating expansive numbers equivalent to a classical >aria or >scena. As the dramatic situation develops, the score moves into more generalised parody, taking in contemporary use of jangling dissonance (for the wrong number), Wagnerian heroics (the argument with George), an all-too-brief >a capella duet in English glee style (he pleading, she putting him off), a ballad (the call to Pamela), and an earnest aria (Ben's bitter plaint while alone). The later parodies combine the Italian-operatic and the English-quaint, and at the end Lucy's telephone number gets the celestial-apotheosis treatment. The piece is sub-titled *L'amour à trois*, aptly so when Ben's final desperate ploy shows him accepting the principle 'if you can't lick 'em, join 'em'. Menotti milks the situation for humour, stacking the odds to suit his point: with Lucy an obtuse featherbrain and Ben an ineffectual wimp it is no wonder that the telephone comes out on top.

Overview: Comedy and tragedy being two sides of a coin, Menotti's telephone behaves something like Cocteau's/Poulenc's in **La voix humaine**. The initial atmosphere of the opera recalls also the domestic exchanges in Strauss's **Intermezzo**, and for sheer fun the parodies anticipate those of Britten in **A Midsummer Night's Dream** and of Walton in **The Bear**.

Listening

Columbia Y2-35239
Ballet Society Production Orch./Balaban
(Cotlow, Rogier)
1948

THE CONSUL

Three acts
Libretto: The composer
First performance: Philadelphia 1950

Plot: John Sorel, a freedom fighter in a police state, has to flee across the frontier. His wife, Magda, approaches the Consulate of a 'free' country for a visa for herself, their baby son and John's mother – and is blocked with unimaginable bureaucratic obstacles. On her endless visits to the Consulate she becomes familiar with several other applicants, each with an equivalent frustration. Her baby dies; her mother-in-law dies; the secret police torment her. She will never be granted a visa. And so she commits suicide to free John from having to return. As she dies, the telephone rings, unanswered: John is back, and has been arrested.

The opera: Written at the height of McCarthyism, *The Consul* was assumed to be about all those *other* societies where there is no freedom. The irony was probably unconscious, and may have been lost on its first audiences. It was intended as a universal statement, and Magda's single moment of eloquence (Act II) proclaims the ultimate triumph of humanity and freedom. The work is a period piece only partly connected with cold war politics, for what dates *The Consul* is its music: sentimental, even meretricious, self-consciously accelerating into 'melody' gear without a feel for melody. Menotti uses all the tricks of the trade – a French song about the return of a lover, the old mother's lullaby to the moribund child, her portentous statements about being old, the dream-waltz for the petitioners in the Consulate, lurid nightmares, 'modern' mechanical repetitions for the consul's secretary, a vision of death/fear/love/guilt/freedom/you-name-it during the suicide, and, at crucial moments of drama, lavish dissonance. Despite itself, the opera can still pack a punch. But what would Janáček have done with it...?

Overview: *The Consul* lacks the unpretentious skill of **The Telephone** or **Amahl and the Night Visitors**. The shade of Puccini hovers close – the dissonance, the >verismo. But where Puccini is content to make a single statement, Menotti lays it on thick: compare **Suor Angelica**'s dying vision of her child with the crowded stage during Magda's suicide. And when the old mother deliberately displays her dead grandson to a man setting out to find John Sorel, only to say 'Don't tell John', it is clear that Menotti values melodramatic feeling more than dramatic integrity.

Listening

Brunswick LAT 8012/3
Orchestra assembled for recording/Engel
(Neway, Powers)
1950s

AMAHL AND THE NIGHT VISITORS

One act
Libretto: The composer
First performance: New York
(NBC Television Opera Theater) 1951

Plot: Life is increasingly difficult for Amahl, a crippled shepherd boy, and his mother, who are so poor they face having to beg. One starry winter's night, Three Kings – travelling with gifts for the Christ-child – call at the house to rest and to warm themselves. The mother hurries out to collect firewood and summon the neighbouring shepherds, who come with simple gifts, and dance for the kings. When the kings are asleep the mother cannot resist stealing some of King Melchior's gold. She is caught, and Amahl defends her. But Melchior tells her she can keep the gold, because the Christ-child will not need it: his kingdom, built on love alone, is for the poor. Moved, the mother returns the gold; she would like to send a gift, too. Amahl offers his crutch – and finds he can walk without it. There is much rejoicing – clearly, he has been touched by God's love. Playing his pipe, he leaves with the Kings to deliver his gift personally.

The opera: The first opera commissioned especially for television, and now a television classic, *Amahl* is equally popular in the theatre. Its sensitively told story is a winner, the sort that touches the heartstrings no matter what the head believes. As an opera, it is uneven. It is finest in the moments of genuine innocence – the introductory orchestral passage, the comical, sub-Prokofiev procession of the three kings, Amahl's exchanges with Melchior and Kaspar, the moment of simple magic when Amahl sings 'I walk, Mother' on a descending minor third, and, perhaps, the return of Amahl's piping at the end. Without a consistently childlike musical style Amahl lacks characterisation; the mother's irritation with him is inflated into Puccinian emotion; the scene with the shepherds lacks an individual folk quality, and the response to the miracle cries out for true radiance. The major achievement of the opera is in welding fantasy and domestic realism.

Overview: The connection with Puccini has been mentioned, but Menotti sustains little of the concentrated wonderment of the miracle in Puccini's **Suor Angelica**. Nor does he create an unsentimentalised child to join Britten's young characters in **Albert Herring** or **The Turn of the Screw**. But *Amahl* is an opera for adults and children alike, and as such it is to be cherished.

Listening

RCA LSB4075; Victor LSC-2762 (US)
NBC Opera Company/Grossman
(Yaghjian, King, Cross, McCollum, Patterson)
1963

Leonard Bernstein

Born: 25th August 1918/Lawrence, Massachusetts

As a composer, conductor, pianist and publicist, Bernstein is a multi-talented musician whose stage works and own natural personality have made him, more than any other, America's 'Mr Music'. The film versions of his scores for the musicals *On the Town* and *West Side Story*, as well as the sound track for *On the Waterfront*, have become well-known worldwide. Other stage works include the opera *Trouble in Tahiti*, the ballet *Fancy Free*, and the musical *Wonderful Town*. The theatre relationship with the choreographer Jerome Robbins was particularly creative. There are orchestral works and songs, and a notable output of large-scale works in the field of choral music.

Further reading: Peter Gradenwitz – *Leonard Bernstein* (English translation, Leamington Spa 1987).

CANDIDE

Two acts
Libretto: (1956 version) Lillian Hellman, John Latouche, Richard Wilbur, assisted by Dorothy Parker and the composer, after Voltaire; (1973/1982 versions) Hugh Wheeler, John Latouche, Richard Wilbur, Stephen Sondheim, after Voltaire
First performances: Boston 1956; New York 1973; New York 1982 (opera house version)

Plot: Two beautiful, aristocratic Westphalian children, Cunegonde and Maximilian, their lowly cousin Candide and their servant Paquette, blindly accept their tutor Dr Pangloss's philosophy that in this, the best of all possible worlds, everything happens for the best. Candide and Cunegonde are in love; when it is discovered, and they are brutally separated, an endless sequence of catastrophes affects them all. They are (in no particular order) engulfed by sea during an earthquake, enslaved, tortured, lusted after, procured, abducted, marooned, killed, resurrected, flogged, sent to the Jesuits of Montevideo, attacked, no sooner enriched than impoverished, and reunited. With a new philosophy, they give up their cheerful world-view, and cultivate a simple life where they will be self-sufficient.

The opera: *Candide* was revised several times because of its mixed reception. Voltaire's extravagant, picaresque satire of deterministic optimism applies even-handedly to all political systems and religious beliefs. But the satire in Lillian Hellman's original adaptation was not obvious to a public whose self-awareness had been dulled by McCarthyism. The 1973 version was a one-acter with a chamber orchestra; the most recent 'opera house' version is likely to become the definitive one. As often happens, a cult attached itself to an honourable failure, and the sheer brilliance of the overture, with its exuberant cross-rhythms reminiscent of Berlioz, has in any case kept the work before the concert-going public. In *Candide* Bernstein delights in musical scene-setting for his characters' travels, with irresistible Spanish and Latin-American dance rhythms and voluptuous waltzes. His bag of tricks includes Baroque counterpoint, canon and chorale, a side-glance at, among others, the Verdi *Requiem* in the *Auto-da-fe* (What a Day), and a full stare at the Jewel Song from Gounod's **Faust** in the beautiful >aria 'Glitter and Be Gay', these last two numbers being the tours de force of a richly diverse work.

Overview: If *Candide* is to be categorised, it must be as an operetta, not only because the scale and aspiration of much of the music takes it further than the traditional musical, but because it is a work firmly in the spirit of Offenbach, with mainly short-breathed phrases, appealing tunes, and both musical and general satire of vitality and sophistication. It is the love-child of a brilliant creative energy; it founds no new genre, and its successive radical revisions have actually turned it into a different work each time.

Further reading: Essay by Theodore S. Chapin accompanying recording below.

Listening

New World Records NW 340/341
CD: NW340/341
New York City Opera/Mauceri
(Mills, Eisler, Lankston)
1986

WEST SIDE STORY

Two acts
Libretto: Arthur Laurents and Stephen Sondheim, after William Shakespeare
First performance: New York 1957

Plot: In the slums of Manhattan a young Puerto Rican gang, the Sharks, faces the xenophobic white Jets. Maria, sister of the Sharks' leader Bernardo, is meant to marry Chino, but she falls in love with founder Jet Tony just when Bernardo is challenged to a gang fight by the Jets' leader, Riff. Tony tries desperately to limit the extent of the fight. But he is mistrusted, and soon flick-knives are out; Bernardo kills Riff, and Tony kills Bernardo. Afterwards, Chino sets out to avenge Bernardo – but Tony is with Maria, desperate for a new beginning. Anita, Bernardo's girlfriend, is persuaded to warn Tony that Chino is hunting him, but when she approaches the Jets, their vicious racism drives her to tell them Chino has killed Maria. As Tony finds Maria, Chino shoots him. Enraged, Maria denounces the violence, and the Jets and the Sharks carry Tony's body away, together.

The opera: Even though it is not an opera, *West Side Story* is sometimes given the full operatic treatment. The orchestral writing for the mimed action in the Prologue and in the Rumble (gang fight) is a tone poem integrating the aggressive jazz and dance idioms of its time; added to the score's thematic complexity, this suggests the thinking of a composer of art music, without undermining the essential nature of the musical. Bernstein deliberately avoided 'the operatic trap' – the climactic moment when Maria rounds on the rival gangs would not even shape up as an >aria. The great melodic outburst in 'Maria' and the tense love duet between Anita and Maria ('A boy like that') break new ground for a musical, and originality abounds in the splendid, restless 'Something's coming', in the ambiguous rhythms of the stunning 'America', and in the shaping of the vocal line of the Jet Song and of 'Cool', with its tight, short phrases. But 'Tonight', for all its key-shifts and its ensemble treatment, is exactly what its

context requires. So are the other fine melodic numbers, the brilliant Latin American dances, and the uproarious 'Gee, Officer Krupke'.

Overview: Dramatic integrity in the American musical, foreshadowed in Jerome Kern's *Show Boat*, became established with *Oklahoma!* and *Carousel* (Rodgers) and the works of Kurt Weill, and *West Side Story* is probably its finest example. In a way that Bellini's **I Capuleti ed i Montecchi** or Gounod's **Roméo et Juliette** cannot do, it serves the same function as an updated or politicised production of the Shakespeare play, bringing the timeless Romeo and Juliet story into sharp modern focus (unlike Cole Porter's *Kiss Me Kate*, a conventional treatment of Shakespeare's *The Taming of the Shrew*). Only Frank Loesser's *Guys and Dolls* approaches a comparable combination of vitality and technique.

Listening

1 CBS JS32603 4 JST32603
 Original cast recording
 1957
2 DG 415 253-1GH2 4 415 253-4GH2
 CD: 415 253-2GH2
 Specially assembled studio orchestra/ Bernstein
 (Carreras, Te Kanawa, Troyanos, Ollman, Horne)
 1985

Philip Glass

Born: 31st January 1937/Chicago, Illinois

An avant-garde minimalist composer influenced in the 1960s by Indian and jazz musicians, Glass has achieved considerable popularity on the fringe of mainstream classical music as well as rock music. He has written a number of music theatre works, notably the group including *Einstein on the Beach*, *Satyagraha* and *Akhnaten*, plus *The Photographer* and *CIVIL warS*, and the film score for *Koyaanisqatsi*.

Further reading: Philip Glass – *Music by Philip Glass* (ed. by Robert T. Jones, USA 1987).

Christopher Robson (centre) in the title role of David Freeman's production of *Akhnaten* (English National Opera 1985)

AKHNATEN

Three acts
Libretto: The composer, assisted by Shalom Goldman
First performance: Stuttgart 1984

Plot: On the death of his father, Amenhotep IV becomes Pharaoh of Egypt. Supported by his mother Tye and his wife Nefertiti, he overthrows the priesthood of Amon and establishes the new, monotheistic worship of Aten (the sun), calling himself Akhnaten and building the city of Akhetaten as his new capital. The way of life he creates is loving and inward-looking, and he refuses to send troops to protect the outlying areas of Egypt's empire. A coalition of the old priesthood and his own allies destroy Akhetaten, and Akhnaten himself disappears. The ruins of Akhetaten are visited today by tourists, unaware that the spirits of its

Pharoah, his wife and his mother are still present in the city.

The opera: *Akhnaten* is one of the few works broadly described as 'minimalist' to be included in the opera repertory. Glass prolongs blocks of mesmeric >ostinato so that each shift in the pattern is instantly recognisable. Set against this there is speaking, chanting, dance and mime. With relatively little singing, the effect when it comes is ravishing (note the trio of Akhnaten, Tye and Nefertiti ending Act I and the duet between Akhnaten and Nefertiti in Act II), the play of interweaving vocal lines creating a sense of movement and a lustrous texture. The work is a frieze or a staged ceremony rather than a dynamic sung play, offering scope for an imaginative production which can convey simple warm spirituality at the same time as a pervasive nostalgia for its loss. Glass worked with an Egyptologist on the libretto, incorporating ancient Egyptian, Hebrew and Akkadian texts, but leaving unanswered the questions raised by the developing interest in *Akhnaten* in the 1980s – interest in his political, religious and aristic significance as well as his unusual physical development of breasts, belly and thighs.

Overview: Essentially *Akhnaten* is music theatre, forging its own path in that area first defined by Schoenberg's *Pierrot Lunaire* (not originally intended for staged performance) and Stravinsky's *Histoire du Soldat*, where Glass's contemporaries such as Berio, Davies, Birtwistle and Stockhausen have also been active. Visually it is sumptuous; musically it is spare, and extremely accessible.

OPERA SINGERS

THESE ENTRIES are a (necessarily) selective sample of singers you may hear on the recommended recordings or see in performance. They are intended to give a flavour of what is or was important and individual about each, with some of their major roles. The exclusion of historical greats like Caruso, Gigli, Melchior, Supervia, Tauber, Lotte Lehmann and Jurinac, etc. is based not on talent but on relevance to a contemporary audience. Opera titles have sometimes been shortened to the main index word (eg Ballo = Un ballo in maschera).

THOMAS ALLEN British baritone (1944–). The best English baritone born this century: highly intelligent, with a focused and vibrant voice, underpinned by excellent dramatic technique. Particularly strong in Mozart roles and as Britten's *Billy Budd*; distinguished in the French baritone repertoire.

JUNE ANDERSON American soprano (1952–). Her large voice possesses great agility and facility, but sometimes lacks vocal colour. Good in the roles Joan Sutherland made famous: *La fille du régiment*, *Semiramide*, *Lucia di Lammermoor* and *Handel*.

IRINA ARKHIPOVA Russian mezzo (1925–). One of the great post-war mezzos, her extraordinarily powerful and bounteous voice exemplifies the Russian voice at its best, with a depth of tone even in high passages. She is still singing – well – in her sixties: her great roles include *Carmen*, Ulrica (*Ballo*), Azucena (*Trovatore*), plus the classic Russian mezzo roles: Pauline (*Queen of Spades*), Olga (*Eugene Onegin*) and Marfa (*Khovanshchina*).

GABRIEL BACQUIER French baritone (1924–). Like Arkhipova, still singing in his sixties – a remarkable and powerful singer-actor with tremendous presence and a special gift for comedy. Roles: Golaud in *Pelléas*, both Leporello and the title role in *Don Giovanni*, *Don Pasquale*, and early Italian roles.

JANET BAKER British mezzo (1932–). A sublime artist who has carved out for herself a unique and uncategorisable repertoire, she has delivered some of the most memorable of all British opera performances. Her singing displays profound musicianship, with both intensity and stillness. Excellent in Handel, Gluck, Mozart, Strauss and Britten.

AGNES BALTSA Greek mezzo (1944–). Exciting, immediate and magnetic, clear-voiced and intelligent. All the great lyric roles, including much florid Rossini: a good Romeo (Bellini's *Capuleti*) and Oktavian (*Rosenkavalier*) and a gutsy *Carmen*.

GABRIELA BEŇAČKOVÁ Czech soprano (1947–). Her lustrous and ample voice coupled with a radiant manner is particularly effective as Tatyana (*Eugene Onegin*) and in Smetana, Janáček, Tchaikovsky and Verdi roles.

TERESA BERGANZA Spanish mezzo (1935–). She maintains an almost classical simplicity and elegance of delivery which is intensely musical. She had few equals as *Cenerentola* in the 60s and 70s; and also gained many admirers as Rosina (Rossini's *Barber*), Cherubino (*Figaro*) and recently *Carmen*.

CARLO BERGONZI Italian tenor (1924–). The last genuine operatic stylist with a very individual timbre. The epitome of Italian vibrancy in all the Verdi tenor roles.

JUSSI BJÖRLING Swedish tenor (1911–60). The supreme lyric tenor of the century. Effortless, pure, aristocratic, never vulgar. All the major Verdi and Puccini roles, especially Pinkerton (*Madam Butterfly*), Gustavus (*Ballo*), Manrico (*Trovatore*), plus Gounod's *Faust*.

RENATO BRUSON Italian baritone (1936–). Currently the only distinguished Italian baritone. Although he has a limited compass of voice, he applies elegance and a controlled intelligence with distinction. Good Donizetti, Verdi, and particularly *Simon Boccanegra*.

GRACE BUMBRY American contralto (1937–). A sensual and exciting presence who has not lived up to her promise, and whose flirtations with soprano roles have led to insecurities. Venus (*Tannhäuser*), Amneris (*Aida*) and Eboli (*Don Carlos*).

MONSERRAT CABALLÉ Spanish soprano (1933–). Has had a long career, much of it at less than her full potential. A versatile and dynamic range with long full phrases (she has extraordinary reserves of breath). For a short period she was the great soprano of the Italian lyric repertoire and also of rediscovered >bel canto roles. Good as Donizetti's *Lucrezia Borgia*, *Anne Bolena* and *Ariadne*.

224

MARIA CALLAS Greek soprano (1923–77). In the sphere of Italian opera, Callas was one of the most potent forces in music drama: a genuine musical genius in addition to her dramatic and vocal talents. Her naturally beautiful voice had some inbuilt flaws. Extraordinarily versatile, she gained an unequalled respect from critics in *Médée* and in >bel canto roles like *Norma* and was a supreme *Tosca*.

PIERO CAPPUCCILLI Italian baritone (1929–). A reliable, solid and well-produced voice, lacking great individuality: best in Verdi roles, such as *Rigoletto*, *Simon Boccanegra* and Renato (*Ballo*).

JOSÉ CARRERAS Spanish tenor (1946–). A dark lyrical voice which sometimes loses its burnish when over-extended. Gifted as Rodolfo (*La bohème*), *Don Carlos*, Don José (*Carmen*), Nemorino (*L'elisir*).

MARIA CHIARA Italian soprano (1939–). Has never quite assumed the post-Renata Tebaldi mantle that people thought she would. Her natural, full and shining voice shows well as *Aida*, Amelia (*Ballo*) and Desdemona (*Otello*).

BORIS CHRISTOFF Bulgarian bass (1918–). The first important Eastern European bass after Shalyapin, he stamped his personality on the roles of *Boris Godunov* and Philip II (*Don Carlos*). A strong stage presence and an immense, gritty and melancholy voice.

FRANCO CORELLI Italian tenor (1921–). Like Bergonzi, he proved that Italy could still produce good post-war tenors. His voice was not always used with consistent taste but was unequalled in its brilliance and power: *Andrea Chénier*, Manrico (*Trovatore*), Canio (*Pagliacci*), Turiddu (*Cavalleria*) and *Werther*.

FIORENZA COSSOTTO Italian mezzo (1935–). A clear voice with an easy power which allows her sometimes to substitute volume for subtlety: Amneris (*Aida*), Ulrica (*Ballo*), Santuzza (*Cavalleria*).

ILEANA COTRUBAS Romanian soprano (1939–). Uneven but at her best one of the most poignant and delicate of sopranos. A vulnerable singer, very empathetic. Roles: Violetta (*Traviata*), Tatyana (*Eugene Onegin*), Mélisande (*Pelléas*) and the Mozart roles.

RÉGINE CRESPIN French soprano (1927–). Although her voice had flaws, she was capable of impressive grandeur. A superb stylist, she excelled in Wagner roles and as the Marschalin (*Rosenkavalier*), where she displayed a glowing, 'womanly' quality. Good actress

VICTORIA DE LOS ANGELES Spanish soprano (1923–). An extraordinarily convincing singer, one of the most naturally beautiful and radiant voices of the century. Ideal for Puccini, the French roles and some Spanish roles, which she particularly developed. The perfect Mimi (*La bohème*), *Madam Butterfly* and a surprisingly seductive and witty *Carmen* under Thomas Beecham.

HELGA DERNESCH Austrian (mezzo) soprano (1939–). A fascinating example of someone who experienced a crisis in her singing, but has reemerged as a powerfully rich mezzo in all the Strauss and Wagner mezzo roles, and as a great Marfa in *Khovanshchina*.

PLACIDO DOMINGO Spanish tenor (1934–). Committed, intelligent, ambitious and continually developing in every respect. Has the widest repertoire of any tenor, and splendid (but not limitless) vocal skills, which sometimes lack an individual colour. Spent three years with the Israel National Opera, mastering many roles in Hebrew. A great *Otello*, *Samson*, Hoffmann, Don José (*Carmen*), and *Lohengrin*.

BRIGITTE FASSBAENDER German mezzo (1937–). An immediate, vibrant and (at its best) irresistible voice with great individuality, although not always totally secure. A controlled and poised technique. Successful in >travesty roles – Cherubino (*Figaro*) and Sextus (*La clemenza di Tito*), the Composer (*Ariadne*), Oktavian (*Rosenkavalier*). Also good as Dorabella (*Cosi*).

DIETRICH FISCHER-DIESKAU German baritone (1925–). He may ultimately be remembered more as a lieder singer, although he has handled – with distinction – a comprehensive set of baritone roles including Renato (*Ballo*) and Pizarro (*Fidelio*). Has also worked on many contemporary roles such as *Doktor Faust* (Busoni) and *Mathis der Maler*.

KIRSTEN FLAGSTAD Norwegian soprano (1895–1962). The archetype of the resplendent Nordic singer: a wide and grand voice, suited to major Wagner roles, plus Gluck and Beethoven in which she conveyed great humanity.

225

OPERA SINGERS

MIRELLA FRENI Italian soprano (1935–). Captivating and charming, she has sung successfully throughout a long career, including roles not apparently suited to her. Good as Tatyana (*Eugene Onegin*), *Adriana Lecouvreur*, Maria (*La fille du régiment*) Amelia (*Simon Boccanegra*) and especially Mimi (*La bohème*).

NICOLAI GEDDA Swedish tenor (1925–). Extremely versatile and linguistically adept. He is a musicial tenor who has sung everything from Bach to Samuel Barber. Even if his voice lacks personality, his standards are high and reliable. Roles: *Hoffmann*, both Berlioz's and Gounod's *Faust* and Don José (*Carmen*).

NICOLAI GHIAUROV Bulgarian bass (1929–). Towards the end of a long career he has lost some of the original beauty of his voice, which is bigger and rounder than Christoff's, although Christoff was the more powerful actor. Good *Boris Godunov* and Philip II (*Don Carlos*) as well as Silva (*Ernani*), Il Padre Guardiano (*Forza*) and Gremin (*Eugene Onegin*).

TITO GOBBI Italian baritone (1913–84). The male match of Callas in musical ability, his voice demonstrated amazing character and burning intelligence, although in later years some dryness crept in. Classic roles include Iago (*Otello*), *Falstaff*, *Simon Boccanegra* and Scarpia (*Tosca*).

RITA GORR Belgian mezzo (1926). Of the great post-war mezzos (including Arkhipova, Ludwig and Resnik), Gorr is possibly the most exciting and powerful, with a thrilling, metallic sound, also capable of subtlety. Her Amneris (*Aida*) is among the best on record, plus Dalila (*Samson et Dalila*), Fricka (*The Ring*), Iphigénie (en Tauride), Ortrud (*Lohengrin*); she created Mother Marie in *Dialogues des Carmélites*.

EDITA GRUBEROVA Czech soprano (1946–). Efficient, competent but not outstandingly individual, she is accomplished in high >coloratura roles such as *Lucia di Lammermoor* and Zerbinetta (*Ariadne*).

MARILYN HORNE American mezzo (1929–). In her rediscovery of >bel canto roles, a mezzo equivalent of Joan Sutherland. A dark voice of agility and vast compass, occasionally spoilt by vulgarity of style, replacing subtlety with force. Roles: Arsace (*Semiramide*) both Adalgisa and the title role in *Norma*, and Handel and Rossini roles.

GUNDULA JANOWITZ German soprano (1937–). A pure and poised voice matching musical intelligence with an understated style which some erroneously interpret as lacking dramatic quality. Roles: *Ariadne*, Pamina (*Magic Flute*) and the Countess in *Figaro*.

GWYNETH JONES British soprano (1936–). Natural warmth and communicative vocal power, sometimes uncontrolled, but over ridden by a sheer hell-for-leather determination to give everything to a role: Brünnhilde (*The Ring*) and other Wagner roles, plus *Elektra* and *Aida*.

RENÉ KOLLO German tenor (1937–). An ex-operetta singer who has found a way of projecting his essentially lyrical voice in roles that would seem too heavy for him, using intelligence and authority on stage. All the Wagner tenor roles.

ALFREDO KRAUS Spanish tenor, of Austrian descent (1927–). Excellent technique with a slightly detached and nasal style; very versatile, especially in >bel canto roles, and *Werther*. Recently, highly admired in French tenor roles.

CHRISTA LUDWIG German mezzo (1928–). One of the most distinguished post-war singers, an opulent mezzo voice used with great sensuality and musical style, plus a command of the higher notes allowing her to conquer soprano roles like Verdi's Lady Macbeth, and Leonore (*Fidelio*). As a mezzo, strong in the Wagner dramatic roles, Amneris (*Aida*) and many others.

SHERRILL MILNES American baritone (1935–). A genuinely vibrant example of a vibrant American/Italian baritone. Although not particularly dramatic, a commanding and musical presence: all the leading Verdi baritone roles, plus *Don Giovanni* and *Hamlet*.

EVGENY NESTERENKO Russian bass (1938–). Not a large voice but dark, focused and used with powerful musicianship. Roles include *Ruslan*, Gounod's *Faust*, Zaccaria (*Nabucco*) and Basilio (*Barber*).

BIRGIT NILSSON Swedish soprano (1919–). Shiningly brilliant, endless stamina and tremendous presence: the Wagnerian soprano of the latter half of this century. Also remarkable as

Databank

Turandot, Elektra, Salome and the Dyer's Wife (Die Frau ohne Schatten).

JESSYE NORMAN American soprano (1945–). A rich voice and statuesque presence, she is an institution, perhaps at the cost of simplicity. A versatile concert singer, her limited repertoire includes Ariadne, both Purcell's and Berlioz's Dido, Cassandra (The Trojans) and Madame Lidoine in Dialogues des Carmélites.

ELENA OBRAZTSOVA Russian mezzo (1939–). Impressive natural gifts; some limits in stage ability and musical taste. Roles: Charlotte (Werther), Azucena (Trovatore), Carmen, Santuzza (Cavalliera) and Dalila (Samson et Dalila).

LUCIANO PAVAROTTI Italian tenor (1935–). Strong, intelligent, natural tenor, possibly promoted above his natural status by show-biz hype, but capable of exercising great charm and appeal. Probably the best diction of any current Italian singer. Particularly important as Idomeneo, Nemorino (L'elisir), Rodolfo (La bohème) and Riccardo (Ballo).

PETER PEARS British tenor (1910–86). A distinctive rather than beautiful voice, used with a kind of genius, consummate intelligence and musicianship. Benjamin Britten's muse, he helped make the Britten repertoire great, creating Albert Herring, Vere (Billy Budd), Aschenbach (Death in Venice) and many others. In his early days roles included Vašek (Bartered Bride) and David (Meistersinger).

LUCIA POPP Czech soprano (1939–). An adorable performer, with warmth and radiant appeal in her voice; a great stage presence. Particularly admired in Mozart roles such as the Countess (Figaro), Pamina – and earlier The Queen of Night – in Magic Flute, and Strauss roles including Arabella and the Marschallin (Rosenkavalier).

HERMANN PREY German baritone (1929–). A long career and a sympathetic, smooth voice covering many roles, including Papageno (Magic Flute), the Count (Figaro), Storch (Intermezzo) and recently Beckmesser (Meistersinger).

LEONTYNE PRICE American soprano (1927–). Velvety, rich, vibrant and smokey voice; the first black singer to conquer the world and arguably the most beautiful Aida of the century. Other roles: the two Leonoras (in Forza and Trovatore), Tosca and the Mozart roles.

MARGARET PRICE British soprano (1941–). The leading Mozart soprano of the day; her voice possesses brightness, size, purity and style. Acclaimed as The Countess (Figaro), Ariadne, and notable as Desdemona (Otello), Elisabeth (Don Carlos) and Amilia (Ballo).

SAMUEL RAMEY American bass (1940–). Well-formed, medium-sized voice with brilliant >coloratura technique in the florid bass roles of Handel, Mozart, Rossini and Meyerbeer.

REGINA RESNIK American mezzo (1922–). Formerly a soprano, her move to mezzo roles was never ideal, but she is a tremendous and riveting artist with a strong, dark and compelling voice. Impressive as Klytemnestra in Elektra, Carmen, Amneris (Aida), Mistress Quickly (Falstaff) and the Nurse in Die Frau ohne Schatten.

KATIA RICCIARELLI Italian soprano (1946–). Although never secure, her voice has a sympathetic quality with a lot of natural colour when on form. Roles: many Italian >bel canto roles, plus Mimi (La bohème), Desdemona (Otello) and Liù (Turandot).

ELISABETH SCHWARZKOPF German soprano (1915–). One of the supreme dominating stage artists of the century, a highly sophisticated musician/actress who can produce extreme reactions, and who applied care, refinement and intelligence to make her roles distinctive: Fiordiligi (Cosi), the Countess (Capriccio) and the Marschalin (Rosenkavalier).

RENATA SCOTTO Italian soprano (1933–). A gifted and naturally beautiful lyric and >coloratura soprano, forced by ambition into roles not suited to her. However, the results were never uninteresting because of her intelligence, diction, vocal colour and acting ability. Roles: Violetta (Traviata), Manon and Manon Lescaut, Madam Butterfly, Norma and Lady Macbeth

BEVERLY SILLS American soprano (1929–). More important for her role as Director of the New York City Opera than for her singing career, although her attractive voice suited roles such as Lucia di Lammermoor, Manon (Massenet), the Queen of Shemakhan (Golden Cockerel) and Donizetti's three Queens: Maria Stuarda, Anna Bolena and Elizabeth in Roberto Devereux.

ELISABETH SÖDERSTRÖM Swedish

soprano (1927–). Like Nicolai Gedda a great linguist, she has enormous repertoire to which she brings her special mix of vocal authority and stage magnetism, together with intelligent humour, charm and the courage to take on difficult roles. Her favourite role is Emilia Marty (*The Makropulos Affair*); she also stands out as Mélisande (*Pelléas*) and in Mozart, Strauss and Janáček.

JOAN SUTHERLAND Austrian soprano (1926–). Her extraordinary, naturally wonderful voice and her willingness to learn have been well channelled to a deserved success. She has radiance and perfect projection from the highest ranges. Like Melba she has become a household name. Her most famous roles include *Lucia di Lammermoor*, the other >bel canto roles, and much Handel.

KIRI TE KANAWA New Zealand soprano (1944–). As a younger sister she had a gloriously vibrant voice like Victoria de los Angeles, but she has not developed as her talent promised, although she has a particularly active commercial career, partly boosted through singing at the Royal Wedding in 1981. Roles: Countess (*Figaro*), Desdemona (*Otello*), Amelia (*Simon Boccanegra*), *Arabella*.

RENATA TEBALDI Italian soprano (1922–). She stood for the Italian soprano at its best. Although not a commanding actress, she was unequalled for the beauty of her tone and vocal colour with a glowing warmth. Impressive as *Tosca*, *Madam Butterfly*, *Aida*, *Adriana Lecouvreur* and Mimi (*La bohème*).

JOSÉ VAS DAM Belgian bass (1940–). The leading Francophone singer of the day; aristocratic with impeccable technique and ability to range across roles from Gluck's *Agamemnon* to

Wozzeck and *The Flying Dutchman*.

JULIA VARADY Romanian soprano (1941–). An idiosyncratic career because of her marriage to Fischer-Dieskau; although a natural Italian soprano she has done a lot of Strauss. Not a large voice, but plenty of colour and 'Mediterranean' substance. Roles: *Madam Butterfly*, Fiordiligi (*Cosi*), Elvira (*Don Giovanni*), Leonora (*Forza*) and *Arabella*.

JOSEPHINE VEASEY British mezzo (1930–). Fine actress-singer showing total technical confidence and authority, and beautiful tone in roles like Berlioz's Dido (*The Trojans*), Fricka (*The Ring*), Brangäne (*Tristan*) and other Wagner, Mozart, Rossini and early Handel roles. Limited her international career by working principally in Great Britain.

SHIRLEY VERRETT American mezzo (1931–). Never solved certain technical problems, especially as her wide range tempted her to take on soprano roles, but her dark, electric voice had tremendous presence: Eboli (*Don Carlos*), Lady *Macbeth* and Dalila (*Samson et Dalila*).

JON VICKERS Canadian tenor (1926–). One of the strongest post-war stage personalities – a titanic, craggy, slightly untamed voice, treated with great thought and intelligence. An important Canio (*Pagliacci*), plus Siegmund (*The Valkyrie*), *Otello*, Peter Grimes, *Tristan* and *Samson* (Saint Saëns).

GALINA VISHNEVSKAYA Russian soprano (1926–). Not a conventionally beautiful voice, but an individual combination of mannered vibrancy and 'soul' which became slightly wild, but nonetheless always had special quality. Roles: Lady *Macbeth*, *Aida*, *Tosca*, Lisa (*Queen of Spades*), Tatyana (*Eugene Onegin*), Katerina Izmailova (*Lady Macbeth of the Mtsenck District*).

OPERA BOOKS

THE FOLLOWING LIST of books is a selection of titles covering various aspects of opera, including general opera history and criticism; discographical information, dictionaries of opera; lives of opera people; and histories of opera companies. Books dealing specifically with the work of an individual composer or a particular opera are listed at the relevant place in the main entries.

ANNALS OF OPERA 1597–1940 – A listing of every known opera, with basic performance information. Alfred Loewenberg/John Calder/1955, 1970, 1978.

THE CONCISE OXFORD DICTIONARY OF OPERA – A reliable and thoughtful A-Z. Harold Rosenthal and John Warrack/Oxford University Press/1964, 1979.

A HISTORY OF ENGLISH OPERA – The author is always an interesting writer, not only on opera but on music generally. Eric Walter White/Faber & Faber/1983.

HOCKNEY PAINTS THE STAGE – A festive and colourful insight into the designer's role in opera, here concentrating on David Hockney's work for Glyndebourne and the New York Met. Martin Friedman/Thames and Hudson/1983.

HOW TO ENJOY OPERA WITHOUT REALLY TRYING – A deliberately lowbrow, laidback, Oz view of opera. Not to be dismissed. John Cargher/Hill of Content, Melbourne/1986.

KOBBÉ'S COMPLETE OPERA BOOK – The heavyweight of opera reference books, with price to match. Gives plot synopses and commentaries on major operas. Revised and enlarged by the Earl of Harewood; the original was published in 1922, four years after the death of Gustav Kobbé, who was music critic of the New York Herald. Tenth edition/Bodley Head/1987.

THE MAKING OF AN OPERA – A behind-the-scenes description of the creation of Peter Hall's 1977 production of *Don Giovanni* for Glyndebourne. John Higgins/Secker and Warburg/1978.

MAN AND HIS MUSIC Volumes 3 and 4 – A highly original view of music as a whole, full of valuable insight. Material on opera features strongly. Wilfrid Mellers/Barrie and Jenkins/1969.

THE NEW GROVE DICTIONARY OF MUSIC AND MUSICIANS – A consistently high standard of entry. *The* encyclopedia of music – if you can afford it. Edited by Stanley Sadie/Macmillan/1980.

OPERA: A CONCISE HISTORY – An illustrated survey of the history of opera, updated by the editor of Opera magazine. Leslie Orrey, revised by Rodney Milnes/Thames and Hudson/1987.

OPERA AS DRAMA – A strongly thought out and very specific concept of opera. Stimulating and uncompromising, and exciting reading. Joseph Kerman/Random House/1956.

OPERA ON RECORD (three volumes) – An indispensable series for the opera record collector. Each volume contains a selection of essays on the recordings of various operas. The quality of writing varies according to the contributor, but when it is good, it is very very good. Volume 1 covers the blockbusters, Volumes 2 and 3 fill out the repertoire. Edited by Alan Blyth/Hutchinson/1979 (Volume 1), 1983 (Volume 2), 1984 (Volume 3).

A SHORT HISTORY OF OPERA – Although the coverage, and to some extent, the opinions are somewhat dated, still very valuable. Donald J. Grout/Columbia University Press/Second edition 1965.

Books on opera companies:

50 YEARS OF GLYNDEBOURNE: AN ILLUSTRATED HISTORY – Jonathan Cape/1985.
GLYNDEBOURNE: A HISTORY OF THE FESTIVAL OPERA – Spike Hughes/David and Charles/1981.
A HISTORY OF THE ROYAL OPERA HOUSE, COVENT GARDEN 1732–1982 – Royal Opera House/1982.
WELSH NATIONAL OPERA – Richard Fawkes/Julia MacRae Books/1986.

Books on opera people:

THE CALLAS LEGACY – John Ardoin/Duckworth/1987. Also **MARIA CALLAS** – Arianna Stassinopoulos/Weidenfeld/1980.
IN MY OWN KEY – Elisabeth Söderström/Hamish Hamilton/1979.
LORENZO DA PONTE: THE LIFE AND TIMES OF MOZART'S LIBRETTIST – Sheila Hodges/Granada/1985.
MORE THAN A DIVA – Renata Scotto/Robson Books/1986.
MY FIRST FORTY YEARS – Placido Domingo/Weidenfeld/1983.
TITO GOBBI ON HIS WORLD OF ITALIAN OPERA – Hamish Hamilton/1984.

229

GLOSSARY

THE TERMS LISTED in this section of the Handbook are indicated throughout by an arrow symbol (>). Most refer specifically to opera; if not, they have been used in their opera-related sense. Definitions of musical terms (eg pizzicato or scherzo) can be found in musical dictionaries or in fact in any good general dictionary such as the Longman Dictionary of the English Language. Cross-references are in italics.

A CAPPELLA Singing without instrumental accompaniment. Comparatively rare in opera, a cappella is found in choral work generally and in early church music especially; more recently the style has featured in the work of vocal groups like The Swingle Singers, The King's Singers and The Flying Pickets.

ARIA An elaborate song with a formal, balanced structure written for a single voice with instrumental backing. The aria originally came into being as a contrast to *recitative*, allowing a character to indulge in deeper contemplation of their feelings. Arias provide the recognisable hits from any particular opera; in comparison, Wagner's most mature operas are *through-composed*, containing no clear-cut arias (or other numbers). Within the basic definition there are many sub-divisions, ranging from the straightforward aria di sortita (or exit aria, written for a character to sing just before leaving the stage) to the extremes of the aria del sorbetto or sorbet aria, which was written for a minor character, giving the audience a chance to disappear for some quick refreshment.

ARIETTA/ARIETTE A small-scale *aria*, which is much less complex than the full version, often quite simply a charming little song, characteristic of *opéra comique*.

ARIOSO A passage of singing with a freer flowing style than the formal *aria*, arioso gives an opportunity for the most beautiful outpouring of melody, precisely because it breaks free from the restrictions of both the aria form and the more predictable *recitative* pattern.

BEL CANTO The Italian for 'beautiful singing', bel canto is a style of singing which favours a pure and even delivery of the solo melody line. Consequently the insistence on evenness of tone can run the risk of a loss of dramatic expression. The style is natural to operas by Bellini, Donizetti, Rossini and (early) Verdi.

BUFFA/BUFFO See *opera buffa*.

CABALETTA An *aria* or part of an aria with a fast, catchy, almost military rhythm and a feeling of brilliance (eg Leonore's 'Abscheulicher!' from Fidelio). In the 19th century the term was often used for the finale of a multi-sectioned aria, representing a transition from reflection to action: a good example is 'Ah! Non giunge' in La sonnambula or 'Di quella pira' in Il trovatore.

CADENZA Within an aria, an extended flourish generally improvised by singers, although Rossini began to control the whole exercise (see page 30). Clearly related to the cadenza in solo instrumental concertos, but generally shorter.

CASTRATO A male singer castrated in boyhood to preserve the soprano or contralto range of his voice. The use of castrati was most prevalent in operas of the 17th and 18th centuries (the last major composer to write castrato roles was Meyerbeer). The voice thus created had a greater breadth and strength than the natural female voice – in the absence of willing volunteers, the parts are today sung by either a soprano, mezzo-soprano, male counter-tenor or tenor.

CATALOGUE ARIA See *patter number/song*.

CAVATINA A brief solo song, often slow-moving and expressive, with little ornamentation: Figaro sings a cavatina in 'Se vuol ballare' from The Marriage of Figaro.

CHAMBER OPERA Usually a short small-scale work using limited forces. Particularly interesting are the modern versions, some produced in the First World War or its aftermath, when there were just not the resources to create massive productions. By making a virtue out of these constraints, they represented a reaction to the vast textures of the late 19th century, a value carried through into full-length operas like Britten's Turn of the Screw and Stravinsky's The Rake's Progress.

CHROMATICISM A style of composition incorporating notes outside the *diatonic* scale to provide an added element of colour and expressiveness. By Wagner's time it was becoming the order of the day.

Databank

COLORATURA Elaborate ornamentation requiring vocal agiliity. Most commonly associated with a high soprano voice, found in the works of 17th and 18th century composers right up to Donizetti, Bellini and early Verdi. A celebrated example is the Queen of the Night's song of revenge in Mozart's The Magic Flute. Rossini wrote some superb mezzo-soprano coloratura: listen to Rosina's 'Una voce poco fa' from The Barber of Seville.

COMMEDIA DELL'ARTE An Italian comedy genre of the 16th to 18th centuries, using plots based on standard situations and stock characters (Harlequin, Punch, Colombine) with a certain amount of improvisation. Typical plotlines – the trickster, the knock-on effect of disguise, and so on – can be found in many operas: The Barber of Seville, The Marriage of Figaro, L'elisir d'amore. The most blatant use of the commedia dell'arte as a source is Leoncavallo's Pagliacci; it informed Puccini's Turandot, Busoni's Arlecchino, and Strauss's Ariadne auf Naxos among others.

CREDO The central idea of the Credo ('I believe' in one God) from the Christian mass has occasionally been carried over into opera, such as for Iago in Verdi's Otello, where it has a perverse Black Mass use. It was reasonable to assume that both audiences and musicians would be familiar with the religious reference.

DEUS EX MACHINA The Latin phrase translates as 'the god from the machine', and refers to the classical Greek dramatic convention of unexpectedly introducing a Being at the climax of a drama to contrive a solution to a seemingly insoluble plot (Monteverdi's Orfeo is a prime example). The device gave opera a chance to revel in the mechanical marvels of stage machinery, and for audiences to anticipate just how the device would be introduced. When operas were written for court performance, the implication was that the 'deus' was the audience's noble host.

DIATONIC The diatonic scales are the major and minor, which include a given set of notes. Music in the time of Bach and Mozart was basically diatonic; when they introduced an element of *chromaticism*, the effect was shattering.

FUGUE A musical form based around the gradual introduction of different parts ('voices'); each repeating or slightly varying a basic theme. One delight for the listener lies in picking out the individual strands of sound as they are woven together. For opera singers fugues are difficult to perform, and for the conductor the trick is to maintain clarity even at speed.

GESAMTKUNSTWERK This German phrase (literally 'total-art-work') is usually associated with Wagner and his theories of unifying all the arts, particularly relevant to his later great operas.

GRAND OPERA The definition of grand opera has become somewhat vague and opinions vary as to precise use of the phrase. Generally recognised as the typical form of Paris operas in the first half of the 18th century – huge sets, massive crowd scenes, epic historical events (as in Spontini, Meyerbeer), it can also refer to the kind of opera such as Boris Godunov which involves a sense of 'the people' as a political force. In grand opera, the intimate is not excluded, but solo scenes can project characters and their emotions as larger than life.

HELDENTENOR ('Hero-tenor' in German) A tenor with a large dramatic voice able to cope with the demands of heavy, especially Wagnerian, roles: a dying breed, as singers who tackle these roles frequently end up damaging their voices by straining or shouting. The tenor Lauritz Melchior had a ringing, rounded tone; in comparison singers today lack resonance.

INTERMEZZO (plural intermezzi) Literally 'inbetween', a short and light entertainment performed between the acts of an opera or play; see the entry on La serva padrona, page 19. The Bassarids (Henze) contains a strange throwback to the 18th-century intermezzo.

LEITMOTIV (also leitmotif) A group of notes, often an extended phrase, associated with an idea, character, object or situation. Although not created by Wagner, the leitmotiv is most often associated with his complex use of it in his later operas, particularly the Ring cycle.

LIEBESTOD The Romantic idea that a person could could actually die for love (as opposed to dying of a broken heart). It was specifically used to refer to Isolde's final outpouring of song in Wagner's Tristan und Isolde, where she

231

GLOSSARY

dies in exaltation to join her lover.

MELODRAMA Dialogue spoken for dramatic effect.

MOTIF See *leitmotiv.*

NUMBER OPERA An opera made up of separate units (*arias*, duets, trios . . .) separated by *recitative*. although in the hands of composers such as Mozart, opera finales tended to be larger composite units, number opera was customary until the time of the Romantics (Berlioz excepted), who tried to integrate the elements by developing thematic unity. Having moved away from number opera with his operas of the 1850s and 1860s, Verdi eventually abandoned the genre for Otello and Falstaff, deliberately aiming at a continuous stream of melody, and beating Wagner at his own game (see *through-composed*). Stravinsky reverted to the classical number opera pattern in The Rake's Progress.

OPERA BUFFA (plural opere buffe) Any type of comic opera, often incorporating stock characters. A development of the *intermezzo*, opera buffa was much less high-flown than *opera seria*, using everyday characters and making politically/socially satirical comments – a form of opera for and about the common people. The French chapter opener on page 70 gives details of the slightly different opéra bouffe. The word 'buffo' refers to singing in the buffa style.

OPÉRA COMIQUE A genre of opera, light in spirit, which was constantly changing over the years. Opéra comique originated from popular entertainment at 17th-century fairs, with spoken dialogue and familiar songs, and from parodies of earnest *tragédies lyriques*. Subsequently it became a form able at various times to embrace more or less refined vulgarity, social and bourgeois values in romantic village tales: it was dominated in the late 18th century by Grétry. After the French Revolution had introduced more serious elements, the 19th century reverted to amusing and sparkling entertainments (exemplified by Auber's work with Scribe). With Carmen, Bizet brought in genuine realism which hardened the edges and undermined the arbitrary distinction between works performed at the Paris Opéra, where spoken dialogue was banned, and those at the Opéra-Comique, where dialogue was de rigueur.

OPERA SEMISERIA A late 18th-century term for opera mingling aspects of both *opera buffa* and *opera seria.*

OPERA SERIA (plural opere serie) A formula genre, the main style of 18th-century Italian opera. Subjects were heroic, tragic tales drawn from the classics, from historical sources, from Romance epics or from mythology, and plots underlined and maintained the order (the backlash was *opera buffa*). The pure opera seria form was fleshed out by each composer in his own way: it was well served by Handel and reformed by Gluck. Mozart wrote two magnificent examples in Idomeneo and La clemenza di Tito.

OSTINATO A persistent musical pattern, usually an accompanying figure.

PARLATO/PARLANDO As though speaking.

PASTORALE In opera, a genre whose rural theme, a tale of simple folk, implied a glamourising of country life. It could be, and later was, parodied for its artificial innocence and bucolic charm (Offenbach's Orfée aux enfers).

PATTER NUMBER/SONG A comic song deriving its humour from the inclusion at high speed of the maximum possible number of words ('La vendetta' in The Marriage of Figaro); subsequently much featured in Gilbert and Sullivan. The catalogue aria follows a similar pattern with a rapid listing of items.

PROGRAMME MUSIC Instrumental music which suggests or represents images, incidents, or even a complete story. Very much a 19th-century phenomenon, reflecting the literary influences on Romantic composers and their cultivation of late 18th-century 'affect'.

RECITATIVE The conversational singing of a narrative text, allowing a composer and librettist to advance the plot between the more reflective *arias* which focus on one point of emotion. The division between the two styles was most obvious in the *number opera*. Called 'semplice' or 'secco' when accompaniment was minimal, 'accompagnato' if the backing was more expressive.

REFORM OPERA One of those operas by Gluck in which the music and the drama work for each other, eschewing the gratuitous accretions of previous popular styles.

RESCUE OPERA An opera in which the whole plot hinges on a dramatic and exciting rescue of a character – particularly popular with audiences of the 1790s, itself a dramatic decade, and indicative of a reaction against sentimental pastoral elements and the charming *opéra comique*. The genre was still alive and well in Smetana's Dalibor (1868).

ROMANCE/ROMANZA In opera, a simple unadorned aria or song, frequently tender in content, and particularly appropriate to the needs of *opéra comique*.

SCENA A solo in which the singer progresses through various stages of emotion incorporating a considerable dramatic range, so allowing the composer to exploit varying writing styles. Compare Médée's decision to kill her own children (Cherubini) with Norma's *not* to kill hers (Bellini) – both are classic scenas.

SERIAL/SERIALISM A compositional concept using the series of twelve notes, and giving them all equal importance, as opposed to traditional harmony which gives greater power to certain notes (eg the 'doh') and certain chords (eg the tonic). Serialism, developed by Schoenberg and Berg, thus dispenses with traditional ideas of harmony and melody: it requires singers with an exceptionally fine sense of pitch.

SINGSPIEL A German opera style of folksy musical numbers interspersed with spoken dialogue, influenced by the *opéra comique* and English ballad opera. Its most typical composer was Hiller, and its very German-ness made it a precursor of the German Romantics such as Weber (see the German chapter opener, page 130).

SPECTACLE In the context of opera, spectacular scenic and crowd displays – a particular obsession with French audiences.

SPRECHGESANG ('Speech-song')/**SPRECHSTIMME** ('Speech-voice') Used by Schoenberg and Berg for speaking at a specified pitch, a voice style somewhere inbetween actual singing and speaking.

STROPHIC ARIA An aria in which each verse follows the same musical pattern.

TESSITURA The natural range in which a voice lies most comfortably: a soprano has a high tessitura. The term can also be applied to a piece of music, meaning its basic range of notes.

THROUGH-COMPOSED When applied to an opera, refers to composing with no artificial stopping points (compare *number opera*). Dramatically the style should reflect the flow of events and emotions, but in fact through-composed works have of necessity to contain some breaks: a *totally* unbroken flow is likely to be too demanding for all involved. In fact, Wagner's works are full of predictable, but never quite final, cadences which act as springboards to the next section.

TRAGÉDIE LYRIQUE A fixed form developed by Quinault and Lully, appropriate to the opera needs of their time, combining dance, singing, scenery and drama based on tragic, epic and mythological subjects.

TRAVESTY/TROUSER ROLE (also breeches part) A male role sung by a woman. There are many examples in opera: Oscar in Verdi's Un ballo in maschera, Oktavian in Strauss's Der Rosenkavalier, the Schoolboy in Berg's Lulu. There is a double twist in Arabella (Strauss), where Zdenka, a woman sung by a woman, is dressed as a man for the purposes of the plot. In Italian *opera buffa*, female characters were occasionally played by men.

TWELVE-TONE SYSTEM See *Serial/serialism*.

VERISMO Thought of simply as the 'naturalistic' school of opera, verismo in fact presented a slice of low life, with violence an essential element, often taking place on stage. The music too set out to shock.

OPERA INFORMATION

THIS SECTION lists information sources for the further exploration of opera, principally opera magazines and major international opera companies (indicating whether a friends group or mailing list exists), festivals and independent bodies. The listing is based on the latest information available at time of going to press, but will inevitably be subject to change. Amendments and suggestions for inclusion should be sent to: The Opera Handbook, Longman Group UK Limited, Longman House, Burnt Mill, Harlow, Essex CM20 2JE.

UNITED KINGDOM

Magazine

OPERA MAGAZINE
Monthly
1A Mountgrove Road
London N5 2LU
01 359 1037
Subscriptions:
OPERA, DSB
14/16 The Broadway
Wickford
Essex SS11 7AA
0268 766330

Companies etc.

DORSET OPERA
Abbot's Acre, Sherborne
Dorset DT9 3JF
0935 812030
Friends
Short festival late August

D'OYLY CARTE OPERA
COMPANY
20 Stukeley Street
London WC2 B5LR
01 405 2030
Friends
Band parts for Gilbert and
Sullivan available for hire

ENGLISH BACH FESTIVAL
15 South Eaton Place
London SW1W 9ER
01 730 5925

ENGLISH NATIONAL
OPERA
London Coliseum
St. Martin's Lane
London WC2N 4ES
01 836 2699/0111
Mailing list (£3.75)
Friends and Young Friends
(under 26), contact
01 836 0111 ×442

ENGLISH TOURING OPERA
Music Centre
University of Warwick
Coventry CV4 7AL
0203 523523
Touring to unconventional
venues/Education
programme
Friends

GLYNDEBOURNE
FESTIVAL
OPERA/TOURING OPERA

Glyndebourne, Lewes
East Sussex BN8 5UU
0273 812321
Annual programme book

KENT OPERA
Pembles Cross
Egerton, Ashford
Kent TN27 9EN
023 376 406/407/558
Mailing list/
Newsletter/Friends

NEW SADLER'S WELLS
OPERA
Sadler's Wells Theatre
Rosebery Avenue
London EC1R 4TN
01 278 6563
Mailing list/Friends
Specialises in light opera

NEW SUSSEX OPERA
15 Coronation House
Newhaven
East Sussex BN9 9PD
0273 513101
Cavatina magazine

NEXUS OPERA
2D Belsize Park Gardens
London NW3 4LD
01 586 9411

OPERA FACTORY
37 Agamemnon Road
London NW6 1EJ
01 431 1471

OPERA LIBERA
3 Iveagh Road
Guildford
Surrey GU2 5PU
0483 570602
Mailing list
Concentrates on intimate
productions, especially for
the National Trust

OPERA NORTH
Grand Theatre
46 New Briggate
Leeds LS1 6NU
0532 445326/439999
Mailing/list/Friends

OPERA RARA
OPERA RARA RECORDS
LTD
25 Compton Terrace
London N1
01 359 1777

Library of 19th century Italian
opera available for research
upon application: phone for
appointment/Record club

OPERA 80
11 Lower John Street
London W1R 3PE
01 439 6589 (administration)
01 439 0978 (press/publicity)
Mailing list
Friends of Opera 80

THE ROYAL OPERA
Royal Opera House
Covent Garden
London WC2E 9DD
01 240 1200
Box Office: 48 Floral Street,
London WC2
01 240 1066/1911 (telephone
booking)
Mailing list
Friends of Covent Garden (at
above address)

SCOTTISH OPERA
39 Elmbank Crescent
Glasgow G2 4PT
041 248 4567
Home base:
Theatre Royal
Hope Street
Glasgow G2 3QA
041 332 3321
Yearbook
Bimonthly newspaper
Scottish Opera News/
Friends

WELSH NATIONAL OPERA
John Street
Cardiff CF1 4SP
0222 464666
Friends

Festivals

THE ALDEBURGH
FESTIVAL OF MUSIC AND
THE ARTS
June
The Aldeburgh Foundation
High Street, Aldeburgh
Suffolk IP15 5AX
072 885 2935
Mailing list (£3 for two
years)/Friends

BRIGHTON FESTIVAL
May

Databank

The Festival Office
Marlborough House
4 Old Steine, Brighton
East Sussex BN1 1EQ
273 29801

BUXTON FESTIVAL
July/August
Crescent View
Hall Bank, Buxton
Derbyshire SK17 6EN
298 70395
Mailing list/Festival Society

CONTEMPORARY MUSIC
FESTIVAL –
HUDDERSFIELD
Mid-November
Department of Music
The Polytechnic
Queensgate
Huddersfield
West Yorkshire HD1 3DH
484 22288 ×2103
Music theatre and chamber
opera
Planning joint project with
Opera North for 1988–1990
Festivals
Mailing list

EDINBURGH
INTERNATIONAL
FESTIVAL
August
1 Market Street
Edinburgh EH1 1BW
31 226 4001
Opera is always a major part
f the festival

LONDON INTERNATIONAL
OPERA FESTIVAL
May/June
4 Prince of Wales Mansions
Prince of Wales Drive
London SW11 4BL
1 720 7610
Also refer to:
BRITISH ARTS FESTIVALS
ASSOCIATION
3 Orchard Road
London N6
1 348 4117

Video source
LONGMAN VIDEO
Longman House
Burnt Mill
Harlow, Essex CM20 2JE
279 26721

AUSTRALIA
Magazine
OPERA AUSTRALIA
Level 7, 84 Pitt Street
Sydney

Companies etc.
THE AUSTRALIAN OPERA
The Opera Centre
480 Elizabeth Street
Surry Hills NSW 2010
2 699 1099
Annual handbook/Australian
Opera Guild

THE STATE OPERA OF
SOUTH AUSTRALIA
20 Rowlands Place
Adelaide SA 5001
8 212 6080
Friends

SYDNEY OPERA HOUSE
TRUST
Sydney Opera House
Bennelong Point
PO Box 4274
Sydney, NSW 2001
2 250 7111
Friends (The Bennelong
Club)

VICTORIA STATE OPERA
370 Nicholson Street
Fitzroy
Victoria 3065
3 417 5061
Friends/The VSO News

WESTERN AUSTRALIAN
OPERA COMPANY
PO Box 7052
Cloisters Square
Perth, WA 6000
9 321 5869
Friends/Opera News

AUSTRIA
Companies
VEREINIGTE BÜHNEN
WIEN
Linke Wienzeile 6
1060 Vienna
222 588300
Mailing list

WIENER STAATSOPER
Opernring 3
1010 Vienna
5324 2655

Festivals
BREGENZ FESTIVAL
July/August
PO Box 119, 6901 Bregenz
5574 22811

SALZBURG FESTIVAL
Salzburger Festspiele
July/August
PO Box 140, 1510 Salzburg
6222 425 41

BELGIUM
Companies
OPERA NATIONAL
4 rue Léopold
1000 Brussels
2 217 2211

OPERA ROYAL DE
WALLONIE
1 rue des Dominicains
4000 Liege
41 235 910

OPERA VOOR VLAANDREN
Schouwbergstr, 9000 Ghent
91 253 377

CANADA
Companies
CANADIAN OPERA
COMPANY
O'Keefe Center
Toronto, Ontario
416 872 2262

COUNCIL FOR BUSINESS
AND THE ARTS IN CANADA
PO Box 7
Suite 1507 the Simpson Tower
401 Bay Street
Toronto, Ontario M5H 2Y4
416 869 3011

EDMONTON OPERA
ASSOCIATION
#202, 11456 Jasper Avenue
Edmonton, Alberta T5K OM1
403 482 7030
Quarterly magazine

L'OPERA DE MONTREAL
Place des Arts
1501 rue Jeanne-Mance
Montreal H2X 1Z9

PROFESSIONAL OPERA
COMPANIES OF CANADA
Mr Morley Workun
c/o McIntosh Workun &
Chernenko
1200, 10117 Jasper Avenue
Edmonton, Alberta T5J 1W8
403 428 1575
Quarterly newsletter –
Operaction

VANCOUVER OPERA
1132 Hamilton Street
Vancouver, British Columbia
604 682 2871

Festival
FESTIVAL OTTAWA
July
PO Box 1534, Station B
Ottawa, Ontario K1P 5W1
613 996 5051

OPERA INFORMATION

EASTERN EUROPE

Companies

NATIONAL THEATRE —
PRAGUE
Národní Divaldo
PO Box 865, 112 30 Praha
Czechoslovakia
2 144 111

SLOVAK NATIONAL
THEATRE
Slovenské Národné Divaldo
Gorkého 4, 815 86 Bratislava
Czechoslavakia
7 333 083 6

STANISLAW MONIUSZKO
GRAND THEATRE
Fredry 9, 60 967 Poznan 176
Poland
544 78/582 91
Mailing list

STATE THEATRE IN BRNO
Dvorákova 11, 657 70 Brno 1
Czechoslovakia
274 21 25
Friends/Mailing list

EIRE

Companies

CORK CITY OPERA
Cork Opera House
Emmet Place, Cork
20022

IRISH NATIONAL OPERA
193 Ceannt Fort
Mountbrown
Dublin 8

Festival

WEXFORD FESTIVAL
OPERA
October/November
Theatre Royal
High Street, Wexford
053 22240/22144
Each year includes a rare or
seldom performed opera
General mailing list/Friends

FRANCE

Magazines

L'AVANT-SCENE OPERA-
OPERETTE
Monthly
(each issue includes a
complete libretto and
extensive background on a
selected opera)
1 rue Lord Byron
75008 Paris
142 225 65 20

OPERA INTERNATIONAL
Monthly (eleven issues a
year)
Administration:
122 Champs-Elysées
75008 Paris
1 42 25 31 62
Editorial:
10 Galerie Véro-Dodat
75001 Paris
1 42 33 32 03

OPERA POUR TOUS
Monthly
14 rue Vital-Foucher
92370 Chaville
1 47 50 47 42

Companies etc.

OPERA DE LYON
Place de la Comédie
69001 Lyon
7 82 80 950

OPERA DU RHIN
19 place Broglie
67008 Strasbourg
88 36 45 668

OPERA MUNICIPAL DE
MARSEILLE
2 rue Molière
13001 Marseille
91 55 21 09/14 99

OPERA DE NICE
4 & 6 rue St-François-de-
Paule, 06300 Nice
93 80 59 83

THEATRE NATIONAL DE
L'OPERA
8 rue Scribe, 75009 Paris
1 42 66 50 22
L'Opéra de Paris
L'Opéra-Comique
Minitel: 36.15 + COM 21

Festivals

FESTIVAL D'AIX EN
PROVENCE
July
Palais de l'ancien
Archevêché
13100 Aix-en Provence
42 23 37 81

FESTIVAL DE MUSIQUE DE
SAINT-CERE
July/August
PO Box 59
46400 Saint-Céré
65 38 29 08

ORANGE FESTIVAL
Maison du Théâtre
Place des Frères-Mounet
84100 Orange
90 34 24 24

HONG KONG

HONG KONG ARTS
FESTIVAL SOCIETY
January/February
13th Floor, Hong Kong Arts
Centre
2 Harbour Road,Wanchai
Hong Kong
5 295 555
Souvenir book

ISRAEL

ISRAEL NATIONAL
OPERA
69 Ibn-Gevirol Street
Tel Aviv 64162
3 438 546/226 629

ITALY

Companies

TEATRO ALLA SCALA
Via Filodramatici 2, Milan
2 809129

TEATRO COMUNALE DI
BOLOGNA
Ente Lirico
Teatro Comunale
Largo Respighi 1
40126 Bologna
51 529947 (press office)/
529011

TEATRO COMUNALE
GIUSEPPE VERDI – TRIESTE
Ente Autonomo
34121 Trieste
40 68311/65700

TEATRO LA
FENICE/TEATRO
MALIBRAN
Campo S Fantin 2519
30124 Venice
41 78 65 41

Festivals

ARENA SFERISTERIO
July/August
Piazza Mazzini 10
62100 Macerata
733 40735

FESTIVAL DEI DUE MONDI
– SPOLETO
Via del Duomo 7, Spoleto
743 28 120

VERONA FESTIVAL
July/August
Ente Lirico Arena di Verona
Piazza Bra 28
37100 Verona
45 28151

Databank

JAPAN

JAPAN OPERA
FOUNDATION
1-28-17 Kitashinjuku
Shijuku-ku, Tokyo 160
3 69 70 20

LATIN AMERICA
Companies

COMPAÑIA NACIONAL DE
OPERA
Palacio de Bellas Artes
Avenida Hidalgo #1, 3er piso
Mexico DF 06050
905 521 36 68/518 63 02

CORPORACION CULTURAL
DE LA ILUSTRE
MUNICIPALIDAD DE
SANTIAGO
Agustinas 794
PO Box 18, Santiago de Chile
Chile
2 335689/712900
Mailing list/Friends groups

TEATRO COLON DE
BUENOS AIRES
Cerrito 618, Buenos Aires
Argentina

THE NETHERLANDS
Company

NETHERLANDS OPERA
De Nederlandse Opera
Waterlooplein 22
1011 PG Amsterdam
20 255454

NEW ZEALAND
Companies etc.

CANTERBURY REGIONAL
OPERA TRUST
PO Box 845
Christchurch
3 60989

DUNEDIN OPERA
COMPANY
PO Box 533
Dunedin
24 777 419

MERCURY OPERA
PO Box 257
Newton, Auckland
9 33869

WELLINGTON CITY OPERA
TRUST
PO Box 6588
Te Aro, Wellington
4 844 434

PORTUGAL

TEATRO NACIONAL DE
SAN CARLOS – LISBON
Rua Serpa Pinto 9
1200 Lisboa
1 368408/368610/365914

SCANDINAVIA
Companies

DEN JYSKE OPERA
The Jutland Opera
Musikhuset
Thomas Jenses Allé
8000 Aarhus C
Denmark
6 13 72 66

DEN NORSKE OPERA
Norwegian National Opera
Storgaten 23, 0184 Oslo 1
Norway
2 42 94 75
Friends/Yearbook

FINNISH NATIONAL OPERA
Bulevardi 23-27
PL 188, 00181 Helsinki
Finland
90 12921

ROYAL DANISH OPERA
The Royal Theatre
PO Box 2185
1017 Copenhagen K
Denmark
1 32 20 20

ROYAL SWEDISH OPERA
Kungliga Teatern
8 10322 Stockholm
Sweden

STORA TEATERN
Box 53116
31 40015 Göteborg
Sweden

Festival

SAVONLINNA OPERA
FESTIVAL
July/August
Olavin Katu 35, 57130 S
Finland
57 22684/12063

SPAIN
Companies

COMPANIA LIRICA DEL
TEATRO DE LA ZARZUELA
Jovellanos 4, Madrid 14

GRAN TEATRE DEL LICEU
C/ Sant Pau 1, Barcelona 1
3 18 92 77

SWITZERLAND
Magazine

OPERNWELT
Monthly
Orrell Füssli + Friedrich
Verlag, Dietzingerstrasse 3
8003 Zurich
1 466 77 11

Companies

BASLER THEATER
PO Box 4010, Basel
61 22 11 30
Mailing list/Monthly
newsheet

GRAND THEATRE DE
GENEVE
11 boulevard du Théâtre
1211 Geneva 11
22 21 23 18

STADTTHEATER BERN
Nägeligasse 20
3011 Bern

STADTTHEATER LUZERN
Theaterstrasse 2
CH 6002 Luzern
41 23 33 63

OPERNHAUS ZURICH
Falkenstrasse 1
CH 8008 Zürich
1 251 69 20
1 251 69 21
Newspaper Opernhaus
Zürich (bimonthly)/Yearbook

USA
Magazines

OPERA NEWS
Monthly (May-November)
Bimonthly (December-April)
Metropolitan Opera Guild
1865 Broadway
New York, NY 10023
212 582 7500

THE OPERA JOURNAL
Quarterly
University of Mississippi
MS 38677
601 232 7474

Companies

CINCINNATI OPERA
ASSOCIATION
1241 Elm Street – Music Hall
Cincinnati OH 45210
513 621 1919 (administration)
Opera Guild/Newsletter two
to three times a year
Opera Festival (June)

GREATER MIAMI OPERA
ASSOCIATION
1200 Coral Way

Miami FL 33145
305 854 1643
Friends/Newsletter – The
Voice – three times a year

HOUSTON GRAND OPERA
Jones Hall
615 Louisianna
Houston Texas 77002
713 5460240
713 227 2787

KENTUCKY OPERA
631 South Fifth Street
Louisville KY 40202
502 584 4500

LYRIC OPERA OF
CHICAGO
20 North Wacker Drive
Chicago IL 60606
312 332 2244

METROPOLITAN OPERA
Metropolitan Opera House
Lincoln Center
New York NY 10023
212 799 3100

NEW YORK CITY OPERA
New York State Theatre
Lincoln Center
New York NY 10023
212 370 5633

OPERA AMERICA
633 E Street NW
Washington DC 20004
Newsletter
Source of information on US
professional opera
companies

OPERA COMPANY OF
BOSTON
PO Box 50
Boston MA 02112
617 426 5300

OPERA COMPANY OF
PHILADELPHIA
1500 Walnut Street
Philadelphia PA 19102
215 732 5814
Guild and the Voice
newsletter

PITTSBURGH OPERA INC.
600 Penn Avenue
Heinz Hall
Pittsburgh PA 15222
412 281 0912
Biannual publication:
Renaissance

SAN DIEGO OPERA
PO Box 988
San Diego CA 92112
619 232 7636
Educational programme
Verdi Festival (June)

SAN FRANCISCO OPERA
War Memorial Opera House
301 Van Ness Avenue
San Francisco CA 94102
415 861 4008

SEATTLE OPERA
PO Box 9248
Seattle WA 98109
206 443 3299

Festivals

COLORADO OPERA
FESTIVAL
June-August
PO Box 1484
Colorado Springs CO 80901
303 473 0073

LAKE GEORGE OPERA
FESTIVAL
July/August
PO Box 425
Glen Falls NY 12801
518 793 3858

SANTA FE OPERA
July/August
PO Box 2408
Santa Fe NM 87504
505 982 3851

Video source

NVC OPERA SERIES
Homevision
5547 N. Ravenswood Avenue
Chicago IL 60640

WEST GERMANY
Magazine

DAS OPERN GLAS
Eleven issues a year
Lappenbergsallee 45
2000 Hamburg 20
40 850 33 95

ORPHEUS
Monthly
Livländische Strasse 27
1000 Berlin 31
30 853 32 87

Companies

DEUTSCHE OPER AM
RHEIN
Opernhaus Düsseldorf,
Heinrich-Heine-Allee 16A
4000 Düsseldorf 1
211 899 30 88

DEUTSCHE OPER BERLIN
34-37 Bismarcker-Strasse
1000 Berlin 1

HAMBURGISCHE
STAATSOPER
Postfach 302448
2000 Hamburg 36
40 35680

OPER DER STADT KÖLN
PO Box 18 02 41
Offenbachplatz 2
5000 Köln 1
221 2210/20761
Friends/Mailing list

OPER FRANKFURT
Städtische Bühnen
Untermainanlage 11
Frankfurt
69 25 62 529

STAATSOPER MÜNCHEN
Gartnerplatz Theater
800 München

STATSTHEATER KASSEL
Friedrichsplatz 15
3500 Kassel
5 611 09 40

STAATSTHEATER
STUTTGART
Oberer-Schlossgarten 6
7000 Stuttgart 1
711 203 24 44

Festivals

BAYREUTH FESTIVAL
July/August
PO Box 2320, 8580 Bayreuth
921 20221

EUTINER SOMMERSPIELE
July/August
PO Box 112, 2429 Eutin
45 21 21 61

HANDEL FESTSPIELE
June
Badisches Stadttheater
Baumeisterstrasse 11
7500 Karlsruhe 1
721 6 02020

MUNICH OPERA FESTIVAL
Bayerische Staatsoper
PO Box 745
8000 München 1
89 21851